D1570530

Kentucky Obituaries,

1787-1854

Compiled by

G. GLENN CLIFT

With an Index by
Anita Comtois

Originally published in
The Register of the Kentucky Historical Society,
Vols. 39-41, 1941-1943
Excerpted and reprinted, with an Added Index, by
Genealogical Publishing Co., Inc.
3600 Clipper Mill Rd., Suite 260
Baltimore, Maryland 21211-1953
1977, 1979, 1984, 1993, 2000, 2006
Reprinted by permission of
The Kentucky Historical Society
Frankfort, Kentucky

Library of Congress Catalogue Card Number 76-57789
International Standard Book Number 0-8063-0758-7
Made in the United States of America

OBITUARIES

Compiled and Edited by G. Glenn Clift

INTRODUCTION

This volume of genealogical notes together with the first book—*Kentucky Marriages 1797–1865* (published in the *Register* April, 1938–October, 1940)—was taken from newspaper files owned by and housed in the Lexington Public Library. The original purpose of the compilation was to make the finished work available only to users of the above-mentioned newspapers, in an effort to minimize usage of this valuable source material. With their publication in the *Register* it is hoped the records will prove of worth to a larger audience.

The obituary notices have been edited to include (a) the name of the person deceased, (b) place of residence, (c) wife or husband, parentage or other survivor or suvivors and (d) date of death. In many instances obituaries too lengthy for inclusion were published by the newspapers. Such notices have been edited for their genealogical value and the word *Obituary* appended, this to enable the researcher to secure the complete necrology if desirable.

For purpose of bibliography an abbreviation of the name of the newspaper from which any notice is taken is given with that notice. The notation following any obituary refers in every instance to the year named in the obituary. As below, in the first entry, KG 10/6 designates the (Lexington) *Kentucky Gazette,* October 6, 1787. The abbreviations used in this first installment denote: KG (Lexington) *Kentucky Gazette* and R *The* (Lexington, Ky.) *Reporter.*

1787

Mrs. Elizabeth Downing, consort of John Downing, of Louisville. Died Thursday, Aug. 9, 1787, aged 25 years. KG 10/6.

1788

Mrs. Maria Irwin, consort of Samuel Irwin, of Danville. Died Sept. 25, 1788. KG 10/11.

John Whitelodge. Died Oct. 11, 1788. KG 10/18.

1789

Major Isaac B. Dunn, of Lexington. Suicided June 28, 1879. Buried in the public burying ground there. KG 6/28.

1792

Mrs. Sarah Gano, consort of Rev. John Gano. Died at Frankfort, Apr. 17, 1792. Buried near the Baptist meeting house at the Forks of Elkhorn. KG 4/28.

1795

Thomas Reeder. Died May 29, 1795. He was Clerk of Bourbon County He married a daughter of J. Edwards, Esq. KG 6/6.

Daniel Boyd. Executed in Lexington, May 29, 1795. KG 5/30.

Col. William Ward, of Lexington. Died "a few days ago." See *Stewart's Kentucky Herald* 8/18.

1796

Christopher Kiser. Was "late deceased" when his buildings on High Street, Lexington, were consumed by fire Saturday, Jan. 23, 1796. KG 1/23.

Sarah, consort of Rev. Moses Bledsoe. Died near Lexington, July 26, 1796, in child bed. She was 33 years of age. KG 7/30.

1797

Betsey Nelson Baylor, daughter of Capt. Walker Baylor, of Lexington. Died Tuesday, Jan. 31, 1797, aged 10 years. KG 2/8.

General Thomas Barbee. Died in Louisville, Feb. 21, 1797. KG 2/25.

James Parker, merchant of Lexington. Died Mar. 6, 1797. He was buried Mar. 7 in the burying ground at Mr. Rankin's Meeting House. KG 3/8.

Major Hugh Brent, of Lexington. Died May 24, 1797. KG 5/27.

Zachariah Worthy, of Kentucky. Died July 22, 1797, aged 56 years. His will named the following: Dorothy Worthy, Rebecca Worthy, John Worthy, Timothy Worthy. Executors: Rev. John Obadiah and Rev. Henry Harrison. Teste: John Sessamy, Henry Wholesome and Titus Thompson. KG 10/14.

Gideon Davis Pendleton. Killed at Post St. Vincents, in September, 1797, in a duel with Joshua Harbin. KG 10/4.

Richard Lake, attorney-at-law of Lexington. Died Sunday, Dec. 23, 1797. He was buried the same day in the Baptist Burying Ground. His funeral was attended by the Lexington Lodge of Free Masons, of which fraternity he was a member. KG 12/26.

1799

Betty Bledsoe, wife of Joseph Bledsoe, a minister. She died Feb. 7, 1799, and was buried Feb. 9, in Lexington. KG 2/21.

John Lewis, of Jessamine county. Died Apr. 3, 1799, "at the Havanna." KG 7/25.

Capt. William Kennedy, of Campbell county. Died May 16, 1799. KG 7/25.

Col. George Nicholas, professor of law and politics in the Transylvania University. Died July 25, 1799, in Lexington. (This date could be June 25, 1799.) KG 8/1.

Col. John Campbell, a senator from Fayette county to the State Legislature. Died Oct. 19, 1799. KG 10/19.

David Bell. Died at the Clark county residence of Mrs. ———— Gist. KG 12/15/1799.

Ralph Nailor, formerly of Kentucky. Died in Dec., 1799, in Jones county, N. C. He was a mill-right. KG 1/11/1803.

1800

Robert Parker, county surveyor for Fayette county. Died at his seat, six miles from Lexington, Tuesday night, March 5, 1800. KG 3/5.

As[r]ael Batterton, of Woodford county. Died Tuesday, October 14, 1800, by a knife wound inflicted by a German resident. KG 10/14.

Col. William Campbell, of Muhlenberg county, and late Senator in the State Legislature from that District. Died Nov. 20, 1800. KG 11/20.

1801

Miss Susanna Clayton Starling, of Mercer county, daughter of Col. William Starling. Died Sunday, Aug. 16, 1801, aged 15 years. KG 8/24.

John McNair, a tavern keeper of Lexington. Died Aug. 30, 1801, leaving a large family. He was a first settler of Lexington. KG 9/7.

James Bliss, attorney-at-law of Lexington. Died on Wednesday, Sept. 16, 1801. KG 9/21.

William Fullerton, of near Lexington. Died during the week of Sept. 14, 1801. He was originally from Philadelphia. KG 9/21.

Mrs. Harriet Beatty, consort of Col. Cornelius Beatty, of Lexington. She died Nov. 19, 1801, after a brief illness. KG 11/20.

1802

Mrs. ———— Craig, consort of Elijah Craig, of Georgetown. Died April 18, 1802. KG 4/30.

Joseph Smith, student, of Lexington. Died Apr. 30, 1802. KG 4/30.

John Hargy, of Lexington. Died Saturday, June 5, 1802, and was buried the following day in Lexington. KG 6/11.

Mrs. Nancy Truitt, consort of Mr. J. Truitt. Died in Lexington, Sunday evening, June 13, 1802. KG 6/18.

Mrs. ———— Oliver, consort of Joseph Oliver, of Shelby county, formerly of Lexington. Died in former place Tuesday, June 15, 1802. KG 6/18.

Mrs. ———— Wright, consort of Israel Wright, of Lexington. Died Wednesday, June 23, 1802. KG 6/25.

Miss Eliza Marshall, only daughter of Humphrey Marshall. She was killed by lightning on Friday, July 2, 1802. KG 7/9.

Mrs. Sally McDowell, consort of Major John McDowell of Fayette county. Died Wednesday night, Aug. 4, 1802. KG 8/6.

Mrs. Margaret Ashby, consort of Capt. Nathaniel Ashby, of Fayette county. Died Monday, Aug. 2, 1802. KG 8/6.

Mrs. ——— McDaniel, of Bourbon county, and two of her children. Died during a storm Tuesday evening, Sept. 7, 1802. KG 9/10.

Robert Dickson, an editor of the Kentucky Gazette. He died Sept. 12, 1802, of cancer of the groin. He was 37 years of age. He was buried in the Presbyterian cemetery at Newton, Bucks county, where he died. KG 10/5.

Richard Terrell, of Jefferson county. Died in Lexington, Sunday evening, October 3, 1802. KG 10/5.

Miss Eliza Edwards, daughter of William Edwards, of Lexington. Died Friday, Oct. 8, 1802, aged 8 years. KG 10/12.

Capt. James Moody, of Lexington. Died Saturday night, Oct. 30, 1802. KG 11/2.

Joseph Tilford, of Lexington. Died Saturday, Nov. 6, 1802. He was buried the following day in Lexington. KG 11/9.

General Benjamin Logan, of Shelby county. Died Saturday evening, Dec. 11, 1802, of a stroke of apoplexy. KG 12/14.

1803

Miss Nancy Cox, daughter of Benjamin S. Cox, of Fayette county. Died March 11, 1803, aged 20 years. KG 3/29.

Mrs. Maria Taylor, consort of William Taylor, of Jessamine county. Died Saturday evening, Mar. 24, 1803. KG 3/29.

The Rev. John Brown. Died Mar. 24, 1803. KG 3/29.

Rev. James Crawford, minister of the Lexington Presbyterian church. Died at his home Wednesday night, Apr. 13, 1803. KG 4/19.

Samuel P. Wallace, infant son of Thomas Wallace, of Lexington. Died Sunday night, July 2, 1803. KG 7/12.

Joseph Hudson, infant son of Joseph Hudson, Sr. Died Saturday Sept. 10, 1803. KG 9/13.

Abel Holmes, Son of Lloyd Holmes, of Lexington. Died in Trenton, N. J., in September, 1803, aged about 24 years. KG 9/27.

David L. Holmes, son of Lloyd Holmes, of Lexington. Died October 10, 1803. See above. KG 10/11.

Mr. Thomas Hicks, at Lancaster, Penna. He was a native of England. He died in December, 1802, while on his way to Kentucky. Left quite an estate to an unknown brother then living in Kentucky. KG 10/11.

Judith Carter, wife of Job Carter, of Fayette county, late of Lancaster county, Va. She died Friday, Dec. 2, 1803, and was buried the day following at Mr. Edward Payne's, senr. KG 12/20.

Andrew Holmes, of Lexington. Died Saturday, Dec. 10, 1803. Buried in the town burying ground. KG 12/13

1804

Otho Beatty, of Franklin county. Died Wednesday, February 8, 1804. KG 2/14.

Mrs. Pricella Bright, consort of Mr. Nicholas Bright, of Lexington. Died Saturday night, Feb. 11, 1804. Buried at Lexington. KG 2/14.

Mrs. Nancy Gilliam, consort of Thomas Gilliam, of Fayette county, and daughter of Richard Downton and Mary, his wife. She died Feb. 17, 1804, in child bed, at the age of 23 years. She left two children. KG 2/21.

John Baptiste Kalb, of Lexington. Died Feb. 18, 1804. KG 2/21.

John Harrison, an aged resident of Lexington. Died very suddenly on Saturday, May 26, 1804. KG 5/29.

Robert Megowan, an aged resident of Lexington. Died May 17, 1804. KG 5/22.

Mrs. Elizabeth Moseby, wife of Capt. John Moseby, of near Georgetown, Scott county. Died July 18, 1804. KG 7/24.

William Lowrey, formerly of Lexington, Ky. Died July 17, 1804, as a result of a gun would inflicted during a duel fought with a Mr. Hurd, from Georgia. The duel took place at Kaskaskias. He was a son of Nathaniel Lowrey, of Lexington. KG 8/7.

Nicholas Bright, of Lexington. Died Friday morning, Aug. 10, 1804. KG 8/14.

Elizabeth Story, daughter and only child of William Story, of Georgetown. She died Thursday, Aug. 30, 1804, of cholic. She was buried in Lexington the following day. KG 9/4.

Mrs. Frances Scott, consort of Gen. Charles Scott, of Woodford county. Died Saturday, Oct. 6, 1804. KG 10/9.

Elenor Leavy, infant daughter of William Leavy, of Lexington. Died Thursday, Oct. 6, 1804. KG 10/9.

James Madison Moore, son of the Rev. James Moore, of Lexington. Died Sunday, Oct. 14, 1804. KG 10/16.

Gen. John Caldwell, Lieutenant-Governor of Kentucky. Died Friday evening, November 9, 1804. KG 11/13.

Frederick Zimmerman, Esq., of Jessamine county. Died when thrown from his horse "with such violence that it put a period immediately to his existence," on Thursday evening, Dec. 11, 1804. KG 12/18.

Mrs. Sanders, consort of Col. Robert Sanders, of Scott county. Died Saturday evening, Dec. 23, 1804. KG 12/25.

Mrs. Jane Maxwell, of near Lexington. Died Friday, Dec. 28, 1804, at a very advanced age. She was the mother of John Maxwell. KG 1/1/1805.

Miss Mahalah Ayres, daughter of Samuel Ayres. Died Saturday, Dec. 29, 1804. KG 1/1/1805.

Mr. Burton Ayres. Died Sunday, Dec. 30, 1804. KG 1/1/1805.

Patrick McCullough, an early adventurer and long resident of Lexington. Died Monday, Dec. 31, 1804. KG 1/1/1805

1805

Alexander Adams, one of the first settlers of Lexington. Died Saturday morning, Jan. 12, 1805, aged 85 years. KG 1/15.

Peter January, Sr., of Lexington. Died Monday night, Jan. 21, 1805. KG 1/22.

Mrs. Anne Starks, consort of John Starks, of near Lexington. Died Jan. 26, 1805. KG 1/29.

Thomas Martin, son of Major John Martin, of Clark county. Died Feb. 16, 1805. KG 2/26.

Mrs. Barbara Springle, consort of Jacob Springle, of Fayette county. Died Friday evening, March 8, 1805. KG 3/12.

Alexander MacGregor, of Lexington. Died Monday, Apr. 8, 1805. KG 4/9.

James Marshall, son of Col. James Marshall, of Brook county, Va. Died Friday morning, May 10, 1805. KG 5/14.

Col. Robert Sanders, of Scott county. Died May 17, 1805. KG 5/21.

George G. Boswell, sheriff of Scott county. Died Wednesday, May 22, 1805. KG 5/28.

Mrs. Ann Henry. Died Monday morning, July 15, 1805, at an advanced age. KG 7/16.

Mrs. Eve, of Lexington. Died by hanging herself Saturday, July 20, 1805. KG 7/23.

John Strode, Sen., of Strode's Station. Died August 18, 1805. "As honest a man as ever God made." KG 8/20.

Francis Lea, formerly of Lexington where he was a young Silversmith. Died in Frankfort, Monday morning, Sept. 9, 1805. KG 8/24.

Patrick Gullion, of Lexington. Died Tuesday morning, Oct. 8, 1805. He was supposed to be nearly 100 years old. KG 10/10.

Richard Butler, of the U. S. Army. He was a resident of Fayette county, and died Saturday, Oct. 19, 1805. KG 10/24.

Mrs. Kay, consort of James Kay, of Scott county. Died Tuesday, Nov. 5, 1805. KG 11/7.

Mrs. Sally Marshall, daughter of Robert Carstarphan, who lived about six miles from Lexington on North Elkhorn. She died at Capt. Bullards, at the mouth of Cumberland, on Aug. 8, 1805. From advertisement in KG 12/5.

William W. Downing, of Lexington. Died from inflammation of the brain Monday, Dec. 16, 1805. KG 12/19.

1806

Mrs. Ann Payne, consort of Edward Payne, of Fayette county. Died Jan. 11, 1806, aged 78 years. She had been married to Edward Payne for fifty years. KG 1/16.

Col. David Robinson, of Lexington, an early settler. Died March 7, 1806, aged 77 years. KG 3/8.

Mrs. ———— Pope, consort of John Pope, of Lexington. She died March 12, 1806. KG 3/12.

Miss Elizabeth McCalla, daughter of Andrew McCalla, of Lexington. Died Tuesday morning, April 1, 1806. KG 4/2.

Patrick Watson, son of Capt. Patrick Watson, formerly of Clark county. Died in Havanna, in August, 1805. KG 4/2/1806.

Mrs. Margaret L. Downing, consort of Dr. R. W. Downing, of Lexington. Died Thursday morning, Apr. 10, 1806. KG 4/12.

Maria Blythe, daughter of the Rev. James Blythe. Died Saturday, Apr. 12, 1806. KG 4/16.

Thomas Lewis West, son of Mrs. Edward West, of Lexington. Died Monday evening, April 14, 1806. KG 4/16.

Major John Crittenden, of Woodford county. Died Tuesday, March 30, 1806, when a tree fell on him. KG 5/3.

Edward Payne, died Saturday evening May 17, 1806, aged 80 years. KG 5/20.

Capt. Henry Marshall, one of the early settlers of Lexington. Died Friday, May 30, 1806. KG 5/31.

Walter Chiles, of Shelby county. Died Tuesday, June 24, 1806, aged 65 years. KG 6/28.

Mrs. Mary Nicholas, relict of the late George Nicholas, of Lexington. Died Tuesday morning, July 1, 1806. KG 7/1.

Archibald Milam, of Scott county. Died at his place, 'Shannon's Mill,' June 12, 1806. KG 7/1.

John Clark, of Fayette county. Died Thursday June 26, 1806. KG 7/1.

Joseph Walker, of Scott county. Died July 10, 1806, aged 84 years. KG 7/15.

Jacob Dinchman, of Lexington. Died Saturday morning, July 19, 1806. KG 7/22.

Mrs. Rebecca Barr, consort of Robert Barr, of Fayette county. Died July 19, 1806, leaving 'a numerous family of children.' KG 7/22.

James Hutchinson, of Scott county. Died July 28, 1806, aged 66 years. He was buried July 29, at 10 o'clock a. m., 'in Col. Collin's grave-yard.' KG 8/5.

John R. Shaw, of Lexington. Killed Saturday, Aug. 17, 1806, by a blast being used in a well for Lewis Sanders, near Lexington. See page —, obituary notice for John R[obert] Shaw, well-digger, who was killed Sept. 6, 1813. KG 7/25.

Green McCreery, son of Elijah McCreery, of Clarke county. Killed in a fall, Friday morning, Aug. 29, 1806, aged 3 years. KG 9/4.

Mrs. Polly Taylor, consort of George G. Taylor, of Clark county. Died Sept. 24, 1806. KG 9/25.

John Stevenson, merchant, of Adair county. Died Saturday, Sept. 14, 1806. KG 9/29.

Edward Fugate, of Bourbon county. Died Sept. 28, 1806. KG 10/6.

Elizabeth Lowrey, granddaughter of Nathaniel Lowrey, of Lexington. Died Saturday morning, Oct. 11, 1806, aged 6 years. KG 10/13.

Susannah, infant daughter of Doctor Michaag, of Lexington. Died Oct. 26, 1806. KG 10/27.

Miss Jane Hawthorn, sister of Messrs. James and Thomas Hawthorn, of Lexington. Died Sunday evening, Oct. 26, 1806. KG 10/27.

Hon. John Breckinridge, Attorney-General of the United States. Died Sunday morning at 8 o'clock, Dec. 14, 1806, of an infection of the stomach. KG 12/14.

1808

Edward Porter, brother of Capt. Porter, of Paris. He died Sunday, Apr. 3, 1808, when attacked by a party of Indians as he traveled on a trading expedition up the Tennessee River. R 5/7/1808.

Mr. ————— Hervy, of Mason county. Died Apr. 3, 1808, during the attack mentioned above. R 5/7.

Colonel Thomas Hart, an old and very respected resident of Lexington. Died Thursday evening, June 23, 1808. R 6/25.

William Price, of Jessamine county. Buried Sept. 9, 1808, with military funeral honors. KG 9/26.

1809

Hon. Allan M. Wakefield, one of the circuit judges of Kentucky. Died Dec. 10, 1808. R 1/12/1809.

Mrs. Hannah Higgins, of Mercer county. Died 'some time ago' in December, 1808, aged 97 years. She was the wife of Robert Higgins, deceased, who had died 'some years ago,' aged 110 years. They left six children, 48 grandchildren and 26 great grandchildren. KG 1/3/1809.

Hezekiah Harrison, of Fayette county. Died Jan. 10, 1809, at an advanced age. R. 1/12.

Capt. Daniel Wilson, Sr., of Henderson county. Died in January, 1809. R 1/30.

Mrs. McCreary, consort of the Rev, James McCreary, of Henderson county. Died in January, 1809. R 1/30.

Mrs. Gano, consort of Dr. I. F. Gano, of Frankfort. She died in January, 1809. KG 1/24.

Mrs. Mary S. Clifford, consort of John D. Clifford, and daughter of William Morton, of Lexington. Died Mar. 2, 1809. KG 3/14.

John Moore, Sr., father of the Rev. James Moore, of Lexington. Died Feb. 16, 1809, at an advanced age. KG 3/21.

John Tucker, of Bourbon county. Died Friday, Mar. 31, 1809, when his powder mill, located about five miles from Paris, blew up. There were about 7,000 pounds of powder on hand. KG 4/4.

John Jones, of Bourbon county. Died Friday, Mar. 31, 1809, when John Tucker's mill exploded. See above. KG 4/4.

Mrs. Mary Dewees, of Lexington. Died Thursday night, June 30, 1809. KG 7/4.

Charles Mason, of Frankfort. Died Friday, July 14, 1809. KG 7/18.

Capt. George Mansel, of Fayette county. Died of cholic, July, 1809. KG 7/18.

Major Thomas Love, of Frankfort. Died Sunday, July 30, 1809. KG 8/15.

Jacob Erwin, of Lexington. Died Thursday night, Aug. 10, 1809. KG 8/15.

Mrs. Rachel Barton, of Fayette county. Died Aug. 19, 1809, aged 84 years. Buried in Lexington, beside her late husband. KG 8/22.

Capt. Kenneth McCoy, a Revolutionary Soldier. Died Aug. 17, 1809. KG 8/22.

Thomas Lewis, of Fayette county. Died while on his way to Virginia, Thursday, Sept. 7, 1809. His body was returned to Lexington and interred at his farm near that city. KG 8/12.

George W. Nicholas, son of the late Col. George Nicholas, of Lexington. He was a Midshipman on board the U. S. Frigate, Essex, off New York. Died Sunday, Sept. 3, 1809. KG 10/31.

Thomas Hart, of Lexington. Died Sunday night, Nov. 26, 1809, aged 37 years. KG 11/28.

Dr. Samuel McKee. Died Sunday, Nov. 5, 1809. KG 11/28.

Col. James F. Moore, senator from Jefferson and Bullitt counties. Died Thursday evening, Dec. 14, 1809. KG 12/19.

1810

Miss Jane Robards, daughter of William Robards, of Jessamine county. Died Thursday night, Feb. 22, 1810. KG 2/27.

Nathaniel Lowry, of Fayette county, an old and respected citizen. Died Saturday morning, Aug. 11, 1810. KG 8/14.

Benjamin Burbridge, of Clark county. Died Sunday, Oct. 7, 1810. KG 10/9.

Alexander Frazer, a native of Ireland, but for several years a resident of Lexington, Ky. Died Nov. 7, 1810. KG 11/13.

1811

Mrs. Sarah Maxwell, consort of John Maxwell, of Lexington. Died March 4, 1811, aged 53 years. KG 3/5.

Hugh Meglone, merchant of Lexington. Died Friday, March 8, 1811. KG 3/12.

Daniel M. C. Payne, of Fayette county. Died Sunday, May 5, 1811. KG 5/14.

Mrs. Mary Postlethwait, consort of John Postlethwait, and daughter of 'our present venerable governor' (Charles Scott). Died Saturday evening, June 6, 1811. KG 6/18.

Samuel B. Clarke, of Fayette county. Died Monday, Sept. 2, 1811, aged 21 years. KG 9/3.

Mrs. Pheby Rose, consort of James Rose, of Lexington. She died Sept. 3, 1811. KG 9/10.

Henry Purviance, of Lexington. Died Tuesday, Sept. 10, 1811. KG 9/17.

Henry Brown, of Lexington, lately of Baltimore, Md. He died Monday morning, Sept. 16, 1811. KG 9/17.

John Kinkead, of Harrodsburg. Died Sept. 11, 1811, aged 17 years. KG 9/24.

Capt. James Speed, of near Danville. Died Oct. 3, 1811. He was an early settler of that vicinity. KG 10/1.

Miss Mary Davenport, sister of Samuel T. Davenport, of Lexington Died Thursday night, Oct. 17, 1811. KG 10/22.

Dr. Caleb Baker Wallace, son of the Hon. Caleb Wallace, of Kentucky. Died at Black Swamp, N. C., Sept. 4, 1811, aged 25 years. KG 10/22.

Mrs. Elliott, consort of the Rev. James Elliott, late of Virginia. Died Wednesday, Nov. 20, 1811. KG 11/26.

Mrs. Frances Letitia Levett, consort of A. B. Levett, of Lexington. Died Saturday, Nov. 23, 1811. KG 11/26.

James Rose, shoemaker of Lexington. Died Nov., 1811. KG 12/3.

Gen. Jonathan Clark, of Jefferson county. He died Nov. 25, 1811, aged 61. He was a soldier in the Revolution. KG 12/17.

1812

Robert Campbell, of Lexington. Died Sunday, Jan. 9, 1812, aged 58 years. He was a native of Ireland, and a soldier in the American Revolution. KG 1/21.

George Frick, of Lexington. A hatter, late of Lancaster, Pa. Died Saturday, Jan. 18, 1812. KG 1/21.

Mrs. Catharine Henly, consort of Thomas Henly, of Lexington. Died Saturday morning, Feb. 1, 1812. KG 2/4.

James Dishman, of Lexington, late of Port Royal, Va. He died Saturday, Feb. 1, 1812. KG 2/4.

Mrs. Harriet Long, consort of Samuel Long, Esq., of Lexington. Died Feb. 27, 1812, aged 24 years. She left three small children and her husband. KG 3/3.

George Washington Pleasants, of Woodford county. Died on Wednesday evening, Apr. 8, 1812, aged 23 years. He was one of the editors of the *Palladium*. KG 4/21.

Dr. Alexander M. Edmiston, of Lancaster, Ky., and only son of Capt. John Edmiston, of Fayette county. Died Saturday, July 11, 1812, aged 25 years. KG 7/21.

Mrs. Mary Rankins, consort of Samuel Rankins, of Lexington. Died Sunday, July 19, 1812. KG 7/21.

Lewis Lunsford Hayden, of Jessamine county. Died July 17, 1812, aged 19 years. KG 7/28.

Dr. R. W. Downing, for a number of years a practicing resident of Lexington. Died Thursday, Aug. 20, 1812. KG 8/25.

Mrs. Mary Anne Witherspoon, consort of Dr. John R. Witherspoon, and daughter of Gen. Robert Todd. Died at Wappataw, near Lexington, Aug. 25, 1812, aged 19 years. KG 9/1.

Major William Gordon Forman, of the Mississippi Territory. Died in Lexington, Ky., while on his way to New Jersey, Sept. 22, 1812. He left his only child, a little girl of four years, who was traveling with him. KG 10/6.

George Buck, of Lexington. A native of England. Died Dec. 14, 1812, aged 64 years. KG 12/22.

Col. John M. Scott. Died Sunday evening, Dec. 27, 1812. See obituary in KG 12/29.

1813

John Bibbs, of Fayette county, lately of Charlotte county, Va. His body was found Sunday, Jan. 14, 1813, in a field in W. William's pasture, or racefield, about one mile from Lexington, near the Georgetown road. According to the verdict of the coroner of Fayette county, Benjamin Stout, he had been murdered and robbed of $5,000 in bank notes. KG 1/26.

Henry Riddle, of Lexington. Died in January, 1813, from wounds received at the battle of Massissinewa. KG 1/26.

Salem Piatt, of Lexington. Died in January, 1813, from a wound received at the battle of Massissinewa. A public demonstration was held for Piatt and Riddle (see above) in Lexington, Feb. 22, 1813. KG 1/26.

Joshua Pilcher, of Lexington. Died Saturday evening, March 13, 1813, when shot through the head by a careless volunteer, on parade. Mr. Pilcher was standing in the Markethouse at the time of the fatal accident. KG 3/16.

Mrs. Mary Armistead Howard, consort of Governor Howard. She died at at the house of John T. Mason, of Lexington, March 21, 1813. Her husband had "gone to answer the call to duty and had departed for his territory when the end came." She was buried the next day in the Episcopalian Burying Ground at Lexington. KG 3/20.

Lewis West, a citizen of Lexington. Died Friday, Apr. 9, 1813. KG 4/13.

John Allen, Esq. Died in the battle at the River Raisin, on Jan. 22, 1813. KG 5/4.

Andrew Barbee, of Lexington. Died Thursday evening, July 1, 1813, when thrown from his horse. KG 7/6.

1813

John R. Shaw, well-digger and stone quarrier, of Lexington. Died Monday evening, Sept. 6, 1813, when blownup in a well he was digging for Robert Wilson. He was the author of the biography bearing his name. KG 9/7.

John Jordan, Jr., Post Master of Lexington. Died Thursday, Sept. 9, 1813. He was an early settler of Lexington. KG 9/14.

General Charles Scott. Died Friday, October 22, 1813, aged 74 years. KG 10/26.

Lieut. Isaac Bickley, of Kentucky. Died in Louisiana, near St. Mary's Parish, Sept. 26, 1813, aged 20 years. KG 10/26.

Capt. Samuel Price, son of Samuel Price, of Lexington. He died in Ohio, in November, 1813. KG 11/15.

Lieut. Richard Price, son of Samuel Price, of Lexington. (See above.) He died in Cincinnati, Ohio, in Nov., 1813. KG 11/15.

Major Levi Hukill, of Lexington. Died Sunday morning, Dec. 5, 1813. Obituary. KG 12/6

William Satterwhite, of Lexington. Died Sunday, Dec. 26, 1813. Buried the Tuesday following in the Presbyterian Cemetery, with Masonic honors. Obituary. KG 1/10/1814.

1814

William Bobb, of Lexington. Died Saturday, Jan. 8, 1814. He left a widow and three small children. KG 1/10.

George Anderson, merchant of Lexington. Died Wednesday, Jan. 19, 1814. KG 1/24.

Miss Caroline Smith, daughter of the President of Princeton College. She died Friday, Jan. 21, 1814, at the Fayette county, Ky., residence of Mr. J. C. Breckenridge. KG 1/24.

Thomas Holloway, of the firm of Holloway, Bain and Steel, of Lexington. Died Friday, Jan. 21, 1814. KG 1/24.

Mrs. Agnes Steel, relict of Robert Steel, of Lexington. Died Sunday morning, Feb. 5, 1814, at an advanced age. KG 2/21.

Mrs. Elizabeth McCullough, wife of Archibald McCullough, of Lexington. Died Mar. 6, 1814, aged 81 years. KG 3/28.

Archibald McCullough, of Lexington. Died Mar. 18, 1814, aged 96 years. This old gentleman and his wife (see above) were natives of Ireland and had been married 63 years. KG 3/28.

General Robert Todd, of Lexington. Died at the home of his son, Dr. John Todd, in March, 1814, aged 57 years. Obituary. KG 3/28.

Mr. Francis Downing, of Lexington. Died in March, 1814, aged 90-odd years. KG 3/28.

John Happy, of Lexington. Died in March, 1814. KG 3/28.

Mrs. Sarah Hudson, relict of the late Joseph Hudson, of Lexington. Died in March, 1814. KG 3/28.

Mrs. Margaret Elder. Died in March, 1814, aged 70-odd years. KG 3/28.

Mrs. Elizabeth Price, wife of Samuel Price. Died in Mar., 1814, aged 70-odd years. KG 3/28.

John Cock. Died in Mar., 1814, aged 62 years. KG 3/28.

John Elder, of Lexington. Died near here, in April, 1814. KG 4/4.

George Adams, of Lexington. Died in Apr., 1814. KG 4/4.

John Wilson, of Lexington. Died in Apr., 1814. KG 4/4.

Alexander Smith, Sr., of Fayette county. Died in Apr., 1814. KG 4/4.

Mrs. Susan Bell, wife of Thomas Bell, of Woodford county. She died Monday, Apr. 4, 1814, aged 53 years. KG 4/11.

John Monroe, of Georgetown. Died in Apr., 1814, aged 60-odd years. KG 4/11.

Daniel Comstock, of Lexington, formerly of Providence, R. I. Died in April, 1814. KG 4/11.

John Rucker, Sr., of Fayette county. Died Apr. 23, 1814, aged "62 years or upwards." KG 5/2.

Col. William Johnson, of Scott county, second son of Colonel Robert Johnson. Died Monday evening, Apr. 25, 1814. Obituary. KG 5/2.

Mrs. Mary Brand, relict of the late J. W. Brand, of Lexington. Died Saturday, May 21, 1814. KG 5/23.

Col. Roger Thompson, of Mercer county. Died Aug. 17, 1814, aged 72 years. KG 8/29.

David Demaree, of Shelby county. Died Aug. 21, 1814. KG 8/29.

Mrs. Elizabeth R. Hanna, consort of John H. Hanna and daughter of the Hon. Thomas Todd. Died at Frankfort, Aug. 23, 1814. KG 8/29.

John Savary, a native of Lyons, France, but recently of Bourbon county, Ky. Died Aug. 24, 1814, at Galliopolis, Ohio. Obituary. KG 9/19.

Lieut. Col. John B. Campbell, of the 11th Regt. U. S. Army. Died at Williamsville, Aug. 28, 1814, of wounds received at the battle of Chippewa. KG 9/19.

Capt. George Frazer. Died Thursday, October 6, 1814, aged 60 years. Obituary. KG 10/10.

Rev. John P. Campbell. Died near Chillicothe, Ohio, Nov. 4, 1814. KG 11/14.

Daniel White, eldest son of Daniel White, late of Lexington. Drowned November 19, 1814, while attempting to ford the North Fork of Licking. KG 11/28.

1815

Andrew Steele, of New Orleans, formerly of Fayette county, Ky. He was Judge of East Baton Rouge Parish. Died Feb. 13, 1815. Obituary. KG 3/13.

Rev. Mr. Launer Blackman. Drowned in the Ohio river, at Cincinnati, June 6, 1815. KG 6/26.

Philip Barton Key, of Georgetown (Md.?). Died July 28, 1815. Obituary. KG 7/28.

Capt. John Hamilton, of Fayette county. Died Sept. 13, 1815, at Cape Giradeau, on the Mississippi river. He was a military hero. KG 9/25.

General George Trotter. Died in the vicinity of Lexington, Oct. 13, 1815, aged about 37 years. Obituary. KG 10/16.

Mrs. Jane Wood, consort of Major James Wood, of Fayette county. Died Oct. 5, 1815, aged 55 years. KG 10/16.

John Shelby, son of his Excellency Governor Shelby. Died Wednesday, Oct. 11, 1815, a young man. KG 10/16.

Col. Robert Johnson, of Gallatin county. Died Sunday, Oct. 15, 1815, aged 71 years. Obituary. KG 10/23.

Hon. John Sevier, of Tenn. Died Oct. 16, 1815, at Fort Strother. Obituary. KG 10/23.

Brig. Gen. Richard M. Gano. Died Sunday morning, Oct. 22, 1815, aged 41 years. Obituary. KG 10/30.

Richard Corwine, of Maysville. Printer and one of the editors of the *Maysville Eagle*. Died Dec. 19, 1815. KG 12/25.

Mrs. Mary Ann Castleman, wife of David Castleman, of Lexington, and youngest daughter of the late John Breckinridge. Died Feb. 9, 1816, aged 21 years and 5 days. R 2/14.

1816

Mrs. Margaret Trotter, consort of Col. James Trotter, of Fayette county. Died Feb. 19, 1816. KG 2/26.

Mrs. Mary Letcher, consort of Robert P. Letcher, and daughter of William Oden. Died March 9, 1816. R 3/27.

Mrs. Sarah Sneed, consort of Achilles Sneed, clerk of the Court of Appeals, Frankfort. Died Mar. 16, 1816. R 3/27.

Colonel Joshua Baker. Died Monday, Apr. 8, 1816, aged 54 years. R 4/10.

Hon. Richard Stanford, of Georgetown. Representative in Congress from N. C. Died Sunday, Apr. 21, 1816, aged about 47 years. KG 4/22.

William Essex, book-seller, of Lexington. Died Saturday morning, June 15, 1816. KG 6/17.

William S. Vance. Drowned while bathing in Town-Fork of Elkhorn, Saturday, June 22, 1816. He was 24 years old. KG 7/1.

Peter I. Robert, of Lexington. Died Monday, July 1, 1816. KG 7/8.

Ezra Boyer. Died July 4, 1816, when stabbed by a rioting Negro. KG 7/8.

Richard Dounton, farmer of Fayette county. Died Thursday, July 11, 1816, at an advanced age. KG 7/22.

Derick Peterson January, attorney-at-law, of Port Gibson, Mississippi Territory, and formerly of Lexington, Ky. Died July 14, 1816. KG 8/5.

Colonel John Davis, of Gallatin county. Died Aug. 25, 1816. R 10/9.

James T. Steele, of Hopkinsville. Died in Oct., 1816. R 10/9.

Samuel Hunt, of Lexington, late of Massachusetts. He was the father of the editor (?) of the *Reporter*. He died Tuesday, Oct. 8, 1816, aged 71 years. R 10/16.

Mrs. Mary Moore, consort of Capt. Thomas P. Moore, of Harrodsburg. Died Friday, Dec. 6, 1816. Obituary. R 12/18.

J. B. Borland, merchant of Lexington. Died Friday, Dec. 13, 1816. R 12/18.

Mrs. Caroline Rucker, consort of L. E. Rucker, of Woodford county. Died in December, 1816. R 12/25.

Mrs. Margaret B. Sproule, consort of C. Sproule, of Frankfort. Died in December, 1816. R 12/25.

1817

Mrs. Susannah Pryor, of Jessamine county. Died Saturday, Jan. 25, 1817, aged almost 70 years. KG 2/3.

Miss Eleanor Kinkead Lindsay, daughter of Henry Lindsay, of Scott county. Died June 17, 1817, aged 20 years. KG 6/5.

Mrs. Eleanor McCullough and Mrs. Jane Luckie, of Lexington. Killed by lightning while attending church at the Presbyterian church on Sunday, July 20, 1817. R 7/23.

Francis W. Ingram, son of the late William Ingram, of Henderson county. Died July 6, 1817, aged about 19 years. R 7/23.

John W. Vaughan, of Cairo, Tenn., formerly of Lexington, Ky. Died Friday, Sept. 19, 1817. Buried from the Episcopal Church, in the latter place. R 10/1.

Moses Hawkins, of Woodford county. Died Friday night, Oct. 10, 1817. R 10/15.

Mrs. Agatha Alexander, consort of William Alexander, of Woodford county. Died in October, 1817. R 11/5.

John Hamilton, merchant of Versailles. Died Sunday, Oct. 26, 1817. R 11/5.

John W. Blair, of Hopkinsville. Died in October, 1817. R 11/5.

Peyton R. Pleasants, of Frankfort. Died in Woodford county, Sunday morning, Nov. 9, 1817. He had just been married. R 11/19.

James Huston, eldest son of William Huston, of Lexington. Died Sunday, Nov. 30, 1817. R 12/3.

Anson Turner, manager of the White Lead Factory, Lexington. Died Sunday, Dec. 14, 1817. R 12/17.

Mrs. Lucy Le Grand. Died Dec. 1, 1817, aged 71 years. R 12/17.

1818

James Carson. Died Jan. 12, 1818. R 1/21.

Capt. Mann Satterwhite, of Fayette county. Died Friday morning, Jan. 16, 1816. R 1/21.

Hugh Crawford. Drowned while attempting to cross a mill pond, Saturday, Jan. 17, 1818. R 1/21.

Thomas Burling, a printer of the *Reporter,* Lexington. He died Feb. 3, 1818, leaving a wife and child. He was a native of New York. R 2/4.

General George Rogers Clark, of Locust Grove. Died Friday, February 13, 1818, aged 66 years. Obituary. R 2/25.

John Williams, of Woodford county. Killed by his son, Milton Williams, March 13, 1818. He was almost 60 years of age. R 3/25.

George G. Ross, of Lexington. Died Wednesday, Apr. 15, 1818, aged 31 years. R 4/22.

Col. Christopher Greenup, of Frankfort. Died Monday, April 20, 1818, aged 69 years. Obituary. R 5/6.

Mrs. Eliza Pope, consort of John Pope, of Frankfort, Secretary of State. She died April 24, 1818. R 5/6.

General Thomas Posey. Died at Shawneetown, March 20, 1818. R 5/6.

Captain Robert Megowan, of the late firm Buck, Bradford and Megowan, Lexington. Died Wednesday, May 13, 1818. R 5/20.

Mrs. Lydia Allen, wife of John Allen, of Fayette county. Died in May, 1818. R 5/20.

William Carson, of Lexington. Died in May, 1818. R 6/3.

Mrs. Julian Misner, of Lexington. Died in May, 1818. R 6/3.

Mrs. Jane Shields, of Lexington. Died in May, 1818. R 6/3.

Mrs. Louisa Bain, of Lexington. Died in May, 1818. R 6/3.

Charles McIntire, of Russellville, Ky. Died in New Orleans, May 24, 1818. Obituary. R 6/17.

Elisha Warfield, of Fayette county. Died Thursday morning, July 16, 1818, aged 78 years. He was a native of Maryland. R 7/29.

James Ragland, Sr., of Clark county. Died July 18, 1818, aged 75 years. He had been a resident of Clark since 1788. R 7/29.

Mrs. Ann Hart, relict of the Capt. N.G.S. Hart, of Lexington. She died in Philadelphia, July 10, 1818. Obituary. R 7/29 and R 8/26.

Mrs. Fanny D. Berry, daughter of Major Herman Bowman, of Woodford county, and consort of Dr. R. B. Berry. Died at her Fayette county residence Saturday, Aug. 1, 1818, aged 17 years. R 8/12.

Henry P. Smith, attorney-at-law, Harrodsburg, and son of Jesse Smith, of Mercer county. Died Aug. 8, 1818. R 8/19.

Col. Richard Davenport, of Danville. Died in Aug., 1818. Obituary. R 8/26.

James Hughes, of Frankfort. Died at Blue Licks, in August, 1818. Obituary. R 8/26.

Col. William Neely, of Jefferson county, Miss. Died in Winchester, Ky., Aug. 27, 1818. He married Mrs. ———— Irvine, widow of Dr. ———— Irvine, who was killed at the River Raisin. R 9/2.

Rev. William Wallace, pastor of the Presbyterian Church at Paris. Died Thursday, Sept. 10, 1818, aged 33 years. R 9/6.

Francis Drake, of Lexington. He died Friday, Sept. 11, 1818, aged 50 years. R 9/16.

John Prentiss, Sr. Died Saturday, Sept. 12, 1818, aged 75 years. R 9/16.

Mrs. Louisa C. W. Keets. Died in Washington county, near Springfield, in October, 1818. R 10/14.

Mrs. Mary Thompson, consort of Major George C. Thompson, of Mercer county. Died November 10, 1818. R 11/18.

William Flower, son of Richard Flower, of Lexington. He was an English emigrant. Died in November, 1818, aged 21 years. R 11/18.

Robert Rodes, of Madison county. Died Nov. 20, 1818, aged 59 years. Obituary. R 12/2.

1819

William Alexander, of Woodford county. Died Sunday evening, Jan. 17, 1819, aged 90 years. Obituary. R 1/20.

General Matthew Walton, of Springfield. Died Tuesday, Jan. 12, 1819. R 1/27.

Col. William Irvine, of Richmond, Ky. Died Jan. 20, 1819, aged 56 years. Obituary. R 2/3.

John C. Grosjean, M.D., died at the residence of the late Judge Allen, Wednesday, Feb. 3, 1819, aged 27 years. R 2/10.

James Essex, formerly of Lexington. Died at Darien, Ga., in March, 1819. Obituary. R 3/24.

Joseph Craig. Died Mar. 6, 1819, aged 78 years. R 3/24.

Mrs. Eliza Pittman, consort of Daniel Pittman, of Lexington. Died Friday, Mar. 12, 1819. R 3/31.

William Frazer, of Fayette county, late of Spottsylvania County, Va., died in April, 1819. R 4/7.

Miss Olivia M. B. Maccoun, eldest daughter of James Maccoun. Died Saturday, Apr. 24, 1819. R 4/28.

Vivion Goodloe, of Woodford county. Died Apr. 25, 1819, aged 59 years. R 5/5.

David Love, of Lexington. Died in St. Louis, Mo., May 16, 1819. R 5/19.

Mrs. Ann Essex, of Lexington. Died May 21, 1819. R 5/26.

Miss Juliann Lee, daughter of General Henry Lee, of Mason county. Died Sunday, May 23, 1819. R 5/26.

Mrs. Elizabeth Duke, consort of Thomas Duke, of Washington, Ky. Died Tuesday morning, May 25, 1819. R 5/26.

Capt. Stoughton Gantt, of the U. S. Army. Died Sunday, May 23, 1819. R 5/26.

Col. George McAfee. Died at his residence in Mercer county, on Salt River, May 28, 1819, aged 42 years. Obituary. R 5/9.

Major Anthony Bartlett, of New Castle, Henry county. Died June 1, 1819. R 5/6.

John Maxwell, of Lexington. Died Thursday, July 2, 1819, at an advanced age. He was a first settler of Kentucky. R 7/7.

Dr. Henry Skinner, of Eddyville. Died June 23, 1819, aged 34 years. Obituary. R 7/14.

Francis Buckner, of Christian county. Died June 30, 1819, aged 62 years. Obituary. R 7/14.

Sarah H. Cook, of Fayette county. Died July 18, 1819, aged 25 years. R 7/28.

James Berthhoud, of Shippingport. Died at Henderson, July 14, 1819. He was a native of France. R 7/28.

Mrs. Rebecca Bradford, relict of the late Benjamin Bradford, of Nashville, Tenn. Died in Lexington, Ky., Saturday, July 31, 1819. R 8/4.

Thomas Whitney, an old resident of Lexington. Died Friday, Aug. 6, 1819. R 8/11.

Mrs. Nancy Jacob, consort of John J. Jacob, of Louisville. Died in Lexington, Friday morning, Aug. 13, 1819. R 8/18.

Richard Marsh, of Lexington. Died Aug. 12, 1819. R 8/18.

Cary L. Clarke, of Georgetown. Died July 23, 1819. R 8/18.

Thomas Rodman, of Jefferson county. Died June 27, 1819, aged 47 years. R 8/18.

Col. George Walker, of near Nicholasville. Died Aug. 19, 1819, aged 50 years. R 8/25.

Mrs. Polly Lewis, consort of Gabriel Lewis, of Russellville. She died in August, 1819. R 8/25.

Mrs. Eliza Keene, consort of Dr. Marcellus Keene, of Georgetown. Died Friday morning, Aug. 20, 1819. R 9/8.

Capt. William Warren, of Lincoln county. Died Sept. 3, 1819, aged 80 years. He had been a resident of Lincoln since 1779. R 9/8.

Mrs. Margaret Fletcher, daughter of the late Colonel George Nicholas, and consort of Col. Thomas Fletcher, of Bath county. She died in Owingsville, at the residence of Col. Thomas Deye Owings, Sept. 1, 1819. R 9/8.

Jacob Johnson, of Lexington, formerly of Philadelphia, Pa. Died Sept. 7, 1819. R 9/15.

Isaac Outter, Sr., of Mason county. Died in September, 1819, aged 71 years. R 9/15.

Alfred Turner, son of James Turner, of Tenn. Died at Smithfield, Ky., in Sept., 1819. R 9/22.

Col. John Lenthicum. Died near Bardstown in Sept., 1819. R 9/22.

John Brackett, of Shelby county. Died in Sept., 1819, aged 76 years. He was one of the first settlers of Kentucky. R 9/22.

Mrs. Lettice Haslett, consort of William F. Haslett, of Woodford county. Died in September, 1819. R 9/22.

Dr. William Baldwin, of the U. S. Navy. Died Wednesday, Sept. 22, 1819. Obituary. R 9/29.

Mrs. Amelia Steele, consort of Richard Steele. Died at Versailles, Sept. 15, 1819, aged 34 years. R 9/29.

William P. Sinclair, of Scott county. Died in September, 1819. R 9/29.

Major Benjamin Eggleston, of Hopkinsville. Died in September, 1819. R 9/29.

Col. William Cannon, of Caldwell county. Died in September, 1819. R 9/29.

Major Jordan Harris, of Caldwell county. Died in Sept., 1819. R 9/29.

Daniel Bennett, of Scott county. Died in Sept., 1819, aged 76 years. R 9/29.

David M. Percefull, of Bardstown, formerly of Lexington. Died in Sept., 1819, while still a young man. R 9/29.

Mrs. Sarah Thompson, consort of William Thompson, of Maysville. Died in October, 1819. R 10/16.

Capt. John M. Young. Died at the Fayette county residence of John Glover, Saturday morning, Oct. 2, 1819, aged 33 years. R 10/16.

Gen. Samuel Hopkins, of Henderson county. Died in Oct., 1819. R 10/6.

Samuel Ewing, of Fayette county. Died in Oct., 1819, at an advanced age. R 10/13.

Mrs. Julia Barclay, consort of J. G. Barclay, of Louisville. Died in October, 1819. R 10/13.

Elijah Groaddus, of Hopkinsville. He was a merchant. Died in October, 1819. R 10/20.

Mrs. Sarah Garner, consort of Jeremiah Garner, of Bowling Green. Died in November, 1819. R 11/10.

Mrs. Catherine Springer, of Frankfort. Died in November, 1819. R 11/10.

Andrew Campbell, of Green county. Died in Nov., 1819, aged 54 years. R 11/10.

Capt. Moses Daulton, of Washington county. Died in Nov., 1819, aged 60 years. R 11/10.

Capt. James Finnie, of Union county. He was one of the first settlers of Kentucky. Died in November, 1819. R 11/17.

Capt. William Farrow, of Fleming county. Died October 17, 1819, aged 80 years. He was a native of Prince William county, Virginia. Obituary. R 11/17.

Richard Bell, of Henry county. Died in Dec., 1819. R 12/8.

Mrs. Nancy Fry, consort of Capt. John Fry, of Lexington. Died Sunday, Dec. 5, 1819. R 12/8.

Dr. Michael Ryan, of Maysville. Died in Dec., 1819. R 12/8.

James Megowan, of Lexington. Died Dec. 9, 1819. R 12/15.

Mrs. Lydia Hosmer, relict of Dr. John Hosmer, of Natchez, Miss., formerly of Lexington, Ky. Died in Dec., 1819. R 12/15.

Capt. William Sutton, of Scott county. Died in Dec., 1819. R 12/22.

Preston Breckenridge, of Fayette county. Died in Dec., 1819. R 12/22.

Mrs. Margaret Keiser, of Lexington. Died Dec. 28, 1819, at a very advanced age. R 12/31.

1820

Walter Alves, of Henderson county. Died Jan. 24, 1820. R 1/19.

Benjamin Howard Payne, son of Edward Payne, of Fayette county. Died Feb. 22, 1820. R 3/1 and 3/8.

Dr. George Chamblin. Died in New Orleans, Feb. 13, 1820. Obituary. R 3/8.

George Shindlebower, of Lexington. He was a well known musician. Died Saturday morning, Mar. 18, 1820. R 3/22.

Col. Abraham Bird, of Fayette county. Died in March, 1820, aged 88 years. R 3/22.

Major James Fisher, of Fayette county. Died Wednesday, April 12, 1820, aged 70 years. Obituary. R 5/3.

James Dunlap, of Lexington. Died Saturday, Apr. 29, 1820. R 5/3.

John D. Clifford, of Lexington. Died Monday, May 8, 1820, aged 42 years. R 5/10.

James Monroe Breckinridge, youngest child of Mrs. Mary H., widow of John Breckinridge. Died at the residence of Dr. Louis Marshall, Thursday, Apr. 19, 1820, aged 14 years. R 5/10.

John Madison, of Frankfort, Auditor of Kentucky. Died on Saturday, May 13, 1820. R 5/17.

Rev. James McChird, pastor of the Market street Presbyterian Church, Lexington. Died in Fayette county, Monday morning at 11 o'clock, May 29, 1820. Obituary. R 5/31.

Samuel Dodge, third son of David Dodge, of Winchester. Died May 21, 1820, aged 19 years. R 5/31.

Thomas S. Brand, of Lexington. Died Sunday morning, June 11, 1820, aged 9 years. R 6/14.

Patterson Bain, Jr., son of Capt. P. Bain, of Lexington. Died Saturday, June 10, 1820. R 6/14.

Mrs. Morton, consort of William R. Morton, of Lexington. Died Thursday morning, June 29, 1820. R 7/5.

Mrs. Magdalane Lotspeich, of Lexington. Died Friday morning, July 7, 1820, aged 67 years. R 7/12.

Col. Richard Dallam, of Butler county. Died June 27, 1820, aged 80 years. R 7/12.

James Boggs, Sr., of Madison county. Died in August, 1820. He was a hero of the American Revolution. R 8/23.

David C. Irvine, of Madison county. Died in August, 1820. R 8/23.

William Grimes, Jr., of Madison county. Died in August, 1820. R 8/23.

Thomas Mastin, of Franklin county. He was murdered in August, 1820. R 8/30.

Mr. X. J. Gaines, of Lexington, editor of the *Castigator*. He died in August, 1820. R 8/30.

Miss Ann Hosmer, daughter of Dr. Hosmer, formerly of Lexington. Died in Natchez, Miss., Aug. 16, 1820, aged 18 years. She was the last survivor of the family. Obituary. R 9/6.

Jonathan Robinson, of Lexington. Died in New Orleans, on Aug. 16, 1820. R 9/6.

Miss Nancy McCall, daughter of William McCall, of Fayette county. Died in Vincennes, Ind., Aug. 25, 1820, aged 28 years. R 9/13.

Miss Elizabeth Drake, of Lexington. Died Sunday, Sept. 10, 1820, aged 16 years. R 9/13.

John Hart, of St. Louis, late of Lexington, Ky. He was the last surviving son of Col. Thomas Hart, dec'd. He died Sept. 3, 1820, aged 31 years. R 9/20.

Robert Latham, of Russellville. Died in New Orleans in September, 1820. R 10/4.

Thomas Wash, of Logan county. Died on his way home from Greenville Springs, in September, 1820. R 10/4.

Enoch Barr, of Washington (Ky.?). Died at the residence of Robert Barr, in September, 1820. R 10/4.

Colonel Daniel Boone, discoverer and first settler of Kentucky. Died Tuesday, September 26, 1820, at Charette Village, in Missouri, where he was buried. R 10/23.

Captain Bragg, of Lewis county. Died Sunday, Oct. 14, 1820. R 10/23.

Dr. Alexander Patrick, of Woodford county. Died in October, 1820. R 10/23.

Abraham Varnum, of Lexington. Died Monday, Oct. 30, 1820, aged 23 years. R 11/6.

Mrs. Sarah Clifford. Died Friday, Nov. 3, 1820, at an advanced age. R 11/6.

Mrs. Catharine Foster, wife of John M. Foster, Register of the Land Office, and daughter of Governor John Adair. She died November 16, 1820. R 12/4.

Franklin Trotter, son of George Trotter, of Lexington. Died at Augusta, Ga., Nov. 20, 1820. Obituary. R 12/11.

Joshua Brown, of Fayette county. Died Dec. 21, 1820. R 12/25.

Mrs. Laura G. Prentiss, consort of the late Thomas G. Prentiss. Died Dec. 18, 1820. R 12/25.

Mrs. Sarah Richardson, consort of Capt. J. C. Richardson, of Fayette county. Died Wednesday, Dec. 27, 1820, aged 68 years. R 1/1/1821.

Mrs. Martha Satterwhite, relict of William Satterwhite, of Lexington. Died Saturday, Dec. 30, 1820. R 1/1/1821.

Capt. Henry King, Sr., of Jessamine county. Died in Dec., 1820. R 1/1/1821.

Mrs. Rebecca Woods, consort of James Woods, of Breckinridge county. A native of Ireland; she died Dec. 12, 1820, aged 59 years. R 1/1/1821.

1821

Mrs. Mary Tandy, consort of Willis Tandy, of Fayette county. She died in Feb., 1821. R 2/19. The *Lexington* (Ky.) *Public Advertiser* recorded that she was the only daughter of Rev. Robert Cloud, and that she died Jan. 18. 1821, aged 24 years.

Mrs. Bledsoe, consort of Capt. Richard Bledsoe, of Fayette county. Died in Feb., 1821. R 2/19.

Capt. William Crow, of Lincoln county. Died Jan. 23, 1821, aged 68 years. He was one of the first settlers of Kentucky. R 2/19.

Dr. John Watson, of Woodford county. Died Apr. 12, 1821. Obituary. R 4/16.

Mrs. Gist, consort of Henry Gist, of Paris, Ky. Died in April, 1821. R 4/16.

Benjamin Smith, of Fayette county. Died May 8, 1821, aged 63 years. R 5/14.

OBITUARIES

The abbreviations used denote:

KG—(Lexington) *Kentucky Gazette.*
R—(Lexington) *Kentucky Reporter.*

1821

Miss Eliza West, daughter of Capt. W. West, of Lexington. Died Wednesday May 9, 1821. R 5/14.

Samuel T. Davenport, of Kentucky. Died in Detroit, Mich., April 25, 1821, aged 31 years. R 5/14.

William Garnet Brown, of Woodford county. Died May 10, 1821, aged 19 years. He was a son of Oliver Brown. Obituary. R 6/4.

John H. Clark, of Louisville. Died in June, 1821. R 6/11.

Mrs. Eliza S. Akers, consort of Peter Akers, of Flemingsburg, editor of the *Flemingsburg Star*. Died in June 1821. R 6/18.

Thomas Ellis, of Fayette county. Killed by a fall from his horse, Monday June 11, 1821, aged about 60 years. R 6/18.

P. D. Mariano, a resident of Lexington since 1818. He was a native of Italy, and died in Washington, D.C., Sunday evening June 10, 1821, aged 37 years. Obituary. R 7/9.

Capt. William Allen, of Fayette county. Died July 27, 1821. R 7/30.

Mrs. Patsey Henley, consort of Ozborn Henley, late Steward of Transylvania University. Died in Lexington Aug. 1, 1821. R 8/6.

Miss Elizabeth C. Owen, of Versailles. Died July 29, 1821. R 8/6.

Mrs. Nancy Mitchell, consort of John Mitchell, and daughter of the late Daniel Boone. Died in July or August, 1821, and is supposed to have been buried in Mason county. R 8/6.

Mrs. Patterson, consort of John Patterson, of Lexington. Died Friday August 3, 1821. R 8/6.

Major John Harrison, of Louisville. Died in July, 1821, aged 67 years R 8/6.

Capt. James L. Heran, of Lexington. Died Sunday evening, Aug. 21, 1821, aged 32 years. R 8/13.

Roderic Perry, of Woodford county. Died Aug. 9, 1821, aged 45 years. R 8/20.

Mrs. Smith, a native of Scotland. Died at Transylvania, Aug. 8, 1821, aged 107 years. She married at 45, had nine children and lived to see her great, great grand children. R 8/20.

Edmund Rice, of Jefferson county. Died in August, 1821, aged 87 years. R 8/20.

Aaron Ross, of Maysville. Died in Aug., 1821. R 8/20.

Dr. Harvey S. Bradford, of Scott county, and formerly of Port Gibson, Miss. Died August 5, 1821. R 8/20.

Thomas Kennedy, of Covington. Died in August, 1821, aged 80 years. R 8/20.

Mrs. Dulcenea Payne, consort of Col. Jilson Payne, of Montgomery county. Died Aug. 15, 1821, aged 50 years. See obituary in R 8/20.

Capt. Joseph Bickley, of Mason county. Died Aug. 31, 1821, aged 27 years. Obituary. R 9/3.

William Breckenridge, youngest son of the late Captain Alexander Breckenridge, of Lexington. Died Aug. 30, 1821. R 9/10.

William Cochrane, a cashier of the United States' branch Bank of Lexington. Died Monday at noon, Sept. 10, 1821. Obituary. R 9/10.

John W. Payson, of Lexington. Died in Shippingport, Sept. 10, 1821. R 9/10.

Daniel Neill Brawford, formerly a professor at Transylvania University. Died in Jefferson county, Mo., in August, 1821. R 9/10.

George Robinson, of Carlisle, Ky. Died in September, 1821, aged 58 years. R 9/10.

James Ely, Jr., of Elizabethtown, Ky. Died in September, 1821. R 9/24.

Thomas McCurdy, of Logan county. Died in September, 1821. R 9/24.

Mrs. Priscilla May, wife of William L. May, of Edwardsville. Died in September, 1821. R 9/24.

Gen. Percival Butler, of Gallatin county. Died in September, 1821. He was Adjutant General of Kentucky for many years. R 9/24.

Edmund Butler, youngest son of Gen Percival Butler, of Gallatin county. See above. Died in Sept., 1821. R 9/24.

Mrs. Rebecca Robins, of Mason county. Died in Sept., 1821. R 9/24.

William H. Carter, son of W. R. Carter, of Louisville. Died in Sept. 1821, aged 19 years. R 9/24.

Mrs. Baker, consort of Joseph Baker, of Louisville. She died in Sept., 1821. R 9/24.

Capt. John Talbot, deputy sheriff of Jefferson county. He died on Sept. 12. 1821. R 9/24.

Gen. William McDowell, of Bowling Green. Died Sept. 19, 1821, aged 59 years. R 10/1.

Mrs. Eliza McDowell, consort of W. S. McDowell, of Bowling Green. See above. Died September 19, 1821. R 10/1.

Mrs. Ann Garner, consort of John Garner, Sr., of Bowling Green. Died Sept. 19, 1821. R 10/1.

Mrs. Mary Lea, of Mason county. Died in Sept., 1821, aged 73 years. R 10/1.

Mrs. George Chamblin, of Bourbon county. Died Monday Sept. 23, 1821, aged 73 years. R 10/1.

Robert Barr, one of the first settlers of Lexington. He died in Franklin, Mo., Sept. 8, 1821, aged 72 years. Obituary. R 10/1.

Leonard Young, of Fayette county. Died Tuesday October 2, 1821, at an advanced age. Obituary. R 10/8.

Mrs. Jane Wilkins, consort of Charles Wilkins, of Lexington. Died Thursday evening Oct. 18, 1821. R 10/22.

Wingfield Bullock, of Shelbyville. Died Oct. 13, 1821. R 10/22.

Mrs. Nancy Garrett, consort of Capt. Ashton Garrett, of Mount Sterling. Died Oct. 17, 1821. R 10/22.

Col. William Hardin, of Hardinsburg. Died July 22, 1821, aged 77 years. Obituary in R 10/22.

James Campbell, formerly of Lexington. Died at Philadelphia, October 29, 1821. R 11/19.

Archibald Gordon, Jr., son of A. Gordon, of Indiana. Died in Fayette county in November, 1821. R 11/19.

Hugh Miller, of Harrison county. Died in Nov., 1821, leaving his widow and six children. R 12/3.

Mrs. Heddleston, consort of William Heddleston, of Cynthiana. Died in November, 1821. R 12/3.

Mrs. Richard Thompson, of Bardstown. Died in Nov. 1821. R 12/3.

Henry Turner, formerly of Fayette county. Died at Natchez, in November, 1821. R 12/3.

Mrs. Mary Keen, Sr., of Fayette county. Died at S. Keen's in Lexington, Saturday Dec. 1, 1821, aged 78 years. R 12/3.

Joseph Kincaid, of Woodford county. Died in Nov., 1821, at an advanced age. R 12/3.

Col. Thomas Dollarhide, a Senator from Pulaski county. Died at Frankfort in November, 1821. R 12/3.

Mr. Pricella Calmes, consort of Gen. Marquis Calmes. She died in November, 1821. (November 18, 1821.) R 12/17.

1822

James Kelly, of Bourbon county. Died on the last Saturday in Nov., 1821, aged 84 years. He was a native of Ireland. R 1/7/1822.

Col. James Garrard, formerly Governor of Kentucky. Died on Saturday night Jan. 19, 1822, at Mount Lebanon, his residence in Bourbon county, aged 74 years. Obit in R 1/28.

Mrs. Catharine Bedford, consort of Henry Bedford, of Fayette or Bourbon county. Died Jan. 14, 1822. R 1/28.

Mrs. Mary Marshall, wife of A. K. Marshall. Died Jan. 28, 1822. Buried Tuesday Jan. 29, in the family burying ground at the Marshall farm, at Washington, Ky. R 2/11.

Miss Mary, eldest daughter of J. T. Mason, of Lexington. Died Sunday Feb. 17, 1822, aged 13 years. R 2/25.

Miss Joanna, youngest daughter of John Wigglesworth. Died Feb. 20, 1822, aged 14 years. R 2/25.

James Berry, of Madison county. A pioneer of Kentucky. Died in February, 1822, aged 70 years. R 2/25.

Mrs. Eliza Huey, consort of Samuel Huey, of Falmouth, Ky. Died in February, 1822. R 2/25.

Joseph Best, of Pendleton county. Died in February, 1822, at an advanced age. R 2/25.

Joseph K. Glenn, of Pendleton county. Died from a fall from his horse, in February, 1822. R 2/25.

John Woodward, of Winchester. A native of Ireland. Died on Feb. 22, 1822. Obit. R 2/25.

William Payne, of Franklin county. Died in Feb., 1822. R 3/4.

Robert Dearing, of Franklin county. Died by a fall from his horse, in February, 1822. R 3/4.

James Scott, eldest son of the late Rev. Archibald Scott, of Virginia. Died in Shelby county in Feb., 1822. R 3/4.

Mr. W. H. S. Faw, of Washington, Ky. Died in Feb., 1822. R 3/4.

Major John Jouett, of Bath county. Died in March, 1822. See obituary in R 3/11.

Mrs. Hester Andrews, consort of John Andrews, of Fleming county. Died at the Fayette county residence of Col. James McDowell Friday Mar. 22, 1822. R 3/25.

Llewellyn J. Hawkins, of Frankfort. Died in April, 1822, aged 21 years. He was a member of the Senior Class at Transylvania University. R 4/15.

Charles Humphries, Jr., of Lexington. Died Sunday morning Apr. 14, 1822. R 4/15.

Mrs. Susannah E. Graves, consort of James Graves, of Lexington. Died in April, 1822. R 4/15.

Joseph Bosworth, of Lexington. Died Wednesday Apr. 24, 1822. He was a son of Benagah Bosworth. R 4/29.

Allen B. Magruder, of Montville, La., formerly a resident of Lexington. Died March 16, 1822. R 4/29.

William Logan, of Lexington. Died at the Jessamine county home of his father, in May, 1822. R 5/6.

David McIlvain, of Shelbyville. Died at his father's home in Fayette county in May, 1822. R 5/13.

Mrs. Mary O. Rodes, wife of J. C. Rodes, of Lexington. Died Wednesday June 5, 1822. R 6/10.

Miss Catharine E. Richardson, of Lexington. Died Friday June 7, 1822. R 6/10.

James A. Trotter, eldest son of Samuel Trotter, of Lexington. Died June 23, 1822. R 6/24.

Miss Virginia Jouett, youngest daughter of Capt. John Jouett, late of Bath county. Died in Mount Sterling, June 16, 1822. R 6/24.

Miss Sophronia Burrus, youngest daughter of the late Col. Charles Burrus, of Alabama. She died in Lexington, Ky., Monday evening July 1, 1822. R 7/8.

Mrs. Mary Stephens, consort of Luther Stephens. Died on Monday July 8, 1822. R 7/15.

Miss Caroline I. Barr, daughter of the late Robert Barr. Died Monday evening July 8, 1822. R 7/15.

Mrs. Mary Ashton, consort of Richard Ashton, of Lexington. Died Wednesday July 3, 1822. R 7/15.

Benjamin Stout. Died Sunday July 14, 1822. R 7/15.

Daniel Ryan, Jr., proprietor of the Jessamine Paper Mill. Died Friday July 12, 1822. R 7/15.

Dr. Joel Miller, of Louisville, formerly of Lexington. He died July 14, 1822. R 7/22.

Dr. Alexander J. Mitchell, of Frankfort. Died Friday July 26, 1822. R 7/29.

Thomas Daugherty, of Lexington, Clerk of the House of Representatives of the United States. Died in Lexington Friday morning August 9, 1822. R 8/12.

John C. Wooldrige, of Frankfort, Agent for the Penitentiary. Died Monday night Aug. 5, 1822. R 8/12.

Col. Philip White, of Franklin county. Died Aug. 22, 1822, aged 58 years. R 8/26.

Henley W. Moore, of Russellville. Died in August, 1822. See R 8/26.

James Haden, of Logan county. Died in Aug., 1822. R 8/26.

John Kennedy, of Logan county. Died in Aug., 1822. R 8/26.

Edward C. Owings, of Paris, Ky. Died in Aug., 1822. R 8/26.

Newton Curd, of Mercer county. Died in Aug., 1822. R 9/2.

Mrs. Martha Littell, consort of William Littell, of Frankfort. Died in August, 1822. R 9/2.

Miss Courtney January, daughter of Thomas January, of Lexington. Died Aug. 28, 1822. R 9/9.

Theoderick Berkley, of Frankfort. Died in Sept., 1822. R 9/9.

William H. Chinn, of Frankfort. Died in Sept., 1822. R 9/9.

George Ratliffe, of Frankfort. Died in Sept., 1822. R 9/9.

Richard Blanton, of Frankfort. Died in Sept., 1822. R 9/9.

Joseph Addison Woodson, printer, of Glasgow. Died in Aug., 1822. R 9/9.

Miss Lucy Curd, daughter of the late James Curd, of Jessamine county. Died in August, 1822. R 9/9.

Mrs. Hannah Holderman, consort of Jacob Holderman, of Aetna Furnace, Ky. Died Sept. 2, 1822, aged 32 years. R 9/16.

Martin Smith, of Greenup county, Ky., formerly of Virginia. Died Sept. 1, 1822, aged 68 years. Obituary in R 9/16.

Reverend John Price, of Jessamine county. An early settler of Kentucky. Died Sept. 10, 1822, aged 77 years. R 9/16.

Mrs. Elizabeth Dickinson, consort of Thomas I. Dickinson. Died Thursday Sept. 12, 1822. R 9/16.

Charles C. Cox, of Lexington, late of Woodford county. He died Thursday Sept. 12, 1822, aged 22 years. Obituary in R 9/23.

Major William Croghan, of Locust Grove, Ky. Died in Sept., 1822. R 9/30.

John Hackley, of Bardstown. Died in Sept., 1822. R 9/30.

Robert Housley, of Bardstown. Died in Sept., 1822. R 9/30.

Samuel J. Postlethwait, second son of Capt. John Postlethwait, of Lexington. Died in Sept., 1822. R 9/30.

Thomas W. Lowry, of Lexington. Died in Sept., 1822. R 9/30.

James Richey, of Fayette county. Died in September, 1822, aged 31 years. R 9/30.

Mrs. Martha Steel, of Shelby county. Died in September, 1822, aged 74 years. R 9/30.

Capt. Thomas Warren, of Christian county. Died in Sept., 1822, leaving a widow and large family of children. R 10/7.

George C. Harlan, of Mercer county. Died in Sept., 1822, R 10/7.

John Anderson, of Lexington. Died Oct. 6, 1822. R 10/7.

Mr. C. Crow, a grocer of Lexington. Died in Oct., 1822. R 10/7.

Major Walker Baylor, of Bourbon county. Died in Sept., 1822. Long obituary in R 10/14.

John Todd Russell, of Lexington. Died in October, 1822, in Gallatin county. R 10/14.

Mrs. Elizabeth Taylor, consort of Col. Edmund Taylor, of Frankfort. Died Oct. 7, 1822. R 10/14.

George Wood, of Lexington. Died on passage to England in October, 1822. R 10/21.

Samuel E. Richards, of New Jersey. Died in Lexington, Ky., in October, 1822. R 10/28.

Hiram Shaw, hatter of Lexington. Died in Oct., 1822. R 10/18.

Mrs. Payne, consort of Henry Payne, of Fayette county. She died in October, 1822. R 10/28.

Mrs. Mary Jeffries, consort of S. Jeffries, of Winchester. Died in Clark county on October, 1822. R 10/28.

Capt. John Thomson, son of Asa Thomson, of Fayette county. Died in Missouri Sept. 18, 1822. Obituary in R 10/28.

William Woolfolk, Sr., of Jefferson county. Died in Oct., 1822, aged 70 years. R 10/28.

John G. Gray, of Gallatin county. Died in Oct., 1822, aged 38 years. R 10/28.

Mrs. Mary L. Hart, wife of Capt. Thomas P. Hart, of Fayette county. Died Friday morning Oct. 31, 1822. R 11/4.

James Hughes, of Nicholas county. A Senator from Nicholas and Bracken counties. Died in October, 1822. R 11/4.

1822-23

Rev. Robert Wilson, pastor of the Presbyterian Church at Washington, Ky. Died in October, 1822, leaving a wife and nine children. R 11/11.

Daniel Eppes, of Frankfort, late of Petersburg, Va. Died Wednesday Nov. 20, 1822. R 12/2.

Thomas G. Jones, of Winchester. Died in Dec., 1822. R 12/16.

Martin Duralde, Sr. Died at Attakapos, La., in December, 1822, aged 86 years. R 12/23.

Col. Michael Jones, of Kaskaskia. Died in Nov., 1822. R 12/23.

Edmund Irvine, of Richmond. Shot by Mr. Mattingly, editor of the *Republican,* Tuesday Dec. 16, 1822, the wound proving fatal. R 12/23.

William Lane, merchant of Carlisle, formerly of Winchester, and Lexington. Died in December, 1822. R 12/23.

Joel Emmory, of Madison county. Died in May, 1822, aged 106 years. R 12/23.

Thomas Prather, of Louisville, late president of the Louisville Branch Bank. Died in Feb., 1823. R 2/10.

W. L. McConnell, of Lexington. Died Apr. 19, 1823. R 4/21.

Mrs. Mary Hawkins, widow of the late P. Hawkins, of Lexington. Died April 17, 1823. R 4/21.

John Higbee, of Fayette county. Died April 28, 1823, aged 65 years. R 4/28.

Mrs. Emily Anderson, consort of Capt. William Anderson, of Fayette county. Died Sunday May 4, 1823. R 5/12.

Bryant Ferguson, of Fayette county. Died Thursday May 8, 1823, aged 88 years. He had been a resident of Fayette county since 1785. R 5/12.

Charles Bickley, a young graduate of Transylvania University. Died May, 1823, at the home of his father in Mason county. R 5/19

Mrs. Ruth Frazer, consort of Dr. Joel Frazer. Died May 11, 1823, at the residence of Mrs. Ruth Warfield, near Cynthiana. R 5/19.

Thomas Cavandaugh, of the U.S. Army. Died in May, 1823, while on his way to his mother's in Clark county, Ky. R 6/2.

Mrs. Mary Desha, consort of Benjamin Desha. Died in May, 1823, at the Mason county residence of her father, William Bickley. R 6/2.

1823

Lucretia H. Clay, third daughter of Henry Clay. Died on Wednesday June 18, 1823, aged 15 years. R 6/23.

Crowford Masterson, of Danville. Suicided Monday July 8, 1823. R 7/14.

Cornelius Coyle, of Lexington, a native of Ireland. Died July 17, 1823. R 7/21.

Thomas M. Prentiss, of Lexington. School-master and former librarian of the Lexington Library. Died Friday July 18, 1823. R 7/21.

Absalem Cavins, of Franklin county. Died Aug. 9, 1823. R 8/18.

Miss Maria Von Phul, of Edwardsville, Ill., formerly of Lexington, Ky. Died in August, 1823. R 8/18.

Capt. Abraham Ward, of Frankfort. Died in Aug., 1823. R 8/25.

Thomas Barr, of Fayette county. Died Aug. 1, 1823, at New Orleans. He was about 45 years of age. R 8/25.

Dr. William Nelson, oldest son of Capt. Thomas Nelson, of Lexington. Died in August, 1823, at Petite Gulph, on the Mississippi River. He was a graduate of Transylvania Medical College. R 8/25.

Francis M. Taylor, late a student at Transylvania University. Died Aug. 26, 1823, aged 20 years, at his father's in Shelby county. R 9/8.

John P. Aldridge, of Jefferson county. Died in Aug., 1823. R 9/8.

Mrs. Nancy Bates, widow of Alvin Bates, dec'd., of Jessamine county. Died Monday Sept. 1, 1823. R 9/8.

Reuben Ewing, of Logan county. Died in Sept., 1823. R 9/15.

James Mosby, of Russellville. Died in Sept., 1823. R 9/15.

Russell Lewis, of Frankfort, formerly Deputy Sheriff of Franklin county. Died in September, 1823. R 9/15.

Gwyn R. Tompkins, of Fayette county. Died Sept. 16, 1823. R 9/22.

Mrs. Elizabeth Smith, widow of the late Capt. Rowley Smith, of Shennandoah county, Va. Died in Todd county, Ky., July 26, 1823, aged 70 years. R 9/22.

Thomas Ficklin, of Scott county. Died September 18, 1823, aged 81 years. R 9/29.

1823

Mrs. ——————— Bradley, daughter of Thomas Ficklin, of Scott county. Died in September, 1823. R 9/29.

Mrs. Helen H. Johnson, wife of William Johnson. Died at Great Crossings in September, 1823. R 9/29.

Mrs. Sarah Dallam, of Hopkinsville. Died in Sept., 1823, a few days before the death of her father, Francis Dallam, of the same place. R 9/29.

Mrs. Nancy Dougherty, relict of the late Thomas Dougherty, of Lexington. Died Sept. 24, 1823. R 9/29.

Col. James Innis, of Blue Spring on North Elkhorn. Died Wednesday Sept. 24, 1823. R 9/29.

Joseph Singer, of Fayette county. Died Sept. 26, 1823. R 9/29.

William Arnold, of St. Louis. Died in Sept., 1823, aged 32 years. He was a native of Ireland. R 9/29.

William Stokes, of St. Louis. Died in Sept., 1823. He was a native of England. R 9/29.

Sanford Keen, of Lexington. Died Saturday morning Oct. 4, 1823, aged 38 years. Obituary in R 10/6.

Laurence Leavy, of Louisville. Died Thursday Oct. 2, 1823, aged 25 years. He was a son of William Leavy, of Lexington. Obituary in R 10/6.

Mrs. Sarah Cavins, of Scott county, consort of Absalem Cavins. She died in September, 1823. R 10/6.

Gen. Martin D. Hardin, of Franklin county. Died in Oct., 1823. R 10/13.

Rev. Joseph B. Lapsley, of Warren county. Died in Sept., 1823. R 10/13.

Cuthbert S. Anderson, of Frankfort. Died in Logan county in October, 1823. R 10/13.

James Hawkins, of Woodford county. Died Oct. 7, 1823, aged 39 years. Obituary in R 10/20.

Mrs. James Hawkins, widow of James Hawkins, of Woodford county. She died Oct. 9, 1823, aged 35 years. See above. Obituary in R 10/20.

Mr. Mary B. Kendall, consort of Amos Kendall, editor of the *Frankfort Argus,* and daughter of the late William Woolfolk, of Jefferson county. Died Monday Oct. 13, 1823. R 10/20.

J. N. Destrehan, of New Orleans. Died in October, 1823. R 10/27.

Major Joseph Anderson, of Murfreesborough, Tenn. Died in October 1823. R 10/27.

1823

Reverend Ambrose Bourne, of Todd county. Died in Oct., 1823. R 10/27.

James Stone, of Fayette county. Died Monday Oct. 6, 1823. Buried on the Tuesday following at 11 o'clock in the family burying ground of William Stone. Obituary in R 10/27.

John H. Barnes, clerk of the Circuit and County Courts of Estill county. Died Oct. 2, 1823, at Irvine. R 10/27.

Dr. Joseph Crockett, Jr., of Nicholasville. Died at the residence of Daniel B. Price, Oct. 15, 1823, aged 37 years. Obituary in R 11/10.

Jesse D. Winn, of Fayette county. Died Oct. 22, 1823, aged 72 years. R 11/24.

Martin Whiting, of Natchez. Died in Nov., 1823. R 11/24.

Mrs. Reed, consort of Thomas B. Reed of Natchez. Died in November, 1823. R 11/24.

Joshua Humphries, of Lexington. Died Nov. 23, 1823. R 11/24.

Mrs. Mary Hardin, consort of Gen William Hardin, of Frankfort, keeper of the Penitentiary. Died Dec. 7, 1823. R 12/22.

Capt. Edward Howe, of Woodford county. A Revolutionary soldier. He died Dec. 16, 1823, aged 80 years. R 12/22.

Thomas Bullitt, of Louisville. Died Dec. 10, 1823, aged 47 years. R 12/22.

Mrs. Margaretta McCall, of Surrogate, Sulphur Well in Clark county. Died Dec. 22, 1823, aged 48 years. She left her husband and ten children. R 12/30.

Mrs. Sarah Keen, consort of Oliver Keen, of Lexington. Died Tuesday Jan. 20, 1824. R 1/26.

Richard Allen, of Fayette county. Died Thursday Jan. 22, 1824, at an advanced age. R 1/26.

Joseph Cabell Breckinridge. His funeral sermon was delivered "in McChord's church" Sunday Feb. 8, 1824, at three o'clock. R 2/2.

Abraham Stout Barton, of Lexington. Died Tuesday Jan. 27, 1824. R 2/2.

Mrs. West, consort of Edward West, of Lexington. She died Saturday February 7, 1824. R 2/9.

1824

Reverend Henry Toler, minister of the Baptist church at Versailles. Died in Woodford county, Tuesday Feb. 3, 1824. R 2/16.

Mrs. Eliabeth Lee, consort of the late Major John Lee, of Woodford county. Died in Russellville, in Feb., 1824, at an advanced age. R 2/16.

John Whitney, of Georgetown. Died in Feb., 1824. R 2/16.

Hon. John Rice Jones, Judge of the Supreme Court of Missouri. Died in February, 1824. R 2/23.

Richard Young, Jr., of Jessamine county. Died in February, 1824, aged 22 years. R 2/23.

Jacob Keller, of Fayette county. Died Feb. 21, 1824. R 2/23.

John Moore, of Fayette county. Murdered Wednesday night, Feb. 18, 1824, by his son John Moore, Jr. R 2/23.

General Thomas Overton, of Nashville, Tenn. A soldier of the Revolution. Died in Feb., 1824, aged 72 years. R 3/8.

Mr. Francis Marshall. Died Mar. 6, 1824, aged 26 years. R 3/15.

Thomas Bridges, eldest son of John Bridges, of Lexington. He died in March, 1824, of wounds received from a Negro who was attempting to rob his father's home. Obituary in R 3/22.

Hon. William Lee Ball. Died in March, 1824, aged 45 years. Obituary in R 3/22.

Mrs. S. Humphreys, consort of C. Humphreys, of Lexington. Died on March 23, 1824. R 3/29.

Mrs. Elizabeth Atchison, consort of John Atchison, of Fayette county. Died March 20, 1824. R 3/29.

Mrs. Elizabeth B. Reed, consort of M. J. Reed, of Jessamine county. Died March 20, 1824, aged 28 years. R 3/29.

Reverend James Elliot, of Woodford county. Died Tuesday morning, March 30, 1824, aged 62 years. R 4/5.

William Anderson, of Clay county. Died March 24, 1824, aged 23 years. R 4/9.

Mrs. Jane Irvine, of Lexington. Died Tuesday morning April 20, 1824. R 4/26.

Mrs. William West, consort of William West, of Lexington. Died Saturday April 24, 1824. R 4/26.

Dr. James Wilson, of Woodford county. Died in April, 1824, aged 30 years. R 4/26.

Reverend Mr. Willett, pastor of the Roman Catholic congregation of Lexington. Died Tuesday evening Mar. 4, 1824. R 5/20.

James McCormie, of Paris and Maysville. Murdered Saturday May 10, 1824, by David and Bob Shields. R 5/17.

Jeremiah Neave, of Cincinnati, formerly of Lexington and a native of England. Died May 15, 1824, aged 59 years. Obituary in R 5/17.

Caleb Baker, of Prince Edward county, Va. A soldier of the American Revolution. Died Mar. 10, 1824, aged 90 years. R 5/24.

James W. Forbes, of Frankfort. Died at New Orleans May 1, 1824. R 5/24.

Capt. Samuel Price, of Versailles. Died May 30, 1824, aged 84 years. He was formedly of Lexington. R 6/7.

Miss Matilda S. Russell, daughter of Colonel William Russell of Fayette county. Died in June, 1824. R 6/7.

Mrs. Hannah Baltzell, consort of Gen. George Baltzell, of Frankfort. Died Wednesday May 27, 1824. R 6/7.

Mr. ———— West, of New Orleans. Died at Capt. Weisiger's, in Lexington, in June, 1824, aged 25 years. R 6/7.

Edward, youngest son of B. Bosworth. Died Thursday evening June 10, 1824, aged 12 years. R 6/14.

Robert A. Sturgus, of Richmond, Ky. Died June 8, 1824. R 6/14.

William Kenner, of New Orleans. Died in June, 1824, aged 48 years. R 6/21.

Mrs. Ann Matheny, consort of James Matheny. Died July 22, 1824. R 7/26.

Mrs. Margaret January, of Paris. Died July 20, 1824, aged 77 years. She was a native of Scotland. R 8/9.

John V. Bradford, of Lexington. A young man of promising talent as an artist. Died Friday night, Aug. 20, 1824. R 8/23.

Col. William Williams, of Madison county. Died in August, 1824, aged 45 years. R 8/23.

Simeon Bledsoe, merchant of Cross Plains. Died at Lexington in August, 1824. R 8/23.

Robert C. Parker, of Cincinnati, formerly of Lexington. Died in August, 1824. R 8/23.

Mrs. Pricilla Gorham, consort of John Gorham, of Fayette county. Died in August, 1824. R 8/23.

John H. Todd, of Frankfort. Died Monday night Aug. 30, 1824, aged 28 years. Obituary in R 9/6.

Charles Thom(p)son, of Philadelphia. Died in Aug., 1824, aged 95 years. R 9/6.

Lewis C. Ellis, of Fayette county. Died in Sept., 1824. R 9/6.

Major William Simpson, formerly of Lexington. Died in August, 1824, at Fredericksburg, Gallatin county. R 9/6.

Dr. William Foushee, of Richmond, Va. Died in September, 1824, aged 75 years. R 9/20.

Samuel Ayers, of Danville, and formerly of Lexington. He died on Thursday September 16, 1824. R 9/20.

Mrs. Sarah O. Crittenden, consort of John J. Crittenden, of Frankfort. She died September 14, 1824. R 9/20.

Dr. Samuel C. Smith, of Kentucky. Died of Yellow Fever in New Orleans, in September, 1824. R 9/27.

Dr. Walter B. Wilkerson, of Kentucky. Died of Yellow Fever in New Orleans, in September, 1824. R 9/27.

John Gwathmey, of Kentucky. Died of Yellow Fever in New Orleans in September, 1824. R 9/27.

Joseph F. Piper, of Russellville. Died in September, 1824. R 9/27.

John Wilgus, of Russellville. Died in September, 1824. R 9/27.

William Littell, LL.D., compiler of *Littell's Laws of Kentucky.* Died Sunday morning September 26, 1824. R 10/4.

Mrs. Marshall, the lady of Humphrey Marshall, of Frankfort. Died in September, 1824. R 10/4.

Dr. Samuel H. Littlejohn, of the U.S. Army. Died Sept. 19, 1824. R 10/4.

John Patrick, Sr., of Madison county, Ky. Died at Monroe, Tenn., in September, 1824, aged 58 years. R 10/11.

Willis A. Lee, of Frankfort. Died in October, 1824. R 10/18.

James Pleasants, Sr., father of the present (1824) Governor of Virginia. Died in September, 1824, in Goochland, Va., aged 86 years. R 10/18.

Capt. Collin Bosworth, formerly of Lexington. Died at Iberville, Miss., September 5, 1824. R 10/25.

Mrs. Collin Bosworth, wife of Capt. C. Bosworth, above, formerly of Lexington. She died at Iberville, Miss., Sept. 30, 1824. R 10/25.

Mrs. Sarah Cooper, of Fayette county. Died October 23, 1824. R 10/25.

Dr. Ephriam Frazer, of Mayslick. Died in October, 1824. R 10/25.

Samuel Ayres. Born in Essex county, Virginia. Emigrated to Kentucky in 1784. Died October 16, 1824. See page —— (44). He was 57 years of age. R 10/8.

Mrs. Ann Dudley, consort of the Reverend Ambrose Dudley, of Fayette county. Died Sunday morning November 7, 1824. R 11/5.

Francis Baker. Murdered near Mayslick, in November, 1824, by Isaac Desha. Buried in Shannon cemetery, Mason county. See issues of R and KG for November, 1824, *et seq.*

Miss Mary Humphreys, eldest daughter of Charles Humphreys, of Lexington. Died Thursday night Nov. 23, 1824, aged 19 years. R 11/29 and 12/6.

Thomas T. Barr, of Fayette county. Died Saturday Nov. 27, 1824, R 11/29.

William Akin, merchant of Danville. Died in Fredericktown, Md., in November, 1824. R 11/29.

William Lewis, formerly of Jessamine county. Died at the Mercer county residence of Mr. Rochester, in November, 1824, aged 93 years. R 11/29.

Thomas Reed, of Lexington. Died Friday November 26, 1824. R 11/29.

Capt. Elisha Catlett, of Owingsville, Bath county. Died November 13, 1824, aged 45 years. R 11/29.

General William Henry, of Christian county. Died November 23, 1824. R 12/13.

Thomas Barr, Sr., of Fayette county. Died Saturday Dec. 6, 1824, aged 77 years. R 12/13.

Dr. Frederick Ridgely, formerly of Lexington. Died in Dayton, Ohio, Sunday November 21, 1824, aged 68 years. R 12/13.

Mrs. Ann Gabriella Hawkins, consort of John Hawkins, Sr., of Hopkinsville. Died Dec. 20, 1824. R 1/17/1825.

Mrs. Mary Parrish, consort of Timothy Parrish, dec'd., of Clark county. Died Dec. 27, 1824. R 1/3/1825.

Lieut. Merit Scott, of Lexington, of the U.S. Army. Died on Wednesday Dec. 29, 1824. R 1/3/1825.

Benjamin Rush, son of the late Dr. Rush. and brother of our present (1824)

Minister to Great Britian. Died at New Orleans, December 17, 1824. KG 1/27/1825.

Samuel Lamme, of Harrison county. An old soldier of the American Revolution. Died in December, 1824, "upwards of 75 years." KG 1/3/1825.

1825

Mrs. Eliza Dill, wife of Gen. James Dill, and daughter of Major General Arthur St. Clair, of the Revolutionary Army. She died at Lawrenceburg, Ind., Jan. 16, 1825, aged 62 years. KG 2/10/1825.

Mrs. Elizabeth Allen, consort of William Henderson Allen, of New Castle. Died in January, 1825. R 2/14.

Dr. John L. McCullough, formerly of Lexington. Died Jan. 20, 1825, aged 32 years. Obituary in R 2/14.

Thomas January, of Lexington. Died Wednesday morning, January 26, 1825. R 1/31.

Dr. John M. Harney, son-in-law of the Hon. John Rowan, of near Bardstown. Died Jan. 15, 1825. R 1/31.

Samuel Meredith, of Fayette county. Died Jan. 21, 1825, aged 59 years. R 1/31.

Reverend Ambrose Dudley. Died at the Lexington residence of Dr. B. W. Dudley, Thursday morning at 6 o'clock, January 27, 1825, aged 72 years. R 1/31.

Joseph Allen, of Fayette county. Died Monday Jan. 24, 1825, aged 60 years. KG 2/3.

John S. Herring, of Virginia. Died at Mrs. Keen's Tavern, in Lexington, Sunday January 9, 1825. R 1/10.

Mrs. Amanda M. F. Sharpe, consort of John M. Sharpe, of Lexington. Died Friday Feb. 11, 1825. R 2/14.

Thomas Jefferson Tibbatts, son of Thomas Tibbatts, of Lexington. He died Feb. 19, 1825, aged 22 years. Obituary in R 2/21.

Benjamin W. Patton, of Hopkinsville. Died Feb. 11, 1825. R 2/21.

Mrs. Margaret P. Wickliffe, consort of Robert Wickliffe, of Lexington. Died Wednesday February 23, 1825. R 2/28.

William Stone, of Fayette county. Died Feb. 1, 1825. KG 2/3.

Mrs. Pamelia, consort of Patrick H. Herndon, of Fayette county. She died at the Fayette county residence of Edward H. Herndon, on Sunday Feb. 5, 1825. KG 2/10.

Sarah Ann, infant daughter of John Henry. Burned to death Feb. 5, 1825. KG 2/10.

Levi Outen, of Lexington. Died Feb. 15, 1825, aged 81 years. KG 2/17.

David Stout, son of John W. Stout, of Lexington. Died at the residence of P. Bain, February 4, 1825. KG 2/17.

Mrs. Eliza Coleman Elley. Died in Shelbyville, on her way to Fayette county, February 16, 1825, aged 20 years on the day of her death. KG 2/24.

General William Lewis, late of Jessamine county. Died near Little Rock, Arkansas, Jan. 17, 1825, aged 58 years. Obituary in KG 3/17.

William Galt, of Richmond, Va. Died in March, 1825, aged 68 years. Obituary in R 4/25.

Joshua Collins, of Versailles, lately of Philadelphia. A resident of Versailles, Ky., since 1816. Died March 16, 1825. R 3/21.

George Trotter, Jr., son of George Trotter, Sr., of Lexington. Died at the residence of Col. James Trotter, March 30, 1825. KG 4/7.

William Warren, Sr., of Lincoln county. Died Thursday April 14, 1825. R 4/25.

Garrard Ficklin, of Mercer county. Died April 15, 1825. R 4/25.

Miss Charity Cross, daughter of John Cross, of Fayette county. Died May 6, 1825. KG 5/12.

Walter Connell, of Lexington. Died Sunday morning May 15, 1825. R 5/16.

Mrs. Robert Wilson, consort of Robert Wilson, of Lexington. Died Friday June 3, 1825. R 6/6.

Elias B. Caldwell, of Washington City. Died in June, 1825. Obituary in R 6/20.

William F. Graves, Sr., of the Irish Station, in Nicholas county. He died in June, 1825, at an advanced age. R 6/20.

M. Birkbeck, of Illinois. Died in June, 1825. R 6/27.

Col. William Russell, of Lexington. Died July 3, 1825, aged 66 years. Obituary in R 7/4 and R 7/11.

Mrs. Ann Robinson, of Fayette county. Died at the residence of the Rev. William H. Rainey, Thursday morning June 30, 1825, aged 80 years. R 7/4.

Reverend John Summerfield, of the Christian Church. Died in June, 1825. R 7/4.

James Lyle, of Fayette county. Died in July, 1825, aged 20 years. R 7/11.

Capt. J. C. Buckner, formerly of Georgetown. Died in Lexington in July, 1825. R 7/11.

Mrs. Eliza P. Todd, consort of R. S. Todd, of Lexington. Died in July, 1825. R 7/11.

Mrs. Helen Foster, consort of John Foster, of Mississippi. Died in Lexington, Ky., in July, 1825. R 7/11.

Mrs. Martha Morrison, relict of the late Major John Morrison, of Fayette county. Died in July, 1825. She was the first white woman in the town of Lexington. She arrived here in 1779. R 7/11.

Mrs. Alice Pilcher, consort of Benjamin Pilcher, of Lexington. She died in July, 1825. R 7/11.

William Gibbons, of Lexington. Died in July, 1825. R 7/11.

N. M. Stephens, of Fayette county. He died Sunday morning July 24, 1825. Obituary in R 8/1.

Miss America Kilgore, consort of the Editor of the *Advertiser,* in Danville. She died Monday July 18, 1825, aged 21 years. R 8/1.

Miss Florida Pope, eldest daughter of John Pope, of Washington county. Died at the Lexington residence of Rev. Mr. Hall, in July, 1825. R 8/1.

Reverend John Lyle, of Paris, Ky. Died in July, 1825, aged 55 years. R 8/1.

Woodson Durrett, of Mason county. Died in July, 1825, aged 47 years. R 8/1.

Thomas McClanahan, Grand High Priest of the Grand Royal Arch Chapter of Kentucky. Died Thursday July 28, 1825, in Louisville. Obituary in R 8/8.

John Harvey Wallace, M.D., of Lexington. Died in August, 1825, aged 24 years. Obituary in R 8/15.

Mrs. Maria Owings, consort of Thomas D. Owings, of Owingsville. Died Aug. 9, 1825. She was the eldest daughter of George Nicholas, dec'd. R 8/15 and R 8/22.

Miss Eliza H. Clay, daughter of Henry Clay, of Lexington. Died at Lebanon, Ohio Thursday Aug. 18, 1825, aged 12 years. R 8/22. For note concerning her grave see OR Nov. 6, 1858.

Mrs. Eliza Jane, wife of Col. William A. Dunham, and daughter of James Nephew, of Darien, Ga. Died in August, 1825. R 8/22.

Samuel Duncan, of Fayette county. Died Aug. 25, 1825, aged 65 years. R 9/5.

William B. Long, of Huntsville. He was editor of the *Democrat.* He died August 17, 1825. R 9/5.

Mrs. Abbey Wilson, consort of Samuel S. Wilson, of Jessamine county. Died June 1, 1825, aged 28 years. R 9/5.

Mrs. Susan Clark, consort of the Honorable James Clark, of near Winchester. She died September 1, 1825, aged 33 years. R 9/5 and R 9/12.

Francis Preston, infant son of R. J. Breckinridge. Died at Abingdon, Va., July 14, 1825. R 9/12.

John O'Sullivan Bear, Count of Bearhaven, brother of Barbara O'Sullivan Bear, of Lexington, Ky. Drowned April 14, 1825, in a shipwreck. Obituary in R 9/26.

Achilles Sneed, of Frankfort, Clerk of the Court of Appeals. Died Sunday September 18, 1825. R 9/26.

William Ruggles, of near Danville. Suicided Tuesday morning, September 27, 1825. R 10/3.

Henry Hancock, of Great Crossing. Suicided Monday September 26, 1825. R 10/3.

Miss Jane Hale, of Woodford county. Suicided in September, 1825. R 10/3.

Mrs. Louisa Taylor, consort of Col. Edmund H. Taylor, of Frankfort. Died Friday October 7, 1825. She had been married but one year. R 10/10.

Mrs. Duralde, wife of Martin Duralde, of Lexington, and eldest daughter of Henry Clay. She was a native of Lexington and died on September 18th, 1825, while still young. Obituary in R 10/17.

William P. Foster, of Natchez. Died September 20, 1825. R 10/17.

Mrs. Harriet Drake, wife of Daniel Drake, Professor of the Theory of Medicine at Transylvania University. She died in Cincinnati, Sept. 30, 1825. R 10/17.

Carter Henry Harrison, second son of Robert C. Harrison, of Fayette county. Died Oct. 9, 1825, aged 29 years. Obituary in R 10/24.

James H. McLaughlin, of Hopkinsville. Died October 7, 1825. Obituary in R 10/24.

Cuthbert Bullitt, of Louisville. A native of Shenandoah county, Va., and resident of Louisville since 1802. Died in October, 1825, aged 62 years. R 11/7.

Mrs. Sarah Ann Gibbons, of Lexington. Died in November, 1825, at an advanced age. R 11/7.

Allen Davis, an old inhabitant of Lexington. Died in November, 1825. R 11/7.

Alfred Howard, son of Col. Leslie Combs, of Lexington. Died Sunday night, November 13, 1825, aged 2 years. R 11/14.

John Pope, of Jefferson county. Died Monday October 31, 1825, aged 25 years. R 11/14.

Mrs. Winifred Ewing, consort of Col. Young Ewing, of Christian county. Died November 4, 1825, aged 57 years. R 11/14.

1826

Capt. James Coleman, of Woodford county. Died in November, 1825, aged 76 years. A native of Virginia and a captain of the Virginia line during the Revolutionary War. R 11/28.

John H. Wilkins, editor of the *Commonwealth,* printed at Versailles. Died Nov. 22. 1825. R 12/5.

Thomas Oliver, of St. Genevieve, a former resident of Kentucky. Died December 17, 1825. R 1/9/1826.

Nathaniel Scott, of Garrard county. Died in January, 1826, while sitting on his horse. P.S.: He didn't fall off. R 1/16.

Captain C. Banks, of Mount Sterling. Died in Jan., 1826. R 1/16.

John Logan, of Shelby county. Died Jan. 6, 1826. R 1/16.

Robert Todd, R.S., of Jefferson county. Died in January, 1826, aged 36 years. R 1/16.

Mrs. Rebecca Dudley, consort of Jeptha Dudley, of Frankfort. Died Jan. 21, 1826. R 1/23.

John Shackleford, son of Samuel Shackleford, of Lincoln county. Murdered at the mouth of Salt River in January, 1826. R 1/30.

Mrs. Mary Pindell, consort of Major Thomas H. Pindell, of Lexington. Died Sunday morning Feb. 5, 1826. R 2/6.

Mrs. Elizabeth Bibb, consort of H. G. Bibb, of Russellville. Died in January, 1826. R 2/13.

Hon. Thomas Todd, Circuit Judge of the United States. He died in Frankfort, in February, 1826. R 2/13.

Mrs. Charlotte Chambers Palmer, wife of J. F. Palmer, of Maysville. Died in January, 1826. R 2/13.

Adam Stephens, of Louisville, formerly of Martinsburgh, Va. Died in January, 1826. R 2/13.

James Edmunds, of Barren county, formerly of Virginia. He died in January, 1826, at an advanced age. R 2/13.

Miss Frances Ann Luke. Died at the Mason county residence of her mother, Mrs. A. K. Marshall, in February, 1826, aged 16 years. R 2/20.

William Harding, one of the first settlers of Kentucky. He died in February, 1826. R 2/20.

Capt. Vanallen Prewitt, of Scott county. Died in February, 1826. R 2/20.

Charles C. Sharp, son of Richard Sharp, of Lexington. Died Feb. 23, 1826. In an issue of the *Argus,* Eliza T. Sharp, widow of above, wrote a long letter charging the editor of the *Constitutional Advocate,* P. H. Darby, with instigating and assisting in the murder of her husband, because Darby and Sharp differed in politics. R 2/27 and R 3/27.

Capt. Richard Apperson, of Franklin county. A soldier in the Revolution. Died in February, 1826. R 2/27.

Thomas Murphy, merchant of Louisville. Died on the boat *Belvidere* on her passage to New Orleans, Feb., 1826. He was about 34 years of age. R 2/27.

Robert Porter, of near Falmouth, Ky. A soldier in the Revolution. Died in Feb., 1826, aged 77 years. R 2/27.

Robert H. Carrington, of Cumberland. Died in February, 1826. R 2/27.

Zachariah Smith Taylor, of Mercer county. Died in February, 1826. R 2/27.

John Everett, of Boston, Mass., formerly a professor at Transylvania University. Died Feb. 12, 1826, aged 26 years. Obituary in R 3/6.

Samuel T. Fitzhugh, of Louisville. Died in February, 1826. R 3/6.

Mrs. Harriet O'Fallon, consort of Col. John O'Fallon, of St. Louis. Died in February, 1826. R 3/6.

William Paton, Post Master of Paris, Ky. A native of Virginia and soldier in the Revolution. Died in Feb., 1826, aged 71 years. R 3/6.

William Wheeler, of Bourbon county. Died in Feb., 1826. R 3/6.

Jefferson Fountain, of Frankfort. Died in March, 1826, aged 27 years. R 3/13.

Mrs. Rachel Gray, of Frankfort. Died in March, 1826, aged 90 years. R 3/13.

John Pool, of Fayette county. A soldier in the Revolution. Died in March, 1826, aged about 80 years. R 3/13.

Capt. Richard Bledsoe, of near Athens, Fayette county. He died February 22, 1826. R 3/13.

Mrs. Mary Alison, of Shelbyville. Died in March, 1826, aged 74 years. R 3/13.

Mrs. Elizabeth Wilson, of Shelby county. Died in March, 1826. R 2/13.

Samuel Joseph Cinn, formerly of Philadelphia. Died in March, 1826. R 3/13.

Dr. Walter Warfield, of Lexington. Died Sunday morning March 12, 1826, aged 66 years. R 3/13.

John A. Smithers, of Lexington. Died March 8, 1826. R 3/13.

Mrs. Pauline Hickey, consort of Col. Thomas M. Hickey, of Lexington. Died March 9, 1826. R 3/13.

General Thomas Fletcher, of Bath county. Died Mar. 13, 1826. R 3/27.

Charles Spillman, of Garrard county. Died Mar. 15, 1826, aged 80 years. R 3/27.

William M. Talbott, of Jessamine county. Died March 22, 1826, aged 25 years. R 4/3.

Edward H. Garrard, son of Gen. James Garrard, of Bourbon county. Died in April, 1826, aged 18 years. He was a member of the Senior Class of the Union Philosophical Society at Transylvania University. R 5/1.

Richard Biddle, High Sheriff of Bourbon county. Died on the 25th of April, 1826, at an advanced age. R 5/1.

Algernon Sidney Taul, son of Col. Michah Taul, of Clark county. Died May 1, 1826, aged 22 years. Obituary in R 5/8.

Thomas Throckmorton, Sr., of Nicholas county. Died in May, 1826. R 5/22.

Michajah Bland, of Maysville. Died in May, 1826. R 5/22.

Mrs. Mary Morton, consort of George W. Morton, of Fayette county. Died May 23, 1826. R 5/29.

Mrs. Rebecca R. Pollock, consort of William Pollock, of Fayette county. Died June 1, 1826. R 6/5.

William Humphries, son of Charles Humphries. Died Thursday June 1, 1826, aged 19 years. He was a member of the Senior Class and the Transylvania Whig Society at Transylvania University. R 6/5.

Pierre Louis Morel, of New Orleans. Died May 18, 1826. R 6/12.

Miss Mary Howard, infant daughter of Major William T. Berry, of Lexington. Died June 5, 1826, aged 7 years and 6 month. R 6/12.

Abraham Whitacar, of Lexington, formerly of Baltimore. He died June 6, 1826. R 6/19.

John Barry, father of Major W. T. Barry, of Lexington. He died Saturday June 1, 1826, aged 84 years. He was a soldier of the American Revolution. R 7/3.

Nelson Nicholas, editor of tne *Kentucky Whig.* Died Monday morning July 10, 1826. R 7/10.

Capt. James G. Trotter. Died Saturday morning July 15, 1826, aged 24 years. R 7/17.

Mrs. Nancy Clay, consort of Sidney P. Clay, of Bourbon county. Died June 25, 1826. R 7/17.

James Matson, of Bourbon county. Died June 29, 1826, aged 80 years. R 7/17.

Major Joseph Ashurst, of Fayette county. Died July 2, 1826. R 7/17.

David Morrison, of Cynthiana. Died Sunday July 11, 1826. R 7/17.

Gabriel Hughes, of Bourbon county. Died from injuries received when he accidently walked through an upper floor window on the night of July 6, 1826. He was 29 years of age. R 7/17.

Isaac Shelby, of Lincoln county. Died Thursday afternoon, July 18, 1826, aged 76 years. Obituaries in R 7/24 and R 7/31.

John Smith, Manufacturer, of Lexington. Died July 29, 1826. R 7/31.

Horatio Cozens, of St. Louis. Murdered in July, 1826, by French Strother, of that city. R 7/31.

Col. Walter B. Alexander, of St. Louis. Died in July, 1826. R 7/31.

Stephen Rector, of St. Louis. Died in July, 1826. R 7/31.

Mrs. Langhorne, consort of Major Maurice Langhorne, of Maysville. Died in July, 1826. R 7/31.

Mrs. Judith Key, of Mason county. Died in July, 1826, aged 85 years. R 7/31.

John Blake. Wounded by Reuben Rankin while riding the Paris-Lexington stage. Died Thursday night Aug. 10, 1826. KG 8/11.

William McBee, of Lexington. Murdered Wednesday night, Aug. 9, 1826, by T. Park. R 8/14.

Mrs. Genevieve Blanchard, consort of Horace F. Blanchard, of Woodford county. Died in Lexington Saturday night, August 12, 1826. R 8/14 and R 8/21.

Mrs. Weighard, consort of George Weighard, of Lexington. Died Saturday August 12, 1826. R 9/14.

Col. James Johnson, of Scott county. A member of Congress. Died August 13, 1826. R 8/14 and R 8/21.

General James Winchester. Died in Tenn., in August, 1826. R 8/14.

Mrs. Mary Barbour, of Barbourville, Va., mother of the Secretary of War, James Barbour, of Virginia. She died July 31, 1826, aged 76 years. R 8/21.

Joseph Higgens, a native of Ireland. Died at the residence of James Royle, near Lexington, Ky., in August, 1826. R 8/28.

Edward Le Page, of Concinnati. Died in Aug., 1826. R 8/28.

Capt. Daniel Hughes, of Hindostan, Ind. Died in August, 1826. R 8/28.

Gerard Jones, formerly of Paris, Ky. Died at Evansville, Ind., in August, 1826. R 8/28.

Mrs. Rachel Sedwell, of Bourbon county. Died in August, 1826, aged 83 years. R 8/28.

Henry Thomas, of Bourbon county. Died in August, 1826. R 8/28.

Zachariah Fowler, of Madison county. Died in Aug., 1826. He was 30 years of age. R 8/28.

Mrs. Polly Stone, consort of Dudley Stone. Died in August, 1826. R 8/28.

Edwards Broaddus, of Madison county. Died in Aug., 1826. R 8/28.

Thomas Cornelison, of Madison county. Died in August, 1826. R 8/28.

Mrs. Elizabeth Cornelison, wife of Thomas Cornelison, above, of Madison county. She died in August, 1826. R 8/28.

Samuel Robertson, of Madison county. Died in August, 1826. R 8/28.

Robert P. Henry, of Hopkinsville. A member of Congress. He died in August, 1826. R 9/4.

Dr. Rezin H. Dorsey, of Louisville. Died in Aug., 1826. R 9/4.

Mrs. Ann Maris Carr, consort of W. C. Carr, of St. Louis. Died in August, 1826. R 9/4.

Mrs. Mary Standeford, of Bourbon county. Died in Aug., 1826. R 9/4.

Samuel Schwartzwelder, of Paris, Ky. Died in Aug., 1826. R 9/4.

Samuel Griffith, a representative elected from Harrison, and in favor of the new court. Died Monday Aug. 28, 1826. R 9/4.

Mrs. Eliza Holt, consort of Dr. David Holt, of Fayette county, and daughter of the late Dr. A. Todd, of Paris. She died Thursday morning August 31, 1826. R 9/4.

Thomas Hart, Jr., son of the late Capt. N. G. S. Hart, of Lexington. Died in August, 1826. R 9/4.

Rev. John H. Ficklin, of Scott county. Died August 21, 1826, aged 56 years. R 9/4.

Major Armistead Morehead, of Bowling Green. Died in Aug., 1826. R 9/4.

Capt. Hugh Wilson, of Maysville. Died August 17, 1826, aged 42 years. Obituary in R 9/4. See also R 8/28.

Richard C. Anderson, Minister to Columbia. One of the first white men in the Western country. Died July 24, 1826. Obituary in R 9/11.

Mrs. Elizabeth Cummens, wife of Charles Cummens, of Lexington. Died in Philadelphia, Aug. 16, 1826. R 9/11.

John H. Coleman, lately of Paris. Died at Athens, Alabama, in Sept., 1826. R 9/11.

Mrs. Nancy T. Spears, consort of Abram Spears, of Bourbon county. Died in Sept., 1826. R 9/11.

John Adamson Coleman and Roger Lindsay, infant children of Alexander M. Dunn and Lady, of Mississippi. Died in Lexington, Ky., in September, 1826. They were consigned to one grave here September 15, 1826. R 9/18.

Miss Maria, daughter of Charles Wickliffe, of Lexington. Died in September, 1826. R 9/18.

Martin Blake, of Louisville, formerly of Boston, Mass. Died in September, 1826. R 9/25.

James Humphries, of Lexington. Died Thursday September 21, 1826. R 9/25.

Miss Margaret Lewis, daughter of Mrs. Jane Lewis, of Lexington. Died September 25, 1826. Buried Tuesday Sept. 26, in the Catholic Cemetery at Lexington. R 9/25.

Andrew Cutter, of Cincinnati, formerly of Boston. He died in September, 1826, aged 37 years. R 10/2.

Mrs. Frances Conn, consort of Capt. William Conn, of Bourbon county. Died in October, 1826. R 10/9.

Col. James Elliston, of Grant county. Died in September, 1826. R 10/9.

Mrs. Lydia Wheeler, widow of the late George Wheeler, of Culpepper county, Va., died in Bourbon county, Kentucky, in October, 1826, aged 50 years. R 10/9.

OBITUARIES

Note: The abbreviations used denote:

A—*Argus of Western America*
KG—*Kentucky Gazette*
R—(Kentucky) *Reporter*

1826

Nicholas Glesner, of Bardstown. Died in September, 1826. R 10/9.

Mrs. Harriet Griffith, wife of John T. Griffith, of Natchez. Died in September, 1826. R 10/9.

Mrs. Kise, wife of William Kise, of Fayette county. Died September 27, 1826. R 10/9:

William Kise, of Fayette county. Died Sept. 29, 1826. R 10/9. See above.

Thomas Marshall, Jr., of Winchester, Va. Died in Sept., 1826, half an hour before the death of his wife, Catharine. He was 28 years of age, she 22. R 10/9.

Mr. Francis Downing, of Fayette county. Died in October, 1826, in Madison county. R 10/9.

Miss Rachel Runyon, daughter of Mr. A. R. Runyon, of Mayslick. Died in October, 1826. R 10/9.

George W. Blackburn, son of William B. Blackburn, of Versailles. Died in October, 1826. R 10/9.

Andrew Blair, of Mason county. Died in Sept., 1826. R 10/9.

Nathan Gulick, of Mason county. Died in Sept., 1826. R 10/9.

David Riley. Died at the mouth of Salt River in September, 1826. R 10/9.

Zachariah Herdon (Herndon?), of Scott county. Died in September, 1826. R 10/9.

John A. Miller, of Georgetown. Died in Sept., 1826. R 10/9.

William Doggett, of Shelby county. Died in Sept., 1826, aged 28 years. R 10/9.

Mrs. Susan Roberts, of Logan county. Died in Sept., 1826, aged 70 years. R 10/9.

Philip Washburn, of Logan county. Died in Sept., 1826. R 10/9.

John Washburn, of Logan county. Died in Sept., 1826. R 10/9.

Miss Nancy Davis, daughter of Harrison Davis, of Logan county. Died in September, 1826. R 10/9.

Whiting Washington, of Logan county. Died in Sept., 1826. R 10/9.

Maxwell Proctor, of Logan county. Died in Sept., 1826. R 10/9.

Robert Cashey, of Greene county. Murdered Sept. 12, 1826, aged 82 years, by Malcom Worley, aged 25 years. R 10/9.

Col. Robert Burruss, of Todd county. Died in Oct., 1826. R 10/16.

William C. Watts, of Hopkinsville. Died in Oct., 1826. R 10/16.

John Mordock, of Mississippi. Died in Maysville, Kentucky, in October, 1826. R 10/16.

Mrs. Elizabeth Strong, of Danville. Died in Oct., 1826, aged 77 years. R 10/16.

William Brown, of Richmond, Ky., formerly of Bolton, England. Died in October, 1826, aged 62 years. R 10/16.

Abraham Irvine Lyle, of Bowling Green. Died in Sept., 1826. R 10/16.

James M. Hickman, of Franklin, Mo., formerly of Paris, Ky. Died in Sept., 1826. R 10/16.

Mrs. Betsey Beckett, of Bourbon county. Died in October, 1826. R 10/16.

Capt. Marquis D. Richardson, a native of Fayette county. Died Oct. 3, 1826, in Toliver county, Ga. He was 34 years of age. R 10/23.

Col. Richard C. Anderson, of Jefferson county. An aid to Gen. Lafayette in the Revolutionary War. Died October 16, 1826. R 10/23.

Capt. Edmund Hopkins, of Henderson county. Died in Sept., 1826. R 10/23.

Montgomery Swope, of Henderson county. Died in Sept., 1826. R 10/23.

James William, son of W. H. Ingraham, of Henderson county. Died in September, 1826. R 10/23.

Miss Sarah Towler, of Henderson county. Died in Sept., 1826. R 10/23.

Mrs. Lucinda, wife of George Barnard, of Henderson county. Died Sept. 17, 1826. R 10/23.

Levi Bailey, of Carlisle. Died in Oct., 1826. R 10/30.

George Schultz, of Maysville. Died in Ripley, Ohio, in October, 1826. R 10/30.

Mrs. Margaret Ward, consort of William Ward, of Missouri. Died in Bourbon county, Ky., in October, 1826. R 10/30.

Benjamin Hardesty, of Bourbon county. Died in Oct., 1826. R 10/30.

Nathaniel Sanders, Sr., of Gallatin county. A soldier in the Revolution. Died in Oct., 1826, aged 84 years. R 10/30.

Jesse Rutherford, of Fayette county. Died in October, 1826. R 10/30.

George Smith, of Shelby county. Died in Oct., 1826, aged 68 years. R 11/6.

Col. William Steel, of Woodford county. Died in October, 1826, aged 71 years. One of the first settlers of Kentucky. R 11/6.

Samuel Lippincott, aged 43 years, and his son, Atkinson Rose Lippincott, aged 18 years, both of Rio Brassos, Texas. Died in October, 1826. R 10/30.

Alexander Barrett, of Bourbon county. A native of Virginia and a soldier in the Revolution. Died in Oct., 1826, aged 72 years. R 11/6.

Benjamin Taylor, of Paris, Ky. Died in Oct., 1826. R 11/6.

Robert McConnell Wheelwright, of Lexington. Died November 3, 1826. R 11/6.

Mrs. Nancy Duke, consort of Thomas Duke, late of Kentucky. Died in Texas in October, 1826. R 11/6.

Richard Sharpe, Jailor, of Lexington. Died in Novemer, 1826. R 11/20.

Mrs. Theodosia Taylor, consort of Benjamin Taylor, of Woodford county. Died in November, 1826. R 12/4.

John Williams, of Georgetown. Died in Nov., 1826, at an advanced age. R 12/4.

Mrs. Deborah Summers, consort of William Summers, of Mason county. Died in November, 1826. R 12/4.

James Machie, of Mayslick. Died in Nov., 1826. R 12/4.

David L. Ward, of Jefferson county. Died in Nov., 1826. R 12/4.

John Price, of Lexington. A native of England. Died in December, 1826. R 12/4.

Mrs. Lucinda Love, consort of James Y. Love, of Lawrenceburgh. Died in November, 1826. R 12/4.

Mrs. Julia E., consort of Dr. A. F. Davis, of Augusta, Ky. Died in December, 1826. R 12/11.

William Watkins, of Breckinridge county. Died December 16, 1826, aged 69 years. Obituary R 12/25.

Dr. Preston W. Brown, of Jefferson county. Murdered Friday September 22, 1826, by Randall W. Smith. R 10/2.

J. O. Beauchamp. Executed at Frankfort, at 1:30 o'clock, July 7, 1826, for the murder of Col. S. P. Sharp. See story in R 7/10.

1827

Mrs. J. O. Beauchamp. Killed by her husband, July 7, 1826. Story in R 7/10.

Mrs. Taliaferro, consort of Hay Taliaferro, of Winchester. Died Dec. 24, 1826. Obituary in R 1/6 1827.

James Bennett Wheeler, of Georgia. Died at George Dunlap's, in Fayette county. Ky., Jan. 1, 1827. R 1/10.

Mrs. Elizabeth Pearson, consort of Isaac Pearson, of Harrodsburgh. Died in December, 1826. R 1/10 1827.

Andrew Thorp, of Mason county. Died in December, 1826, aged 69 years. A soldier in the Revolution. R 1/10 1827.

Mrs. Edgar, of Harrison county, mother of J. T. Edgar, of Maysville. Died in December, 1826. R 1/10 1827.

Hon. John Haywood. Died Dec. 22, 1826. Obituary in R 1/10. 1827.

Mrs. Amanda, consort of Dr. J. E. McDowell, and daughter of Gen. Robert Pogue, of Fleming county. Died in Jan., 1827. R 1/13.

Richard A. Maupin. Died January 13, 1827. R 1/20.

Rowland Thomas, clerk of the Henry county Circuit and County Courts. Died at New Castle in January, 1827. R 1/24.

Mrs. Polly Lamme, widow of the late Jonathan Lamme, of Fayette county. Died January 23, 1827. R 1/24.

Miss Susannah Agnes Tibbatts, daughter of Thomas Tibbatts, of Lexington. Died Jan. 21, 1827. Obituary in R 1/24.

John Trott, of Louisville. Died Jan. 28, 1827. R 1/31.

Asa Park, an artist, formerly of Newton. Died Monday morning Jan. 29, 1827 (in Lexington?). R 1/31.

Charles Sharp, of Lexington. Died Feb. 8, 1827. R 2/10.

Dr. Charles Orr, of Lexington. A medical student from Chester District, S. C. Died February 8, 1827. R 2/10.

Samuel Offutt, of Jessamine county. Died Jan. 25, 1827, aged 76 years. An inhabitant of Kentucky since 1801. R 2/10.

George Coons, Sr., of Fayette county. Died March 1, 1827. R 3/3.

William H. Stockdell, of Georgetown. Stabbed by William B. Crawford, March 6 and died March 12, 1827. R 3/14.

John W. Chinn, of Burlington, Ky. Died at the Bourbon county residence of John M. Vonn, Feb. 29, 1827, aged 28 years. R 3/14.

Jacob McConathy, of Lexington. Died Mar. 29, 1827. R 3/31.

Mrs. Mary M. Brown, relict of William Brown, dec'd., of Woodford county. Died in March, 1827, aged 80 years. R 3/31.

Mrs. Catharine Beach, consort of James Beach, of Lexington. Died Sunday March 25, 1827. R 3/31.

John McAlister, of Franklin, Tenn. Drowned Mar. 26, 1827. R 4/11.

Frederick Dickson, of Franklin, Tenn. Drowned in March, 1827. R 4/11.

Mrs. Jane Sharp, relict of the late Richard Sharp, Sr., of Lexington. Died Apr. 17, 1827, at an advanced age. R 4/21.

General John Preston, of Fincastle, Va. Died in March, 1827. R 4/28.

Davis Chinn, of Bourbon county. Died in March, 1827. R 5/9.

Mrs. Clarkson, consort of Peter Clarkson, of Bourbon county. Died in May, 1827. R 5/9.

Mrs. Rebecca, consort of Levi Owen, of Scott county. Died in April, 1827. R 5/9.

Mrs. Ann Ferguson, consort of the late Bryant Ferguson. She died May 16, 1827, aged 86 years. R 5/26.

Amos Cole, of Woodford county. Killed in May, 1827. See story in R 5/19.

Rev. Samuel K. Nelson, of Danville. Died in May, 1827, in Tallahassee, Florida. R 6/9.

Peter Hull, of Lexington. Died July 14, 1827. Obituary in R 7/18.

Samuel H. Woodson. Died at Chaumiere, the residence of D. Meade, in Jessamine county, Saturday morning July 28, 1827, aged 50 years. R 8/1.

Halstead Brown. Died in Lexington, July 30, 1827. R 8/4.

Col. James Trotter, an old and highly respected citizen of Lexington. Died Sunday Aug. 5, 1827. R 8/8.

Edward Worthington, Midshipman. Died at Norfolk, Va., Aug. 1, 1827. Obituary in R 8/8.

Matthew H. Jouett, of Lexington. Died Friday afternoon, August 10, 1827. Obituary in R 8/15.

Isaac Thom, of Louisville. A native of New Hampshire. He died Thursday Aug. 9, 1827. R 8/15.

Colonel Robert Patterson, one of the first emigrants to Kentucky. Died at the residence of his son, near Dayton, Ohio, August 5, 1827, aged 74 years, 4 months and 20 days. R 8/18.

Mrs. Eliza Moore, consort of Dr. Joseph A. Moore, or Versailles. Died Aug. 13, 1827, aged 18 years. R 8/25.

Dr. Horace Holley, late professor at Transylvania College. Died on board the ship *Louisiana* on her passage from New Orleans to New York, in August, 1827. R 8/25. See also *Kentucky Gazette* Aug. 25, 1900.

Daniel, son of John Mitchell. Killed in August, 1827, while working on C. Shultz's steam mill at Maysville. R 8/29.

Mrs. Judith Ann Brown, consort of Mason Brown, of Frankfort. Died in Lexington Tuesday Sept. 28, 1827. R 9/1.

Edward West, an old citizen of Lexington. Died in the last week of August, 1827. R 9/1.

Thomas Oldham, of Lexington. Died in August, 1827. R 9/1.

Nathaniel S. Porter. Died August 30, 1827. R 9/1.

Mrs. Martha Ann Perkins, consort of Dr. J. Perkins, of Mayslick. Died August 21, 1827. R 9/1.

William Darby, a topographical engineer. Died in Maryland, August 30, 1827. R 9/1.

Deacon Hart, of Hamden, Conn. Died from the sting of a bumble bee, Aug. 3, 1827, aged 70 years. R 9/1.

Mrs. Warner, consort of Elijah Warner, of Lexington. Died in September, 1827. R 9/5.

George Taylor, of Clark county. Died in Sept., 1827, aged 47 years. R 9/5.

John Dillard Duval, of Fayette county. Died Sept. 9, 1827. R 9/12.

Clark McAfee, of Mercer county. Died in Sept., 1827. R 9/12.

Mrs. Sarah Coleman, widow of the late Capt. James Coleman, of Woodford county. Died in Sept., 1827, aged 71 years. R 9/15

Joseph Gibbs, of Louisville. Died in Sept., 1827. R 9/19.

Thomas Lewis, of Bourbon county. Died in Sept., 1827. R 9/19.

Robert Payne, of Fayette county. Died in Sept., 1827. R 9/19.

Robert Richardson, of Louisiana, formerly of Richmond, Va. Died in Sept., 1827, aged 66 years. R 9/19.

Ludwell Carey, of Fayette county. Died in Sept., 1827. R 9/19.

Mrs. Matilda Brown, consort of George W. Brown, of Nicholasville. Died August 25, 1827. R 9/19.

Charles Wilkins, of Lexington. Died in Sept., 1827. R 9/26.

John Keen, of Fayette county. Died Sept. 27, 1827. R 9/29.

Jacob Holderman, proprietor of the Iron Works in Hart county. Died in September, 1827. R 9/29.

John Christopher, of Versailles. Died in Oct., 1827. R 10/10.

Mrs. Mary Ann Riley, consort of Jesse M. Riley, of Winchester. Died in October, 1827. R 10/10.

Peter Bonta, of Mercer county. Suicided Oct. 18, 1827. R 10/24.

Daniel P. Cook, of Illinois, late a representative in Congress. Died in Scott county, Ky., at the residence of his father, in October, 1827. R 10/24.

Mrs. Anna Maria Dudley, consort of Dr. B. W. Dudley, of Lexington. Died Tuesday Oct. 23, 1827. R 10/24.

Henry H. Hunt, of Pensacola, Fla., late of Lexington, Ky. Died Oct. 17, 1827, aged 30 years. Obituary in R 10/31.

Waller Overton, of Fayette county. A soldier in the Revolution. Died October 22, 1827, aged 77 years. R 10/31.

Mrs. Croghan, consort of William Croghan, of Locust Grove. Died in October, 1827, aged 24 years. R 11/3.

Frederick William Spence, of Louisville. Died in Oct., 1827. R 11/3.

Rev. Thomas Charlton Henry, of Charleston, S. C. Died Oct. 5, 1827, aged 38 years. Obituary in R 11/3.

Mrs. Annie C. Buck, consort of John L. Buck, of Versailles. Died October 19, 1827, aged 26 years. R 11/10.

Elijah Thornberry, of Scott county. Died Nov. 6, 1827, aged 55 years. years. R 11/14.

George W. Thornberry, son of E. Thornberry (see above.) He died in August, 1827, aged 10 years. R 11/14.

Hon. Henry W. Conway. Killed October 20, 1827, in a duel with Robert Crittenden, Secretary of Arkansas Territory. R 11/24.

William, son of Gen. James Garrard, of Bourbon county. Died in Lexington, Wednesday Nov. 21, 1827, aged 24 years. Obituary in R 11/28.

Richard Young, Sr., of Jessamine county. Died Nov. 16, 1827, aged 54 years. R12/1.

1828

St. George Tucker, of Virginia. Died Nov. 10, 1827. R 12/8.

Hon. Henry Crabb, of West Tenn. Died in Nov., 1827, aged 34 years. R 12/12.

Charles McLear, of Fayette county. A native of Ireland. Died Dec. 2, 1827, aged 40 years. R 12/15.

Daniel McNeil, of Lexington. Found dead Sunday Dec. 16, 1827. Story in R 12/19.

Julius M. Clarkson, of Bourbon county. Died in January, 1828, aged 24 years. R 1/5.

William Lotspeich. Died Jan. 5, 1828, aged 88 years. He died at the residence of his daughter, Mrs. Elizabeth Taylor. R 1/9.

Clifton Rodes, of Barren county. Died Jan. 23, 1828, aged 60 years. Obituary in R 2/6.

Mrs. Lucy T. Thompson, consort of George B. Thompson, of Mercer county. Died Feb. 2, 1828, aged 30 years. R 2/20.

Robert Carlisle, of Woodford county. Murdered Friday morning Feb. 1, 1828. Buried near Washington (Penna.?). Story in R 2/20.

Edward Buckner, of Frankfort, late of Virginia. Died in February, 1828. R 3/5.

Mr. ———— Hopkins, of Georgia. Died in Lexington, Ky., Mar. 3, 1828. R 3/5.

Mrs. Elizabeth Pollard, consort of Capt. John Pollard, of Lancaster. Died in March, 1828. R 4/2.

Alexander Dunlap, of Brown county, Ohio, formerly of Woodford county, Ky. An early settler of Kentucky. Died in Ohio, March 16, 1828, aged 86 years. R 4/2.

Hon. Thomas Montgomery, of Lincoln county. Died in March, 1828. Obituary in R 4/9.

Stephen P. Norton, book binder of Lexington. Died in April, 1828, leaving a wife and several children. R 4/23.

Mrs. Winter, consort of E. I. Winter, of Lexington. Died Wednesday Apr. 23, 1828. R 4/30

Nicholas Talbott, of Bourbon county. Died in May, 1828. R 5/7.

Miss Susan Moore, daughter of William Moore, of Paris, Ky. Died in May, 1828. R 5/7.

W. W. Henning, of Richmond, Va., clerk of the Chancery Court. Died in April, 1828. R 5/7.

Mrs. Cassandra Flournoy, wife of D. Flournoy, of Scott county. Died May 8, 1828. R 5/14.

Richard Monks, Sr., of Lexington. Died May 16, 1828. Obituary in R 5/21.

James Robinett, eldest son of Richard Robinett, of Philadelphia. Died Mar. 31, 1828, aged 34 years. R 5/28.

Mrs. Ann M. Russell, consort of Capt. Thomas A. Russell, of Fayette county. Died May 28, 1828, aged 29 years and 15 days. R 6/4.

Dr. Basil Duke, of Mason county, an aged citizen. Died in May or June, 1828. See R 6/11.

James Cooley, of Ohio, Charge d'Affaires of the United States in Peru. Died February 24, 1828. R 6/11.

Mrs. Rebecca Singleton, consort of Lewis Singleton, of Jessamine county. Died Sunday June 22, 1828. R 6/25.

Joseph Rogers, of Scott county. Died in June, 1828, aged 65 years. R 6/25.

James Grimes, of Fayette county. Died in June, 1828, aged 68 years. R 6/25.

Elias D. Lawrence, of Louisville. Died in June, 1828. R 6/25.

Robert Bowmar, of Woodford county. Died in June, 1828, aged about 88 years. R 6/25.

Gen. John E. King, of Cumberland county. Died in June, 1828, aged 70 years. R 6/25.

William Murphy, Post Master of Maysville. Died in June, 1828. R 6/25.

Jonathan Parrish, of Fayette county. Died in June, 1828. R 6/25.

Mrs. Catharine Ernest, of Lexington. Died in June, 1828. R 6/25.

Mrs. Sarah Brennan, consort of John Brennan, of Lexington. She died Monday June 30, 1828, aged 28 years. R 7/2.

Thomas M. Randolph, of Virginia. Died in June, 1828. R 7/9.

Orville B. Martin, eldest son of John L. Martin, of Fayette county. Died July 15, 1828. R 7/23.

Marquis D. Combs. Died at Thibodauxville. Tuesday July 8, 1828, aged 25 years. R 8/6.

Abraham Cadmus, Jr., merchant of Tuscumbia, Ala., formerly of Newark, N. J. Died in Lexington, Ky., August 20, 1828. R 8/27.

Judge Robert Trimble, of Bourbon county. Died Monday Aug. 25, 1828. R 8/27.

Sarah Anne, daughter of Augustus F. Hawkins, of Lexington. Died Aug. 29, 1828, aged 9 years. R 9/10.

Major D. Ketchum, of the U. S. Infantry. Died at Jefferson Barracks, Mo., in September, 1828. R 9/17.

Rev. Enoch George, of Staunton, Va. Died in September, 1828, aged about 60 years. R 9/17.

Rev. John A Hill, Vicar General of the Diocese of Cincinnati. Died in September, 1828. R 9/24.

Dr. Hugh Steel, editor of the *Illinois Gazette*. Died at Shawneetown, in September, 1828. R 9/24.

Dr. Anderson Watkins, of Augusta, Ga. Died Sept. 16, 1828, in Scott county, Ky., at the home of Lewis Nuckles, his brother-in-law. Long obituary in R 9/24.

Mrs. Meade, consort of David Meade, of Chaumiere, Jessamine county. Died September 28, 1828. R 10/1.

Mrs. Patsey C., consort of Walker Kidd, and daughter of Bird Price, all of Fayette county. Died Sept. 25, 1828. R 10/15.

Hinman Seeley, of Lexington. Died Oct. 25, 1828. R 10/29.

William H. Wood, of Bath county, formerly of Boston. He died Saturday, October 25, 1828. R 10/29.

James H. Graves, of Lexington. Died Oct. 19, 1828. R 10/29.

Capt. James Coleman, of Cynthiana. Died in Nov., 1828, aged 55 years. R 11/19.

Gen. Green Clay, of Madison county. Died in Nov., 1828. R 11/19.

Isaac B. Desha. Suicided in prison, Aug. 15, 1828.(?). See R 12/3.

Mrs. Margaret Bradford, consort of Daniel Bradford, of Georgetown. Died in November, 1828. R 12/3.

Major Charles Morehead, of Logan county. Died in November, 1828. R 12/17.

Mrs. Rachel Cromwell, of Fayette county. Died Dec. 15, 1828, aged about 70 years. R 12/17, 12/24.

John Scott, Sr., an old and respected citizen of Jessamine county. Died December 23, 1828. R 12/31.

Daniel Price, late merchant of Versailles. Died at the residence of Charles Wickliffe, in Lexington, Wednesday, Jan. 7, 1829. R 1/14.

Col. Richard Taylor, of near Louisville. Lieut.-Colonel in the 9th Virginia Regiment in the Continental establishment. Died Jan. 19, 1829, aged 84 years. Obituary in R 1/28.

Capt. Daniel Weisiger, of Frankfort. Died in January, 1829. R 2/11.

Timothy Pickering, of Salem, Mass. Died Jan. 29, 1829, aged 84 years. Obituary in R 2/18.

William H. Smith, student at Transylvania University. Died in February, 1829. See Resolutions in R 2/18.

Major Thomas Sthreshly, of Fayette county. Died Feb. 25, 1829, aged 83 years. R 3/4.

Joseph Patterson, of Fayette county. Born in Augusta county, Virginia. Served in the Revolution and emigrated to Kentucky in 1783. Died Feb. 23, 1829, aged 80 years. R 3/4.

Waddill G. Bruce, of Nicholasville. Died Feb. 24, 1829, aged 45 years and 10 months. R 3/4.

Mr. Chesley Glover, of Montgomery county. A soldier in the American Revolution. Died in February, 1829. R 3/4.

Sidney Bedford, of Bourbon county. Died in February or March, 1829 R 3/11.

David Meade, of Chaumiere, Jessamine county. Died Monday morning, March 9, 1829, aged 84 years. R 3/11.

William Sheely, of Harrison county. Died at the residence of his mother, near Nicholasville, in March, 1829. R 3/11.

Mrs. Caroline Virden, consort of Daniel Virden, of Lexington. Died Saturday, April 4, 1829. R 4/8.

Jacob Ashton, of Dublin Township, Philadelphia county. Died March 1, 1829, aged 84 years. A soldier in the Revolution. R 4/8.

Mrs. Harriett Hurt, consort of Alfred Hurt, of Mount Sterling, and daughter of Robert Grinstead, of Lexington. Died March 31, 1829, aged 22 years. Left her husband and infant child. R 4/8.

Mrs. Martha Bibb, consort of George M. Bibb, of Frankfort. Died in April, 1829. R 4/22.

Robert Francis Kidd, died Tuesday, Apr. 22, 1829, aged 20 years. R 4/29.

Miss Margaret Hume, daughter of George Hume, of Scott county. Died in April, 1829. R 4/29.

Gen. Samuel Finley, of Chillicothe, Ohio. Died at the Philadelphia residence of his son-in-law, Rev. W. L. McCalla, in April, 1829. He was 77 years of age. R 4/29.

Mrs. Lucy Taylor, consort of Col. Colby H. Taylor, of Clark county. Died in April, 1829. R 5/6.

Mrs. Mary Baxter, consort of William Baxter, of Clark county. Died in April, 1829. R 5/6.

Mrs. Elizabeth Clarke, of Lexington. Died Monday, May 4, 1829, at an advanced age. R 5/6.

Mrs. Patsey W. Duncan, consort of Garnett Duncan, of Louisville. Died at the residence of her father, John L. Martin, Sunday, May 3, 1829. R 5/6.

William Davis, of Montgomery county. Killed by lightning, in April, 1829. R 5/6.

Mrs. Mary Grant, of Lexington. Died May 2, 1829. R 5./13.

Thomas Cavins, of Fayette county. Died May 9, 1829, aged 83 years R 5/13.

Mrs. Mary Ann Hardin, consort of Parker C. Hardin, of Columbia, Ky. Died May 6, 1829, aged 24 years. Obituary in R 6/3.

Miss Mary Metcalfe, of Nicholasville. Died in May, 1829. R 6/3.

Major Carey Nicholas, a native of Kentucky. Died in Tallahassee, Fla., in May, 1829. R 6/3.

William Quarles, died Thursday, Mav 22, 1829, aged 25 years. Obituary in R 6/10.

John Cleves Symmes, of Hamilton, Ohio. Died May 23, 1829. Obituary in R 6/10.

Miss Susan Nelson, of Danville. Died in Jonesborough, Tenn., May 8, 1829. She was the daughter of Rev. Samuel K. Nelson, dec'd., and granddaughter of Governor (Isaac) Shelby. R 6/10.

Mrs. Sarah Kizer, consort of the late Jacob Kizer, of Fayette county. Died at the residence of Benjamin Cromwell, June 11, 1829. R 6/17.

Thomas R. Benning, of Lexington. Shot and killed March 9, 1829, by Charles Wickliffe. See story in R 7/8.

Bird Price, of Fayette county. Died Friday, June 3, 1829, aged 74 years. R 7/8.

Mrs. Amanda Morehead, consort of Charles S. Morehead, of Hopkinsville, and daughter of William Leavy, of Lexington. Died Sunday, July 5, 1829, aged 25 years. Obituary in R 7/15.

W. S. Blair, formerly of the U. S. Army. Died in Frankfort, in July, 1829. R 7/15.

Mrs. Elizabeth Bryant, consort of A Bryant. Died in Frankfort in July, 1829. R 7/15.

Elijah Oliver, shoemaker of Lexington. Killed July 18, 1829, by Mark Boston. R 7/22.

John Williams, second son of Mr. A. F. Hawkins. Died July 17, 1829, aged 3 years. R 7/22.

James Anderson Gaither, of near Bardstown. Died in July, 1829, aged 27 years. R 7/22.

Thomas Reed, of Mason county. Died in July, 1829. R 7/29.

Henry Altie, of Mason county. Died in July, 1829, aged 70 years. R 7/29.

Charles Schmidt, of Maysville. Died in July, 1829. R 7/29.

Mrs. Maria Williams, consort of Col. John Williams, of Mount Sterling Died in July, 1829. R 7/29.

Leslie Combs, infant son of John Tilford, merchant of Lexington. Died Friday, July 24, 1829. R 7/29.

Robert Bedford, of Bourbon county. Died in July, 1829. R 8/5.

Mrs. Antoinette C. Offutt, consort of Dr. Azra Offutt, of Jessamine county. Died July 19, 1829. R 8/5.

Mrs. Mary Ellis Todd, wife of George Todd, of Frankfort. Died in August, 1829. R 8/12.

George Madison Thompson, eldest son of George C. Thompson, of Mercer county. Died in August, 1829. R 8/12.

Samuel Scott, formerly of Lexington. Died in Louisville in August, 1829. R 8/12.

Col. A. Muldrow, of Woodford county. Died Aug. 24, 1829. R 8/26.

John W., infant son of Charlton Hunt, of Lexington. Died August 16, 1829. R 8/26.

Gabriel Allen, of Bourbon county. Killed in August, 1829, by a company of Negroes. Story in R 8/26.

Mrs. Eleanor Turner, consort of John Turner, of Jessamine county. Died August 25, 1829. R 9/2.

Miss Sarah Liter, daughter of Henry Liter, of Jessamine county. Died in August, 1829, aged 15 years. R 9/2.

Joseph Buchanan, M.D., of Louisville. Died Thursday, Sept. 3, 1829. R 9/9.

Mrs. Rachel Highbee, consort of James P. Highbee, of Jessamine county. Died Sept. 7, 1829. R 9/16.

John Christian, of Bowling Green. Died in September, 1829. He was about 23 years of age. R 9/16.

Samuel Capbell, of Bowling Green. Died in Sept., 1829. R 9/16.

Hugh Morrison, of Shelby county. Died in Sept., 1829, aged 75 years. R 9/16.

Mrs. Eleanor Taylor, consort of Nathaniel Taylor, of Jefferson county. Died in Sept., 1829. R 9/16.

John Bledsoe, of Fayette county. A patriot of the Revolution. Died Sept. 1, 1829, aged 74 years. R 9/16.

Mrs. Ann Barr, wife of William Barr, of Versailles. Died Sept. 19, 1829, aged 21 years. R 9/30.

Mrs. Ann Catharine Keiser, consort of Benjamin Keiser, of Lexington. Died Sept. 25, 1829. R 9/30.

Maria, infant daughter of Phillip Spare, of Lexington. She died Sept. 26, 1829. R 9/30.

Miss Cordelia Gatewood, daughter of P. Gatewood. Died in Fayette county at the residence of James Wood, Sept. 24, 1829, aged 24 years. R 9/30.

Mrs. Catharine Kennedy, consort of Robert Kennedy, of Winchester. Died in September, 1829. R 9/30.

Mrs. Elizabeth Nelson, of Campbell county. Died in Fayette county Saturday, Sept. 26, 1829. R 9/30.

Benjamin Ayres, of St. Louis, formerly of Lexington, Ky. He died September 10, 1829. R 9/30.

Mrs. Sophia Clay, consort of Porter Clay, of Lexington. Died September 28, 1829. R 9/30.

Seneca McCrackin, of Franklin county. Died Sept. 9, 1829, aged 73 years. He was one of the early settlers of the Western country, which he explored in the year 1776. R 9/30.

Richard Flower, of near Albion, Ill. Died in Sept., 1829, aged 68 years. R 10/7.

Miss Frances Graves. Died at the residence of Dr. Dudley, October 12, 1829. R 10/14.

Charles Wickliffe, of Lexington. He died Friday, October 9, 1829, from wounds received in a duel with George James Trotter, editor of the ***Kentucky Gazette.*** He was 21 years of age. R 10/14.

William D. Jackson, of Bourbon county. Died in October, 1829. R 10/14.

Mrs. Elizabeth Cosby, consort of Abner Cosby, of Millersburg. Died in October, 1829. R 10/14.

Major John Whistler, of the U. S. Army. Died at Bellefonatin, Mo., in September, 1829, aged 71 years. R 10/14.

Capt. Job H. Pike, of Lexington, formerly of Providence, R. I. Died October 19, 1829. R 10/21.

James B. January, one of the oldest members of the Lexington Bar. Died Oct. 16, 1829. R 10/21.

Mrs. Nancy H. Rainey, daughter of the Rev. William H. Rainey, of Harrison county. Died Oct. 16, 1829, aged 18 years. She was from Aberdeen, Ohio. (*Mrs.* evidently typographical error.) See R 10/28.

Joseph William Edmiston, of Washington, Ala., formerly of Lexington, Ky. Died in October, 1829. R 10/28.

Mrs. Mary H., consort of Horace F. Blanchard, of Shelby county. Died Oct. 21, 1829. R 11/4.

Elijah Warner, of Lexington. Died in Philadelphia in October, 1829. R 11/4.

Jefferson Neilson, of Louisiana. A graduate of Transylvania University, Lexington. Died Oct. 25, 1829, aged 24 years. R 11/18.

Isaac Hughes Tyler, of Louisville. Died at Baton Rouge, La., Oct. 25, 1829. He had been married but three days to the daughter of the Hon. Mr. Gurley, of Louisiana. R 11/18.

William V. Rector, of Little Rock, Ark. Died Sept. 16, 1829. R 11/18.

William Day, formerly of Madison county. Died in Clark county at the residence of Ambros Christy in November, 1829. R 11/25.

Hon. Thomas B. Reed, congressman from Mississippi. Died in Lexington, Ky., November 26, 1829. Obituary in R 12/2.

D. P. Buckner, of Georgetown. Died in Lexington Nov. 28, 1829. R 12/2.

Mrs. Elizabeth Watkins, widow of Henry Watkins, her second husband. Died in Woodford county Dec. 4, 1829, aged 80 years. Henry Watkins died ten days before. She was the mother of Henry Clay. R 12/9. (She was Elizabeth Hudson, of Hanover county, Va. She married John Clay, father of Henry Clay, in 1765 when she was 15 years of age. She married Henry Watkins, 26-year-old planter and militia captain, in 1784, almost a year after the death of John Clay.)

William Clark, of Warren county. Died in Dec., 1829, aged 45 years. R 12/9, 12/16.

Col. Joseph Crockett, of Jessamine county. Died Dec. 19, 1829. He was a soldier in the Revolution. R 12/16.

Major James Smiley, of Bardstown. Died in December, 1829, aged 71 years. R 12/16.

Maximilian Young, a citizen of Kentucky. Died in New Orleans in December, 1829. R 12/16.

Joseph H. Cross, formerly of Orange county, N. J. Died in Lexington, Ky., Dec. 9, 1829, aged 27 years. R 12/16.

Capt. Francis G. West. Died Dec. 17, 1829. R 12/30.

Luke Usher, of Lexington. Died in December, 1829, aged about 65 years. R 12/30.

Patrick H. Darby, of Brandenburg, Ky. Died in Dec., 1829. R 12/30.

Richard Hawes, Sr., of Daviess county. Died in December, 1829, aged 59 years. R 12/30. (See *Register*, vol. xxvii, p. 635, which says Richard Hawes, Sr., was born Feb. 3, 1772, and died Nov. 29, 1829.)

Miss Maria Ellen, daughter of Samuel Gwathmey, of Louisville. Died in Dec., 1829, aged 16 years. R 12/30.

Rev. William Staughton, D.D., President of Georgetown College. Died Saturday, December 12, 1829. R 12/30.

David Culberton, of Lincoln county. Suicided in December, 1829. R 1/13/1830.

Daniel McLaughlin. Executed at Flemingsburg, Dec. 11, 1829, at 2 o'clock. R 1/13/1830.

Dr. Benjamin Mason, of Garrard county. Died Dec. 17, 1829. R 1/13/1830.

Dr. W. A. Ficklin, a graduate of Transylvania University. Died at Thebodeauxville, La., Dec. 16, 1829, aged 24 years. R 1/13/1830.

Walter Brasher Crutcher, of Frankfort. Died January 21, 1830, aged about 23 years. R 1/20.

Dr. Samuel Brown, late Professor of Theory and Practice of Medicine at Transylvania University. Died 10 miles from Huntsville, Ala., at the home of Thomas G. Percy, Dec. 12, 1829. He was 61 years of age. Obituary in R 2/3.

Patrick C. Snoddy, of S. C., a member of the Medical Class at Transylvania University. Died Jan. 31, 1830. R 2/3.

Simon Beckham, of Frankfort. Died Feb. 5, 1830, at an advanced age. A 2/10.

Mrs. Elizabeth Pendleton, consort of John T. Pendleton, of Franklin county. Died February 14, 1830. A 2/17.

Mrs. Helen Higgason, consort of Thomas C. Higgason, of Shelby county, and daughter of Col. Samuel Stone, of Oldham county. She died Jan. 23, 1830, aged 29 years. A 2/17.

Mrs. Virginia R., consort of Albert G. Ballard, of Henry county, and daughter of Thomas Smith, Sr. Died Feb. 4, 1830, aged 23 years. Obituary in A 2/17.

Mrs. Mary Edrington, consort of Benjamin Edrington, of Frankfort. Died February 22, 1830, aged 54 years. A 3/10.

Mrs. Elizabeth Keenon, of Paris. Died March 16, 1830, at an advanced age. A 3/24.

Mr. Francis McConnell, of Fayette county. Died March 6, 1830. KG 3/12.

Elias Tapp, of Mayslick. Died March 3, 1830. KG 3/12.

Mrs. Ann Anderson, consort of Larz Anderson, of Louisville. Died Feb. 22, 1830. She was the only daughter of William Pope, KG 3/12.

John Bradford, of Lexington. Died March 20, 1830, aged 83 years. "The moral philosopher of the West." Obituary in KG 4/2.

David Harris, Sr., of Woodford county. Died May 23, 1830. Obituary in R 6/2.

William Vance, of Bowling Green. Died in May, 1830. R 6/2.

Major Valentine Peers, of Maysville. Died at the residence of his son-in-law, Lewis Collins, Saturday, June 19, 1830. He was a soldier in the Revolution. Obituary in R 6/23.

Major Alexander Parker, of Frankfort, formerly a merchant of Lexington. Died in July, 1830. R 7/7.

Edmund Taylor, second son of George W. Anderson. Died Thursday, July 1, 1830. R 7/7.

Col. John Watts, of Bedford county, Va. Died in June, 1830, aged 75 years. R 7/7.

Major Gabriel Tandy, of Harrodsburgh. Died in July, 1830. R 7/7.

Benjamin Kendrick, Sr., of Bourbon county. Died in July, 1830, aged 73 years. R 7/14.

Mrs. Cynthia Ann Grooms, of Frankfort. Died in July, 1830. R 7/28.

William Montgomery, of Franklin county. Died in July, 1830, aged about 60 years. R 7/28.

Mrs. Eleanor Carson, consort of William Carson, of Rockcastle county. Died July, 1830. R 7/28.

Col. Richard Taylor, of Frankfort. A soldier in the American Revolution. He died in July, 1830, aged 60 years. R 7/28.

Fielding Bradford, youngest son of John Bradford, decd., of Lexington. Died at Lawrenceburgh, Ky., while on his way from his residence in Louisiana to Lexington. Died in July, 1830. R 7/28.

Dr. James Walker, dentist of Lexington, lately from Pennsylvania. Died July 22, 1830. R 7/28.

Mrs. Sarah Morton, consort of William Morton, of Lexington. Died July 25, 1830, aged 76 years. R 7/28.

Mary Ann Robb, daughter of Major Joseph Robb. Died Saturday Aug. 7, 1830, aged 21 years. R 8/11.

Mrs. Nancy Bledsoe, consort of Robert Bledsoe, of Eatonton, Ga. Died Friday June 4, 1830. R 8/11.

Dr. Christopher Clarke, of Madison county. Died July 18, 1830, aged 76 years. Obituary in R 8/11.

Capt. Samuel Tudor, of Madison county. Died in July, 1830, aged 38 years. R 8/11.

Madison Fox, son of Capt. Samuel Fox, of Madison county. Died in New Orleans, July 6, 1830. R 8/11.

D. L. Stone, son of Dudley Stone, of Madison county. Died July 6, 1830, in New Orleans. R 8/11.

John Hayes, of near Bardstown. Found dead near Cox's Creek, July 24, 1830. R 8/11.

John H. Morton. Died Sunday August 15, 1830. R 8/18.

William B. Collins, of Louisville, formerly of Lexington. Died in August, 1830. R 8/18.

Mrs. Jane Penn, wife of John Penn, of Bourbon county. She died in August, 1830, aged 31 years. R 8/18.

Jonas Markee, of Bourbon county. Died in August, 1830, at an advanced age. R 8/18.

Mrs. Susan Hall, wife of Thomas Hall, of Mason county. He died in August, 1830. R 8/18.

John Reitzer, a resident of the Mason county Poor-house. Died in August, 1830, supposed to be 115 years of age. He was a native of Holland. R 8/18.

Ambrose Graves, of Mo., formerly of Lexington, Ky. Died in August, 1830. R 8/18.

Benjamin Howard Dudley. Died in Clarksville, Tenn., in August 1830, aged 24 years. R 8/18.

Mrs. E. B. Proctor, consort of Thomas S. Proctor, of Lancaster, Ky. Died July 31, 1830, aged 31 years. R 8/18.

1830

Mrs. Catharine B. Martin, consort of J. L. Martin, of Fayette county. Died Saturday August 21, 1830. R 8/25.

Dr. Charles Henry Warfield, eldest son of the late Dr. Walter Warfield. Died Sunday August 22, 1830. R 8/25.

Solomon Spears, of Bourbon county. Died in Aug., 1830. R 8/25.

Mary Matilda Eldridge, daughter of Mr. W. W. Eldridge, of Paris, Ky. Died in August, 1830. R 8/25.

John Baldwin, of Scott county. Died in August, 1830, aged about 60 years. R 8/25.

Mrs. Mary Yoder, consort of Capt. Jacob Yoder, of Spencer county. Died Aug. 21, 1830, aged about 55 years. R 9/8.

Mrs. Philadelphia Frazer, relict of William Frazer, of Fayette county. Died Monday August 23, 1830. R 9/15.

Mrs. D. Eliza Marshall, wife of Dr. Alexander Marshall, of Danville. Died in September, 1830. R 9/15.

Dr. E. P. Steele, late from South America. Died in July, 1830, on the 31st of the month, in Green county, Ala. R 9/15.

Benjamin Gratz, Jr., eldest son of Benjamin Gratz. Died Thursday Sept. 16, 1830, aged 10 years. R 9/22.

William Russell, of Grantico, La., a native of Kentucky. Died Wednesday August 18, 1830. R 9/22.

William Pritchartt, merchant of Lexington. Died Tuesday Sept. 28, 1830. R 9/29.

Charles Humphreys, one of the oldest members of the Lexington Bar. Died Oct. 2, 1830, aged 55 years. R 10/6.

Levi Gist, of Franklin county, Ala. Died in Lexington, Ky., where he was born and educated. Died at the residence of Samuel Trotter, Sept. 29, 1830, aged 40 years. Obituary in R 10/6.

Dr. Robert Best of Lexington. Died Oct. 5, 1830. R 10/6.

Mrs. Ann Russell, relict of Col. William Russell, of Fayette county. Died Sept. 27, 1830. R 10/6.

Colonel Gabriel Slaughter, former Lieutenant Governor and Acting Governor of Kentucky. Died in Mercer county in September, 1830. R 10/6.

John W. Hundley, of Jefferson county. Died in September, 1830. R 10/6.

Dr. Lawson F. Caldwell, of Lincoln, N. C. Died in Lexington, Ky., Oct. 3, 1830. He was a graduate of Transylvania Medical College. R 10/13.

Mrs. Mary B. Merrill, consort of Col. Benjamin Merrill. Died Wednesday October 6, 1830. R 10/13.

John Tompkins, of Glasgow, formerly of Fayette county. Died in former place in October, 1830. R 10/20.

Joseph Robb, of Fayette county. Died near Lancaster, Ohio, Oct. 14, 1830, aged about 60 years. Obituary in R 10/20.

David Alexander, of Woodford county, late of the Parish of Concordia, La. Died in Oct., 1830, aged 43 years. R 10/20.

Hon. John McLean, U. S. Senator from Illinois. Died at Shawneetown, Ill., Oct. 13, 1830. R 11/3.

William N. Young, a native of Lexington. Died in New Orleans October 9, 1830. R 11/3.

Mrs. Deborah M. Breckinridge, wife of William T. Breckinridge, and daughter of General Robert S. Russell, of Fayette county. Died at Vicksburgh, Miss., in October, 1830. She left her husband and four small children. R 11/3.

Mrs. Ann Brown, wife of James Brown, late Minister Plenipotentiary of the U. S. A. to France. Died Oct. 19, 1830. R 11/3.

Mrs. Catharine Trotter, consort of Samuel Trotter. Died Saturday November 13, 1830. R 11/17.

Mrs. Elizabeth Allen, wife of Samuel C. Allen, of Louisville. Died in November, 1830. R 11/17.

William Wilson, of Russellville. Died in Nov., 1830. R 11/17.

Miss Mary Ann Davidson, daughter of Major James H. Davidson, of Logan county. Died in Franklin, Ky., in Nov., 1830. R 11/17.

Rev. J. C. Porter, Pastor of the Episcopal Church at Natchez. Died in November, 1830. R 11/24.

Martin Hawkins, of Scott county. Died in November, 1830, at an advanced age. R 11/24.

Mrs. Sarah Slaughter, wife of Philip C. Slaughter, of near Bardstown. Died in November, 1830, aged 39 years. R 11/24.

Joseph, second son of Edward H. Herndon, of Bourbon county. Died Friday December 3, 1830. R 12/8.

Miss Caroline Brashear, daughter of Dr. Walter Brashear, of Attakapas, La. Died Oct. 18, 1830, aged 19 years. R 12/22.

Henry Warfield, of Cynthiana. Died in Dec., 1830. R 12/22.

Miss Clementine Russell, daughter of James Russell, of Franklin county. Died in December, 1830. R 12/22.

1831

Mrs. Ann Redmon, of Bourbon county. Died in December, 1830, aged 71 years. R 12/22.

Mrs. Mary Dulin, consort of Edward Dulin, of Fleming county. Died in December, 1830. R 1/5/1831.

Henry Muzy, of Logan county. Died in December, 1830, aged 80 years. R 1/5/1831.

Abraham Worthington, of Missouri, late of Fleming county, Ky. Died in Missouri in December, 1830, R 1/5/1831.

Francis Downing. Died January 9, 1831. R 1/12.

William Prentiss, of Lexington, Ky. He was born in Cambridge, Mass., and died at Capt. Postlethwait's Inn, in Lexington, Jan. 16, 1831. He was 77 years of age. R 1/19.

Capt. Abraham Venable, of Fayette county. Died January 30, 1831, aged 73 years. R 1/19.

Anthony V. Carr, of the Osage Agency. Died in December, 1830. R 1/19.

Matilda Curle Allison, daughter of Samuel Allison, of Richmond. Died in January, 1831. R 1/19.

Paulina H. Boswell, daughter of George Boswell, of Lexington. Died Saturday January 22, 1831, aged 4 years. R 1/26.

Mrs. Sarah D. Hart, wife of Capt. Thomas P. Hart, and daughter of Capt. John Postlethwait. Died at the latter's residence Friday January 28, 1831. R 2/2.

Mrs. Eleanora E. S. Richards, wife of Dr. William Richards, of La., and daughter of Dr. Keene, of Georgetown, Ky. Died in La., in January, 1831. Obituary in R 2/9.

Robert Lockridge, of Nicholas county. Died in Jan., 1831. R 2/2.

William Kelley, of Clark county. Died in January, 1831, aged 35 years. R 2/2.

Robert Garnett, of Cumberland county. Died December 31, 1830, the date being the anniversary of the 94th year of his age. See obituary in R 2/2.

William Denning of Mifflin township, Penna. The first man ever to make a successful attempt to manufacture a wrought iron cannon. He died in December, 1830, aged 94 years. Story in R 2/2.

John Loveless, of Shelbyville. Died on February, 1831, aged about 35 years. R 2/9.

Mr. W. Ritchie, Jr., of Clark county. Died in February, 1831. R 2/9.

A. Hatten, of Clark county. Died in February, 1831. 'He was upwards of 100 years old.' R 2/9.

Mrs. Ellen Darnaby, wife of James Darnaby, of Fayette county. Died in Feb., 1831, aged 37 years. R 2/9.

Peter Francisco, a Revolutionary hero. Died at Richmond, Va., January 17, 1831. R 2/9. (Note: For an account of Peter Francisco's great strength and Border fame see story in the LOR April 25, 1855.)

Col. John Pickett, of Mason county. Died in Cincinnati, O., Friday January 20, 1831. R 2/9.

James D. Offutt, of Scott county. Died Thursday Feb. 3, 1831. R 2/9.

Mrs. Sarah Glover. Died Jan. 11, 1831, aged 80 years. R 2/9.

John G. Keenon, of Paris. Died in Feb., 1831, aged 33 years. R 2/16.

Mrs. Sarah Buchanan, wife of George Buchanan, of Louisville. Died in February, 1831. R 2/16.

Hugh Riley, of Henry county. Shot accidently and killed by Thomas J. Bartlett, a constable of Henry county. Died Feb. 1, 1831. Story in R 2/23.

Mrs. McNitt, wife of Robert McNitt, of Lexington. Died in February, 1831. R 2/23.

Mrs. Eliza Fleming, wife of W. P. Fleming, of Fleming county. Died in February, 1831. R 2/23.

William H. Taylor, of Mercer county. Died in February, 1831, at an advanced age. R 2/23.

Capt. Nicholas Lafon, of Woodford county. Died in February, 1831, aged about 70 years. R 2/23.

Robert Bailey, of Shelby county. A soldier in the American Revolution. Died in February, 1831, aged 83 years. R 2/23.

Gen. Thomas Baird of Shelby county. Died in February, 1831, aged 48 years. R 2/23.

Mr. Alcee Fortier, of La. Died at Throckmorton's Inn, in February, 1831, aged 18 years. Obituary in R 2/23.

Elizabeth Offutt, widow of Samuel Offutt, of Jessamine county. Died February 21, 1831, aged 70 years. R 3/2.

Rhoda, youngest child of Mr. G. W. Anderson. Died Friday February 25, 1831. R 3/2.

Mrs. Elizabeth M. Clarke, consort of E. Clarke, of Lexington. Died Monday March 14, 1831. R 3/16.

William H. Nicol, of the U. S. Army. Died at Jefferson Barracks in March, 1831. R 3/23.

Mrs. America D. Taliaferro, consort of Dr. Robert Taliaferro, of Paris. Died in March, 1831. R 3/23.

Mrs. Hester Briggs, consort of James T. Briggs, of Warren county. Died in March, 1831. R 3/23.

James M. Parrish of Lexington. Died in March 1831. R 3/23.

Archibald Allan, of Louisville. Died in March, 1831. R 3/23.

Gen. William Lytle, of Cincinnati. Died in March, 1831, aged 61 years. R 3/30.

Mary Whitlock Harvie, daughter of John Harvie, of Frankfort. Died March 24, 1831, aged about 16 years. R 3/30.

Mrs. Sophronia Steffee, wife of John Steffee, of Georgetown. Died in March, 1831. R 3/30.

Mrs. Harriett Caldwell, wife of Rev. S. B. F. Caldwell, of Scott county Died in March, 1831. R 3/30.

Mrs. Mary Ann Bibb, consort of the Rev. Richard Bibb, of Russellville. Died in March, 1831. R 4/6.

Jacob Trumbo, of Bath county. Died in March, 1831, aged 57 years. R 4/6.

Mrs. Sally Anderson, widow of Amos Anderson, of Shelby county. Died in March, 1831, aged 58 years. R 4/6.

Gen. Joseph Winlock, of Shelby county. Died in March, 1831. He was 73 years of age. R 4/6.

Mrs. Isabella Lake. Died at the Maysville residence of her son-in-law, William Henry, in March, 1831, aged 78 years. R 4/6.

Joseph Ellen Robb, infant son of Abraham T. Skillman, of Lexington. Died March 26, 1831, aged 8 months and 9 days. R 4/6.

Mrs. Mary Dupuy. Died at the Woodford county residence of Alexander McClure April 2, 1831, aged 90 years. Obituary in R 4/13.

Mrs. Charlotte S. Backus, wife of George Backus, of Louisville. Died in April, 1831. R 4/20.

Major Thomas Stone, of Nelson county. Died in Mar., 1831. R 4/20.

Thomas C. Owings, of Paris. Died in April, 1831. R 5/4.

John Mason, of Fayette county. Died at George Hunt's on April 11, 1831, aged 87 years and 7 months. R 5/11.

Mrs. Ann Wingfield, wife of Samuel Wingfield, of Versailles. Died in May, 1831. R 5/11.

Elder Thomas Adams. Died in Lexington, at the residence of James Searles, May 8, 1831. R 5/11.

George Miller, formerly of Washington City. Died in Lexington Monday May 9, 1831. R 5/11.

Mrs. Margaret Clark, wife of George W. Clark, of Fayette county. Died in May, 1831. R 5/18.

Mrs. Catharine Price, relict of Daniel Price, of Woodford county. Died in May, 1831. R 5/18.

Thomas C. Clay, of Bourbon county. Died in Milledgville, Ga., in May, 1831, aged 26 years. R 5/18.

Col. William P. Anderson, of Winchester, Tenn. Died in May, 1831, aged 56 years. R 6/1.

Mrs. Margaret Sullivant, consort of Joseph Sullivant, of Ohio. Died at the residence of her father, Col. Joseph McDowell, near Danville, Ky., in May, 1831. R 6/8.

Mrs. Louisa A. Herndon, consort of John B. Herndon, of Logan county. Died in May 1831. R 6/8.

William E. Arnold, of Paris, Ky. Suicided May 22, 1831, aged 19 years. R 6/8.

Mrs. Elizabeth M. Todd, of Fayette county. Died Saturday June 11, 1831. She was the youngest daughter of the late Rev. J. Moore. R 6/15.

Major Shadrach Penn, Sr., of Scott county. A soldier in the Revolution. Died in June, 1831, aged 80 years. R 6/15.

James A. Frazer, formerly of Lexington. Died in June, 1831. Obituary in R 6/15.

Alben Kelbough, of St. Louis, formerly of Lexington, Ky. Died June 1, 1831. R 7/6.

William Cunningham. Died in Hanover county, Va., in June, 1831, aged 54 years. R 6/29.

Samuel McDowell, of Bowling Green. Died in Mercer county, in June, 1831. R 6/29.

James True, High Sheriff of Fayette county. Died Sunday July 3, 1831. R 7/6.

Walker Sanders, of Shelby county. Died at the residence of M. Flournoy in June, 1831. R 7/6.

Mrs. Eleanor H. Davis, consort of Allen Davis. Died June 29, 1831, aged 21 years. R 7/6.

Ezekiel Glover, of Louisville. Died in July, 1831, aged 52 years. R 7/13.

Andrew Wills, of Nashville. Died in June, 1831. R 7/13.

William F. Pope, of Louisville. Died at Little Rock, Ark., of a wound received in a duel in February, 1831. Died June, 1831. R 7/13.

Robert P. Gatewood, only son of Peter Gatewood, of Fayette county. Died June 29, 1831, aged 16 years. R 7/13.

Rev. O. B. Ross, of the Lexington Methodist Episcopal Church. Died Thursday Aug. 4, 1831. R 8/10.

Alexander Campbell Lamme, infant son of Milton Lamme. Died Aug. 5, 1831, aged 3 years and 4 months. R 8/10.

Mrs. Louisiana McMurray, daughter of Dr. Cloud, of Lexington, Ky. Died there July 20, 1831, aged 21 years. R 8/17.

Mrs. Bullock, consort of Waller Bullock, of Fayette county. Died August 4, 1831. R 8/17.

Mrs. Martha McPheeters, consort of Charles McPheeters, of Fayette county. Died July 29, 1831. R 8/17.

Mrs. Nancy T. Randolph, consort of J. H. Randolph, and daughter of the late Rev. James Moore. Died Aug. 7, 1831. R 8/17.

Mrs. Letitia P. Porter, consort of Gen. P. B. Porter, and daughter of the late John Breckinridge, of Fayette county. Died at Black Rock, N. Y., in July, 1831. R 8/17.

Mrs. Carr B. Bailey, formerly of Flemingsburgh, Ky. Died in Missouri in July, 1831. R 8/17.

Mrs. Amanda M. Berry, consort of Newton Berry, of Jessamine county. Died in July, 1831, aged 20 years. R 8/17.

Randolph Harris, of Fayette county. Died July 31, 1831, aged 80 years. Obituary in R 8/17.

Benjamin Lawrence, of Lexington. Died Aug. 23, 1831. R 8/24.

Mrs. Lucinda Dupuy, wife of Lemuel W. Dupuy, of Shelby county. Died in August, 1831. R 8/31.

Miss M. Spear, daughter of Mrs. S. Spear, of Shelbyville. Died in August, 1831. R 8/31.

Mrs. Margaret Allen, wife of Joseph F. Allen, of Shelby county. Died in August, 1831. R 8/31.

Mrs. Hannah Cardwell, relict of George Cardwell, of Shelby county. Died in August, 1831. R 8/31.

OBITUARIES

The abbreviations used denote:

O—*Lexington* (Kentucky) *Observer*
OR—*Lexington* (Kentucky) *Observer & Reporter*
R—*The* (Lexington, Kentucky) *Reporter*

1831

Mrs. Elizabeth Gwinn, of South Frankfort. Died in August, 1831, aged 55 years. R 8/31.

Louis Arthur Anderson, only son of the Hon. Richard Anderson, of Louisville. Died in August, 1831. R 8/31.

Mrs. Elizabeth Ormsby, of Frankfort. Died in August, 1831. R 8/31.

Mrs. Ann E. Barrow, widow of Willie Barrow. She died in Nashville in August, 1831. R 8/31.

Jefferson Curle, of Madison county. Died in August, 1831, aged 28 years. R 8/31.

Mrs. Catharine Gray, wife of Richard Gray, of Fayette county. Died in Aug., 1831, aged 74 years. R 9/7.

Miss Elizabeth F. Bisland, of Mississippi. Died at the Bourbon county, Ky., residence of Mrs. Caldwell in August, 1831. R 9/7.

Stephen Price, of Warren county. Died in August, 1831, aged 20 years. R 9/7.

Charles Wahrendorff, of St. Louis. Died in Aug., 1831. R 9/7.

Col. A. S. Drake, of Lexington. Died Sept. 6, 1831. R 9/14.

Mr. Scarlett Smith, of Lincoln county. Died in September, 1831, aged 70 years. R 9/14.

Gilon Haun, of Lancaster. Died in September, 1831, aged 30 years. R 9/14.

Mrs. America Alford, consort of Nathaniel Alford, of Garrard county. Died in September, 1831. R 9/14.

Capt. William West, of Lexington. Died Monday night, September 19, 1831, at an advanced age. R 9/21.

Samuel S. Brooking, of Hart County. Died in Sept., 1831. R 9/21.

Mrs. Julia Ann H. Hines, consort of F. W. Hines, and daughter of the Rev. Spencer Cooper. Died Sept. 26, 1831. R 9/28.

William Leavy, merchant of Lexington. Died Sept. 21, 1831, at an advanced age. R 9/28.

Thomas Coke, of Louisville. Died in Sept., 1831. R 9/28.

Samuel Filson, of Fleming county. Died in September, 1831, aged 74 years. R 9/28.

Mrs. Harriett Smith, consort of William Smith, of New Castle. Died in September, 1831. R 9/28.

Capt. William Douglas, of Louisville. Died in Columbus, Miss, in September, 1831. He had been appointed by the President to value and sell the cattle belonging to the emigrating Choctaw Indians. R 9/28.

Miss Almira Gatewood, daughter of Peter Gatewood, of Fayette county. Died Sept. 5, 1831, aged 18 years. R 10/5.

Alfred W. Carr, of Lincoln county. Died in Sept., 1831. R 10/5.

Joseph Barbee, of Fayette county. Died Oct. 1, 1831, from a cut on the knee inflicted by a hemp knife. R 10/5.

John Christy, son of John Christy of Clark county. Died in Lexington Saturday October 8, 1831. R 10/12.

Richard Downton, of Fayette county. Died in Oct. 1831, leaving his wife and several children. R 10/12.

John Adair Hardin, eldest son of Mark Hardin of Shelbyville. Died in Mercer county at the residence of Judge Bridges, in October, 1831, aged 22 years. R 10/12.

William Rousseau Cox, M.D. Died at Natchez in September, 1831. R 10/19.

James S. Stevenson, of Pittsburgh, late a member of Congress. He died in October, 1831. R 10/26.

James Harper, cashier of the United States Branch Bank of Lexington. Died October 25, 1831. R 11/2.

George Madison, son of the late Governor Madison. Died in Franklin county in October, 1831. R 11/2.

William R. Dickinson, late of Steubenville, Ohio. Died in Austin's Settlement, Texas, August 27, 1831. R 11/2.

Dr. Azra Offutt, of Jessamine county. Suicided October 26, 1831. R 11/2.

Mrs. Frances G. Ellicott, consort of Addison T. Ellicott, formerly of Jefferson county. Died Nov. 6, 1831, at the Clark county residence of her father, Joel Hickman. She was (?) yeas of age. R 11/16.

James Robinson, of Bourbon county. Died in November, 1831. R 11/30.

Amos Francis, of Bourbon county. Died in November, 1831, aged 20 years. R 11/30.

Thomas H., eldest son of George W. Anderson, of Lexington. Died Friday November 25, 1831. R 11/30.

Mrs. Margaret Todd. Died November 21, 1831, aged 57 years. She was thrown from her carriage when her horses ran away. R 12/7.

Hon. Henry Davidge, of Gallatin county. Died in November, 1831, aged 62 years. R 12/7.

Miss Elizabeth Chenault, of Madison county. Died in November, 1831. R 12/7.

James Boggs, of Fayette county. Died in December, 1831, leaving his wife and one child. R 12/7.

Benjamin Mills, lawyer of Kentucky. Died December 6, 1831. He was from Frankfort. Obituary in R 12/14.

Miss Eliza Ann Pinckard, of Lexington. Died December 19, 1831. R 12/21.

Martin Baum, of Cincinnati. Died in December, 1831, at an advanced age. R 12/28.

Alexander McCoy, of New Orleans. Died in December, 1831. R 12/8.

Mrs. Harriet K. Clark, consort of Gen. William Clark. Died in St. Louis in December, 1831. R 1/11/1832.

John Wilie, of New Orleans. Died December 13, 1831. R 1/6/1832.

Mary Louiza, infant daughter of John D. Eblin, of Lexington. Died December 29, 1831. R 1/4/1832.

William Ferril Baird, of Tennessee, a member of the Medical Class at Transylvania University, Lexington. Died January 1, 1832, aged 23 years. R 1/4.

Sarah Elizabeth, daughter of Col. Thomas H. Bradford, of Scott county. Died Thursday December 29, 1831, aged 4 years. R 1/6/1832.

Susan Mary, second and last child of Col. Thomas Bradford, of Scott county. Died January 9, 1832, aged 2 years. See above. OR 1/13.

William Hall, of Bourbon county. Died Jan. 4, 1832, aged 58 years. R 1/11.

Alexander Bell, of Louisville, formerly of Lexington. He died December 20, 1831. OR 1/13/1832.

Patrick Shields, of Lexington. Died in the vicinity of Russellville December 28, 1831, aged 44 years. OR 1/13/1832.

Mrs. Mary H., consort of John S. Van de Gaff, of Scott county. Died January 9, 1832, aged 24 years. OR 1/13.

James M. Pike, formerly of Lexington, Ky. Died in Nashville, Tenn., January 7, 1832. OR 1/20.

Reuben Samuel, of Franklin county. Died in Jan., 1832. OR 1/20.

Archibald Curle, of Madison county. Died in January, 1832, at an advanced age. OR1/20.

Dorthea Ripley, of Virginia. A celebrated female preacher. Died in January, 1832, aged 64 years. R 1/25.

Zephemiah Watson, of Mason county. Died in January, 1832, aged 80 years. R 1/25.

Jeremiah Martin, Jr., son of Col. J. Martin, of Maysville. Died in Natchez, Miss., in January, 1832, aged 21 years. E 1/25.

Robert G. Dudley, son of Col. William Dudley, who fell in the battle at Fort Meigs in May, 1813. Died in Marion county December 26, 1831. OR 2/3/1832.

Mrs. Elizabeth Julia Blackburn, consort of Rev. George Blackburn, of Woodford county. Died Jan. 28, 1832, aged 40 years. R 2/1.

Col. Robert Carter Nicholas, eldest son of the late George Nicholas. Died Dec. 1, 1831, at Brassori, Province of Texas. R 2/1.

Henry Clay Kennedy, youngest son of Mr. M. Kennedy. Died in February, 1832, aged about 3 years. R 2/1.

John E. Heron, of Hardiman county, Tennessee. Died in Fayette county, Kentucky, February 10, 1832. R 2/1.

Amos Martin Rogers, a member of the Medical Class of Transylvania University. Died February 19, 1832. He was from Spartanburgh District, South Carolina. O 2/24.

Mrs. Elizabeth Darnaby, consort of Capt. John Darnaby, of Fayette county. Died January 24, 1832, aged 75 years. O 2/24.

James Weir, of Lexington. A native of Ireland. Died February 24, 1832. O 3/2.

Miss Mary Morton LeGrand, daughter of Abner LeGrand. Died March 18, 1832, aged 16 years. O 3/23.

Robert Marshall McNitt, Jr., of Lexington. Died March 22, 1832. O 3/23.

Charles Norwood, Sr., of Lexington. Died March 22, 1832, at an advanced age. O 3/20.

Mrs. Ann Thompson, of Lexington. Died March 24, 1832. O 3/30.

Mrs. ——— Potter, of Lexington. Died March 25, 1832. O 3/30.

George Hampton, of Lexington. Died March 28, 1832. O 3/30.

Col. Allen Withers, of Scott county. Died in March, 1832, aged 38 years. O 3/30.

James Lemon, of Lexington. A soldier in the Revolution. Died April 28, 1832, aged 82 years. Obituary in O 5/10.

Mrs. Sarah Brown, consort of George J. Brown, of Nicholasville. Died May 6, 1832. Obituary in O 5/17.

Mrs. Sarah M. Sercy, consort of Col. William W. Sercy, of Rutherford county (Tenn.?). Died April 29, 1832, aged 50 years. O 5/17.

Mrs. Hannah Taylor, of Fayette county. Died May 16, 1832, aged 78 years. O 5/24.

Mrs. Z. Mason, consort of Samuel H. Mason, of Rodney, in Mississippi. Died at New Orleans May 2, 1832. O 5/24.

Jacob Sodowsky, of Fayette county. A soldier in the American Revolution. Died May 19, 1832, aged 79 years. OR 5/24/1832.

Elizabeth Sodowsky, consort of the late Jacob Sodowsky, of Fayette county. See above. She died in Jessamine county May 30, 1832, aged 69 years. OR 5/31.

James B. Barr, of Winchester. Died May 27, 1832. OR 5/31.

James Briscoe, of Scott county. Died May 30, 1832. OR 5/31.

Mrs. ———— Bohannon, wife of Dr. Richard Bohannon, of Versailles. Died June 7, 1832. OR 6/13.

Mary Eliza, daughter of Richard Downing, of Fayette county. Died on Monday June 11, 1832, aged aout 7 years. OR 6/13.

Henry Clay Todd, son of Col. Charles S. Todd, of Shelby county. Died May 30, 1832, aged about 2 years. OR 6/13.

Charles Stewart Todd, son of Col. Charles S. Todd, of Shelby county. Died May 31, 1832, aged 4 years. See above. OR 6/13.

Susan Hart Todd, daughter of Col. Charles S. Todd, of Shelby county. See above. She died June 6, 1832, aged about 10 years. OR 6/13.

Rev. Robert Marshall, of Fayette county. Died June 16, 1832, aged 72 years. He had been in the Ministry 42 years. OR 6/21.

Jane, daughter of James E. Davis, of Lexington. Died June 18, 1832, aged about 3 years. OR 6/21.

Stephen H. Desforges, of Lexington. Died June 27, 1832, at an advanced age. OR 6/28.

Mrs. Elizabeth Jane Hull, consort of Jacob Hull, of Lexington. Died July 1, 1832. OR 7/5.

Capt. James Pace. Killed in August, 1832, in Clark county, supposedly by John Ramsey. Story in OR 7/12.

Joseph Logan, son of Archibald Logan, of Lexington. Died July 7, 1832. OR 7/12.

Robert E. Coleman, of near Harrodsburg. Murdered in July, 1832, by two of his slaves. Story in OR 7/26.

George Trotter, Sr., of Fayette county. Died July 25, 1832, aged 73 years. OR 7/26.

Mrs. Nancy Elliott, consort of John Elliott, of Scott county. Died July 18, 1832, aged 55 years. OR 7/26.

Mrs. Sarah H. Barton, relict of the late A. S. Barton, of Fayette county, and daughter of Col. Benjamin Merrill. Died July 27, 1832. OR 8/2.

Thomas B. Riely, of Mississippi, son of John Riely, of Paoli, Indiana, and brother-in-law of one of the editors of the *Lexington Observer & Reporter*. Died in Mississippi July 1, 1832, aged 27 years. OR 8/2.

Thomas Layton, son of Thomas K. Layton, of Lexington. He died July 27, 1832, aged about 2 years and 6 months. OR 8/2.

Julius Layton, brother of Thomas Layton, above. Died July 26, 1832, aged six months. OR 8/2.

Bennett P. Sanders, M.D., of Rodney, Mississippi, formerly a resident of Lexington, Kentucky. Died July 5, 1832. OR 8/2.

Samuel Greenup, of Scott county. Died July 27, 1832, aged about 50 years. OR 8/2.

Gustavus Keene, of Lake Providence, La., formerly of Scott county, Kentucky. Died July 6, 1832. OR 8/9.

Col. Richmond Dedmon, of Fayette county. Died July 28, 1832, aged 77 years. OR 8/16.

Sarah Ann, eldest daughter of John Clugston, of Fayette county. Died August 5, 1832, aged 8 years. OR 8/23.

Sarah Jane, eldest daughter of George Clugston, of Fayette county. Died Aug. 11, 1832, aged about eight years. OR 8/23.

H. H. Eaton, assistant professor at Transylvania University. Died in Lexington August 15, 1832, aged 23 years. OR 8/23.

Samuel Brown Brand, son of John Brand, of Lexington. Died August 23, 1832. OR 8/30.

Mrs. Eliabeth Garrard, relict of the late Col. James Garrard, of Bourbon county. Died August 29, 1832, aged 82 years. OR 9/6.

John W. Coleman, of Woodford county. Died Aug. 19, 1832, aged about 30 years. OR 9/6.

General Samuel South, of Fayette county. Died Aug. 24, 1832, aged 65 years. OR 9/13.

Mrs. Susannah Hart, widow and relict of the late Colonel Thomas Hart. Died in Lexington August 26, 1832, aged 86 years. She had 7 children, 2 only surviving her. One of the latter was Lucretia Hart, Mrs. Henry Clay. OR 9/6.

Mrs. Catharine R. Irwin, consort of William Irwin, of Lexington. Died Sept. 3, 1832. OR 9/13.

H. Hulbut Eaton, A.M., Professor of Chemistry at Transylvania University. Died Aug. 17, 1832. OR 10/11.

Mrs. Elizabeth Herndon, wife of John Herndon, and daughter of Major Rodes Thompson, of Scott county. Died Monday October 8, 1832. OR 10/11.

Francine, aged 3 years and Mary Eliza, aged 11 months and 25 days, daughters and only children of John H. Robb, of Lexington. They died Saturday morning Oct. 5, 1832. OR 10/11.

Abraham S. Van De Graff, of Scott county. Died October 2, 1832, aged 70 years. OR 10/11.

Mrs. Ann Elder, of Lexington. Died October 10, 1832, at the residence of William Oldham. OR 10/18.

Mrs. Goddard, consort of Michael Goddard, of Georgetown. Died October 9, 1832. OR 10/25.

Mrs. Maria Hampton, relict of George Hampton. Died Oct. 23, 1832. OR 10/25.

Mrs. Mary Ann Trotter, consort of George James Trotter, editor of the *Kentucky Gazette,* and daughter of the Reverend Nathan H. Hall. Died Friday October 26, 1832. OR 11/1.

James Morrison, merchant of Maysville. Died of cholera October 21, 1832. OR 11/1.

Mrs. Margaret Butler McKinney, consort of Major John McKinney, Jr., of Versailles. Died Oct. 18, 1832, aged 43 years. Long obituary in OR 11/8.

Mrs. Bohannon, of Frankfort. Died of cholera Tuesday Nov. 6, 1832. OR 11/15.

Mrs. Mary Ann Gray, of Frankfort. Died of cholera Tuesday November 6, 1832. OR 11/15.

James, infant son of William R. Morton, of Lexington. Died November 14, 1832. OR 11/15.

Helen Judith, daughter of Spencer Cooper, of Fayette county. Died Nov. 14, 1832, aged 6 years. OR 11/15.

Mrs. Jane Scott, wife of John Scott, of Gallatin county. Died Nov. 5, 1832, aged 57 years. OR 11/15.

Mrs. Hawks, wife of M. H. Hawks, of Lexington. Died Nov. 17, 1832. OR 11/22.

Charles Carroll, of Carrolton. Died Nov. 14, 1832, aged 96 years. Obituary in OR 11/22 and OR 11/29.

Reverend Mr. Osgood, of Hopkinsville. Died of cholera in November, 1832. OR 11/22.

William M. Ford, of Hopkinsville. Died of cholera in November, 1832. OR 11/22.

Robert C. Brigham, clerk of Livingston county Circuit Court. Died of cholera in November, 1832. OR 11/22.

Andrew McCalla, of Lexington. Died Nov. 28, 1832, at an advanced age. OR 11/29.

Dr. John B. Duke, of Paris. Died Nov. 17, 1832, aged 28 years. OR 11/29.

Jacob Todhunter, of Jessamine county. Died Dec. 3, 1832, aged 73 years. OR 12/6.

Alfred Shelby, of near Danville, youngest son of Governor Shelby. Died Saturday December 8, 1832. OR 12/13.

Joseph Miller, youngest son of the late John Andrew Miller, of Scott county. Died in Georgetown in Nov., 1832. OR 12/13.

Mrs. Margaret Worthington, consort of Isaac Worthington, of Mississippi, and daughter of Richard Higgins, of Lexington, Ky. Died in the latter place December 15, 1832. OR 12/20.

Mrs. Sally Higgins, consort of R. Higgins, of Lexington. See above. Died Wednesday Dec. 19, 1832, aged about 60 years. OR 12/27.

Edward Shippen, cashier of the U. S. Branch Bank of Louisville. Died Dec. 23, 1832. OR 1/3/1833.

Mrs. Margaret Featherston, consort of Richard Featherston, of Fayette county. Died at the residence of her mother, in Jessamine county, December 25, 1832, aged about 30 years. OR 1/3/1833.

Hon. Thomas J. Crittenden. Died at Louisville December 27, 1832, aged 45 years. Obituary in OR 1/10 and 1/3/1833.

James Teague, of Lexington. Died Dec. 30, 1832, at an advanced age. OR 1/10/1833.

Cuthbert Petty, of Fayette county. Died Jan. 1, 1833, aged 30 years. OR 1/10.

1833

William C. Dunn, of Fayette county. Died Jan. 9, 1833, aged 50 years. OR 1/17.

Ruth Ann, eldest daughter of Benjamin Warfield, of Fayette county. Died Jan. 10, 1833, aged 18 years. OR 1/17.

Mrs. Charlotte Williams, consort of Bayless Williams, of Lexington, and daughter of Thomas Holt, of Jefferson county. Died Jan. 19, 1833. OR 1/24.

James W. Palmer, editor and publisher of the *Louisville Price Current*. Died Jan. 18, 1833. OR 1/24.

Mr. J. Desgranges, a native of France but for many years a citizen of Lexington, Ky. Died Feb. 5, 1833, aged 73 years. OR 2/7.

Maria Pendleton, daughter of Prof. John E. Cooke, of Lexington. Died Jan. 26, 1833, aged 2 years. OR 2/7.

John Norton, Jr., son of George Norton of Fayette county. Died Feb. 27, 1833, aged about 20 years. OR 2/28.

John Peters, of Woodford county. Died Feb. 24, 1833, aged 70 years. OR 2/28.

Lucius Manluis, aged 2 years, and Augustus, aged about 6 months, children of Judge Turner, of Fayette county. They died February 13, 1833. OR 2/28.

Edwin Welsh, of Lincoln county. Suicided March 2, 1833. Died at Cheney's Tavern, near Shelbyville. See story in OR 3/7.

Col. Anthony New, of Todd county. Died March 2, 1833, aged 87 years. A Soldier in the American Revolution. OR 3/21.

Major John Jennings, of Lancaster, Ky. Died March 11, 1833, aged 34 years. OR 3/21.

Jacob Ladd, of Clark county. Suicided March 8, 1833. OR 3/21.

Dr. Richard Pindell, of Lexington. Died March 20, 1833, aged 78 years. Obituary in OR 3/28.

Mrs. Mary Stevenson, consort of Job Stevenson, of Georgetown. Died March 20, 1833. OR 3/28.

William Hewett, of Georgetown. Died March 28, 1833, at a very advanced age. OR 4/3.

Phoebe Catharine Wood, daughter of Benjamin C. Wood. Died in Lexington March 28, 1833. OR 4/3.

William Virden, of Lexington. Died Sunday March 31, 1833. He was 20 years of age. OR 4/3.

John S. Walker, of Lexington. Died March 30, 1833. OR 4/3.

William Fisher, of Fayette county. Died Apr. 1, 1833, aged 44 years. He left his wife and 5 children. OR 4/10

Samuel Pilkington, of Lexington. Died Apr. 22, 1833. OR 4/25.

Israel Colvert, of Lexington. Died Apr. 22, 1833. OR 4/25.

Nathaniel Herndon, of Madison county. Died Apr. 15, 1833, aged about 42 years. He left his wife and 8 small children. OR 5/25.

William Challen, of Lexington. Died Apr. 15, 1833, aged 71 years. A long poem was penned in his memory in OR 4/25.

Miss Lucretia Calvit, of Mississippi. Died at the Lexington, Ky., residence of Mrs. Mentelle April 28, 1833, aged 16 years. OR 5/2.

Mrs. Susannah Shaw, of Lexington. Died Apr. 2, 1833, aged 66 years. OR 5/2.

Miss Heathy Potter. Died at the Lexington residence of her brother, Charles A. Potter, May 8, 1833, aged 22 years. OR 5/9.

Mrs. Sally Rogers, wife of John Rogers, of Fayette county. Died May 5, 1833. OR 5/9.

Mrs. Charlotte S. Ritchie, consort of Dr. James Ritchie, of Fayette county. Died at the residence of her father, John L. Mart, May 14, 1833. OR 5/16.

Jonathan Bryan, of Clark county. Died May 6, 1833, aged 66 years. OR 5/16.

John Atchison, of Fayette county. Died May 13, 1833, aged aout 45 years. OR 5/16.

George R. Payne, son of James Payne, dec'd. Died May 13, 1833, aged 23 or 24 years. OR 5/16.

Catharine H. and Ann C. Morgan, infant daughters of C. C. Morgan, of Fayette county. Died May 10, 1833. OR 5/16.

Catharine G. Hunt, daughter of John W. Hunt, of Lexington. Died May 14, 1833, aged 18 or 19 years. OR 5/16.

Edmund Shackelford, of Jefferson county, Miss. Died of cholera April 30, 1833. He was a native of Virginia. OR 5/23.

William Shackelford. Died of cholera May 2, 1833, aged 17 years and 4 months. OR 5/23.

Sarah Ann Allen, eldest daughter of Elder Thomas M. Allen, of Fayette county. Died May 14, 1833, aged 14 years and 4 months. OR 5/23.

Mrs. A. W. Bowie, of Vicksurg, Miss., formerly of Lexington, Ky. Died May 2, 1833, aged about 30 years. OR 5/23.

Henry Lindsay, of Scott county. Died May 25, 1833, aged 67 years. OR 5/30.

Following is a list of deaths in the CITY OF LEXINGTON, Kentucky from June 1 to August 1, 1833. Most of these deaths were caused by cholera. Persons whose names are preceded by a star (*) died of other diseases. This list was reported to the City Council of Lexington by a committee appointed for that purpose, consisting of Messrs. Leavy, Layton, McKinney and Gough. It was published in the *Lexington Observer and Reporter* Thursday August 22, 1833. Note: Only the names of white residents are given here. For the Negroes see above noted issue of OR.

Ward No. 1

1st. On Main Street. *Miss Eleanor Leavy; Mrs. Agnes Bell, widow, at Mrs. Gatewood's; Michael Fishel; Thomas C. Blincoe; Mrs. Logan, wife of A. Logan; Miss S. Shields, daughter of the late John Shields; *Henry Kelly, Mrs. Katherine Kelly, wife of Henry Kelly; Joseph Laudeman; Mrs. Susan Laudeman, wife of George W. Laudeman; Dr. Joseph Challen; Mrs. Ann Usher, widow; Miss Elizabeth Kid; Benjamin Cobb, son of the late David Cobb; Mrs. Lanckart, wife of Lewis Lanckart; Joseph Lanckart, infant son of Lewis L.

2nd. On Mill Street. Mrs. Lydia Jones, widow; Charle Winn, son of J. Winn.

3rd. Main Cross Street. Mrs. Catharine Loney, wife of Hugh Loney; Mrs. Catharine Loney, mother of same; Mrs. Bridges, widow of John B.; Mrs. Elizabeth Bradley, wife of Andrew B.; Mrs. Winney Thomas, widow; Mrs. Williamson, wife of Lewis H. Williamson; Miss Mary Ann Nixon; Moses S. Hall; Samuel Thompson; Mrs. Harriet Berryman; Mrs. Walker, wife of John Walker —at Mrs. Price's; Mrs. Sarah Steele, widow of Solomon S.

4th. On Water Street, and in Manchester, being the same continued. William Dougherty; Miss Patsey Rodden; Elisha Hunter; Mrs. Isabella Lowery, widow; Mrs. Isabella Boswell; Marianne S., daughter of Mrs. Sampson, widow; Henrietta, daughter of same; Bushrod Sampson, son of same; John Stoddard, at W. Dukemineer's; Robert Page (overseer W. W. Ater & Co.); Mrs. Eliza Ater; James F. Royle, son of J. Royle; Mrs. Nancy Grinstead, widow; Mrs. Turner, wife of J. Turner; William, infant son of Elizabeth Rutherford.

5th. On and near High Street. Mrs. Christana McQuillan, widow of F. McQuillan; Willis Higginbotham, at J. Milward's; Nathan Putnam; Mrs. Huchinson, widow of William Hutchinson; Andrew and Francis Hutchinson, twin sons of same.

WARD NO. 2

1st. Cheapside and Market Street. Joseph Towler (Cashier Bank U. States.); John C. Blades.

2nd. Mill Street. Mrs. Judith C. Scott, widow of Gov. Chas. Scott, dec'd., died at Mrs. Gratz's; Henry C. Gist, died at same; Mrs. John Murphy; W. C. Noke; Bayless Williams; Roger McGraw, died at Mrs. Connell's; William T. Smith; Dr. John Steele; Mrs. Seeley, widow of Benjamin Seeley; Benjamin Seeley; James A. Brooks; Alexander W. Dillon, student of Medicine; Mr. Patterson, of Ohio, at James A. Brook's; Mons'r Xaupi, at Mr. Brooks'; Robert White, overseer for J. Hamilton; Mrs. White, wife of preceding. Catharine, infant daughter of Col. Morgan, at J. W. Hunt's.

3rd. On Main Street. Miss Virginia Pinckard, daughter of A. W. Pinckard; Mrs. Elizabeth Young, wife of Leavin Young; Mrs. Weible, widow, at L. Young's; Miss Rosanna F. Tod; Mrs. Jane Byrne, wife of John Byrne; Miss Joanna Lanckart, daughter of Joseph Lanckart; Joseph Ficklin Wainscott, son of G. W.; Mary L. Cloud, daughter of Dr. C. W. Cloud; *Rev. Dr. Cloud; Rebecca Hudgens, at P. Elliott's; Jane Monroe; Mrs. M. Close, at Simpson's.

4th. Main Cross Street. Mrs. Diana Ashton, wife of Richard Ashton; Miss Margaret Asby; Mrs. Elizabeth January, widow of James B. January; John G. Ashby; Dr. Solomon F. Hoagland; Capt. Matthias Shryock; Miss Jane Chinn, daughter of R. H. Chinn; Dr. James Webb, died at M. T. Scott's; *Mrs. Winney Scott, wife of M. T. Scott; Mrs. Poston.

6th. On Short Street. Dr. Joseph Boswell; Mr. Thompson, a stranger; Mrs. Mary Ball, daughter of C. Wickliffe; Mrs. Susannah Wickliffe, wife of C. Wickliffe, Sen.; Mrs. Spicy Bunnell, wife of J. Bunnell; *Miss Rebecca Shrock, daughter of J. Shrock; Wallace Johnson; Frederick Field, hatter; Miss Caroline Shaw, daughter of John R. Shaw.

6th. Second Street. Robert Grooms; George Roberts; Maria O'Haver; *Luther C. Grimes, son of Benjamin Grimes.

7th. Lunatic Asylum. Edward Kindred, Madison county; R. Randolph, Greensburg, Ala.; Philip Sumery, Logan county; Susan Dougherty, Mason county; Abigail Bateman, same; Jesse Holtzclaw, Fayette county; Frederick Jones, same; Jane Holmes, Jefferson county; Elizabeth Plummer, Scott county; Susan Browning, Logan county; Jonathan Polk, Simpson county; Dow Halfacre, Pendleton county; Elizabeth Hunter, Logan county; David Snow, Nashville, Tenn.; Darius Jackson, Fleming county; Robinson Coward, Jefferson county; William Henson, Nelson county; William Davenport, Mercer county;

Nelson P. Wilcox, Caldwell county; Jacob Cooper, Breckinridge county; Madelina Miller, Spencer county; Richard Pope, Logan county; Charles Jackson; Shelby county; John Mason, Casey county; Mary O'Connell, Bardstown, Ky. Alfred Lain, Fayette county; Mary Haburn, Breckinridge county; John Armstrong, Scott county; Mary Iredell, Barren county; Courtney Knapp, Bourbon county; John Haberry, Mercer county; Mary Lemon, Harrison county; Joseph Erwin, Miss.

Ward No. 3

Robert Scott; Joseph Ellison; John G. Boyer; Ann Boyer, wife of J. Boyer; James M. Boyer; Baldwin Boyer; Harvey M. Seeley; *Elizabeth McKenney, wife of Gerard McKenney, of fever. William Wingate; Nancy Plunkett; Catharine Haley, sister of Larkin Haley; Sarah Carter and child, wife of Landon Carter; Richard Johnson, at J. Lewis's; Edward Ashley; James H. Brown; William Douglass; Richard O. Thompson; James Fletcher; Nancy Bailey, wife of David Bailey; Malerida Winscot, wife of G. Winscot; Elizabeth Huston, wife of William Huston; Elizabeth Landrum; Sarah Shelton, widow; Frances, daughter of S. Freeman; Elizabeth, daughter of M. T. Woods; Benjamin Woodruff; Sarah Duvall, widow; Elizabeth Smith, wife of Rev. B. B. Smith; Elizabeth, daughter of Enoch Clark; James Talbot and wife; Catherine B. Cook, widow; Jane Anderson, sister of Capt. William Anderson; Catharine Nunan, at Mrs. Coyle's; Elizabeth A. Orrick, wife of J. C. Orrick; Gen. Thomas Bodley; James B. Bodley; James McIntosh; Margaret Warfield, complaint not known; Elizabeth Weigert, widow of P. A. Weigert; Charles West; Sarah Holloway, wife of James Holloway; Andrew F. Price; George Boswell; Abraham Walker; *Mrs. Fowler, wife of Capt. John Fowler, of Cancer; *Mrs. Beckley, of Dropsy; Thomas T. Skillman; Lewis A. Thompson; Elizabeth Studman, wife of T. Studman; A. Studman, daughter of do; John P. Harrison; John B. Miller, son of Isaac Miller; Catherine Woodruff, widow; Francis Head; Mary Steele, widow; Maria Stone, wife of George W. Stone; Margaret Stone, widow.

Ward No. 4

Reverend James Bunch; Mrs. Brown; Jacob Cole; William Cook and wife; Mrs. M. Cornwall; Ann Crow; Miss Sarah W. Craig; Miss Susan D. Craig; Benjamin Carcuff; Anthony Dumesnil and wife; Miss Dowdell; Videl Davis; Adel Davis; Miss Polly Edger; William Frain; Lewis P. Garrett George A. Garrett; John Griffith; Miss Elizabeth Hawkins; William Heydell; Mrs. Huggins; Daniel Hukle and wife; Mrs. Thomas Hukle; William B. Hudson; Mrs. Joseph H. Hervey; Mrs. Johnson; Thomas W. Jones; Mrs. Nancy King; *Peter H. Leuba; Benjamin Floyd; Mrs. Martha McCalla; Alison McChord, of Cahawba, Ala., died at A. Garrett's; Mrs. Myers; Anthony Guant; Mrs. E. McConathy; John Megowan; Mrs. J. G. Norwood, and her infant child; Robert Norish; Francis O'Neal; Mr. Pittman; Mrs. Peel; Mrs. Grace Price; John Postlethwaite; Duncan Postlethwaite; Miss Maria Peck; Miss F. A. Petterson; Barnet Rucker and wife; Vardy Renfro; Nathaniel Rutherford; Thomas Sparke and wife; Philip Spare and wife; Mrs. Sourbright; Lewis Sayre; William Tegway, a stranger of Mrs. Metcalfe's; Mr. Van Horn; Marnix Virden; Robert Wilson; Jacob Weigart; Mrs. N. Warner, Margaret Warner and Nancy Warner, Mother and Daughters of D. Warner; Francis Walker, Sr., and wife; Francis Walker, Jr.; James T. Berryman; Elijah H. Drake; Samuel Trotter

SUMMARY OF DEATHS IN LEXINGTON FROM

JUNE 1—AUGUST 1, 1833

	Whites	Slaves	Free-Blacks	Total
Ward No. 1	51	26	5	82
Ward No. 2	87	57	3	147
Ward No. 3	60	73	21	154
Ward No. 4	74	28	17	119
	272	184	46	502

Mrs. John Armstrong, of Maysville. Died of cholera in May, 1833. OR 6/6.

Johnston Armstrong, of Maysville. Died of cholera in May, 1833. OR 6/6.

Mrs. Eliza Jane Boyer, consort of Alfred Z. Boyer. Died June 4, 1833, aged 25 years and 5 days. OR 6/6.

H. H. Gaylord, of Maysville. Died of cholera in May, 1833. OR 6/6.

Mrs. Hodge, of Maysville. Died of cholera in May, 1833. OR 6/6.

Miss Charlotte Hull, of Maysville. Died of cholera in May, 1833. OR 6/6.

Emily Huston, daughter of William Huston, of Maysville. Died of cholera in May, 1833. OR 6/6.

Elizabeth, Isabella, and Andrew, three children of Mr. Andrew M. January, of Maysville. Died of cholera in May, 1833. OR 6/6.

Rev. Samuel Johnston, Pastor of St. Paul's Church of Cincinnati. Died of cholera May 22, 1833. OR 6/6.

Mrs. Newman, of Maysville. Died of cholera in May, 1833. OR 6/6.

Joshua Reese, of Maysville. Died of cholera in May, 1833. OR 6/6.

Jones B. and John K. Thompson, of Scott county. Died in June, 1833. OR 6/6.

Following is a list of deaths resulting from cholera in Flemingsburg, Kentucky. From OR June 27, 1833:

June 6, 1833. William McCord, printer, a native of Lebanon, Pa. James H. Jones; Mrs. Wallace, consort of Thomas Wallace. Mrs. Houston, consort of Dr. Houston.

June 10. Dr. Edward Dorsey. Miss Lucy Ann Fleming, daughter of Thomas Fleming. George Houston, aged about 15 years and Miss Minerva Houston, son and daughter of Dr. Houston.

June 11. Dr. William H. Howe. Henry Ward, journeyman blacksmith. Mrs. Dent, consort of Isiah Dent, hatter. Peter F., son of Thomas Bowles, aged about 3 years. Col. James Harrison, of Fleming county.

June 12. Mrs. Saffern, relict of Thomas Saffern. Two daughters of the late Capt. James Sanders.

June 13. Mary Ann, daughter of Dr. Houston.

June 14. Mrs. Elizabeth Gorman, consort of David Gorman. Col. William Goddard, of Maysville.

June 15. William, eldest son of James Eckles, of Flemingsburg. Miss Bond, of Baltimore. She died at the residence of J. D. Early, in Flemingsburg. Miss Maria T. Roe.

June 23–27. Simeon Floyd, mail contractor. Mrs. Daukins, wife of William Daukins. Dr. Robert Tilton, of Elizaville. Captain Gallagher, of Elizaville.

Joshua Worthy, of Fayette county. Died June 2, 1833. OR 6/6.

Mary Susette, infant daughter of Thomas C. Orear, merchant of Lexington. Died May 29, 1833. OR 6/6.

Miss Mary Robertson, of Lancaster. Died of cholera in June, 1833. OR 6/27.

Mrs. Elizabeth Eckles, wife of James Eckles, of Flemmingsburg. See above. She died June 9, 1833. OR 6/27

Mrs. J. B. Holtzclaw, of Georgetown. Died of cholera in June, 1833. OR 6/27.

Mrs. Priscilla Wall, of Cynthiana. Died of cholera in June, 1833. OR 6/27.

Mrs. Pullen, of Georgetown. Died of cholera in June, 1833. OR 6/27.

Isaac Ware, son of Thomas Ware, of Cynthiana. Died of cholera in June, 1833. OR 6/27.

Mrs. Rachel Kimbrough, of Cynthiana. Died of cholera in June, 1833. OR 6/27.

William Laney, of Cynthiana. Died of cholera in June, 1833. OR 6/27.

Thomas Ramsay, of Cynthiana. Died of cholera in June, 1833. OR 6/27.

Wesley Broadwell, of Cynthiana. Died in June, 1833. He was a merchant. OR 6/27.

George Hord, of Mason county. Died of cholera at the residence of Belvin Ross in June, 1833. OR 6/27.

Jeremiah Tarlton, of Scott county. Died of cholera in June, 1833. OR 6/27.

Daniel Duncan, of Scott county, formerly of Paris, Ky. Died suddenly, of appoplexy, June 20, 1833. OR 6/27.

Mrs. Myers, of Winchester. Died of cholera in June, 1833. OR 6/27.

William L. Miller, of Winchester. Died of cholera in June, 1833. OR 6/27.

Isaac Shrere (Shrites?), of Winchester. Died of cholera in June, 1833. OR 6/27.

Mrs. Boulling (Bouling), of Winchester. Died of cholera in June, 1833. OR 6/27.

James Gentry, Sr., of Winchester. Died of cholera in June, 1833. OR 6/27.

Mrs. Jefferson Murray, of Winchester. Died in June, 1833, of cholera. OR 6/27.

Joseph H. Dearborn, of Winchester. Died of cholera in June, 1833. OR 6/27.

Mrs. Thomas Mathers, of Winchester. Died of cholera in June, 1833 OR 6/27.

Mrs. William Eastham, of Georgetown. Died of cholera in June, 1833. OR 6/27.

Elijah H. Drake, of Lexington. Died of cholera at the residence of his father-in-law, Clifton Thomson, June 24, 1833. OR 6/27.

Peter H. Leuba, a native of France. Died at the Fayette county residence of Mr. B. A. Hicks, June 26, 1833. OR 6/27.

Jeff. Sutton, of Fayette county. Died of cholera in June, 1833. OR 7/4.

John Todd, of Fayette county. Died of cholera in June, 1833. OR 7/4.

Mr. G. Saddler, of Fayette county. Died of cholera in June, 1833. OR 7/4.

Joseph Pullum, of Fayette county. Died of cholera in June, 1833. OR 7/4.

John Huston, of Fayette county. Died of cholera in June, 1833. OR 7/4.

Miss Huston, of Fayette county. Died of cholera in June, 1833. OR 7/4.

Miss Sally Ann Ellis, of Fayette county. Died of cholera in June, 1833. OR 7/4.

John Foster, of Fayette county. Died of cholera in June, 1833. OR 7/4.

Thomas Power, of Fayette county. Died of cholera in June, 1833. OR 7/4.

John Kent, of Fayette county. Died of cholera in June, 1833. OR 7/4.

James Harvey, of Fayette county. Died of cholera in June, 1833. OR 7/4

Mrs. E. Darnby, of Fayette county. Died of cholera in June, 1833. OR 7/4.

Mrs. Prewitt, of Fayette county. Died of cholera in June, 1833. OR 7/4.

Miss Hunter, of Fayette county. Died of cholera in June, 1833. OR 7/4.

Joseph Earn, of Fayette county. Died of cholera in June, 1833. OR 7/4.

Marcus Cary, of Fayette county. Died of cholera in June, 1833. OR 7/4.

Daniel White, of Fayette county. Died of cholera June 29, 1833, aged 72 years. OR 7/4.

Virginia Cirode Catharine, infant daughter of John D. Hager, of Fayette county. Died of cholera June 16, 1833. OR 7/18.

Henry Kelly. Died July 21, 1833, at a very advanced age. OR 7/25.

Miss Ellen Leavy, daughter of the late W. Leavy. Died July 22, 1833. OR 7/25.

Miss Mildred Ann, daughter of Walker Kidd, of Fayette county. Died of cholera July 10, 1833. OR 7/25.

Miss Charlotte Wallace, daughter of Col. Harp, of Fayette county. Died of cholera July 5, 1833, aged 16 years. OR 8/1.

Mrs. Jane Smith, consort of Joseph Smith, of Fayette county. Died of cholera Aug. 1, 1833, aged 37 years. OR 8/7.

Capt. Joseph McCann, of Fayette county. Died July 31, 1833. OR 8/7.

Elias Myers, of Winchester. Died of cholera June 16, 1833. OR 7/4.

John Blaydes. Died in Clark county of cholera in June, 1833. OR 7/4.

Following is a list of the white persons who died of cholera in Paris, Kentucky, during June and July, 1833. The list was taken from OR 7/11.

Jonathan Willett; George W. Williams' daughter; Mrs. Lyon; Mrs. Judith Bryan; Mrs. Gaither; Mrs. Moore and son; Peter Sharer, Sr.; Parker, son of Mrs. Andrews; Jonathan Dearborne and his son, William; Samuel D. Scott; Mrs. Ann Kennedy; Peter Kizer; Richard Samuel; Mrs. James Paton; Thomas Burden; Dr. N. Warfield's daughter, Sophia; Thomas Hardwick; Mrs. William M. Samuel; Mrs. Hinton; Mrs. Charles Brent; Mr. Isaac Avery; Samuel Beeler; Erasmus Gill; Richard Holmes; Mrs. James McCann; Mr. Praul; George Davis; Richard Turner.

Citizens of Paris who died in Bourbon county.

G. P. Bryant; Dr. Davis; Eliabeth Leer; Mary Ann, daughter of Jonathan Massie; Miss Susan Croxton; Mrs. Barkley; Mrs. John G. Martin; G. W. Williams' son.

Col. Abraham Buford, of Scott county. Died of cholera June 26, 1833. OR 7/4.

Mrs. G. P. Rice, of Danville. Died of cholera in June, 1833. OR 7/4.

John B. Thompson, senator in the State legislature from Mercer county. Died of cholera in June, 1833. OR 7/4.

Basil Q. Rigg. Died in the explosion of the steamboat *Lioness,* May 19, 1833, aged 33 years. Obituary in OR 7/4.

Robert Hutchinson, of Newtown, Scott county. Died of cholera in July, 1833. OR 7/11 and 7/18.

Henry Landers, of Mt. Sterling. Died of cholera July 4, 1833. OR 7/11.

Martha Ann, eldest daughter of Dr. John Slavens, of Mt. Sterling. Died of cholera July 6, 1833. OR 7/11.

The following, residents of Athens, Ky., died of cholera during June and July, 1833. OR 7/11:

John Taylor; Mary Todd, daughter of Samuel Todd; Nelly Valaningham; Jefferson Erskin; Mrs. Boyd, wife of Alexander Boyd and James, son of Richard Muir.

Following is a list of deaths (Whites) from cholera in Lancaster, Kentucky, Kentucky, during June and July, 1833. The first case appeared Wednesday June 19: the epidemic proved fatal to 69 citizens.

William Cooke, Sr.; William Pollard; Mrs. Dr. Tillett; Elijah Sartain; Alexander McDonald; Thomas Pratt and wife; John Pollard; Mrs. Edmond Anderson; Darius McKee; Miss Sarah McKee; Patience Wilmot, daughter of S. S. Wilmot; Sarah J. Cooke, daughter of William Cooke; James Tillet, a child of Mr. Matheny's; Mrs. Reynolds; Mrs. Emily George; Joseph Woodruff and wife; Miss Mary Woodruff; William Lillard; S. S. Wilmot; Dr. William Gill; Ray Smith; Charles S. Bledsoe; Mrs. David Sutton; Seymore C. Gice; Mrs. Gresham; Mary Lusk, daughter of Samuel Lusk.

In Garrard County died.

Dr. Joseph V. Gill and wife; John Aldridge, Sr., and wife; General Benjamin Letcher; Robert Gill; Daniel G. Bledsoe; Elizabeth Gill; George Thompson; Alexander Collier; Fothergale Hutcherson; Mrs. Beverly Brown and daughter; Mrs. Patience Crow; James Pope, child of C. S. Bledsoe; Mrs. Augustine Jennings; James Aldredge; Miss Nancy Bland; Mrs. Dunn; John Bryant; Old Mr. Parks and his wife.

William H. McCaslin, of New Castle, Ky. Died of cholera July 1, 1833. OR 7/11.

Capt. Benjamin Branaham, of New Castle. Died of cholera in July, 1833 OR 7/11.

John Bryant, of Garrard county (see above.) He was born in Powhatan County, Virginia, January 1, 1760, and served in the Revolution. He moved to Kentucky in 1781, settling in Garrard county in 1786. He died of cholera July 4, 1833. OR 7/11.

Alexander W. Dillon, student of Medicine at Transylvania University. Died at the Bourbon county residence of his mother, June 30, 1833. OR 7/11.

Miss Mary King, daughter of William King, formerly of Fayette county. Died in Hendricks county, Ind., June 16, 1833. OR 7/11.

Samuel Allison, inn-keeper, of Richmond, Ky. Died of cholera during the week of July 9, 1833. OR 7/18

Following is a list of deaths resulting from cholera in Lawrenceurg and Anderson county during June and July, 1833. From OR 7/11.

James G. White's child; Lewis P. Hensley; Moses Bell; James Brown; Durett Riddle; Charles Cane; James B. Bell; John Carter's child; John Walker, Sr.; Nathan Railback's child; James Hutton; Joseph W. Misner; Martin Parker, Sr.; Presley White's son; Rev. John Penny; William Conner; Miss McKinney; George Hunt; John Howard's child; Dr. Smith's child; Rev. J. T. Mills' daughter; Mrs. Elizabeth McBrayer; George Bastow's two children; Joshua Carter, Sr.; Miss Elizabeth Massie; James Paxton, Sr.; James McMichael's son; Thomas Wright's child; Dr. Witherspoon's child; Martin Parker, Jr.; Mr. Allen;

James Story; Nelson C. Johnson; Mr. Edgeman; M. D. King; William Abbott; Miss Ethrington; Matthew Gault; William Rout; Ezekiel Taylor; Miss Ferguson; Mark Lillard; Henry Searcy; F. L. Conner's son; Mrs. Mary Barne; Dr. William W. Penny; William B. Wallace; John B. White's daughter; John G. Holeman's child; Howard Sutherland's child; W. W. Penny's child; Mrs. Mary Collins; James McBrayer's daughter; Mrs. Foree's child.

Cholera not cause of death of the following who also died during the epidemic: James Hutton's child; Randall Walker's child; Charles B. Robinson; Jeremiah Hanks; Mrs. Sarah Lillard.

Alexander Whitehead, of Frankfort. Died of cholera in July, 1833. OR 7/18.

Washington Carter, of Frankfort. Died of cholera in July, 1833. OR 7/18.

Thomas Long, of Cumberland county. Died in Frankfort, of cholera, in July, 1833. OR 7/18.

James Duncan, of Scott county. Died of cholera July 15, 1833. OR 7/18.

Christian Hager, Jr. Died at the Woodford county residence of his father, of cholera, June 27, 1833. He was 28 years of age. OR 7/18.

Mrs. Elizabeth Hager. Died June 27, 1833, aged 83 years. OR 7/18.

Col. Christian Hager, of Woodford county. Died of cholera July 14, 1833, aged 50 years. OR 7/18.

John E. Shropshire, of Bourbon county. Died in July, 1833. OR 7/18.

John Haun, of Scott county. Died in July, 1833. OR 7/18.

Miss Mary Elizabeth Rodes, daughter of Col. W. Rodes, late of Scott county. Died at the Fayette county residence of Waller Bullock, July 14, 1833. OR 7/18.

Mrs. Toppass, consort of James Toppass, of Scott county. Died Thursday July 11, 1833. OR 7/18.

Mrs. Eliza Clay, wife of L. B. Clay, of Bourbon county, and daughter of John Ward, of Winchester. Died in latter place in July, 1833. OR 7/25.

Mrs. Ward, wife of John Ward, of Winchester. See above. She died July 16, 1833. OR 7/25.

Dr. Leroy C. Downey, of Winchester. Died July 16, 1833. OR 7/25.

James K. Taylor, of Clark county. Died July 21, 1833. OR 7/25.

Tarlton Chiles. Died July 21, 1833. OR 7/25.

James Cowan, Commonwealth's Attorney for (Lexington) Judicial District. Suicided in July, 1833, Story in OR 8/1.

Mrs. Rachael Crockett, consort of Capt. Newbold Crockett, of Fayette county. Died July 19, 1833, aged 52 years. She died of Dysentery. A short time before her death two of her grandchildren died of the same disease. These were: Susan Rachel, infant, only daughter of Thomas W. Crockett and Mary Catharine, infant, only daughter of James Byrns. OR 8/1.

Mrs. Susan Shelby, relict of Governor Isaac Shelby, of Lincoln county. She died July 23, 1833, aged 70 years. Obituary in OR 8/1.

Mrs. Caroline M. Brown, consort of George W. Brown, of Nicholasville. Died July 7, 1833. Obituary in OR 8/1.

Mrs. Frances Whaley, consort of James Whaley. Died July 20, 1833, aged 53 years. OR 8/1.

Capt. Benjamin Branham, of New Castle, formerly of Scott county. Died of cholera in July, 1833. OR 8/7.

Col. John Rodman, of New Castle, State Senator for Henry county. Died of cholera in July, 1833. OR 8/7.

Willis Long, postmaster at New Castle. Died of cholera in July. 1833. OR 8/7.

Mrs. Davis, wife of Benjamin Davis, of Scott county. Died Monday August 5, 1833, of cholera. OR 8/7.

James McCalla, of Scott county. Died of cholera July 29, 1833. OR 8/7.

Capt. William L. Rowan, eldest son of Hon. John Rowan. Died of cholera at Federal Hill, near Bardstown, July 26, 1833, at 3 o'clock. OR 8/7.

Mrs. Eliza Rowan, consort of Capt. William L. Rowan, see above. She died of cholera at Federal Hill July 26, 1833, at eight o'clock. OR 8/7.

Col. Atkinson Hill Rowan, second son of Hon. John Rowan. Died of cholera at Federal Hill July 26, 1833, at eleven o'clock. See above. OR 8/7.

Miss Mary Jane Steel, grand daughter of Hon. John Rowan. Died of cholera at Federal Hill July 26, 1833, at two o'clock p.m. OR 8/7.

Mrs. Elizabeth Kelley, consort of Judge Kelley, and sister of the Hon. John Rowan. Died at Bardstown in July, 1833. OR 8/7.

Mrs. Catharine Hawkins, wife of Cleon Hawkins, of Georgetown, and daughter of Elijah Craig. Died July 31, 1833. OR 8/7.

Samuel Hall, son of Rev. N. H. Hall. Died August 1, 1833. OR 8/7.

Mrs. Eliza Morton, wife of William R. Morton, of Lexington, and daughter of the late John Bradford. Died August 1, 1833. OR 8/7.

Major Samuel Spotts, of New Orleans. Died July 11, 1833, of cholera. Obituary in OR 8/7.

Dr. John W. Hunt, of New Orleans, son of J. W. Hunt, of Lexington. Killed July 25, 1833, in a duel with a Mr. Conrad. Story in OR 8/15.

Richard Ashton, of Lexington. Died August 12, 1833, at an advanced age OR 8/15.

Miss Sarah L. Trotter, daughter of the late Samuel Trotter. Died Wednesday August 14, 1833. OR 8/15.

Mrs. Mary Ann Richardson, wife of John C. Richardson, and daughter of Mrs. Elizabeth R. Parker, all of Fayette county. Died Aug. 6, 1833. OR 8/15.

James Garrard, infant son of Major Thomas A. Russell, of Fayette county Died August 10, 1833. OR 8/15.

OBITUARIES

Note.—The abbreviations used denote:

KG—(Lexington) *Kentucky Gazette*

OR—*Lexington* (Ky.) *Observer & Reporter*

1833

Mrs. Sarah Wells, relict of Isaac Wells, of Fayette county. Died July 25, 1833, aged 79 years. OR 8/15.

David W. Watson, of near Union Meeting, Fayette county. He died in August, 1833, aged 30 years. Obituary in OR 8/15.

James M. Boswell, son of the late Gen. William E. Boswell. Died July 30, 1833, at the Harrison county residence of his mother. He was 18 years of age. OR 8/15.

Joseph Palmer, of Winchester. Stabbed and killed by Joel V. Collins, in the summer of 1833. OR 8/21.

Hon. William P. Roper, of Flemingsburg. Died Aug. 18, 1833. OR 8/21.

Dr. Owen W. Bush, of Raymond, Miss., a native of Clark county, Ky. Died July 14, 1833, aged about 24 or 25 years. Obituary in OR 8/21.

David Terrance, of Scott county. Died Aug. 22, 1833, at an advanced age. OR 8/29.

Miss Margarett Polk, of near Newtown, Scott county. Died Aug. 21, 1833. OR 8/29.

Hezekiah Offutt, of Harrison county. Died Aug. 20, 1833. OR 8/29.

Lewis Hale, of Woodford county. Died in August, 1833. OR 8/29.

Mr. W. M. Ferguson, of Fayette county, formerly a merchant of Winchester. Died Aug. 8, 1833, aged 40 years. OR 8/29.

Arthur P. Buckner. Died in Benton, Miss., July 31, 1833. OR 9/5.

Mrs. Margaret Finnell, wife of Benjamin W. Finnell, of Scott county. Died Aug. 27, 1833. OR 9/5.

William Morton, Sr. Died at the Lexington residence of William R. Morton in September, 1833, aged 22 years. OR 9/5.

Mrs. Margaret G. Holland, consort of Dr. Robert C. Holland, and daughter of the late Samuel Trotter. Died Aug. 24, 1833. OR 9/5.

Miss Sarah McCracon, daughter of Thomas McCracon, of Lexington. She died Aug. 22, 1833. OR 9/5.

Miss Elizabeth Christy, daughter of John Christy, of Clark county. Died Sept. 3, 1833, aged 26 years. OR 9/12.

Major Morgan A. Heard, of Russellville, Ky. Died Sept. 5, 1833. OR 9/15.

Mrs. Amanda F. Brown, wife of William Brown, Jr., of Georgetown, and daughter of the late Jeremiah Tarlton. Died at the residence of her mother in Scott county in September, 1833. OR 9/15.

Orlando Breckinridge, only son of William T. Breckinridge. Died at the Fayette county residence of his grandfather, Gen. Robert S. Russell, Sept. 5, 1833, aged 6 years. OR 9/15.

Elizabeth Howard, infant daughter of Edward C. Payne, of Shelby county. Died Sept. 6, 1833. OR 9/15.

Col. Benjamin Whaley, of Bourbon county. *A soldier in the Revolution.* Died at the Bourbon county residence of his son-in-law, Mr. Moreland, Sept. 7, 1833, aged 74 years. Obituary in OR 9/15.

Dr. Aylett Hawes, of Rappahannock county, Virginia. Died Aug. 31, 1833, aged 65 years. Obituary in OR 9/19.

Mrs. Rachel Frances Hill, wife of James Hill, of Scott county, and daughter of John Finnell, late of Orange county, Va. She left two small children, one an infant six months of age. Died in Scott county Sept. 12, 1833, aged 26 years. OR 9/19.

Mrs. Henrietta Buford, wife of Charles Buford, of Scott county. Died at Flat Rock, N. C., Aug. 31, 1833. OR 9/19.

Charles Buford, infant son of James K. Duke, of Scott county. Died Sept. 10, 1833. OR 9/19.

Mrs. Nancy Robb, wife of John H. Robb, of Lexington. Died Sept. 11, 1833. OR 9/19.

Ezekiel T., infant son of the Rev. William B. Christie, of Mansfield, Ohio. Died at Lexington, Ky., Sept. 12, 1833. OR 9/19.

John W. Ball, of Fayette county. Died Sept. 12, 1833. OR 9/19.

Dr. James W. Scott, son of M. T. Scott, of Lexington. Died in Chillicothe Sept. 14, 1833, aged 22 years. OR 9/19.

James Stanley, of Hopkins county. Killed Sept. 13, 1833, by John Hefford. OR 9/26.

Henry Weir, of Lexington. Died Sept. 22, 1833. OR 9/26.

Presly Edwan, of Russellville. Died Sept. 7, 1833, aged about 40 years. OR 9/26.

Mrs. Julia Ann Patterson, wife of Walter R. Patterson, of Lexington. Died Wednesday, Sept. 25, 1833. OR 9/26.

Samuel R. Combs, of Winchester. Killed Tuesday October 1, 1833. Story in OR 10/2.

Mary Ann J. Hunter, of Lexington. Died Sept. 29, 1833. OR 10/2.

Miss Hannah McCalla, of Scott county. Died September 30, 1833. OR 10/2.

Columbus Beatty, son of William Beatty. Died Sept. 30, 1833, aged about 26 years. OR 10/2.

Mrs. Eliza Ann Smith, consort of B. B. Smith, of Georgetown. Died in October, 1833, aged 20 years. OR 10/10.

Dr. Charles V. Swearingin and Bayard Thistle, son of George Thistle. Murder and suicide by Swearingin on Sept. 24, 1833. Story in OR 10/10.

James Brooks, son of William Brooks, of Woodford county, formerly of Georgetown. Died Oct. 6, 1833, aged 27 or 28 years. OR 10/10.

Joseph Nelson Owen, son of Thomas Owen, of Scott county. Died October 6, 1833, aged 26 years. OR 10/10.

Francis S. M. Elgin, son of Joseph Elgin. Died Oct. 6, 1833, aged 21 or 22 years. OR 10/10.

Thomas Bryant, son of James Bryant, of Garrard county. Died October 9, 1833, aged about 16 years. OR 10/17.

Margaret Brand, daughter of John Brand, of Lexington. Died October 13, 1833, aged 12 years. OR 10/17.

Mrs. Elizabeth Bradford, relict of John Bradford, of Lexington. Died Saturday morning October 12, 1833, aged 87 years. OR 10/17.

Col. John Porter, of Butler county. *A soldier in the Revolution* and member elect of the State Legislature. Died September 24, 1833, aged 74 years. OR 10/17.

William Shellars, Sr., of Georgetown. Died October 22, 1833, aged 86 or 87 years. OR 10/24.

Mrs. Jane Warner, consort of Alfred Warner, of Fayette county. Died October 23, 1833. OR 10/24.

Major Benjamin Chambers, of Little Rock, Arkansas, late of Georgetown, Ky. Died Oct. 14, 1833, leaving his wife and six small children, all daughters. OR 10/31.

Mrs. Maria Gatewood, consort of Capt. Robert H. Gatewood, of Montgomery county. Died Oct. 14, 1833. OR 10/31.

Robert Sanders, of Mt. Sterling. Died Oct. 19, 1833. OR 10/31.

Mrs. Sarah Pew, of Lexington. Died Oct. 19, 1833, at an advanced age. OR 10/31.

Mrs. Ann Candy, consort of John Candy, of Lexington. Died October 26, 1833. OR 10/31.

George Vance Pinckard, son of Dr. Pinckard, of Lexington. Died Nov. 1, 1833. OR 11/7.

Mrs. Martha McIntyre, wife of Benjamin McIntyre, of Cynthiana late of Lexington. Died Oct. 30, 1833. OR 11/7.

Haney H. Wilkerson, of Lexington. Died Nov. 6, 1833. OR 11/7.

Patsy Jane Duvall, wife of J. Duvall, of Lexington, and daughter of Michael Gough. Died Oct. 30, 1833. OR 11/7.

Robert Fisher, a student at Transylvania University. Died at the residence of his uncle, Robert Wickliffe, October 31, 1833, aged about 19 years. OR 11/7.

Eben Milton, of Fayette county. Died Oct. 15, 1833. OR 11/7.

Samuel D. Moore, a native of Fayette county, but late of Missouri. Died at the Scott county, Ky., residence of his mother-in-law, Mrs. Tarlton, November 3, 1833. OR 11/7.

Ellen Ann, eldest daughter of Benjamin Harrison, of Woodford county. Died Nov. 6, 1833, aged 15 years. OR 11/7.

Virginial, daughter of John P. Eblia, of Lexington. Died November 19, 1833. OR 11/21.

Mrs. Martha Clugston, wife of William Clugston, of Fayette county. Died Nov. 16, 1833. OR 11/21.

William Poston, of Winchester. Died Nov. 13, 1833, at an advanced age, death resulting from a fall from his horse. OR 11/21.

Col. Young Ewing, of Lagrange, Tenn., for a long time a member of the Kentucky Legislature. Died Oct. 5, 1833. OR 11/21.

Sarah P. Megowan, daughter of Thomas B. Megowan, of Lexington. Died Nov. 22, 1833, aged 8 years. OR 11/28.

Robert Nourse Irwin, son of John M. C. Irwin, of Fayette county. Died Nov. 29, 1833, aged 8 years. OR 12/5.

Miss Mary J., youngest daughter of D. Flournoy, of Fayette county. Died December 2, 1833. OR 12/12.

Junius P. Fenner, student at Transylvania University. Shot and killed December 18, 1833, by Thomas W. Harris, a fellow student. Story in OR 12/19.

William Chappell, of Bullitt county, Ky., *a soldier in the Revolution.* Died at the Lexington residence of Laban Headington, December 12, 1833, aged 74 years. OR 12/19.

Mrs. Patsy Bryant, wife of James G. Bryant, of Garrard county. Died Dec. 26, 1833, aged 45 years. She left her husband and ten children, one being three months of age. OR 1/2/1834.

Mrs. Jane Berry, wife of George Berry, of Scott county. Died Dec. 26, 1833, aged 69 years. OR 1/2/1834.

Joseph N. Cotton, of Versailles. Died at the Fayette county residence of Col. Benjamin Taylor Dec. 29, 1833. OR 1/2/1834.

George M. Smedes, of Fayette county. Died Dec. 26, 1833. OR 1/2/1834.

Mrs. Katherine Sidener, consort of George P. Sidener, Sr., of Fayette county. Died Dec. 18, 1833, aged 54 years. OR 1/2/1834.

Mrs. Sarah Trotter, relict of George Trotter, of Lexington. Died Jan. 8, 1834, at an advanced age. OR 1/9.

Mrs. Emily Whitney, wife of Dr. W. W. Whitney. Died Jan. 2, 1834. OR 1/9.

Joseph Charles, son of Francis McLear. Died Dec. 27, 1833, aged 7 years and 5 months. OR 1/9/1834.

Mrs. Elizabeth Bryant, consort of Jesse Bryant, of Fayette county. Died Dec. 29, 1833, aged 69 years. Obituary in OR 1/9/1834.

John B. Agnew, of Lexington. Died Jan. 15, 1833. OR 1/16.

Mrs. Susan Hart Irvine, consort of Major David Irvine, of Richmond, Ky., and daughter of the late Dr. Ephraim McDowell and grand daughter of the late Governor Isaac Shelby. Died Jan. 13, 1834, aged 31 years. OR 1/23.

Capt. G. McKenney, a native of Virginia, but for many years a resident of Lexington, Ky. Died Jan. 16, 1834. OR 1/23.

William Carter, of Fayette county. Died Jan. 13, 1834, aged 23 years. OR 1/30.

James C. Applegate, of Georgetown. Died Jan. 12, 1834, aged 21 years. OR 1/30.

Cleon Hawkins, merchant of Georgetown. Died Jan. 17, 1834. OR 1/30.

Hugh Alexander, of Scott county. Died Jan. 13, 1834, at an advanced age. OR 1/30.

Col. William P. Fleming, a member of the Senate from Fleming county. Died in Frankfort Jan. 28, 1834. OR 1/30.

Mrs. Judith Rogers, of Fayette county, wife of Elijah Rogers. Died Jan. 31, 1834. OR 2/6.

Elijah Rogers, of Fayette county. See above. He died February 1, 1834. OR 2/6.

Rev. William Hickman, of Franklin county. Died Jan. 24, 1834, aged 87 years. OR 2/6.

Samuel L. Wheelock, of Lexington, Ky., a native of Boston, Mass. Died Feb. 23, 1834, aged 39 years. OR 2/27.

Edward Lovejoy. Died Feb. 11, 1834, aged about 40 years. OR 2/27.

James W. Riely, a printer. Died Feb. 12, 1834, aged 35 years, 9 months and 20 days. OR 3/6.

Dr. Richard Emmons, a native of Boston, Mass. Died Feb. 1, 1834. OR 3/6.

Mrs. Dorothy Kerr, wife of Capt. David Kerr, of Scott county. Died Feb, 21, 1834, aged 71 years. OR 3/6.

General Marquis Calmes, of Woodford county. *A soldier in the Revolution and in the War of 1812.* Died Feb. 27, 1834, aged 80 years. Obituary in OR 3/6.

Richard Thomas, infant son of Dr. John T. Lewis, of Woodford county. Died Mar. 14, 1834, at the residence of Mrs. M. Dowing, in Fayette county. He was one year of age. OR 3/13.

Horatio E. Boyd, of Lexington. Died Mar. 12, 1834. He was from Portland, Maine. Obituary in OR 3/13.

John C. Richardson, Sr., of Fayette county. He emigrated from Virginia to Fayette county about 1789. Died March 23, 1834, aged 81 years. OR 3/27.

Moses Randolph, son of Harvey Maguire, of Lexington. He died March 23, 1834. OR 3/27.

Miss Maria Warren, daughter of the late William Warren, of Georgetown. Died April 3, 1834, aged about 18 years. OR 4/10.

Emily, daughter of Mrs. Nancy Crittenden, of Lexington. She died Wednesday April 2, 1834. OR 4/10.

Mrs. Joyce Garnett, of Lexington. Died at the residence of her son, W. C. Garnett, April 9, 1834. OR 4/10.

Miss Julia Cullen, daughter of John P. Cullen, of Georgetown. Died Apr. 5, 1834, aged about 15 years. OR 4/17.

Mrs. Josephine S. Hunt, of St. Louis. Died in Lexington, Ky., April 13, 1834. OR 4/17.

Col. George Thompson, of Mercer county. Died Apr. 22, 1834, aged 86 years. OR 5/1.

Wesley Walker, of Cooper county, Mo., formerly of Kentucky. Died at the home of Mr. W. Walker, March 30, 1834, aged about 36 years. OR 5/1.

Frederick Kleet, of Campbell county. Died Apr. 24, 1834, aged 40 years. OR 5/1.

Mrs. Naomi Nash, consort of Mr. W. Nash, of Newport, Ky. Died April 23, 1834. OR 5/1.

William Theobald, Sr., of Scott county. Died May 9, 1834, aged 68 years. OR 5/15.

Mrs. Lucinda A. H. Wallace, wife of Dr. C. Wallace, of Lexington. Died May 9, 1834. OR 5/15.

Mr. ———— Shotwell, Sr., of Georgetown. Died May 12, 1834. OR 5/15.

Mrs. Agatha B. Nelson, wife of Capt. John Nelson, of Lexington. Died April 30, 1834, aged 78 years. OR 5/15.

Rev. George W. Ashbridge, Pastor of the First Presbyterian Church of Louisville. Died May 1, 1834. OR 5/15.

Richard Williamson, of Lexington. Shot and killed by his wife Saturday night May 17, 1834. Story in OR 5/22.

Gen. Richard B. New, late speaker of the House of Representatives of Kentucky. Died at Elkton, Todd county, May 12, 1834. OR 5/29.

Sarah Elizabeth, daughter of W. E. Probert, of Lexington. Died May 29, 1834, aged 18 months. OR 6/5.

Mrs. Eliza Henderson, wife of William Henderson, of Georgetown, and daughter of James Betts. Died June 1, 1834. OR 6/5.

Theodore Taylor, of Georgetown. Died in May, 1834. OR 6/5.

James James, American Consul for the ports of Vera Cruz and Alvarado. Died at Puebla, Mexico, April 24, 1834, aged 28 years. OR 6/5.

Mrs. Eliza Ann Berry, consort of Newton Berry. Died at her father's residence in Woodford county June 7, 1834. OR 6/11.

Mrs. Sally Luke, consort of A. B. Luke. Died June 5, 1834, at the Fayette county residence of Mr. Haynes. OR 6/11.

Susan Bell, infant daughter of John Dawson, of Lexington. Died June 13, 1834. OR 6/18.

Minerva, infant daughter of Mr. Notley (?) of Lexington. Died June 16, 1834. OR 6/18.

Mrs. Nancy Miller, consort of Capt. Jacob Miller, of Scott county. Died in June, 1834. OR 6/18.

John F. Anderson, of Louisville, formerly of Lexington. Died of cholera Friday, June 13, 1834. OR 6/18.

Mrs. Agnes P. Ward, consort of John Ward, of Lexington. Died June 19, 1834. OR 6/25.

Mary Louisa, infant daughter of W. W. Graves, of Fayette county. Died June 16, 1834, aged 1 year and 2 months. OR 6/25.

Miss Elizabeth Waters, daughter of Capt. Philamon Waters, formerly of Washington county, Ky. Died June 20, 1834, aged 52 years and 3 months. OR 6/25.

General Marquis de La Fayette, of France. He died May 22, 1834, aged 77 years. He was born Sept. 1, 1757. OR 7/2.

Miss Janette Grinstead, daughter of R. Grinstead, of Lexington. Died June 23, 1834. OR 7/2.

Col. James B. Payne, of Fayette county. Died June 24, 1834. OR 7/2.

Robert Reily, son of John Reily, of Paoli, Ind., and brother-in-law of the proprietor of the *Observer and Reporter.* (N. L. Finnell?) Died in Hardinsburg, Breckenridge county, Ky., June 30, 1834. OR 7/9.

Dr. John P. Declary, of Louisville. Suicided July 4, 1834. Story in OR 7/16.

Mrs. Mary Hawkins, of Fayette county, daughter of Jonathan Rigg. Died Saturday July 5, 1834. OR 7/16. See below.

Jonathan Rigg, of Fayette county. Died July 12, 1834, at an advanced age. See above. OR 7/16.

Joseph Rogers, of Fayette county. Died Sunday July 13, 1834, aged 95 years. He had been a resident of Fayette county "near 50 years." OR 7/16.

Col. John M. McConnell, of Greenup county. Died July 5, 1834. OR 7/6.

Mrs. Mary Elizabeth Payne, wife of Lewis Payne and daughter of Mrs. Mary Keene, all of Fayette county. Died July 3, 1834. OR 7/6.

Edward Rigg, a native of Kentucky. Died in Louisiana on Sunday June 15, 1834, aged 34 years. OR 7/6.

Jonathan Robinson, of Scott county. Died Saturday July 12, 1834, aged 87 or 88 years. OR 7/16.

Albert Humrickhouse, of Virginia. Killed when the stage coach bearing Henry Clay from Harper's Ferry to Winchester overturned July 6, 1834. Mr. Clay was not hurt "though the horses were at half speed descending a hill at the instant the stage capsized." OR 7/23.

Israel Gilpin, of Boone county. *A soldier in the Revolution.* Died July 4, 1834, aged 94 years "on the 11th of October next." Long obitury in OR 7/23.

Thomas Webb, of Clark county, only son of Dr. William Webb. Died Thursday July 17, 1834, aged 21 or 22 years. OR 7/23.

Col. Enoch Prince, of Princeton, Caldwell county. Died in July, 1834. He was a Kentucky Senator. OR 7/30.

Miss Margaret Macbean, daughter of William Macbean, of Lexington. Died August 5, 1834. OR 8/6.

William McCalla, of Lexington. Died Thursday July 31, 1834, aged about 30 years. OR 8/6.

David Bryant, of Fayette county. Died Aug. 6, 1834, aged about 55 years. OR 8/13.

Powhattan, son of Powhattan Ellis, of Natchez, Miss. Died in Lexington, Ky., June 30, 1834, aged 20 months and 6 days. OR 8/13.

John Jennings, of Port Gibson, Miss. Murdered Sept. 9, 1834, by Jacob Skinner. OR 8/13.

Andrew Hawthorne, of Louisiana. Died in Lexington, Ky., at the Lexington Hotel on Monday Aug. 10, 1834. OR 8/13.

Peter G. Winn, son of Dr. Minor Winn, of Pendleton county. Died in Georgetown, Ky., Aug. 14, 1834. OR 8/20.

Joseph D. Jones, a native of Kentucky. Died in Boonville, Mo., July 22, 1834. OR 8/20.

John S. Van De Graff. Died at Greenburg, Ind., in August, 1834. OR 8/27.

Henry R. Clarke, late of Canandagua, N. Y. Died at Winchester, Ky., Saturday Aug. 2, 1834. OR 8/27.

Edward Ritchie, formerly of Philadelphia. Died at his residence, Union Mills, near Lexington, Ky., in August, 1834. OR 9/3.

Col. Hugh Muldrow, of Fayette county, one of the first settlers of Kentucky. Died Aug. 22, 1834, aged 79 years. OR 9/3.

Miss Sarah S. Perkins. Died Monday August 29, 1834, at the Lexington residence of her adopted father, Nathan Burrows. OR 9/3.

Hester, infant daughter of John C. Atkinson. Died Sept. 2, 1834. OR 9/3.

Elijah Patrick, of St. Francis County, Arkansas. Killed in August, 1834, by a Mr. Roland. OR 9/10.

William Smith Craig, son of Lewis Craig. Died at the residence of Charles Norwood, in Versailles, August 28, 1834. OR 9/10.

John Ward, of Winchester. Died Sept. 4, 1834, at an advanced age. OR 9/10.

Lewis H. Bryan, of Clark county. Died Sept. 24, 1834, aged about 40 years. OR 9/10.

David M. Bean, son of Charles Bean, of Clark county. Died Sept. 4, 1834, aged 25 years and 8 months. OR 9/10.

Mrs. Margaret Frazer, of Fayette county. Died Sept. 8, 1834, aged about 30 years. OR 9/17.

Patrick Geohegan, of Lexington. Died Sept. 18, 1834, aged about 55 or 56 years. He left a large family. OR 9/24.

John, infant son of Dr. J. D. Cornell, of Lexington. Died September 23, 1834. OR 9/24.

Miss Harriet Simrall, of Mason county. Died Sept. 21, 1834. OR 9/24.

James Granville, infant son of Josiah Gayle, of Lexington. Died Sept. 23, 1834. OR 9/24.

James G. Brooks, of Natchez, Miss., son of the late James A. Brooks, of Lexington, Ky. Died Aug. 30, 1834, aged about 20 or 21 years. OR 9/24.

Dr. J. H. A. Fehr, late of Lexington. Died of cholera in Louisville in September, 1834. S 9/7.

Thomas Stewart, of Fayette county. Died while on a coon hunt, Tuesday night Set. 30, 1834. He had no family. OR 10/1.

Mrs. Sarah J. A. Waddle, consort of Alexander Waddle, of Clarke county, Ohio, and daughter of the late Samuel H. Woodson. Died at the Jessamine county residence of her mother on Sept. 11, 1834. OR 10/1.

Mrs. Susan Henry, wife of Thomas Henry and eldest daughter of Capt. Robert Dudley. Died in Christian county Sept. 20, 1834, aged 37 years. She left her husband and 3 sons. OR 10/1.

Hon. William H. Crawford. Died eight miles from Elberton, Ga., Oct. 1, 1834. OR 10/8.

John James, infant son of James Nelson, of Lexington. Died Oct. 10, 1834. OR 10/15.

James Hamilton, of Lexington. Died Oct. 1, 1834, aged 78 years. OR 10/15.

James D. McCoy, of Alexandria, La., formerly from Georgetown, Ky. Died Sept. 16, 1834, aged 28 years. Obituary in OR 10/15.

Joseph P. Devore, of Fayette county. Died Sept. 30, 1834, aged about 45 years. OR 10/22.

George Hamilton, Sr., of Fayette county. Died Oct. 9, 1834, aged 84 years. OR 10/22.

Mrs. Martha C. Dudley, wife of Col. Ambrose Dudley, of Fayette county. Died in Cincinnati, of cholera, in October, 1834. OR 10/22.

Miss Mary Cartright, daughter of Henry Cartright, of Bourbon county. Died October 18, 1834. OR 10/29.

William T. Taliaferro, of near Winchester. Died Oct. 21, 1834, aged about 60 years. He left his wife and a large family of children. OR 10/29.

Mrs. Margaret Edmiston, relict of *Capt. John Edmiston,* of Fayette county. He fell at the Battle of *the River Raisin.* She died October 8, 1834. OR 10/29.

Rev. Moore Wisdom, of McNairy county, Tenn. Murdered on August 30, 1834, by a Mr. Ward. OR 11/5.

James Smith, of Lexington. Died November 1, 1834. OR 11/5.

Mrs. ———— Gordon, wife of John Gordon, Sr. Died Friday October 31, 1834. OR 11/5.

John Howard, of Lexington. Died Friday November 7, 1834, aged 103 years. He was born in Goochland county, Va., near Carter's Ferry. His father was Col. Allen Howard. He (John Howard) made a settlement at Boonesborough in June, 1775. See obituary in OR 11/12.

John Linton. Murdered in Mississippi in October, 1834. OR 11/19.

Mrs. Eliza Williams, daughter of William Smith, dec'd. She died in Scott county Nov. 15, 1834. OR 11/19.

Col. John Thomson, of Christian, formerly of Scott county. Died Oct. 29, 1834, at an advanced age. OR 11/19.

Henry H. Whittington. Died at the Versailles residence of Col. William Barr on Monday Nov. 17, 1834, aged 27 years. OR 11/26.

Mr. N. M. Henderson. Died in November, 1834. Obituary in OR 11/26.

John Tilford, infant son of Col. Leslie Combs, of Lexington. Died Nov. 24, 1834, aged 15 months and 12 days. OR 11/26.

Mrs. Nancy Shaw, consort of John R. Shaw, of Lexington. Died Saturday November 22, 1834. OR 11/26.

Rev. Eli N. Sawtell, Pastor of the Second Presbyterian Church of Louisville. Died Nov. 22, 1834. OR 11/26.

Andrew W. Trapnall, of Clarksburg, Va., formerly of Mercer county, Ky. Died Nov. 17, 1834, aged 24 years. Obituary in OR 12/3.

Mrs. Frances Ann Flournoy, wife of T. B. Flournoy, late of Fayette county, Ky. Died on Lake Swan, in Arkansas, Dec. 7, 1834. OR 12/24.

Mrs. Frances Chalk, of Georgetown. Died Dec. 12, 1834, aged 60 years. OR 12/24.

Clifton Rodes Birch, of Scott county. Died Dec. 28, 1834, aged 41 or 42 years. OR 12/31.

1835

Charles E. Bains, Principal Instructor in the Preparatory Department of Transylvania University. A native of England and resident of Lexington, Ky., since 1828. Died Tuesday Jan. 6, 1835, aged about 30 years. Obituary in OR 1/7.

Milton Suggett, son of John Suggett, Sr. Died in Scott county Jan. 19, 1835, aged 40 years. OR 1/12.

Nathaniel Mothershead, Sr., of Scott county. Died Sunday Dec. 28, 1834, aged 80 years. *A soldier in the Revolution.* See obituary in OR 1/12/1835.

Rebecca Ruckel, eldest daughter of John W. Trumbull, of Lexington. Died Feb. 4, 1835. OR 2/4.

Taliaferro Sanders. Died at the Fayette county residence of Peter Gatewood, Jan. 31, 1835, aged about 45 years. OR 2/4.

Robert Crittenden, of Little Rock, Arkansas Territory, and formerly of Kentucky. Died in Vicksburg, Miss., Dec. 17, 1834. OR 2/4/1835.

Hezekiah McCann, of Fayette county. Died Feb. 2, 1835. OR 2/4.

Francis Flournoy, of Scott county. Died Jan. 29, 1835, aged 64 years. Obituary in OR 2/4.

Mrs. Blythe, wife of James Blythe, D.D., President of South Hanover College. Died at South Hanover, Ind., Thursday January 29, 1835. OR 2/11.

Samuel Q. Richardson. Shot in Frankfort, Ky., Sunday Feb. 8, 1835, by John U. Waring. Died Monday Feb. 9, 1835. Story in OR 2/11.

Dr. Lyddall Wilkinson, of Frankfort. Died Feb. 15, 1835. OR 2/18.

Ralph B. Mattingly, of Springfield, Ky., a student at Transylvania University. Died in February, 1835. OR 2/18.

William L. Trotter, son of Samuel Trotter. Died February 13, 1835, aged 27 years. OR 2/18.

Francene Eliza, daughter of Thomas Rankin. Died Feb. 18, 1835. OR 2/8.

William McAdams. Died Feb. 15, 1835. OR 2/18.

J. J. McLaughlin, of Nashville, Tenn., formerly of Hopkinsville, Ky. Died Feb. 5, 1835. OR 2/25.

Hon. David White, of Franklin county. Died Feb. 18, 1835. OR 2/25.

Miss Emily Elder. Died at the Knoxville residence of her brother-in-law, Mr. Oldham, February 8, 1835, aged 22 years.

General Wade, Hampton, of Columbia, S. C. Died March 4, 1835, aged 81 years. OR 3/4.

Levi Ragan, of Lexington. Died March 3, 1835. OR 3/4.

Charles Bratton, of Nicholasville. Stabbed and killed, Mar. 9, 1835, by James P. Major. Story in OR 3/11.

Major John McKinney, Jr., clerk of the Woodford county circuit court. Died in Versailles March 4, 1835. OR 3/11.

Mrs. Elizabeth P. Benedict, consort of the Reverend H. T. N. Benedict, and eldest daughter of the late Rev. John Metcalf. Died at the Jessamine county residence of William S. Scott March 5, 1835, aged 37 years. OR 3/11.

John Maxwell. Died in Lexington at the residence of Mr. H. M. Winslow, Friday March 6, 1835. OR 3/11.

Thomas T. Skillman, one of the proprietors of the *Western Luminary.* Died in Lexington March 10, 1835. OR 3/11.

Benjamin Bosworth, of Fayette county. Killed by an explosion of gunpowder at Westbrook, the farm of Thomas Smith, of Fayette county. Died March 15, 1835. OR 3/18.

Daniel Boyce, son of Col. John R. Dunlap, of Fayette county. Died March 18, 1835, aged 3 years and 7 months. OR 3/25.

Robert McNitt, of Lexington. Died Apr. 4, 1835, aged about 67 years. OR 4/8.

Mrs. Rebecca P. Bayles, wife of Jesse Bayles, and daughter of the late Robert McNitt, of Fayette county. See above. She died April 7, 1835, leaving her husband and an infant child. OR 4/8.

Thomas Outten, of Fayette county. Died Apr. 23, 1835. OR 4/29.

Miss Betsey Thompson Scott, daughter of M. T. Scott, of Lexington, Ky. Died at Baltimore April 14, 1835, aged 22 years. OR 4/29.

Miss Margaret Buzzard, daughter of Solomon Buzzard, of Lexington. Died April 28, 1835, aged about 23 years. OR 5/6.

Presley Talbott, of Jesamine county. Died April 17, 1835, aged 56 years. OR 5/13.

Mrs. Lucy Taylor, consort of Col. Colby H. Taylor, of Clark county, and daughter of Col. James Minor, of Virginia. She died Sunday May 17, 1835. OR 5/20.

Mrs. Magdalena Waltz, consort of Frederick Waltz, of Fayette county. Died May 13, 1835, aged about 64 years. OR 5/27.

Mrs. Mary Brown, wife of George D. Brown, of Georgetown. Died May 24, 1835. OR 5/27.

Miss Catherine Hawkins, of Scott county. Died May 25, 1835, at an advanced age. OR 5/27.

General Robert McHatton, late of Scott county, Ky. Died in Marion county Ind., May 20, 1835. Obituary in OR 6/3.

John Wardlaw, of Fayette county. Died May 27, 1835, aged about 60 years. OR 6/3.

Mrs. Eliza A. B. West, consort of Preston West, of Georgtown, and daughter of James B. Crawford. Died June 5, 1835, aged 26 or 27 years. She left her husband and several small children. OR 6/10.

Mrs. Ruth Warfield, relict of Elisha Warfield. Died May 30, 1835, aged 73 years. OR 6/17.

Mrs. Elizabeth Dunn, relict of C. Dunn, and daughter of Capt. William Duncan, of Clay county, Mo. Died at the Fayette county, Ky., residence of Benjamin Scott June 15, 1835. OR 6/24.

Mrs. Catherine D. Armstrong, wife of John Armstrong, Sr., of Maysville, and daughter of Gen. Thomas Hood, of Anne Arundel county, Maryland. Died June 12, 1835. OR 6/24.

Miss Margaret Young, of Ohio. Died of cholera Saturday June 20, 1835. OR 6/24.

John Mann. Died June 20, 1835. OR 6/24.

Mrs. Jane Grant, wife of John Grant, of Mason county. Died of cholera Saturday June 20, 1835. OR 6/24.

James H. Wallace, Sr., editor of the Madison (Ind.) *Republican and Banner*. He was a native of Mason county, Ky. Died of cholera Wednesday June 17, 1835. OR 7/1.

Honorable Amos Davis. Died June 11, 1835. See obituary in OR 7/1.

Eli Kennady, of Bourbon county. Died of cholera June 29, 1835. OR 7/1.

Mrs. Mary Woolfolk, of Woodford county. Died June 28, 1835, aged 88 years. OR 7/1.

Gen. John H. Rudd, formerly of Bracken county, Ky. Died in Yazoo county, Miss., May 12, 1835. OR 7/1.

John J. Warner, of Lexington. Died Wednesday July 1, 1835, aged about 50 years. OR 7/8.

John W., infant son of James Harrison. Died July 1, 1835. OR 7/8.

Marcus A., infant son of R. H. Chinn. Died June 28, 1835. OR 7/8.

Willis Bradley, of South Frankfort. Died June 24, 1835. OR 7/8.

Hon. Eli Huston, formerly of Kentucky. Died in Natchez, Miss., June 12, 1835. OR 7/8.

Thomas Marshall, eldest son of Chief Justice John Marshall. Killed during a storm in Baltimore, Saturday July 4, 1835. He left his wife and six children. He was buried in the family vault at Oak Hill, Fauquier county, Va. OR 7/15. See below.

Anna Adair, daughter of Dr. William Pawling, of Lexington. Died July 7, 1835. OR 7/15.

William Dougherty, of Lexington. Died July 21, 1835. OR 7/22.

Mrs. Mary Shellers, of Georgetown. Died July 16, 1835. OR 7/22.

Mrs. Lucinda Graves, consort of Harvey C. Graves, of Fayette county, and daughter of Capt. John Garth, of Scott county. Died July 9, 1835, aged 27 years. OR 7/22.

Chief Justice John Marshall. Died in Philadelphia July 6, 1835. Sketch of his life in OR 7/22. See above.

Williams Byrns, late of Fayette county, Ky. Died in Ross county, Ohio, June 11, 1835, of cholera. OR 7/22.

Mrs. Anne Bradford, consort of Col. James M. Bradford, formerly of Franklin county, Ky. Died in Illinois July 8, 1835. OR 7/22.

Mrs. Mary Stewart, consort of Rev. Charles Stewart, of Fayette county. Died June 22, 1835. OR 7/29.

Andrew M., son of Theodore G. Price, of Georgetown. He died July 20, 1835. OR 7/29.

Miss Malinda W. Blair, of Lexington. Died Aug. 1, 1835. OR 8/5.

Major John McDowell. Died in July, 1835. OR 8/5.

Mrs. Eliza Underwood, of Edmonson, Ky., consort of Hon. Joseph R. Underwood, late one of the Judges of the Court of Appeals of Kentucky. Died July 17, 1835. OR 8/5.

Abraham K. Smedes, of Lexington. Died Sunday July 29, 1835. OR 8/5.

Benjamin B. Pritchard, of Montgomery county, Ky. Died at the home of Horace Benton, June 30, 1835, aged 45 years. He was *a soldier in the War of 1812.* He weighed 525 or 550 pounds. Story in OR 8/5.

John Crawford, of Lewis county. Suicided July 31, 1835. OR 8/12.

William H. Spencer, Sr., of Clark county. Died Aug. 2, 1835, at an advanced age. OR 8/12.

The following white citizens of Russellville, Ky., died of cholera during July, 1835. OR 8/12:

Major J. R. Ferbush
James C. Slaughter
Mr. ———— Hilton
Elias Haddox & Lady
Solomon Hardy
William Lacey & Son
James L. Armstrong
M. McGrath
Mrs. William E. Warren
Mrs. Patten
Miss Columbia Burgess
Miss Sarah Sands
William L. Harding
Charles Rhea
Noah White
William Morton
Peyton L. Parrish
W. R. Belt
David Armstrong
Mr. ———— Shafer
Mrs. Hunter
Miss Julia Rice
Miss Elizabeth O'Bannon
R. S. Emmitt
Col. William L. Sands
William L. Lander
James Alderson
Joseph A. Smith
Samuel W. Linebaugh
Reuben Jackman
Francis R. Browning
Mrs. John Roberts
Miss Patsy Underwood

Mrs. Sarah Higgins, consort of Richard Higgins, Jr., of Lexington. Died August 5, 1835. OR 8/12.

Mrs. Deborah Warner, consort of Derrick Warner, of Lexington. Died Aug. 9, 1835. OR 8/12.

Mrs. Ursula T. Dunnington, daughter of William Thornsbury, of Fauquier county, Va., and consort of Dr. William P. Dunnington, from Dumfries, Va. Died at her residence in Millersburg, Kentucky, of cholera June 28, 1835, aged 43 years. She left her husband and six children. OR 8/12.

Josephine Elizabeth, daughter of Dr. William P. Dunnington. See above. Died June 30, 1835, aged 5 years. OR 8/12.

Mrs. Eleanor Bradford, consort of Fielding Bradford. Died in Scott county Friday August 14, 1835. OR 8/19.

Richard S. Lander, formerly of Clark county. Died in Hardinsburg, July 20, 1835, aged about 45 years. Left his wife and six or eight children. OR 8/19.

Mrs. Mary Cabell Satterwhite, wife of Dr. Thomas P. Satterwhite, and daughter of Joseph Cabell Breckinridge, dec'd. She died in Lexington August 13, 1835. OR 8/19.

John Hull, Jr., of Lexington. Died Aug. 20, 1835, aged about 25 years. OR 8/26.

Simeon True, of Scott county. Died August 17, 1835, aged about 45 years. OR 9/2.

The following white citizens of Versailles, Kentucky, died of cholera in August 13, 1835. OR 8/19.

John Fritzlen
Mrs. Elizabeth Moreland and child
Robert Shelton, Sr.
Mrs. Doctor Rhoton
Mrs. Mary Hunter, Sr.
Southy Whittington
Charles Bruce
Granville Crockett
Hugh Ferguson
James Yost
Mr. ——— Davidson
Miss ——— Shackleford
William S. Hunter
Robert Kinkead, Jr.
Henry Christopher
Lawson Carroll
Preston Terrell, Jr.
James Riddle
William Agun
Dr. ——— Stevenson
William Moore
Alexander Peters
Vincent Ross
William Coons
J. Riddle
Preston Terrell, Sr.
Mitchell Conley

Mrs. Mary Ann Lovejoy, of Lexington. Died Aug. 23, 1835. OR 9/2.

Thourt Johnson, of Lexington. Died Aug. 31, 1835, aged about 19 years. OR 9/2.

James Hutchinson, of Doneraille, Fayette county. Died Aug. 14, 1835, aged about 50 years. OR 9/2.

Cornelius Vorhies, of La. Died in Lexington, Ky., Aug. 26, 1835, aged 58 years. OR 9/2.

Mrs. Eliza J. Brown, consort of Preston M. Brown and daughter of William Geers, formerly of Lexington, Ky. Died in Jacksonville, Ill., August 11, 1835. KG 8/29.

James Haggin, of Frankfort. Died Aug. 21, 1835, aged about 56 years. OR 9/2.

Capt. Hudson Martin, of Union county, Ky. Died in September, 1835 OR 9/16.

Benjamin Hickman, child of Richard K. Woodson, of Woodford county. Died at the residence of Mrs. Ann R. Woodson, of Jessamine county, Sept. 12, 1835, aged 2 years. OR 9/16.

Capt. Walker Powell, of Scott county. Died August 31, 1835. OR 9/16.

Philemon B. Price, of Jacksonville, Ill., but late of Georgetown, Ky. Died in Philadelphia Sept. 5, 1835. OR 9/16.

Lewis Barbee, of Lexington. Died Sept. 5, 1835, aged 50 years. He left his wife and several children. KG 9/12.

John James Flournoy, of Campbell county. Died in September, 1835, aged 65 years. Obituary in KG 9/19.

George Hume, of Scott county. Died September 10, 1835, aged 64 years. He was a native of Virginia. OR 9/23.

Mrs. Mary Ann Peers, consort of the Reverend Benjamin O. Peers, formerly of Lexington. Died in Louisville Sept. 8, 1835, aged 40 years. OR 9/23.

Henry N. Norton, son of George Norton, of Lexington. Died on Monday September 21, 1835, aged 20 years. OR 9/23.

John Fry, of Fayette county. Died Sept. 21, 1835, at an advanced age. OR 9/23.

Mrs. Susan Robinson, consort of James F. Robinson, of Georgetown. Died Sept. 17, 1835. OR 9/23.

J. Addison Lyle, son of John Lyle, of Fayette county. Died in Woodford county Sunday Sept. 20, 1835. OR 9/23.

Robert D. Stockton, of Greenup county. Died near Greensburg, Ky., Sept. 11, 1835. OR 9/23.

Alfred C. Hurt, formerly of Lexington. Shot and killed by Nathan Hodge, in Flemingsburg, Sept. 20, 1835. Story in OR 9/30.

Absalom Pollard, of Garrard county. *A soldier in the American Revolution.* Died Aug. 30, 1835, aged 80 years. OR 9/30.

Benjamin Higbee, of Lexington. Died in Cincinnati September 22, 1835. OR 9/30.

James S. Ferguson, of Jessamine county. Died in September, 1835. OR 9/30.

Rev. Minor M. Crosby, of the Methodist E. Church. Died on his way from the Henderson circuit of the Kentucky Conference to his wife's relations in Clark county. Died Sept. 3, 1835, aged 27 years. OR 9/30.

James Stewart, Sr., of Clark county. Died in September, 1835, aged 91 years and 7 months. OR 9/30.

Honorable William T. Barry, United States Minister to Spain. Died in September, 1835, in England. OR 10/21.

Elizabeth Person, daughter of Levi Prewitt. Died Sept. 25, 1835, aged about 3 years. OR 10/7.

Miss Mary E. Norton, daughter of George Norton, of Fayette county. Died Saturday October 10, 1835. She was the fourth child her parents had lost within the short period of three years, the second within two weeks. OR 10/14.

William Winslow, infant son of Col. Alvan Stephens, of Lexington. Died October 6, 1835. OR 10/14.

Mrs. Ann Trueman, consort of William Trueman, of Maysville. Died October 1, 1835. OR 10/14.

James M. Runyon, of Mayslick. Died October 6, 1835. OR 10/14.

Mrs. Rebecca Martin, wife of Samuel Martin, of Maysville. Died October 7, 1835. OR 10/14.

Thomas Gibson Howard, of Mt. Sterling. Died September 29, 1835, aged about 30 years. OR 10/14.

Miss Ianthe C. Story, daughter of John Story, Georgetown. Died October 3, 1835. OR 10/14.

Hay Taliaferro, of Winchester, Ky., a native of Caroline county, Va. Died Oct. 7, 1835. OR 10/14.

Mrs. Mary Blair, relict of Samuel Blair, of Fayette county. Died Oct. 1, 1835. OR 10/14.

Oliver Langdon Leonard, infant son of V. V. Baldwin, of Woodford county. Died Oct. 2, 1835, aged about 20 months. OR 10/14.

James Moore, of Fayette county. Died October 13, 1835, aged 24 or 25 years. OR 10/14.

Mrs. Mary Butler, of Fleming county. Died in Lexington Wednesday October 14, 1835, aged 34 years. OR 10/21.

Mrs. Margaret Ann Krusor, wife of James Krusor, and daughter of Col. Joseph Scrugham, all of Lexington. Died in Lexington Monday Oct. 18, 1835, aged 22 years. OR 10/21.

Francis Williams, son of William Richardson, of Lexington. Died October 23, 1835. OR 10/28.

Downing Craig, son of D. M. Craig. Died Oct. 26, 1835. OR 10/28.

Mrs. Catharine Hunt, consort of John W. Hunt, of Lexington. Died Oct. 17, 1835, aged 57 years. OR 10/28.

James Johnson, formerly of Kentucky. Died at Indianapolis, Ind., October 24, 1835. OR 11/4.

Mrs. Sarah Hewett, consort of the Rev. M. Hewett, of Lexington. Died November 5, 1835. OR 11/11.

George C. Pond, later of Franklin, Mass. Died in Lexington, Ky., Thursday November 5, 1835. OR 11/11.

Col. Robert Scohee, of Clark county. Died Oct. 31, 1835. OR 11/11.

Mrs. F. P. January, wife of Joseph January, of Winchester. Died November 4, 1835. OR 11/18.

William F. Taylor, adopted son of Willis Collins, of Winchester, Ky. Died at the residence of William Taylor, at Point Coupee, La., on October 2, 1835, aged 19 years. OR 11/18.

Capt. John Smith, of Scott county. Died November 9, 1835, aged 73 years. OR 11/18.

Philip Smith, of Scott county. Died Nov. 14, 1835, aged about 55 years. OR 11/18.

Major Benjamin Shackleford, of Lexington. Died Nov. 19, 1835, at an advanced age. OR 11/25.

Mrs. Sarah Ann Fanning, consort of Rev. Talbot Fanning, of Nashville, and daughter of Judge W Shreve, of Nicholasville, Ky. She had been married to Reverend Fanning on November 5, was taken ill Nov. 8 and died at her father's home No. 20, 1835. OR 11/25.

Mrs. Nancy Garrard, consort of General James Garrard, of Bourbon county. Died Nov. 17, 1835, aged 62 years. OR 11/25.

Col. William Duane. Died at Philadelphia No. 24, 1835, aged 76 years. OR 12/9.

Rev. William C. Warfield, formerly of Lexington. Died in Christian county Nov. 2, 1835. OR 12/9.

Mrs. Ann Erwin, consort of James Erwin, of Lexington, and daughter of the Hon. Henry Clay. Died Thursday night December 10, 1835. OR 12/16.

Mrs. Mary Bain, consort of P. L. Bain, and eldest daughter of Thomas Theobalds, keeper of the Penitentiary. Died at Frankfort Dec. 13, 1835. OR 12/16.

Benjamin W. Ford, of Paris, Ky. Died at Vicksburg, Miss., Nov. 24, 1835. OR 12/16.

James, infant son of Thomas Huggins, of Lexington. Died Dec. 21, 1835. OR 12/23.

Mrs. Cross, consort of John Cross, of Lexington. Died Sunday Dec. 20, 1835. OR 12/23.

Samuel Shivel, of Lexington. Died Dec. 20, 1835. OR 12/23.

1836

Thomas N. Rainey, son of William H. Rainey, of Lexington. Died Jan. 6, 1836, aged 3 years, 5 months. An only child. OR 1/13.

Edward Wayland Monett, youngest son of Dr. Monett, of Mississippi. Died in Lexington, Ky., Jan. 2, 1836. OR 1/13.

Mrs. Margaret Rucker, consort of Lewis Rucker, of Georgetown, and daughter of Michael Goddard. Died Jan. 18, 1836. OR 1/20.

Mr. T. T. Rucker, of Lancaster. Died Jan. 8, 1836. OR 1/20.

Mary Williams, daughter of Caleb Williams, of Lexington. Died on January 16, 1836, aged 15 years. OR 1/20.

Capt. Lynn West, of Georgetown. One of the oldest settlers of that place. Died Jan. 26, 1836, aged 66 years. OR 1/27.

Burrell Griffith, of Bourbon county. Died January 26, 1836, aged 29 years and 20 days. OR 1/27.

Mrs. Caroline T. Robbins, consort of Silas W. Robbins, of Montgomery county. Died Jan. 26, 1836. OR 2/3.

Jeptha D. Garrard, of Cincinnati. Died Jan. 27, 1836. Obituary in OR 3/10.

Col. William McMillan, of Clark county. Died Feb. 3, 1836. OR 2/10.

George R. Young, printer, of Lexington. Died Feb. 1, 1836, aged about 28 years. OR 2/10.

Emily, infant daughter of Thomas A McGrath, of Louisville. Died in Lexington Feb. 2, 1836. OR 2/10.

Leslie Combs, Jr., second son of Gen. Leslie Combs, of Lexington. Died Feb. 15, 1836, less than 6 years of age. OR 2/17.

Gen. Edward King, of Cincinnati. Died Feb. 6, 1836. OR 2/17.

Miss Eliza Hostetter, of Lexington. Died Feb. 9, 1836. OR 2/17.

John Bruce, of Lexington. Died Feb. 10, 1836, aged 49 years. OR 2/17.

Dr. Thomas L. Smith, druggist of Lexington. Died Feb. 16, 1836, leaving his wife and 2 children. OR 2/17.

William S. James, of the firm James & Brothers of Lexington. Died Feb. 16, 1836, in Louisville. He was formerly from Philadelphia. OR 2/24.

Abraham S. Barton, a native of Fayette county, Ky. Died in Savannah, Ga., in February, 1836. OR 2/24.

Robert R. Barr, of Lexington. Died Feb. 25, 1836. OR 2/24.

Michael Goddard, Sr., of Georgetown. Died Feb. 26, 1836, aged about 55 years. OR 3/2.

Fielding E. Dickey, of Georgetown. Died Mar. 1, 1836, aged about 35 years. OR 3/2.

Dr. Robert Sayres, of Tenn., a member of the Medical Class of Transylvania University. Died in Lexington, Ky., Feb. 28, 1836. OR 3/2.

Richard Allen Curd, of Lexington. Died March 8, 1836, aged about 35 years. Resolutions in OR 3/9.

Robert Russell, infant son of Elder Thomas M. Allen, of Fayette county. Died March 8, 1836. OR 3/16.

Mrs. Catharine S. Payne, consort of Nathan Payne, of Fayette county. Died Mar. 8, 1836, aged 49 years. OR 3/16.

Mrs. Polly Adams, consort of T. J. Adams, of Georgetown. Died Mar. 10, 1836. OR 3/23.

David Anson, formerly of Zanesville, Ohio. Killed in Louisville on March 8, 1836. OR 3/23.

William Tod, Sr., of Lexington. Died March 21, 1836. OR 3/23.

Charles Wickliffe, of Lexington. Died March 24, 1836, aged 70 years. OR 3/30.

Benjamin Grimes, of Lexington. Died March 24, 1836, at an advanced age. OR 3/30.

Thomas Triplett, of Lexington. Died March 29, 1836, aged about 40 years. OR 4/6.

Mrs. Emeline M. Jones, consort of Major H. Jones, of Versailles. She died at the Woodford County residence of her father, Willis Field, on March 23, 1836. OR 4/6.

Mrs. Allen, consort of Thomas Allen, of Clark county. Died Mar. 26, 1836, aged 55 years. OR 4/6.

Samuel Logan, merchant of Lexington. Killed during a fight in the Lexington Court House. The fight was between John L. and James Turnbull and William R. Logan and Samuel Logan, his brother. Fight took place on Monday and Samuel Logan died Tuesday evening April 5, 1836, aged 24 or 25 years. OR 4/13.

Mrs. Nancy McCoy, wife of Neill McCoy, of Lexington. She was born in the County of Antrim, Scotland. Died March 25, 1836 aged about 61 years. OR 4/13.

John Irvin, infant son of John R. Lyle, of Fayette county. Died Sunday April 10, 1836, aged 2 years and 5 months. OR 4/13.

Joseph Ficklin Grooms, of Lexington, a Medical Student. Died at the residence of Mr. Ficklin April 13, 1836, aged 20 years. OR 4/20.

William H. N. Drake, of Pendleton county. Died mysteriously April 13, 1836. Story in OR 4/20.

Mr. W. C. Spurr, of near Athens, Fayette county. Died April 13, 1836, aged 61 years. OR 4/27.

James F. Shy, of Lexington. Killed April 16, 1836, at the Race Course near the city. He was 13 years of age. OR 4/27.

Mrs. Susan Adams. Died Sunday April 10, 1836, at the Scott county residence of her son, George W. Adams. She was 76 years of age. OR 4/27.

Mrs. Sarah Blackburn, consort of Dr. C. J. Blackburn, of Scott county, and daughter of Oliver Keene, of Lexington. Died April 23, 1836. OR 4/27.

Mrs. Nancy Decret, consort of Joseph Decret, of Winchester, and daughter of the late Jonathan Bryon. Died April 18, 1836. OR 4/27.

Mrs. Nancy Anderson, relict of John Anderson, of Louisville, and daughter of John L. Martin, formerly of Lexington. Died April 15, 1836. OR 5/4.

Mrs. Sheppard, consort of David Sheppard, of Lexington. Died in May, 1836. OR 5/11.

William Williamson, of Fayette county. Died May 7, 1836, aged 73 years. OR 5/12.

William H. Edrington, printer, formerly of Frankfort, Ky. Died in Troy, Miss., May 18, 1836. OR 5/30.

Mrs. Rebecca Blanchard, consort of Asa Blanchard, of Lexington. She died Saturday, May 28, 1836. OR 5/30.

Thomas Carr, Sr., of Fayette county. Died May 31, 1836. OR 6/1.

Mrs. Dorothea Coons, consort of Henry C. Coons, Died June 4, 1836, aged 34 years. KG 6/23.

Wilson, youngest son of Dr. L. P. Yandell, of Lexington. Died June 13, 1836, aged 5 years, 11 months and 1 day. KG 6/23.

Joseph I. Lemon, of Fayette county. Died June 17, 1836. KG 6/20.

Mary Lidia, daughter of Richard Allen, of Fayette county. Died June 9, 1836, aged about 15 months. KG 6/23.

Miss Mary Headington, daughter of Laban Headington, of Lexington. Died June 21, 1836. OR 6/22.

Mrs. Susan Gano Bryan, consort of Capt. William Bryan, of Fayette county. Died June 17, 1836, aged 22 years. KG 6/23.

Mrs. Mary Ann Shelby, consort of Thomas H. Shelby. Died June 23, 1836, aged 37 years. KG 6/30.

Mrs. Mary Louisa Osburn, consort of the Rev. Ephraim Osburn, of Columbia, Tenn., and daughter of Mrs. Julia S. Towler, formerly of Lexington, Ky. Died June 19, 1836. KG 6/30.

Mrs. Eliza Smith, relict of William T. Smith, of Fayette county. Died June 25, 1836. KG 6/27.

Tapman Truett, of Scott county. Died Sunday June 26, 1836, aged about 70 years. OR 7/6.

Charles Cosby, of Madison county. Died June 29, 1836, aged 60 years. OR 7/6.

Mrs. Eliza M. Wilson, consort of John Wilson, formerly of Lexington, Ky. Died in Jacksonville, Ill., June 28, 1836. OR 7/13.

Jeremiah White, Sr., of Fayette county. Died June 22, 1836, aged 74 years. He was one of the earliest settlers of Kentucky. KG 6/27.

Mrs. Eliza McConathy. Died at the Gallatin county residence of James McConathy on Sunday June 19, 1836, aged 36 years. She left her husband and eight children. KG 6/30.

Capt. Oliver Hart, formerly of Lexington, Ky. Died on board the steamboat *Memphis* on her passage from New Orleans in May, 1836. KG 6/13.

General Simon Kenton, of Logan county, Ohio. Died April 29, 1836, aged 82 years. "The Father of Mason County, Kentucky." KG 6/9. (Editor's note: Quotes added, not in death notice.)

Mrs. Hester Higbee, consort of Peter Higbee, Jr., of Lexington. Died Monday June 6, 1836. KG 6/9.

Col. William Ward, formerly of Scott county. Died in Mississippi July 15, 1836. KG 8/4.

Mrs. Clark, consort of Judge James Clark, of Winchester. Died Monday August 15, 1836. OR 8/21.

Mrs. Mary Ann Laudeman, consort of David Laudeman. She died August 14, 1836, aged 21 years. OR 8/21.

John Witherhill, infant son of Mr. F. Montmollin. Died Aug. 17, 1836. OR 8/21.

Mrs. Rosina Elliott, consort of James Elliott, of Lexington. Died August 9, 1836. OR 8/21.

Samuel Glass, only son of Alexander and Mary M. Robinson, of Lexington. Died Aug. 9, 1836, aged 1 year, 7 months and 12 days. OR 8/10.

Mrs. Martha Rankin, relict of the Reverend Adam Rankin. She died at Columbia, Tenn., at the residence of her son, John M. Rankin, July 27, 1836. She was one of the first settlers of Lexington, Ky., and was a resident here for 43 years. OR 8/10.

John Kirkpatrick, a native of Ireland, and long time resident of Lexington, Ky. Died August 5, 1836. OR 8/10.

Mrs. Mary Shelby, consort of General James Shelby, of Fayette county. Died July 30, 1836, aged 49 years. OR 8/10.

Thomas Martin, of Lexington. Died July 26, 1836. OR 7/27.

Virginia Morgan, infant daughter of Samuel A. Young. Died at the Fayette county residence of Col. John Morgan July 22, 1836. OR 7/27.

OBITUARIES

The abbreviations used denote:

KG—(Lexington) *Kentucky Gazette*
OR—*Lexington* (Ky.) *Observer & Reporter.*

1836

Richard Tubman, of Augusta, Ga. Died at Lincolnton, N. C., July 11, 1836. OR 7/27.

Mrs. Rhoda A. Holloway, consort of William P. Holloway, of Lexington. Died July 14, 1836. OR 7/20.

Lawrence Golay, Vevay, Ind. Died Aug. 18, 1836. OR 8/24.

Ephraim Sodowsky, Jr., son of Ephraim Sodowosky, Sr., of Jessamine county. Died Aug. 29, 1836, aged 16 years. OR 8/31.

Mrs. Ann C. Johnson, wife of E. L. Johnson, of Georgetown, and daughter of Judge William Warren, dec'd. Died Aug. 19, 1836. OR 8/31.

Mrs. Lucy N. Woodson, consort of D. M. Woodson, of Carrolton, Ill. Died at the Fayette county, Ky., residence of James Allen, Friday August 19, 1836. OR 8/31.

Hon. David Dickson, member of the House of Representatives from Mississippi. Died at Little Rock, Arkansas, July 30, 1836. OR 8/31.

Alice Peachey, youngest daughter of W. P. and Mary Nicholson, of Baltimore, Md. Died at the Lexington, Ky., residence of M. T. Scott, August 27, 1836. KG 8/29.

Samuel Harris, of Fayette county. Died in September, 1836, aged about 25 years. OR 9/7.

Stephen Chipley, infant son of Dr. J. S. Richardson, of North Carolina, and grandson of Rev. S. Chipley, of Lexington, Ky. Died at latter place August 24, 1836. OR 9/7

Emily Euphania, infant daughter of Dr. E. B. Stedman, of Pittsborough, N. C., and granddaughter of Rev. S. Chipley, of Lexington, Ky. She died August 1, 1836. See above. OR 9/7.

Margaret Robertson Hopper, daughter of the late General Letcher and wife of Seymore Hopper, of Lancaster, Ky. Died on Sunday August 28, 1836. Obituary in OR 9/7.

William Cooper, Sr., of Fayette county. Died Sept. 5, 1836, aged 75 years. OR 9/7.

Rowland M. Thomas of Newcastle, died Aug. 25, 1836. OR 9/7.

Judge George Shannon, formerly of Kentucky. Died at Palmyra, Mo., August 31, 1836. OR 9/14.

James Crawford, of Fleming county. Died in Sept., 1836. OR 9/21.

Sarah Frances, infant daughter of Dr. William S. Hood, of Newtown, Scott county. Died Sept. 5, 1836, aged 18 months and 17 days. OR 9/21.

Nathaniel Ferguson, of Fayette county. Died September 21, 1836, aged about 67 years. OR 9/28.

John W. Anderson, of Mason county, Representative elect from that county to the Legislature. Died Sept. 20, 1836. OR 9/28.

Robert, son of Elijah Noble, of Lexington. Died Sept. 27, 1836, aged 6 or 7 years. OR 9/28.

Thomas Goady, infant son of John Brennan, of Lexington. He died Sept. 22, 1836. OR 9/28

Jane Steele, eldest daughter of John Steele, of Fayette county. Died Sept. 7, 1836, aged 19 years. OR 10/5.

Mrs. Lucy Webb, consort of Col. John V. Webb, of Scott county. Died Sept. 23, 1836, aged 72 years. OR 10/5.

Robert P. Frazer, son of Robert Frazer, of Lexington. Died Sept. 24, 1836, aged 4 years. OR 10/12.

Eliza Coleman Frazer, daughter of Robert Frazer, of Lexington. See above. She died Sept. 27, 1836, aged 3 years. OR 10/12.

Miss Martha Rogers, daughter of Henry Rogers, of Fayette county. Died Oct. 9, 1836, aged 17 years. OR 10/19.

Mrs. Serena L. Smith, consort of Samuel M. Smith, formerly of Winchester, Ky., and daughter of Samuel Hanson. Died at Alexandria, La., Aug. 31, 1836, aged 25 years. OR 10/26.

Samuel M. Smith, of Alexandria, La., formerly of Winchester, Ky. See above. He died Sept. 4, 1836. OR 10/26.

Dr. George Flanagan, formerly of Winchester, Ky. Died in Chicot County, Arkansas, in September, 1836. OR 10/26.

Gabriel Tandy, son of the late Capt. Achilles Tandy, of Fayette county. Died in Boone county, Ky., Sept. 26, 1836. OR 10/26.

Mrs. Sarah Butler, consort of James Butler, and daughter of Joseph Hervey. Died Oct. 21, 1836. OR 10/26.

William Wilgus. Died October 24, 1836. OR 10/26.

Mrs. Amanda Crane, consort of Rev. Simeon H. Crane. Died in Lebanon, Ohio, October 24, 1836. OR 11/2.

Eliza A. Wirt, daughter of John Wirt, of Lexington. Died October 31, 1836. OR 11/2.

Bushrod Taylor, of Lexington. Died Oct. 28, 1836. OR 11/2.

Thomas W. Crockett, of Fayette county. Died Nov. 6, 1836, aged 27 years. He left a wife and one child. OR 11/9.

John William, infant son of David L. Zimmerman, of Fayette county. Died Nov. 13, 1836, aged 2 months and 17 days. OR 11/16.

William Morton, of Lexington. Died Nov. 17, 1836, aged 80 years. OR 11/23.

Stephen T. Breckenridge, of Georgetown. Died Nov. 19, 1836. OR 11/30.

Phil. Thompson. Killed in Owensboro, Daviess county, in November, 1836, by a Mr. Jefford. Story in OR 12/7.

Francis K. Buford, of Woodford county. Killed Sept. 3, 1836. Story in OR 12/7.

Gen. James Allen, of Greensburg. Killed by a fall from his horse Saturday Dec. 10, 1836. OR 12/14.

Mrs. Hewett, consort of John M. Hewett, of Lexington. Died in Fayette county Dec. 18, 1836. OR 12/21.

Tilman Kemper, of Fayette county. Died Dec. 3, 1836, aged 77 years. He was a soldier-patriot of the Revolution. OR 12/21.

Charlton Hunt, of Lexington. Died Dec. 27, 1836, aged about 35 years. Obituary in OR 12/28.

Elisha Bridges, of Lexington. Died Dec. 27, 1836. OR 12/28.

James Gatewood, of Montgomery county. Died Dec. 26, 1836, aged 61 years. KG 1/5/1837.

1837

Mrs. O'Connell, wife of Daniel O'Connell, M.P. Died in January, 1837. KG 1/12.

William Boon, of Lexington. Born in King George county, Va., May 2, 1768. Settled in Kentucky at an early age. Died Jan. 26, 1837. KG 2/9.

Mrs. Isabella Carson, relict of James Carson, of Fayette county. Died Saturday Feb. 4, 1837. KG 2/9.

Willis Field, of Woodford county. Died Feb. 2, 1837, aged 60 years. KG 2/9.

Joseph Stanton, of Miss., a student at Transylvania University. Died Feb. 13, 1837, in Lexington, Ky. KG 2/16.

John D. Willis, Sr., of Scott county. Died in February, 1837, aged 70 years. KG 2/16.

Mary Elizabeth, daughter of John F. Zimmerman, of Lexington. Died Feb. 13, 1837, aged 2 years, 5 months and 5 days. KG 2/16.

Adaliza C., infant daughter of Thomas Monks, of Lexington. Died Friday Feb. 10, 1837. KG 2/16.

Edgar M. Crutchfield, of Fayette county. Died Feb. 18, 1837, aged about 30 years. KG 2/23.

Samuel Glass, of Scott county. Died Feb. 11, 1837, at an advanced age. KG 2/23.

Capt. William J. Keiser, of Lexington. Died in February, 1837. KG 3/2.

Sarah, infant daughter of Tucker Woodson, of Jessamine county. Died Mar. 2, 1837, aged almost 15 months. KG 3/9.

Albert, infant son of Mr. A. G. Meriwether. Died at Washington City, Feb. 16, 1837, aged 13 months and 18 days. KG 3/9.

Capt. Benjamin F. Bradford, of the Texan Army, a brother of the printer of the *Kentucky Gazette* (Thomas F. Bradford). Died at the Lower Blue Licks, Ky., March 10, 1837, aged 28 years. KG 3/16.

Dr. W. Knight, of Georgetown, Professor of Moral and Mental Science, Sc., in Bacon College. Died March 20, 1837. KG 3/23.

Mrs. Rebecca Gough, relict of James Gough, of Woodford county. Died Mar. 14, 1837, aged 48 years. KG 3/30.

Richard Scrugham, eldest son of Col. Joseph Scrugham, of Lexington. Died Mar. 24, 1837, aged 30 years. KG 3/20.

Mrs. Mary Flynt, consort of Henry Flynt, of Lexington. Died March 24, 1837. KG 3/30.

Louis I. Marshall, third son of Judge J. J. Marshall. Died in Louisville in March, 1837, aged 21 years. KG 4/6.

Minos Hearne, late of Lexington. Died in Nicholasville, Apr. 17, 1837. KG 4/20.

.... Elgin, only daughter of Joseph M. Elgin, of Scott county. Died in Lexington Apr. 17, 1837, aged about 11 years. KG 4/20.

William W. Darnaby, son of Col. George W. Darnaby, of Fayette county. Died Apr. 21, 1837, aged 13 years. KG 4/27

Mrs. Rachel Cloud. Died Apr. 30, 1837, aged 78 years. KG 5/4.

John Parker, of Fayette county. Died May 28, 1837, at an advanced age. Obituary in KG 6/1.

Reuben Craig of Scott county, died May 13, 1837, aged 74 years. KG 6/1.

Capt. James Hunter, of Shelbyville. A Revolutionary soldier. D. May 8, 1837, aged 74 years. KG 6/1.

Mrs. Ann E. Wise, wife of Hon. Henry A. Wise, of Accomack county, Va. Died May 4, 1837. KG 6/1.

Mrs. .... Theobald, mother of Dr. .... Theobald. Died on Monday May 29, 1837. KG 6/1.

Mrs. Eliza A. Lee, wife of William M. Lee, and only daughter of James Jenkins, of Fayette county. Died in Lincoln county May 23, 1837, aged 27 years. KG 6/8.

James Craig, infant son of D. M. Craig, of Lexington. Died May 30, 1837. KG 6/8.

Mrs. Mary W. Palmer, relict of J. W. Palmer. Died June 3, 1837. KG 6/15.

Caroline Harrison, daughter of Daniel Bradford, of Lexington. Died June 16, 1837, aged 14 years. KG 6/22.

George W. Hendley, son of John Hendley, formerly of Lexington. Died at Liberty, Mo., May 24, 1837. KG 6/22.

Mrs. Eliza Jane, consort of A. G. Meriwether, and daughter of the late Capt. Richard Sharp, of Lexington. Died in Washington City June 27, 1837. KG 7/13.

Mrs. Eliza Maguire, consort of H. Maguire, of Lexington. Died July 7, 1834, aged 31 years. KG 7/13.

Charles Samuell, youngest son of C. C. Moore, of Fayette county. Died July 29, 1837, aged 3 years. KG 8/3.

John Ford, formerly of Fayette county. Died Aug. 1, 1837. KG 8/3.

Job Stevenson, of Georgetown. Suicided July 10, 1837, aged 55 years. Obituary in KG 8/3.

Miss Amanda, daughter of Augustus F. Hawkins, of Lexington. Died Aug. 6, 1837. KG 8/10.

Brice C. Randall, of Lexington. Died Aug. 6, 1837, aged 66 years. KG 8/10.

Mathew Kenney, of Fayette county. Died Aug. 2, 1837. KG 8/10.

Hon. Samuel H. Harper, Judge of the U.S. Court for the District of La. Died at Madisonville, La., July 18, 1837. KG 8/10.

Mrs. Mary Theodora Chew, consort of Beverley Chew. Died July 21, 1837. KG 8/10.

William Clark, of Lexington. Died Aug. 19, 1837, aged about 55 years. KG. 8/14.

Clarendon Peck, M.D., of Sicily Island, La. He was a son of John Peck, of Lexington, Ky. Died Aug. 1, 1837, aged 25 years. KG 7/14.

Joseph Craig, son of Lewis Dedman, of Fayette county. Died Aug. 16, 1837, aged 5 years. KG 8/31.

Phoebe Fishback, relict of Jacob Fishback, of Clark county. Died Aug. 16, 1837, aged 86 years. KG 8/31.

Mrs. Catharine McIrwin, relict of William McIrwin. Died at the Fayette county residence of her son on Aug. 19, 1837, aged 78 years. KG 8/31.

Hon. John Brown, of Frankfort, father of the editor of the *Commonwealth* and one of the first Senators from Kentucky to the Senate of the United States. Died Tuesday Aug. 29, 1837, aged 80 years. KG 8/31.

Governor John Floyd, of Virginia, a native of Jefferson county, Ky. Died Aug. 16, 1837. KG 8/31.

Capt. John McKinney, of Versailles. Died Aug. 24, 1837, aged 82 years. KG 8/31.

Walker Alsop, of Louisville. Died Aug. 19, 1837. KG 8/31.

Mrs. Lucy Benning, of Fayette county. Died Aug. 28, 1837, aged 89 years. KG 9/7.

Litteberry Laffon, son of James and Elizabeth Laffon (also spelled Laffoon) of Fayette county. Died Sept. 2, 1837, aged 34 years. KG 9/7.

Mrs. Sarah J. Hickey, consort of Simeon Hickey and daughter of the late Francis McDermot, who brought her to Kentucky in 1779. She died at the Lexington residence of her son, the Hon. Thomas M. Hickey, Monday Sept. 11, 1837, aged 71 years. Obituary in KG 9/14.

Capt. Rodham Neale, of Fayette county. Died Aug. 27, 1837. KG 9/14.

Greenberry Spiers, son of Jeremiah Spiers, of Fayette county. Died Sept. 9, 1837, aged 15 years. KG 9/21.

Col. Thomas S. Smith, of Jessamine county. Died Sept. 17, 1837, aged 58 years. KG 9/21.

Francis DeCous, a native of New York. Died Sept. 15, 1837. KG 9/21.

Major Benjamin W. Edwards, of Holmes County, Miss., a native of Bourbon county, Ky. Died Aug. 18, 1837. At the time of his death he was a candidate for Governor of Mississippi. KG 9/28.

Isham Talbott, of near Frankfort. He was a veteran of the Kentucky Bar and formerly a Senator in Congress from this State. He died Monday Sept. 25, 1837. KG 9/28.

Major Joseph Simrall, of Shelbyville, a distinguished officer in the war of 1812. Died Sept. 7, 1837. KG 9/28.

Rev. O. S. Hinckley, of Natchez, formerly of Lexington, Ky. Died Sept. 14, 1837. KG 10/5.

Francis Conner, found dead in his home, about 9 miles from Lexington. Inquest held Oct. 1, 1837. KG 10/12.

William C. Boner, aged 20, and Thomas C. Boner, aged 16 years, sons of William Boner, of Garrard county. Former died Sept. 21 and latter Sept. 24, 1837. KG 10/12.

Robert Irvin, of Fayette county. Died Sept. 22, 1837, aged 27 years. KG 10/12.

Hon. David Barton, of Mo. Died Sept. 28, 1837. KG 10/19.

Lewis Randolph, of Clark county, Arkansas, son of Thomas Mann Randolph, of Virginia. Died Sept. 24, 1837. KG 10/19.

Mrs. Elizabeth Brasfield, consort of Major Wiley R. Brasfield, of Clark county. Died Oct. 21, 1837, aged 66 years. KG 10/26.

Morton Brennan, son of John Brennan, of Lexington. Died October 18, 1837. KG 10/26.

Charles Railey, of Woodford county. Died Oct. 26, 1837, aged 71 years. KG 11/2.

Mrs. Francis McKinney, consort of James G. McKinney. Died October 28, 1837. KG 11/2.

Notley Flournoy, of Franklin county. Died Oct. 29, 1837. KG 11/2.

Miss Virginia Clay Richardson, daughter of G. P. Richardson, of Maysville. Died in October, 1837, aged 5 years. KG 11/2.

Mary Elizabeth, daughter of William A. Verbryke, of Lexington. Died Oct. 26, 1837. KG 11/9.

Nancy Shaw, daughter of John Myers, of Lexington. Died on Wednesday October 31, 1837. KG 11/9.

Mrs. Susan Throckmorton, consort of Major Ariss Throckmorton, of Louisville. Died in October, 1837. KG 11/9.

Samuel Pyke, of Paris. Died November 1, 1837. KG 11/9.

Mrs. Margaret Scofield, of Scott county. Died Nov. 4, 1837, aged 81 years. KG 11/4.

Mrs. Frances B. Young, late consort of Rev. John V. Young, President of Centre College. Died in Lexington on Thursday Nov. 2, 1837. KG 11/9.

Mrs. Mildred Tunstall, relict of Thomas Tunstall, of Frankfort. Died in October, 1837, at an advanced age. KG 11/9.

John Henry Taylor, of Chicot county, Ark. Died October 27, 1837, aged 24 years. Obituary in KG 11/9.

Dr. William Patterson Bain, of Lexington. Died Nov. 11, 1837, aged 30 years. KG 11/16.

Samuel M. Blair, of St. Augustine, Fla., formerly a resident of Fayette county, Ky. Died Aug. 26, 1837, aged about 36 years. KG 11/16.

John Purnell, son of Purnell Bishop, of Lexington. Died on Monday Nov. 13, 1837. KG 11/16.

William Milligan, Sr., of Fayette county. Died Nov. 14, 1837, aged 85 years. KG 11/23.

Col. Abram Bowman, of Fayette county. An officer in the American Revolution. Died Nov. 9, 1837. KG 11/23.

Boon Ingles, of Paris. Died Nov. 9, 1837, aged 53 years. KG 11/23.

Mrs. Eunice Lockwood (late Mrs. Ayres) consort of Caleb Lockwood, of Liberty, Clay county, Mo. Died in Lexington, Ky., November 16, 1837. KG 11/30.

Johanna Todhunter, consort of the late Jacob Todhunter. Died at the residence of P. E. Todhunter Nov. 20, 1837, aged 68 years. KG 11/30.

William Cavins, of Fayette county. Died Nov. 27, 1837, aged 48 years. KG 12/7.

Col. Benjamin Merrell, of Lexington. A soldier in the Revolution. Died Dec. 17, 1837. KG 12/21.

Simon Hickey, of Lexington. He settled here in 1789. He died Dec. 17, 1837, aged 74 years. KG 12/21.

Miss Juliett Thomas, of Georgia. Died in Lexington, Ky., Dec. 18, 1837. KG 12/21.

A. W. P. Parker, a native of Lexington, Ky. Died at Port Gibson, Miss., at the home of his brother, Dr. J. P. Parker, on Dec. 6, 1837. KG 12/21.

1838

John P. Eblin, of Lexington. A student at Transylvania University. Died in Jan. or Feb., 1838. KG 2/22.

Gwynn R. Tompkins, of Fayette county. Died Jan. 5, 1838, aged 34 years. Obituary in KG 1/11.

John Grimes. Died at the Lexington residence of his relative, T. Grant, Dec. 28, 1837, aged 38 years. Obituary in KG 1/11/1838.

Miss Paulina Beach, daughter of James Beach, of Lexington. Died Saturday January 20, 1838, aged 17 years. KG 1/25.

Mrs. Jarret Milligan, of Lexington. Died at the residence of her son, James B. Milligan, in January, 1838, at an advanced age. KG 2/1.

Professor John Eberlie, of Transylvania University. He was a native of Tenn., and died here (Lexington, Ky.) February 2, 1838. (Probably same as John P. Eblin, above). KG 2/8.

Major Arthur L. Campbell, of Louisville. An early settler of Kentucky and fighter in the Indian Wars. He died Jan. 19, 1838, aged 58 years. Obituary in KG 2/15.

William H. Harrison, Jr., son of Gen. William H. Harrison, of North Bend, Ohio. Died Tuesday Feb. 6, 1838, aged 36 years. KG 2/2.2.

Dr. Robert Austin Oliver, of Millersburg, Mo., and a native of Fayette county, Ky. Died Feb. 1, 1838, aged 30 years. KG 3/1.

Mrs. Virginia L. Matthews, consort of Howard Matthews, of Randolph county, Mo. Died about the 1st of February, 1838, aged 19 years. KG 3/8.

Ann, daughter of Hugh Carlan, of Lexington. Died March 7, 1838, aged 17 years. KG 3/15.

Mrs. Elizabeth Pilcher, consort of Edward Pilcher. Died at the Lexington residence of James Hensley, March 1, 1838. KG 3/15.

Thomas E. Hickman, of Winchester. Died Mar. 4, 1838, aged 43 years. KG 3/15.

James M. Gordon, of Mississippi, a student at Transylvania University. Died March 13, 1838. KG 3/15.

Isaac Yarnall, of Fayette county. An early settler of Kentucky. He erected the second Paper Mill in the State. He died March 17, 1838, aged 61 years. KG 3/22.

Col. Henry Beard of Fayette County. Died Mar. 17, 1838, at an advanced age. KG 3/22.

Patterson Bain, of Mississippi, a native of Lexington, Ky. Murdered on his plantation in March, 1838. KG 3/22.

Mrs. Rebecca Elbert, consort of Henry D. Elbert, of Scott county. Died Mar. 25, 1838, aged 64 years. KG 3/29.

Albert G. Garth, of Scott county. Died Mar. 21, 1838. KG 3/29.

Stephen Young, of Lexington. Died Apr. 2, 1838. KG 4/5.

R. A. Ferguson, one time editor of the *Kentucky Gazette.* He was killed by .... Rivers, in Hickman county, in March or April, 1838. Story in KG 4/12.

Gen. William H. Ashley, a citizen of Missouri. Died Mar. 26, 1838. KG 4/12.

Gen. John Woods, of Frankfort. Died Apr. 5, 1838. KG 4/12.

Mrs. Betsey Allen, consort of John Allen, of Fayette county. Died Apr. 10, 1838. KG 4/12.

Benjamin J. Taul, of Clark county. Died Apr. 8, 1838. KG 4/19.

Mrs. Sarah Gatewood, relict of Peter Gatewood. Died at the Fayette county residence of Mrs. Elizabeth Gatewood, on Apr. 14, 1838, aged 96 years. KG 4/26.

Miss Mary, daughter of Mrs. Lucy D. Gatewood, of Lexington. Died April 23, 1838. KG 4/26.

Thomas Fleming, of Lexington. Died April 21, 1838, aged 90 years. KG 4/26.

Worden Pope, of Louisville. Died Apr. 21, 1838, one of the oldest citizens of Louisville. KG 4/26.

Samuel January, of Maysville. Died Apr. 16, 1838, at an advanced age. KG 4/26.

John Wickliffe, of Bourbon county, eldest son of Robert Wickliffe, of Lexington. Died Apr. 30, 1838, aged 28 years. KG 5/3.

Mrs. .... Campbell, widow of Rev. J. P. Campbell, formerly of Jessamine county, and daughter of Col. John McDowell, dec'd., of Fayette county. She burned to death at the Mason county home of Thomas J. Pickett. She was a lady of advanced age. Her daughter, Miss .... Campbell and Mrs. Pickett came to her assistance and were also burned, the former fatally. She died Friday April 27, 1838, a few hours after the death of her mother. KG 5/3.

Josiah W. Dunham. Died Apr. 30, 1838. KG 5/3.

Mrs. Martin Winthrop, consort of Rev. E. Winthrop, of Theological Seminary. Died May 8, 1838. KG 5/10.

Miss Nancy B., daughter of Mrs. Elizabeth Harrison. Died April 30, 1838. KG 5/10.

Mrs. Isabella Clark, consort of Allen H. Clark, of Lexington. Died May 12, 1838. KG 5/17

Mrs. Louisa J. M. Smith, consort of Dr. C. J. Smith, of Harrodsburg, formerly of Lexington. Died May 13, 1838. KG 5/17.

William Huston, of Lexington. Died Monday May 14, 1838, at a very advanced age. KG 5/17.

Mary Elizabeth, daughter of William Newberry, of Lexington. Died Saturday May 12, 1838. KG 5/17.

Mrs. Sarah Ryman, consort of Robert Ryman, of Fayette county. Died May 8, 1838. KG 5/17.

Robert Scott, of near Pittsburg, Pa., formerly of Lexington, Ky. Died Apr. 14, 1838, aged about 67 years. KG 5/24.

Charles Thomas, son of George P. Richardson, of Lexington. Died May 19, 1838, aged 15 months. KG 5/24.

Capt. Ephraim Porter, a soldier of 1776. He was formerly a citizen of Fayette county. Died at Elkton, May 4, 1838, aged 79 years. KG 5/24.

Abraham Bradley. Died May 21, 1838. KG 5/24.

Richard Russell, of New Orleans. Died May 19, 1838. KG 5/31.

Capt. John Nelson. Died May 27, 1838, aged 87 years. KG 5/31.

Mrs. Eliza R. Walker, consort of Dr. Tandy W. Walker, of Oakville, North Alabama, and daughter of Capt. Samuel Patterson, of Fayette county, Ky. Died May 18, 1838. KG 6/7.

William Macbean. Died at the residence of Bernard Gaines, in Woodford county, on May 30, 1838. He was a native of Newmarket, England, and settled in Lexington, Ky., about the year 1798. KG 6/7.

Mrs. Margaretta Brown, relict of the Hon. John Brown, of Frankfort, and mother of the editor of the *Commonwealth*. Died May 28, 1838. KG 6/7.

Mrs. Lucy Roper, relict of the late Judge Roper, of Frankfort. Died June 4, 1838. KG 6/7.

Samuel Smith, of Fayette county, a widely known stock raiser. Died June 2, 1838, aged 43 years. KG 6/7.

Mrs. Eliza Clugston, consort of John Clugston, of Fayette county. Died June 1, 1838. KG 6/7.

Peter McCarton, of Lexington. Died June 5, 1838, at an advanced age. KG 6/7.

Patrick McCausland, of Lexington. Died May 30, 1838, a young man. KG 6/7.

Capt. David Rees, of North Elkhorn, Fayette county. He was a soldier in Revolution and in the Indian Wars. He died May 29, 1838. KG 6/14.

Howard Wickliffe, son of Robert Wickliffe, of Lexington, Ky. He had been living in England (London) and in Edinburgh, Scotland, for the past three years while he studied law. He died in New York the last of May, 1838, and was buried in Lexington, Ky., June 11, 1838. KG 6/14.

Mrs. Isabella Cooper, consort of Capt. William Cooper, of Fayette county. Died June 7, 1838, aged 22 years. KG 6/14.

Jacob Cassell, formerly of Lexington, Ky. Died in Jacksworth, Ill., May 19, 1838. KG 6/21.

John Barton, coroner of Lexington. Suicided Friday June 22, 1838. The newspapers made quite an issue of his suicide, the question being whether he had failed to perform his duty when he did not hold an inquest over his own body, previously, to elicit all the facts concerned with the event. KG 6/28.

David R. MacCoun, a native of Lexington, Ky. Suicided by jumping overboard the steamer Arabian, on the night of June 26, 1838. Story in KG 7/12.

Nancy Garrard, infant daughter of Col. Thomas A. Russell, of Fayette county. Died July 12, 1838. KG 7/19.

Sarah Elizabeth, infant daughter of James Wood, of Lexington. Died July 15, 1838. KG 7/19.

Alexander Walker, of Fayette county. He was one of the oldest residents of the county, having been born and reared at McConnel's Station, about 1 mile below Lexington. He died in July, 1838. KG 7/19.

John S. Hart, son of Mrs. Eleanor Hart, formerly of Lexington, then of Louisville. Killed by lightning July 20, 1838. He was 34 years of age. KG 7/26.

David Duvall, of Winchester. Died July 21, 1838, aged about 21 years. KG 7/26.

Mrs. Mary Lickey, consort of Nathan Lickey, of Clark county. Died July 12, 1838, aged 81 years. KG 7/26.

Thomas H. Hickey, infant son of Col. Francis McLear, of Lexington. Died July 22, 1838. KG 7/26.

John J. Stevenson, of Midway, Woodford county. Died July 27, 1838, aged 27 years. KG 8/2.

Thomas Smith, Sr., of Clark county. Died July 31, 1838, aged 86 years and 3 days. KG 8/2.

John P. Graves, a native of Virginia, and nephew of Capt. W. F. White, formerly of Fayette county. Died in Nashville on July 27, 1838, aged 19 years. KG 8/9.

Walter Dun, of Fayette county. Died Aug. 4, 1838. KG 8/9.

Miss Mary Elizabeth, only daughter of Jepthah Adams, of Fayette county. Died Aug. 3, 1838, aged 9 years. KG 8/9.

Garret D. Wall, an old and respected citizen of Scott county. Died Aug. 9, 1838, at the residence of Benjamin W. Finnell. KG 8/16.

Mrs. Mary Elizabeth Fife, consort of Matthew Fife, late of Philadelphia, and daughter of Elisha I. Winter, of Lexington. Died at the Fayette county residence of her grandfather, Walter Carr, in September, 1838. OR 9/5.

Mr. E. P. Suggett, of Scott county. Died Aug. 12, 1838. KG 8/16.

General James Garrard, of Bourbon county. Died Aug. 1, 1838, aged 65 years. He was Kentucky's second governor. OR 9/5 and KG 9/6.

Mrs. Sarah Berry, consort of Col. Silas Berry, of Scott county. Died in August, 1838. OR 9/5.

Mrs. Rebecca, consort of Henry Ruckel, of Lexington. Died Sept. 7, 1838, aged 41 years. OR 9/12.

Asa Blanchard, of Lexington. Died September 15, 1838, at an advanced age. OR 9/19.

John Higbee, of Fayette county. Died Sept. 24, 1838. KG 9/26.

Capt. George Burbridge, of Scott county. Died Sept. 15, 1838. OR 9/26.

John Harvie, of Frankfort. Died Sept. 20, 1838, at an advanced age. OR 9/29.

John King, keeper of the Lunatic Asylum, of Lexington. Died Aug. 27, 1838, aged 56 years. OR 9/8.

Capt. John Laughlin, of Clark county. Died Aug. 27, 1838, aged 72 years. OR 9/12.

Jacob Warble, of Fayette county. Died Sept. 18, 1838, aged 48 years. He left his wife and 8 children. OR 9/22.

Mrs. Laura Simonds, of Mississippi, widow of Professor Simonds, formerly of Transylvania University, Lexington, Ky. She died Sept. 11, 1838. KG 9/13.

Felix Bieller, son of Felix and Elizabeth L. Bosworth, of Carroll, La. Died in Fayette county, Ky., Sept. 8, 1838, aged 19 months. KG 9/13.

Thomas McOuat (McQuat?), formerly of Lexington, Ky. Died at Indianapolis, Ind., Aug. 25, 1838. KG 9/6.

George M. Elgin, of Georgetown. Died Aug. 30, 1838, aged 37 years. KG. 9/6.

Mrs. Ann West Bain, consort of William E. Bain, of Lexington. Died Sunday September 30, 1838. KG 10/4.

Col. R. E. W. Earl. Died at the Hermitage Sept. 15, 1838. KG 10/4.

Hon. John Green, of near Danville. Died Sept. 30, 1838. KG 10/4.

Henry Walker, of Versailles, a native of Mecklenburg county, Virginia. Died Sept. 26, 1838. KG 10/4.

Capt. Morgan A. Simpson, of Vicksburg. Died in Mount Sterling, Ky., Sept. 10, 1838. KG 10/4.

Morrison Shrock, infant son of Nathaniel M. Shrock, M.D., of Mount Sterling. Died Oct. 7, 1838, aged 9 months. KG 10/11.

Sarah, infant daughter of Thomas B. Megowan, of Lexington. Died November 4, 1838. OR 11/7.

William Breckenridge, of Fayette county, a brother of the Hon. John Breckenridge. Died Nov. 7, 1838, aged 80 years. OR 11/10.

Col. Thomas Wornall, of Clark county. Died in November, 1838, at an advanced age. OR 11/17.

William Anderson, of Louisville. Died Nov. 21, 1838. OR 11/24.

John Riely, of Paoli, Orange county, Ind. A Revolutionary soldier and former resident of Clark county, Ky. Died Nov. 17, 1838, aged 74 years. OR 12/1.

Col. Samuel P. Carson, of N. C. Died at Hot Springs, Arkansas, Nov. 23, 1838. OR 12/1.

Mrs. Sarah Ann McMurtry, wife of John McMurtry, of Lexington, and daughter of Stark Taylor, of Fayette county. Died Nov. 29, 1838. OR 12/8.

Capt. Walter Carr, of Fayette county, a member of the Convention that formed the Constitution of Kentucky. Died Dec. 7, 1838, aged 86 years. OR 12/8.

Horatio Nelson Graves, son of William W. Graves, of Fayette county, and grandson of Col. John Graves, of North Elkhorn. Killed accidently Monday Dec. 3, 1838, aged 21 years, 3 months and 22 days. OR 12/8.

Joseph Foreman, of Fayette county. Died Dec. 9, 1838, leaving his widow and 7 children. OR 12/12.

George Shoemaker, of Lexington. Died Dec. 10, 1838, aged 39 years. He left a widow and 7 children. OR 12/12.

Col. Benjamin Combs, of Clark county. A soldier in the American Revolution. Died Dec. 10, 1838, aged 89 years. OR 12/12.

James Masterson, of Fayette county. One of the first settlers in Kentucky. Died Saturday December 15, 1838, aged 100 years. Obituary in OR 12/22.

Dr. E. W. Coleman, late editor of the *Kentucky Democrat*, Frankfort. Died in Scott county Dec. 18, 1838. OR 12/26.

Lieut. Stephen Tibbatts, of the U. S. Army. Suicided at Louisville Dec. 29, 1838. He was reared in Lexington where his family lived in 1838-1839. OR 1/2/1839.

Churchill Newnem, of Clark county. Killed Christmas Day, 1838, by Arthur Stanhope and John Williams. OR 1/2/1839.

William McCormick. Died Nov. 19, 1838, in Gibson county, Indiana. He was a native of Pennsylvania and one-time resident of Scott county, Ky. OR 1/2/1839.

Abisha A. Baker, late of Colchester, New London county, Conn. Died at Lexington, Ky., at the residence of Thomas B. Megowan on Dec. 31, 1838. OR 1/2/1839.

1839

Mrs. Mary Ann Randolph, consort of John A. Randolph, of Lexington. Died Jan. 15, 1839. OR 1/19.

Mrs. Mary Jane Young, consort of Samuel A. Young. Died Jan. 16, 1839, at the Fayette county residence of her father, Col. John Morgan. OR 1/19.

Mrs. Jane Lee Campbell, wife of John P. Campbell, and daughter of General Thomas Metcalfe, of Forest Retreat, Nicholas county. Died there in January, 1839. OR 1/19.

Miss Isabella Downing, daughter of Joseph Downing, of Fayette county. Died Jan. 19, 1839. OR 1/23.

Mrs. Elizabeth Wilson, consort of David B. Wilson, of Lexington and daughter of Henry Ruckle. Died in Lexington Jan. 19, 1839. OR 1/23.

John L. Menifee, a native of Kentucky and brother of Hon. Richard M. Menifee. Died Jan. 4, 1839, from wounds he received in a duel with Mr. .... McClung. OR 1/23.

Mrs. Susan H. Van Doren, wife of Rev. L. H. Van Doren, President of Columbia College, Mo. Died Jan. 10, 1839, aged 22 years. OR 1/26.

Mrs. Mary Kay, of Fayette county. Died Jan. 20, 1839, aged 81 years. OR 1/26.

William K. and Benjamin H. Harney, children of Elsey Harney. Both died Wednesday Jan. 26, 1839. OR 1/26.

Mrs. Lucretia Pilcher, wife of Capt. Mason Pilcher, formerly of Lexington. Died in La., in January, 1839. OR 1/30.

Mrs. Mary Keiser, of Lexington. Died Jan. 28, 1839, at an advanced age. OR 1/30.

Rev. Richard Bibb, father of the late Hon. George M. Bibb, of Louisville. Died in Russellville Jan. 25, 1839. OR 2/9.

Rev. Spencer Cooper, of Fayette county. Died Feb. 8, 1839. OR 2/13.

Capt. Eben Best, of Garrard county. Died Feb. 4, 1839. OR 2/13.

Judith Kohlhass, of near Sugar Loaf Mountain, in Frederick county, Md. Died Dec. 21, 1838, aged about 79 years; and on Jan. 10, 1839, her husband, Henry Kohlhass, aged about 84 years. OR 2/13/39.

Matthew Thomson, of Clark county. Died Feb. 12, 1839, aged 66 years. Obituary in OR 2/20.

Maslin, son of Bird Smith, of Woodford county. Died Feb. 16, 1839, aged 6 years. OR 2/27.

David Flournoy, of Scott county. Died in February, 1839, aged 86 years. OR 2/27.

John Todd Breck, son of Daniel Breck, of Richmond, Ky. Died Feb. 13, 1839, aged 19 years. OR 2/27.

Major Morgan Neville. Died in Cincinnati March 1, 1839, aged 55 years. OR 3/6.

Elizabeth, daughter of O. F. Dean, of Jessamine county. Died Feb. 24, 1839. Obituary in OR 3/9.

David Smith, Sr., of Fayette county. Died March 8, 1839, aged 59 years. OR 3/13.

Almira, daughter of Charles Gibson, of Lexington. Died Mar. 14, 1839, aged about 4 years. OR 3/16.

David H. Standley, of Louisville. Killed on the route from Sinking to Cloverport by three men, supposed to have been David Scott, James Crosgrove and John Miller. His wife was Jemimah Standley. He died in March, 1839. OR 3/20.

Mrs. Nancy Taylor, wife of Richard Taylor, of Fayette county, and daughter of David McMurtry. Died Feb. 27, 1839. OR 3/23.

Col. Nathaniel Dick, of New Orleans. Died Mar. 5, 1839. OR 3/23.

Miss Caroline Boner, daughter of William and Elizabeth Boner, of Garrard county. Died Mar. 22, 1839, aged 15 years. OR 3/27.

Died on the 17th of March, 1839, Castleman, youngest son of Prof. James C. Cross, aged 8 years; and on the 11th of April, James C., and on the 12th of April, John, aged 13 years, sons of Professor Cross. James C. was 11 years of age. OR 4/17.

E. U. Berryman, a native of Fayette county, where he was born and reared. Married in New York City where he resided several years, and where he died April 9, 1839, aged 41 years. OR 4/20.

General Duncan McArthur. Died at Fruit Hill, near Chillicothe, Ohio, Sunday April 28, 1839, aged 67 years. OR 5/8.

Elder Silas M. Noel, pastor of the First Baptist Church of Lexington. Died May 5, 1839, aged 56 years. OR 5/11.

Joseph Sharp, of Lexington. Died May 6, 1839. OR 5/11.

Ambrose Young, of Fayette county. Died Apr. 28, 1839. OR 5/11.

William, son of James Weir, of Fayette county. Died May 8, 1839, aged 21 months. OR 5/15.

Jesse P. Nelson. Died at White Sulphur Springs in Bath county, May 4, 1839, aged 38 years. OR 5/15.

Mrs. Catharine L. Pinchard, consort of Dr. Thomas B. Pinchard, of Lexington. Died May 16, 1839. OR 5/18.

Thomas Pope, of Garrard county. Died in Lexington at the Brennan's Hotel May 10, 1839. OR 5/18.

Dr. Samuel M. Wilson. Died May 15, 1839. See resolutions of citizens of Mortonsville and vicinity in KG 5/30.

John P. Trotter, of Fayette county. Drowned at Cleveland's Ferry on the Kentucky river May 16, 1839. OR 5/22.

Dr. Thomas Cooper, died at Columbia, S. C., May 11, 1839, aged 80 years OR 5/25.

George Berry, of Scott county. Died May 10, 1839, aged 76 years. OR 5/22.

Mrs. Jane Patrick, of Lexington, relict of Dr. A. Patrick, of Woodford county. Died in Louisville May 24, 1839. OR 6/5.

Baltimore. Died June 8, 1839, aged 2 years and 11 months. OR 6/12.

Mary Anna, daughter of Whittington and Elizabeth King, formerly of Baltimore. Died June 8, 1839, aged 2 years and 11 months. OR 6/5.

Eleanor Wilkinson, infant daughter of Richard W. Downing, of Fayette county. Died May 25, 1839. KG 6/9.

Major W. R. Brasfield, of Clark county. Died May 19, 1839, aged 74 years. OR 6/15.

Asa Cartmel, of Fayette county. Died June 4, 1839, at the residence of Joseph Bryant. OR 6/15.

Col. John V. Webb, of Scott county. Died June 7, 1839. OR 6/15.

Mrs. Eliza A. Stevenson, consort of Rev. Edward Stevenson. Died in Harrodsburg June 7, 1839. OR 6/22.

Miss Amanda Carlan, daughter of Hugh Carlan, of Lexington. Died Wednesday June 19, 1839. OR 6/22.

Mary Eliza, daughter of Joseph Biggs. Died June 19, 1839, aged 2 years, 10 months and 19 days. OR 6/22.

Thomas Henry, son of Thomas Bradley. Died June 29, 1839. OR 6/22.

Mrs. Eliza Caldwell, consort of George Caldwell, of Jessamine county, and daughter of Samuel McDowell. Died June 17, 1839. OR 6/29.

Bernard Gaines, of Woodford county. Died June 23, 1839, at an advanced age. KG 6/27.

J. Black Robinson, merchant, formerly of Lexington, Ky. Died at Nashville, Tenn., June 22, 1839. OR 7/3.

William Phillips, youngest son of John L. Elbert, of Fayette county. Died June 28, 1839, aged about 16 months. OR 7/3.

John Kennard, son of Whittington and Elizabeth King. Died July 1, 1839, aged 11 months and 8 days. OR 7/6.

Dudley C. Campbell, formerly of Lexington, Ky. Died near St. Louis, Mo., June 28, 1839. OR 7/6.

James Birney. Died in Louisville at the residence of his son-in-law, Judge Marshall, July 24, 1839, aged 72 years. OR 7/31.

John W. Russell, of Lexington. Died July 24, 1839. OR 7/31.

Simon Gratz, of Philadelphia. Died July 14, 1839, aged 67 years. (KG 8/11 says he was 57 years of age.) OR 7/27.

Virginia Elizabeth, infant daughter of Thornton P. Pierson, of Lexington. Died July 21, 1839, aged 6 months and 6 days. OR 7/27.

John Rogers, of Fayette county. An early settler of Kentucky. Died June 22, 1839, aged 67 years. OR 7/24.

Miss Rebecca Jane Kennedy, only daughter of Matthew Kennedy, of Louisville. Died in Lexington July 6, 1839, aged 18 years. OR 7/17.

Jesse Fishback, of Clark county. Died July 10, 1839. OR 9/17.

Greenberry Spiers, Sr., of Fayette county. Died July 23, 1839, aged 74 years. (KG 8/1 says he was 84 years of age.) OR 7/27.

Edwin I. Curle, formerly of Madison county, Ky. Died in St. Charles county, Mo., July 20, 1839. KG 8/1.

James McMurtry. Died Monday July 8, 1839, at the residence of his brother-in-law, John W. McKee, Bailey's Landing in Lincoln county, Mo. He was 31 years of age. KG 8/1.

Robin Beatty, of Lexington. Died Aug. 10, 1839, aged 80 years. OR 8/17.

Governor James Clark, of Clark county. Died Tuesday morning at 7 o'clock, August 27, 1839. He was born Jan. 16, 1779. KG 8/29.

Isola, infant daughter of Mr. M. B. Morrison. Died July 25, 1839, aged 8 months and 23 days. OR 7/31.

Capt. James Lusk, of Nicholasville. Long obituary concerning his military life in OR 8/7. He died July 31, 1839, aged 48 years.

Col. Robert Willmott, of Bourbon county. Born in Maryland in 1757; located in Kentucky in 1789. Died August 20, 1839. Long obituary in OR 9/4.

Samuel, son of Caleb Williams, of Lexington. Died Aug. 27, 1839, aged 16 months. OR 9/11.

Solomon Buzzard. Died Sept. 8, 1839, at an advanced age. KG 9/12.

Mrs. Polly W. Johnson, formerly of Scott county. Died at the Lexington residence of E. P. Johnson, Aug. 26, 1839. KG 8/29.

Mrs. Sarah Petty, consort of Ransdale Petty, of Fayette county. Died Sept. 12, 1839. KG 9/19.

Mrs. Susan Frances Honfleur, wife of Juan Honfleur, formerly known in Lexington as Miss Rodgers. She died in Jeffersonville, Indiana, Sept. 5, 1839. KG 9/19.

Daniel M. Thompson, son of Philip Thompson, of Owensborough, Ky. Died at the Lunatic Asylum in Lexington Sept. 22, 1839, aged about 18 years. KG 9/26.

Benjamin Andrews, formerly a resident of Lexington, Ky. Died in New Orleans August 24, 1839. KG 9/26.

Thomas Ross, of Lexington. Died Oct. 7, 1839. He was buried Tuesday Oct. 8 by the Mechanics Infantry of which he was a member. OR 10/9.

Benjamin Chapese, of Bardstown. Died at Elizabethtown Sept. 26, 1839. OR 10/12.

Mrs. Elizabeth Nutter. Died at the Fayette county residence of her son-in-law Capt. Newbold Crockett October 3, 1839, aged about 90 years. OR 10/12.

Williamson C. Jones, of Lancaster, Va., formerly a resident of Lexington, Ky. Died Sept. 10, 1839. OR 10/12.

Matthew Elder, of Morgan county, Ill., formerly a citizen of Lexington, Ky. Died Sept. 11, 1839, aged 67 years. OR 10/12.

Mrs. Margaret Ann, consort of William C. Lyle, of Paris. He was editor of the *Western Citizen*. She died in Paris October 4, 1839. OR 10/16.

Major James Brasfield, of Platt county, Mo., formerly of Clark county, Ky. Died Sept. 22, 1839. OR 10/16.

Robert Houston, of Lexington. Died Oct. 15, 1839. OR 10/16.

Mrs. Agnes Perkins, wife of E. Perkins, of Lexington. She died Oct. 17, 1839. OR 10/19.

Hon. Joseph M. White, born and reared in Kentucky. Died in St. Louis, Mo., at the residence of his brother, Dr. White, October 19, 1839. OR 10/30.

Capt. George Hancock Griffin. Died at Fort Brooke, Tampa, Florida, Oct. 7, 1839. Obituary in OR 11/2.

Rev. Eli Smith, of South Frankfort. Died Oct. 30, 1839. OR 11/2.

John H. Donaldson, of Louisville, formerly of New Orleans. Suicided in November, 1839, aged 46 years. OR 11/13.

Mrs. Anne Allen, consort of Richard Allen, dec'd., of Fayette county. Died at the residence of Richard Higgins, Nov. 9, 1839, aged about 85 years. OR 11/13.

George Weir, of Scott county. Died Nov. 12, 1839. OR 11/13.

Major Abner Gaines, of Boone county. Died Oct. 30, 1839, at an advanced age. OR 11/20.

James Wilson, of Natchez, son of John Wilson, of Lexington, Ky. Died September 20, 1839. OR 11/27.

Mrs. Mary Dudley, of Bourbon county, consort of E. S. Dudley, and daughter of Col. Henry Clay, of Bourbon county. Died Nov. 19, 1839. OR 11/27.

Mortimer R. Wigginton, of New Orleans, formerly of Louisville, Ky. Died in Brazos, Texas, in November, 1839. OR 11/27.

John Barton, of Fayette county. Died Nov. 26, 1839, aged 84 years. OR 11/30.

David Sutton, one of the oldest citizens of Lexington. Died Thursday night December 12, 1839. Obituary in OR 12/14.

Otto James, of Lexington, Ky. Died in Philadelphia, Pa., Dec. 14, 1839. OR 12/18.

H. W. Fontain, of Louisville. Died in Houston, Texas, Nov. 21, 1839. OR 12/18.

Samuel Robinson, Sr., of Fayette county. Died Dec. 14, 1839, aged 86 years. OR 12/25.

1840

John Anderson, of Lexington. Shot and killed Jan. 5, 1840, by Harrison Jeter. Story in OR 1/15

William J. Ashley, formerly of Carlisle, Ky. Died in St. Louis, Mo., January 25, 1840. OR 2/5.

Mrs. Susan Bedford, consort of A. G. Bedford, of Woodford county. Died at the residence of James Byrns, Feb. 22, 1840. OR 2/26.

Mrs. Elizabeth Bridges, wife of W. A. Bridges, of Garrard county. Died Jan. 27, 1840. OR 2/8.

Mrs. Anna Duidwitt, consort of .... Duidwitt, of Lexington, and daughter of Isaac R. Miller. Died March 28, 1840, aged 17 years. OR 4/1.

Capt. John C. Graves, of Fayette county. Died at the residence of his son-in-law, H. Hansbro, April 17, 1840, aged 83 years. OR 4/22.

Thomas F. Harper, formerly of Lexington, Ky. Died in New Orleans, March 15, 1840, aged about 27 years. OR 4/1.

Capt. John Hurst, of Fayette county. One of the first settlers of Kentucky. Died March 24, 1840, aged 70 years. OR 4/8.

John Kennard, Sr., of Lexington, formerly of Baltimore, Md. Died Jan. 8, 1840, aged 63 years. OR 1/11.

Mrs. Ruth Mothershead, of Scott county. Died Apr. 15, 1840, aged 77 years. OR 4/22.

James Rogers of Fayette county. Died Feb. 6, 1840, at an advanced age. OR 2/9.

Miss Elizabeth Ruth Warfield, daughter of Dr. Lloyd Warfield, of Lexington. Died Jan. 9, 1840. OR 1/11.

Mrs. Sarah F. Saunders, consort of J. H. Saunders, and eldest daughter of M. A. Feris, M.D., formerly of Georgetown, Ky. Died in Pettis county, Mo., Jan. 24, 1840. Obituary in OR 2/22.

Capt. John Shrock, of Fayette county. Died Apr. 22, 1840, aged 52 years. OR 4/29.

Jane Mary Vigus, eldest daughter of Mr. D. L. Vigus, of Lexington. Died Feb. 7, 1840, aged 6 years and 9 months. OR 2/12.

George N. Wallace, of Garrard county. Died Feb. 16, 1840, aged 24 years. He left his wife and one child. OR 4/22.

William Dolan, Jr., formerly of Lexington, Ky. Died in Burlington, Iowa, Jan. 9, 1840. OR 1/15.

David Craven, of Jessamine county. Died Nov. 30, 1839, aged 58 years. OR 1/4/1840.

Mrs. Julia Clay, consort of H. Clay, Jr. Died in Louisville, at the residence of her mother, Mrs. .... Prather, Feb. 14, 1840, aged 24 years. OR 2/19.

George Warfield, son of Dr. B. H. Warfield. Died Feb. 8, 1840, aged 16 years. OR 2/15.

Charles J. Hemphill, of Ozark, Franklin county, Ark., formerly of Kentucky. Died Nov. 12, 1839. KG 2/27/1840.

Elijah H. Grooms, of Lexington. Died Jan. 28, 1840, at an advanced age. KG 2/30.

Rev. George McNelly, of the Kentucky Conference of the M. E. Church. Died in Springfield, Tenn., April 16, 1840, aged 48 years. OR 5/2.

James Patterson, Jr., son of Col. James Patterson, of Scott county. Died April 27, 1840, aged 20 years. OR 5/9.

Mrs. Patsey C. Ford, consort of Benjamin B. Ford, of Georgetown. Died May 5, 1840. OR 5/9.

John C. Miller, of Georgetown. Died May 5, 1840, aged 40 years. OR 5/9.

Levi Rice, eldest son of Abram Rice, of Fayette county. Died May 8, 1840, aged 20 years. OR 5/13.

Mr. Francis T. Coburn, of Maysville. Died May 5, 1840, aged 30 years. OR 5/16.

Mrs. Harriet Hawkins, consort of Augustus F. Hawkins, of Lexington. Died May 21, 1840. OR 5/23.

General John Adair, of Mercer county, formerly Governor of Kentucky. Died Tuesday May 18, 1840. OR 5/23.

William Boon, of Lexington. Died May 26, 1840. OR 5/27.

Col. James Robertson, of Louisville. Died May 27, 1840, aged 65 years. OR 6/3.

John W. Clark, Jr., son of John W. Clark, of Lexington. Died June 1, 1840. OR 6/3.

Dr. Benjamin Harrison. Died at his father's residence at North Bend, on Tuesday June 16, 1840, aged 34 years. OR 6/20.

Mrs. Martha Parish, consort of James Parish, of Woodford county. Died June 19, 1840. OR 6/20.

Nathaniel L. Turner, of Lexington. Died June 19, 1840, aged about 30 years. OR 6/20.

Benjamin F. Thomas, of Mt. Sterling. Died June 15, 1840. OR 6/24.

Helen Louisa, only daughter of James M. Beach, of Lexington. Died on Saturday June 20, 1840, aged about 22 months. OR 6/24.

Colonel James Patterson, of Scott county. Died Sunday June 28, 1840, at an advanced age. OR 7/1.

Major Robert McCalla, of near Stamping Ground, Scott county. Died on June 16, 1840, aged 72 years. OR 7/1.

Anna, infant daughter of William W. Ater, of Lexington. Died July 1, 1840. OR 7/4.

Mrs. Emmeline M. Swigert, consort of Jacob Swigert, clerk of the Court of Appeals, Frankfort, and daughter of the late Captain Daniel Weisiger. Died June 25, 1840. OR 7/4.

William Nixon, of Louisville. Died June 26, 1840. OR 7/4.

Col. Henry S. Langford, of Mt. Vernon, Rockcastle county. Killed in July, 1840, by a Mr. Davidson. OR 7/8.

Margaret Bruce, daughter of J. J. Hunter. Died July 3, 1840, aged 2 years, 10 months and 21 days. OR 7/8.

Jacob Hull. Died July 4, 1840. OR 7/8.

Capt. Hubbard B. Smith, one of the oldest settlers of Grant county, and clerk of the Circuit and County Courts since the foundation of the county. He died in Williamstown, June 29, 1840. OR 7/11.

Rezin Bridges, formerly of Lexington. Died near South Union, Kentucky, July 3, 1840, aged 23 years. OR 7/18.

Joseph S. Benham, of the Cincinnati Bar. Died July 15, 1840, aged 43 years. OR 7/18.

Benjamin F. Thomas, of Mt. Sterling. Died July 16, 1840, aged 38 years. OR 7/18.

Juliet Thomas, consort of the late B. F. Thomas, of Mt. Sterling (see above) and eldest daughter of George Howard. She died July 17, 1840. OR 7/18.

William Carr, son of Judge William C. Carr, of St. Louis. Died July 13, 1840, aged about 5 years. OR 7/25.

O'Bannon Pettit, of Frankfort. Died July 11, 1840, aged 33 years, 2 months and 14 days. OR 7/18.

Abraham Vaughan, son of James H. Ware, of Fayette county. Died July 21, 1840, aged 13 months. OR 7/29.

William Wallace, of Fayette county. Died July 25, 1840, aged about 33 years. OR 7/29.

Lawrence, infant son of William A. Leavy, of Lexington. Died July 30, 1840. OR 8/1.

Mrs. Phebe Winn, consort of Owen D. Winn, of Fayette county, and daughter of James Stonestreet, of Clark county. Died Saturday July 18, 1840. OR 8/1.

Mrs. Ann Harrison, consort of Robert Carter Harrison, Sr., of Elk-Hill, Fayette county. Died July 27, 1840, aged 70 years. Obituary in OR 8/12.

John Bean, of Montgomery county. Died July 29, 1840, aged 42 years. OR 8/12.

Miss Eliza McNitt, daughter of Robert McNitt, dec'd., of Lexington. Died Aug. 7, 1840. OR 8/12.

Dr. William Hardman, of Lexington. Died Aug. 14, 1840. OR 8/15.

Abraham Ferguson, of Fayette county. Died July 2, 1840, aged 80 years. OR 8/19.

Bela Metcalfe, son of General Thomas Metcalfe. Died Monday August 10, 1840, aged nearly 30 years. OR 8/19.

Samuel Trotter Leavy, of Louisville, formerly of Lexington. Died Aug. 10, 1840, aged 30 years. Buried Sunday Aug. 16, 1840, in the Presbyterian Cemetery at Lexington. OR 8/19.

Elihu Owings, of Bath county. A native of Maryland and long time resident of Kentucky. Died Aug. 13, 1840, aged 72 years. OR 8/19.

Ambrose F. Dudley, of Madison county. Died Aug. 17, 1840, aged 38 years. OR 8/26.

Capt. John Fowler, of Lexington. One of the first inhabitants of Lexington and for many years representative from Kentucky in the Congress of the United States. He died Saturday August 22, 1840, aged about 85 years. KG 8/27 and OR 8/26.

Dr. Robert Spottswood, of Callaway county, Mo., son of Gen. R. S. Russell, late of Fayette county, Ky. Died Aug. 30, 1840, aged 33 years. Obituary in KG 9/24.

Charles C. Winter, of Sulphur Spring, Pine Woods, Arkansas. Died there at the residence of Peter T. Hickman on Sept. 7, 1840, aged 26 years. He was from Lexington, Ky., and had been a resident of former place for 3 years. KG 10/22.

Samuel Lamme, infant son of Joseph Chew. Died at the residence of his grandfather, Jesse Lamme, October 18, 1840, aged 5 months. KG 10/22.

Thomas Rogers, son of Thomas and Catharine Rogers, of Lexington. Died October 20, 1840, aged 17 years. KG 10/22.

Mrs. Eleanor Loud, consort of Richard Loud, of Fayette county. She was a native of Philadelphia, where she was married. She removed to Kentucky in 1828, and died Nov. 14, 1840, aged 39 years. She left her husband and six children. KG 11/26.

Mrs. Elizabeth Turner, relict of Nathaniel Turner. Died at the Lexington residence of her father, Daniel Bradford, Nov. 19, 1840, aged 33 years. KG 11/26.

James G. Dana, of Frankfort. Died Nov. 19, 1840. Obituary in KG 11–26.

Elizabeth Frances, eldest daughter of General John M. McCalla, of Lexington. Died Dec. 22, 1840, aged 17 years. KG 12–24.

Colonel Josiah Dunham, of Lexington. Died May 10, 1844, at an advanced age. OR 5/11.

Dr. Thomas C. Cropper, of Grand Gulf, Miss., formerly of Lexington, Ky. Died Apr. 25, 1844, aged 35 years. OR 5/11.

Mrs. Eleanor Bennet, consort of James Bennet, of Woodford county. Died May 3, 1844, aged 60 years. OR 5/11.

James E. Quarles, son of James Quarles, of Woodford county. Died in May, 1844, aged 22 years. OR 5/28.

Mary A. Bryan, daughter of Greenberry and Mary A. Spiers. Died at the Woodford county residence of Lawson L. Spiers, May 18, 1844, aged 30 years. OR 5/29.

Thomas Chamberlin, of Lexington. Died May 28, 1844, aged 64 years. OR 5/29.

Miss Amanda C., eldest daughter of Samuel Wilson, of Fayette county. Died June 5, 1844, aged 21 years. OR 6/12.

John B. Reese, of Lexington. Died June 14, 1844. OR 6/19.

Norman Leslie, son of Thomas and Isabella Bradley. Died June 15, 1844. aged 21 months. OR 6/19.

Col. Thomas Buckner, of Kenton county. Died June 19, 1844, aged 49 years. OR 6/29.

Mrs. Sarah Ann Hall, consort of Dr. John R. Hall, of Vandalia, Ill., and eldest daughter of Isaac and Mrs. Rebecca Vanmetre, of Clark county, Ky. Died at the Fayette county, Ky., residence of Rev. N. H. Hall June 22, 1844, aged 19 years. OR 6/29

Mrs. Mary Prall, wife of Garrison Prall, both natives of Hunterdon, N. J. She died Friday June 28, 1844, at the Woodford county residence of her son Capt. John Prall. She was 84 years of age. OR 7/3.

Jefferson Lamme, of Fayette county. Died June 30, 1844, aged 42 years. Obituary in OR 7/10.

John McDowell, son of Capt. John J. McDowell, of Fayette county. Died Monday July 3, 1844, aged about 15 years. OR 7/10.

Col. William Barr, of American Bend, Miss., formerly of Versailles, Ky. Died June 5, 1844, aged 74 years. Obituary and story in OR 7/13.

OBITUARIES

The abbreviations used denote:

KG—(Lexington) *Kentucky Gazette*
OR—*Lexington* (Ky.) *Observer & Reporter.*

1844

Mrs. Mary Ann Sidner, wife of Andrew Sidner of Fayette county, and daughter of James Hearst. Died July 8, 1844, aged 24 years. OR 7/17.

Anson Warner Eames, of Grand Gulf, Miss., for many years a resident of Lexington, Ky. Died July 7, 1844, aged about 24 years. OR 7/20.

Thomas W. Hawkins, of Lexington. Died July 20, 1844, aged 62 years. Obituary in OR 7/24.

Edward Payne, of Fayette county, a native of Virginia. He died July 13, 1844, aged 81 years. Obituary in OR 7/24.

Mrs. Elizabeth R. Duvall, consort of Willis Duvall, and daughter of Robert Hicks, of Fayette county. Died July 7, 1844, aged 24 years. OR 7/27.

Mrs. Harriet Hampton, consort of John A. Hampton, of Lexington. Died at Crittenden, Ky., Monday July 29, 1844. OR 8/3.

Edward A., infant son of Mr. E. W. Dowden, of Lexington. He died July 31, 1844. OR 8/10.

John Stratford Goins, of Lexington. A Negro barber of repute. Died Aug. 10, 1844, aged about 60 years. OR 8/14.

Mrs. Martha Ann Hunt, consort of Wilson Hunt, of Fayette county. Died August 16, 1844. OR 8/17.

Frederick Zimmerman, of Michigan, formerly of Lexington, Ky. Died July 15, 1844, aged 71 years. OR 8/17.

Mrs. Mary Elizabeth Shryock, relict of Capt. Mathias Shryock, of Lexington. Died Aug. 18, 1844, at an advanced age. OR 8/21.

Miss Mary L. Barnett, of Mill Street, Lexington. Died Aug. 21, 1844, aged 21 years. OR 8/24.

William McClelland, of Fayette county. An early settler of Kentucky. Died Aug. 22, 1844, aged 72 years. Obituary in OR 8/28.

Miss Rebecca Price, of Scott county. Died Aug. 7, 1844: and on Aug. 15, 1844, her father, Thomas Price, Sr., aged 61 years. OR 8/28.

Mrs. Mary Stone, relict of George Stone, of Fayette county. She was one of the earliest settlers of Kentucky, having lived in Fayette county "upwards of 50 years". She died Thursday night August 29, 1844, at a very advanced age. OR 8/31.

Hon. William S. Fulton, Senator in Congress from Arkansas. Died at Rosewood, his residence about one mile from Little Rock, Aug. 15, 1844. OR 9/4.

Achilles Eubank, of near Booneville, Mo., formerly of Clark county, Ky. Died August 16, 1844, aged 91 years. OR 9/4.

Miss Caroline C. Boyce, of Lexington, Mo. Died Aug. 22, 1844, aged 16 years. OR 9/14.

William Chilton Allan, son of the Hon. Chilton Allan, of Winchester, Ky. Died Sept. 6, 1844, aged 19 years. "He was one of the most finished scholars of his age in the State, and one of the most promising Sculptors this country has ever produced." OR 9/14.

Hon. George Adams, of near Jackson, Miss. Died Sept. 4, 1844. OR 9/14.

Dr. D. H. Dickinson, of Frankfort Died Sept. 9, 1844. OR 9/14.

Mrs. Margaret Almira Webb, wife of Capt. John V. Webb, of Pettit-saw Bluffs, Mo., formerly of Scott county, Ky. She died Aug. 21, 1844, aged 32 years. OR 9/18.

James Hawkins, of Keene, Jessamine county. Died Sept. 15, 1844, aged 26 or 27 years. OR 9/18.

Mrs. ———— Allen, wife of John Allen, Sr., of Woodford county, and daughter of Col. James Quarles. Died Sept. 11, 1844. OR 9/18.

Miss Hulda Barnett, of S. Mill street, Lexington. Died Sept. 16, 1844, aged 18 years. OR 9/21.

Mrs. Jane Logan Parker, wife of Dr. John T. Parker. Died Sept. 13, 1844. OR 9/21.

Mrs. Catherine C. Humphrey, wife of Edward P. Humphrey, of Louisville, and youngest daughter of the late Thomas Prather. Died in October, 1844, aged 28 years. OR 10/5.

Mrs. Mary O. Wickliffe, consort of Robert Wickliffe, and daughter of Col. John Todd who fell at the Battle of Blue Licks. She was born in Lexington, and died Friday Sept. 29, 1844, aged 63 years. OR 10/9.

Samuel Henderson, of Fayette county. Died October 3, 1844. He had been a resident of Fayette county for 50 years. OR 10/9.

John J. Chambers, son of the Honorable John Chambers, of Iowa (formerly of Washington, Mason county Ky.) He died at the residence of Hugh J. Brent Sept. 30, 1844, aged about 19 years. OR 10/9.

Mrs. Margaret Shackleford, wife of W. H. Shackleford, of Paris, and daughter of John L. Martin. Died Oct. 1, 1844. OR 10/9.

William McConnell. Died at the Fayette county residence of his brother, James McConnell, Sept. 29, 1844, aged 64 years. OR 10/9.

Capt. John W. Moore, of Fayette county. Died Sunday Oct. 13, 1844. OR 10/16.

John Campbell, of Mt. Sterling. Died Oct. 6, 1844, aged 33 years. OR 10/16.

Thomas Glossop, of Lewisport, Ky. Trapped and buried in a Hawesville mine. Died Oct. 4, 1844. Story in OR 10/23.

Rev. John H. Fielding, of St. Charles, Mo., and President of St. Charles College. Died Oct. 14, 1844. OR 10/26.

The following died when the steamer *Lucy Walker* exploded in October, 1844: Samuel M. Brown, postoffice agent, Lexington; Charles Donne, Louisville; James Vanderberg, Louisville; A. E. Edwards, Lexington, and Nicholas, Ford, formerly of Lexington. Story in OR 10/26.

John Porter, merchant of Stephensburg, Ky. Killed Wednesday Oct. 23, 1844, by Marquis B. Brown. OR 10/30.

Mrs. Malvina Arnold, consort of Col. Matthew R. Arnold, of Fayette county, and youngest daughter of the late General Robert S. Russell, of Calloway county and long resident of Fayette county. She died Oct. 28, 1844, aged 35 years. OR 11/9.

Edward C. Owings, of Montgomery county. Died Oct. 29, 1844, aged 41 years. OR 11/20.

John A. Murrell, "the notorious Land Pirate." Died in Pikeville, Bledsoe county (Tenn.?) November 1, 1844. OR 11/27.

Elder Barton W. Stone. Died at Hannibal, Mo., Nov. 8, 1844, aged 72 years. OR 11/27.

Mrs. Sarah Chiles, wife of Richard Chiles, of Fayette county. Died Dec. 6, 1844, aged 70 years. OR 12/14.

Mrs. Rachel Pendleton, wife of Gen. Edmund Pendleton, of Clark county. Died Dec. 5, 1844, aged 45 years. OR 12/14.

Col. Ratliff Boon, of Pike county, Mo. Died Nov. 20, 1844. He was for twelve years a member of Congress from Indiana. OR 12/14.

Mrs. Mary Newton, wife of Thomas W. Newton, of Little Rock, Ark., and daughter of Col. John Allen, dec'd., of Shelby county, Ky. Died Nov. 23, 1844, aged 35 years. OR 12/14.

Samuel Campbell, son of Charles C. and Mary Anne H. Campbell, of Fayette County. Died Nov. 28, 1844, aged 9 months. OR 12/14.

William B. Fleming, of Woodford county. Died Dec. 3, 1844. OR 12/14.

Mrs. Lucy D. Howard, consort of John L. Howard, of Fayette county Died Nov. 18, 1844, aged 38 years. OR 12/14.

Dr. Isaac M. Jennings, of Mortonsville, Woodford county. Died Friday December 5, 1844, aged 36 years. Obituary in OR 12/18.

Dr. Alexander R. Kenney, of Millersburg. Died Dec. 12, 1844, aged 56 years. OR 12/18.

Douglas P., son of D. L. Price, of Fayette county. Died Dec. 9, 1844, aged 21 months. OR 12/18.

George Crutcher, of Lexington. Died Dec. 21, 1844, aged about 40 years. OR 12/28.

Mrs. Sarah Bayles. Died at the residence of her son, Col. Jesse Bayles, Sunday Dec. 22, 1844, aged 79 years. OR 12/28.

Mrs. Mary Tilford, consort of Major John Tilford, of Fayette county. Died Dec. 31, 1844, aged 57 years. Obituary in OR 1/1/1845.

Hon. William Wright Southgate, of Covington. Died Dec. 26, 1844, aged 45 years. OR 1/4/1845.

John B. Overton, of Fayette county. Died Saturday December 28, 1844. He left his wife and several children. OR 1/4/1845.

James William, infant son of William G. Skillman. Died Jan. 5, 1845, aged 3 months and 8 days. OR 1/8/1845.

Mrs. Sophonisba Breckenridge, wife of Rev. Dr. R. J. Breckenridge. She died in Baltimore in January, 1845. Her father was the late Col. Preston of Abingdon, Va. One of her brothers was the Hon. Mr. Preston, Senator from South Carolina. Governor McDowell, of Virginia, married one of her sisters. OR 1/15.

Mrs. Mary Zimmerman, relict of Frederick Zimmerman. Died in Florida, Michigan, Dec. 21, 1844, aged 59 years. OR 1/15/1845.

Thomas H. Fletcher, of Nashville. Died Jan. 12, 1845. OR 1/18.

Nancy Sanders, daughter of John P. Innis, of Fayette county. Died Jan. 21, 1845, aged 6 years and 10 months. OR 1/25.

Mrs. Elizabeth White, relict of Daniel White, of Lexington. Died at the Georgetown residence of Thomas B. White Jan. 25, 1845, aged 60 years. OR 1/29.

Mrs. Elizabeth Darnaby. Died at the residence of her son-in-law, P. E. Yeiser Jan. 31, 1845. OR 2/5.

Mrs. Sarah Inskeep Wilson. Died Feb. 2, 1845, at the residence of M. P. D. Yeiser. OR 2/5.

Alexander R. Macey, of Bowling Green, editor of the *Green River Gazette.* Died Jan. 28, 1845. OR 2/5.

Mrs. Harriet Miller, consort of Washington Miller, of Winchester. Died Jan. 23, 1845, aged 43 years. OR 2/8.

William F. Hockaday, of Winchester. Died Feb. 1, 1845. OR 2/8.

1845

Mrs. Jane Stevenson, of Lexington. Died at the residence of her son, Robert Stevenson, Feb. 8, 1845, aged 95 years She was the second white female in Lexington. OR 2/12.

Mrs Amanda F., consort of Edwin C. Hickman, of Clark county, and daughter of Dr. Robert Best, dec'd. Died Jan. 22, 1845, aged 30 years. OR 2/12.

Col. John T. Woodford, of Clark county. Died Jan. 31, 1845, in his 83rd year. He emigrated from Virginia to Clark county in 1819. He was a son of the gallant and distinguished Col. William Woodford, of the Virginia line in the Revolution, and in whose honor the Kentucky county of the name was so called. Obituary in OR 2/15.

Mrs. Eliza Herndon, consort of A. G. Herndon, of Lexington. Died Feb. 11, 1845, aged 40 years. She left her aged mother, her husband and one child, a daughter. (A. G. Herndon was Augustus G. Herndon.) OR 2/15.

John Ward Scott, infant son of Samuel Scott, of Woodford county. Died Feb. 9, 1845, aged 19 month and 23 days. OR 2/19.

Mrs. Martha Hull, relict of Jacob Hull, Sr., of Fayette county. Died Feb. 17, 1845. OR 2/19.

Miss Sarah Preston, daughter of Hon. William C. Preston, of Columbia, S. C. Died Feb. 8, 1845. OR 2/22.

Mrs. Julia P. McPheeters, wife of Addison McPheeters, late of Manchester, Scott county, Illinois. Died at the Fayette county, Ky., home of James Wardlow, Feb. 12, 1845. OR 2/26.

Frances Cordelia, daughter of James Wood, of Lexington. Died Feb. 22, 1845, aged 12 years. OR 2/26.

Mrs. Eliza Gaunt, eldest daughter of Elder John M. Hewett, of Lexington, Ky. Died in Jacksonville, Ill., Feb. 16, 1845, aged 48 years. Obituary in OR 3/1.

Dr. F. A. Andrews. Died in Flemingsburg, Monday 3, 1845. OR 3/8.

Mrs. Elizabeth Galloway, wife of Joseph Galloway, dec'd., and daughter of Rev James Crawford, one of the early settlers of Kentucky who died in 1803. She died in Lexington March 2, 1845. OR 3/12.

Clifton R. Thompson, member of the Fayette county bar. He was shot and killed in Mt. Sterling March 6, 1845, by his brother-in-law, the Hon. Henry Daniel. Thompson was born and reared in Fayette county. Story and resolutions in OR 3/8 and 3/12.

Garland B., infant son of Mr. G. B. Hale. Died Sunday March 16, 1845. OR 3/19.

Williamson W. Bacon, of Franklin county. Died Tuesday March 18, 1845. OR 3/29.

Eliza, daughter of P. Swigert, of Frankfort. Died March 22, 1845, aged 12 years. OR 3/29.

John James, son of Mr. G. B. Hale, of Lexington. Died March 23, 1845, aged 8 years. OR 3/29.

John Harris, Sr. Died at the Frankfort residence of his son, Monday March 31, 1845, aged 78 years. OR 4/5.

Edwin Cogshell, of Lexington. Died April 13, 1845. OR 4/19.

Thomas Sewall, M.D., of Washington City. Died Apr. 10, 1845, aged 59 years. OR 4/19.

Solomon Hoggins, of Bourbon county. Died Apr. 9, 1845, aged 77 years, 6 months and 10 days. He had been a resident of Bourbon more than 50 years. OR 4/19.

Edward Church. Died at Lexington, Ky., April 22, 1845. He was native of Mass. Obituary in OR 4/26.

Isabelle B., infant daughter of William Newberry, of Lexington. Died April 22, 1845. OR 4/26.

Mrs. Sarah Cunningham, relict of Capt. Isaac Cunningham. Died in Clark county Apr. 12, 1845, at an advanced age. OR 4/26.

William Campbell, late editor of the *Western Visitor*. Died in Covington, April 22, 1845. OR 4/30.

Alpheus W. Bascom, of Maysville. Died Apr. 22, 1845. OR 4/30.

Augustine W. Pinckard. Died Apr. 13, 1845, on the plantation of A. G. Creath, on the Yazoo River (Miss.?). He was formerly a resident of Lexington, Ky. OR 5/3.

Eli A. Bigger, of Clark county. Died May 6, 1845. OR 5/14.

Capt. William Markham, of Bath county. Died Apr. 28, 1845, aged 77 years. OR 5/17.

Mrs. Mildred Dunovan, formerly of Lexington. Died in Maysville May 18, 1845. OR 5/21.

David Dunlop, of Lexington. Died May 19, 1845. OR 5/21.

Louisa Ker, only daughter of John G. Allen, of Lexington. Died May 22, 1845, aged 3 years, 5 months and 10 days. OR 5/24.

Armistead Mason Barry, of Lexington, second son of the Hon. William T. Barry. Died in Newport, Ky., at the residence of his brother-in-law, James Taylor, Jr., May 12, 1845. Obituary in OR 5/28.

Overton S. Ragland, of Fayette county. Died Sunday May 18, 1845. OR 5/28.

Violinda, infant daughter of George T. and Louisa H. Fishback. Died May 29, 1845, aged 7 weeks. OR 6/4.

Alexander Crawford, only son of Rev. James Crawford, who was the second Presbyterian minister who emigrated to Kentucky. Alexander died Wednesday May 28, 1845, leaving but one surviving member of the family. OR 6/4.

John G. Pitts, one-time editor of the *Hopkinsville* (Kentucky) *Gazette*. He drowned near Cat Island, lower Mississippi, May 3, 1845. Story and obituary in OR 6/7.

Benjamin Robinson, of Mt. Sterling. Died May 29, 1845, aged 90 years. He was a soldier in the *American Revolution*. OR 6/7.

Jefferson Wright, of Mt. Sterling, an artist (portrait painter). He died in Louisville May 26, 1845. OR 6/7.

Hannah, wife of Major Lewinski, and daughter of Hugh Carey, of Louisville. Died in Lexington June 2, 1845, aged 29 years. OR 6/7.

Mrs. Elizabeth Chambers, consort of Francis T. Chambers, of Washington, Mason county. Died June 1, 1845. OR 6/7.

Mrs. Lucey Ann White, daughter of Benjamin Hieronymus, of Clark county. Died May 31, 1845. OR 6/7.

Robert Breckenridge, infant son of Tobias and Louisiana B. Gibson. Died June 9, 1845. OR 6/14.

John G. Allen, of Jessamine county. Died June 9, 1845, aged 66 years. OR 6/14.

General Andrew Jackson. Died Sunday June 8, 1845, at 6 o'clock p. m., at the Hermitage. OR 6/14.

Richard M. Price, son of Willis Price, of Fayette county. Died June 3, 1845, aged about 20 years. OR 6/14.

James Calloway, of Natchez, Miss. Died in Louisville, Ky., May 26, 1845. OR 6/14.

Samuel Coolidge, of Lexington, formerly of Watertown, Mass. Died in former city June 18, 1845. OR 6/21.

Charles S. Gatewood, of Montgomery county. A native of Jessamine county; married, first time, the daughter of the late Asa Blanchard and second, a daughter of General Williams, of Montgomery county. He died June 17, 1845, aged 42 years. Obituary in OR 6/25.

Sue, infant daughter of David and Virginia Castleman. Died June 19, 1845, aged 8 months and 15 days. OR 6/25.

Dr. William Webb, of Clark county. Died June 15, 1845, aged 77 years. OR 6/28.

William Roman, of Fayette county. Died Apr. 27, 1845, aged 71 years. OR 6/28.

Mrs. Julia Keith, consort of James W. Keith, of Winchester. Died June 22, 1845. OR 6/28.

Miss Rebecca, daughter of Joseph and Elizabeth Galloway, of Lexington, and granddaughter of the Rev. James Crawford. She died June 29, 1845, aged 23 years. OR 7/2.

James Edward, son of James Virden, of Lexington. Died June 28, 1845, aged 2 years and 6 months. OR 7/2.

Dr. James Fishback, of Lexington. Died June 26, 1845. OR 6/28.

Julius Clarke, formerly of Lexington, Ky., where he was one of the founders and for several years one of the editors of the *Lexington Intelligencer*. He died in Middlebury, Vermont, June 7, 1845. OR 6/28 and 7/5.

Mrs. Jane Moore, consort of George Moore, of Garrard county. Died June 19, 1845, aged 29 years. OR 7/5.

Mrs. Mary Ann, consort of William D. Crockett, of Scott county. Died Monday June 30, 1845, aged about 22 years. OR 7/5.

Wilberforce Lyle, of Madison, Ind., a native of Scott county. Ky. Died June 24, 1845. OR 7/5.

William C. Bell, of Lexington, Ky., agent of the *True American*. Died in Schuykill, Penna., July 1, 1845. He left in Lexington his wife and family. OR 7/9.

Mrs. Sarah George, wife of Alfred George. Died in Fulton, Mo., June 27, 1845, aged 38 years. OR 7/9.

Lucy Julia, daughter of Cornelia D. Winn. Died in Huntsville, Ala., June 29, 1845, aged 1 year and 8 months. OR 7/12.

Benjamin Dudley Reid, infant son of Charles and Lucy Reid. Died in Lexington July 15, 1845. OR 7/16.

Mrs. Innes, consort of Col. Robert Innes, of Fayette county. Died July 15, 1845. OR 7/19.

David McMurtry, of Fayette county. Died July 15, 1845, at an advanced age. OR 7/19.

John A., infant son of John A. Hampton, of Lexington. Died Monday July 21, 1845. OR 7/23.

Robert Tucker, Sr., of Fayette county. Died July 17, 1845, aged 78 years. OR 7/23.

Elizabeth Church, consort of Thomas Church, of Lexington. Died July 22, 1845, aged 90 years. OR 7/26.

Mr. G. L. Johnson, of Lexington. Died July 22, 1845. OR 7/26.

Miss A. B. Robinson, of Scott county. Died at the residence of her brother, J. F. Robinson, Sunday July 20, 1845. OR 7/30.

Miss Catharine E. Lister, daughter of ———— Lister, of Versailles. She died in Lexington July 18, 1845, aged 14 years and 9 months. OR 7/30.

Judge A. M. Davis, of San Augustine, Texas. Died at the Lexington, Ky., residence of Mrs. Layton, July 28, 1845. OR 7/30.

John C. Richardson, of Miss., a native of Fayette county, Kentucky. Died at the residence of his brother, Dr. William H. Richardson, Aug. 3, 1845, aged 59 years. Obituary in OR 8/9.

Mrs. Rebecca J. Young, of Jessamine county. Died July 23, 1845, aged 51 years. Obituary in OR 8/9.

Harriett Jane, infant daughter of W. P. and Margaret McCall, of Clark county. Died in August, 1845, aged 19 months. OR 8/9.

Miss Mary Fletcher, of Booneville, Mo., formerly of Lexington, Ky. She died July 27, 1845. OR 8/9.

Mrs. Elizabeth Davenport, of Crab Orchard, formerly a resident of Lexington, Ky. Died Aug. 5, 1845, aged 65 years. Obituary in OR 8/13.

Miss Browning, the "Kentucky Giantess," of Fleming county. Died July 22, 1845, aged 23 or 24 years. Obituary in OR 8/16.

William M. Scearce, of near Shelbyville. Killed by lightning Monday Aug. 18, 1845. OR 8/16.

James C. Pickett, of the Lexington I. W. Scott & Co. Died at his mother's residence in Lexington Wednesday Aug. 13, 1845. OR 8/16.

Rev. J. E. Jackson, Rector of St. Paul's Church, Henderson, Ky. Died Aug 4, 1845, aged 63 years. OR 8/16.

Mr. A. S. Higgins, of Fayette county. Died Aug. 9, 1845, aged 65 years. OR 8/20.

Mrs. Sophia McCaleb, wife of James F. McCaleb, of Natchez. She was a native of Danville, Ky. Died in August, 1845, aged 31 years. OR 8/20.

Cyrus McCracken, of Palmyra, Mo., formerly of Woodford county, Ky. He died August 9, 1845. OR 8/23.

Zebedee Kendall, eldest son of Amos Kendall. Killed in Washington City, Tuesday August 19, 1845, by William Rufus Elliott. OR 8/27.

Sarah Buford, infant daughter of Henry C. and Susan W. Blackburn, of Woodford county. Died August 16, 1845, aged 2 months and 1 day. OR 8/27.

Dr. Charles Pinkney, of Clinton, La. Died in Lexington, Ky., at the residence of William Elder, Aug. 23, 1845, aged 40 years. OR 8/27.

Luther Stephens, of Lexington. Died Aug. 27, 1845, at an advanced age. Obituary in OR 8/30.

Basil D. Crookshanks, one of the editors of the *Flemingsburg Republican* and formerly connected with the press at Maysville. Died in Flemingsburg, Saturday Aug. 23, 1845. OR 8/30.

John Cotton, second son of Charles Cotton, of Woodford county. Died Aug. 18, 1845. OR 8/30.

William M. Guthrie. Died at Sparta, Ill., Aug. 20, 1845, aged 28 years and 6 months. OR 9/3.

Colonel William Sudduth, of Owingsville, Ky. Died Aug. 28, 1845, aged 80 years. Obituary OR 9/3.

Thomas Jefferson Graves, son of W. W. Graves. Died August 25, 1845, aged 8 years and 8 months. OR 9/3.

Mrs. Rosanna Woodson, wife of Robert E. Woodson, of Nicholasville, Jessamine county. Died Aug. 29, 1845. They had been married little more than one year. OR 9/3.

Mrs. Jane Rodes, widow of John Rodes, of Barren county. She was born in Albermarle county, Va., in 1770, from whence she emigrated with her husband to Kentucky about 55 years ago, and removed to Lexington, Ky., about 1830 where she resided until her death. Obituary in OR 9/6. She died in August, 1845.

Hugh I. Brent, of Paris. Died Sept. 2, 1845, aged 43 years. He was President of the Paris Branch of the Northern Bank of Kentucky. OR 9/6.

Angeline Prentiss, only daughter of Mr. N. P. Long. Died September 3, 1845. OR 9/6.

Mrs. Sarah Jones, consort of John Jones, and daughter of Captain Daniel Gano, of Scott county, where she died Aug. 26, 1845, aged 21 years and 7 months. OR 9/10.

Adam Haun, of Fayette county. Died Aug. 30, 1845, aged 60 years. OR 9/10.

Mrs. Hester Weber. Died at the Lexington residence of her son-in-law, Thomas Ross, Sept. 7, 1845, at an advanced age. OR 9/10.

Dr. William H. Richardson, member of the Medical Faculty of Transylvania University. Died at the Fayette county residence of his son, Louis Richardson, Sunday September 14, 1845. Obituary in OR 9/17.

General Richard Cheatham, of Tenn. Died Sept. 9, 1845. OR 9/17.

Edward Dyer, of Washington City. Died September 8, 1845, aged 53 years. OR 9/17.

Mrs. Sarah Wilmott, consort of John L. Wilmott, of Lexington, and daughter of George Norton. Died Sept. 19, 1845. OR 9/20.

Mrs. Jane Webb, consort of Garland Webb, of Scott county. Died Sept. 14, 1845 OR 9/20.

Joseph M. Elgin, of Scott county. Died Sept. 16, 1845. OR 9/20.

Mrs. Margaret Lamme, consort of Milton Lamme, and daughter of Jesse Lamme, of Fayette county. Died in Mercer county Sept. 20, 1845. OR 9/24.

John Willson, of Knoxville, Tenn., formerly of Scotland. Died at the Fayette county, Ky., residence of Isaac N. Yarnall, Sept. 20, 1845. OR 9/24.

John M. Harrison. Shot during a duel with his brother-in-law, Dr. John L. Taylor. Died Sept. 17, 1845. Story in OR 9/24.

Rev. Joseph Taylor, of Clinton county, Ill. Died at the Lexington, Ky., residence of E. W. Craig, Sept. 23, 1845. Buried in the family cemetery in Franklin county. OR 9/27/1845.

John Watkins, of Scott county, Mo. Died Sept. 11, 1845, aged 59 years: and on Sept. 14, 1845, died his son, John Watkins. OR 9/27.

Hon. John White, of Richmond. Suicided in September, 1845. OR 10/1.

Beverley Allen, of St. Louis. Died in New York, Sept. 12, 1845. OR 10/1.

Mrs. Pocahontas Sloane, relict of Dr. S. C. Sloane, of Palmyra, Mo., and daughter of the late Robert C. Harrison, Sr., of Fayette county, Ky. Died on Sept. 14, 1845. OR 10/1.

Margaret Ann, daughter of Major A. D. Irvine, of Fayette county. Died Sept. 22, 1845, aged 17 years. OR 10/4.

Clarence Birch, youngest son of Henry C. and Susan W. Blackburn, of Woodford county. Died Sept. 28, 1845, aged 3 years, 3 months and 3 days. OR 10/4.

Dr. Burr Harrison, of Nelson county. Died Aug. 3, 1845, aged 70 years. OR 10/5.

Mrs. Theodocia Young, relict of A. H. Young, formerly of Fayette county. Died in St. Louis Sept. 28, 1845, aged 60 years. OR 10/4

Sidney C. George, of Jessamine county. Died Sept. 27, 1845. OR 10/4.

Francis K. Southgate, son of the late Hon. William W. Southgate, of Covington. Died at the residence of Capt. G. F. Keen, Sept. 28, 1845, aged 8 years. OR 10/4.

Miss Martha Overton. Died at the late residence of Waller Overton, in Fayette county, September 17, 1845. OR 10/4.

Francis Bremaker, formerly of Louisville, Ky. Drowned at Baton Rouge, La., Sept. 22, 1845. OR 10/11.

Preston M. Brown, of St. Louis, formerly of Fayette county, Ky. Died October 5, 1845. OR 10/15.

Miss Frances Amanda Wallace. Died at tthe Crittenden county residence of her brother, Arthur A. Wallace, Sept. 17, 1845. OR 10/15.

Mrs. Alice C. Boyd, consort of the Hon. Linn Boyd, of Kentucky. She died in Lafayette county, Mo., October 2, 1845, aged 31 years and 11 days. OR 10/15.

Mrs. Elizabeth D. Tandy, of Lexington, consort of the late Edmund Tandy. Died Sunday Sept. 21, 1845, aged 48 years. Obituary in OR 10/18.

Mrs. Sarah R. Blackwell, consort of Col. Armstead Blackwell, of Clark county. Died Oct. 12, 1845, aged 37 years. OR 10/18.

John W. Dillon, died at the Henderson, Ky., residence of Edmund L. Starling, Oct. 9, 1845, aged about 16 years. OR 10/18.

Walter B. Todd, son of the Hon. David Todd, of Columbia, Mo. Died Sept. 26, 1845, aged 26 years. OR 10/25.

Mrs. Jane Todd, wife of Major Thomas Todd, of Shelby county. Died Oct. 16, 1845, aged 24 years. OR 10/25.

William Hickman, of Bourbon county. Died October 18, 1845, aged 53 years. OR 10/25.

E. S. Thomas, of Cincinnati. Died Oct. 28, 1845, aged 71 years. Obituary in OR 10/29.

Mrs. Mary E. Hicks, wife of Robert Hicks, of Fayette county. Died Oct. 21, 1845, aged 45 years. OR 10/29.

Mrs. Jane S. Harris, relict of John Harris, Sr. Died in Frankfort on October 24, 1845, aged 70 years. OR 11/1.

General Henry Lee, of Mason county. Died October 24, 1845, aged 90 years. OR 11/1.

Mrs. Ann Elizabeth Howard, consort of James Howard, of Montgomery county and daughter of the late Thomas T. Skillman, of Lexington. Died October 29, 1845. OR 11/1.

Elizabeth Mary, daughter of Jonathan D. and Sarah Hager, of Fayette county. Died Oct. 31, 1845, aged 4 years and 3 months. OR 11/5.

Miss Melissa, daughter of Richard H. Chinn, of New Orleans. She died at the Gault House, in Louisville, Ky., October 22, 1845, aged 17 years. OR 11/5.

Mrs. Almira Craig, consort of E. W. Craig, of Lexington. Died Wednesday Nov. 5, 1845. OR 11/8.

Ann Lucinda, daughter of John C. and Elizabeth Noble, of Louisville. Died Nov. 5, 1845, aged 3 years and 6 months. OR 11/12.

William Patterson, a student at Georgetown College. Died Nov. 3, 1845, aged 17 years. OR 11/12.

Malnor G. Coons, of Maysville. Died Nov. 10, 1845, aged 25 years. See obituary in OR 11/15.

Mrs. Mary Russell, relict of John Russell, of Lexington. Died Saturday Nov. 15, 1845. OR 11/19.

Mr. N. M. Bacon, of Owen county. Died at Owenton, Nov. 14, 1845. OR 11/19.

Martha Ann, infant daughter of Mr. J. T. Davidson. Died Saturday Nov. 15, 1845. OR 11/22.

William M. Brand, of Lexington. Died Saturday Nov. 22, 1845; see obituary in OR 11/26.

Elizabeth, only child of Dr. T. D. and Mary Elliot. Died in Washington county, Miss., Nov. 2, 1845, aged 23 years. OR 11/26.

John J. Young, eldest son of William D. Young, of Woodford county. Died Nov. 13, 1845, aged 32 years. OR 11/26.

George William, infant son of John T. and Jane Garrett Nolan, of West Baton Rouge, La. Died Nov. 5, 1845. OR 11/26.

John Carty, Sr., of Lexington. He was a native of New Jersey, an early emigrant to Kentucky, and soldier in Wayne's campaign. He died in Lexington, Ky., Nov. 25, 1845, aged 83 years. OR 11/29.

John W. Boyle, son of the late Judge Boyle, of Fayette county. Died Nov. 25, 1845, aged 30 years. See obituary in OR 11/29.

Mrs. Ann M. Letcher, consort of Dr. William R. Letcher, of Richmond, Ky., and daughter of Gen. Hugh White, of Clay county. Died Nov. 26, 1845. OR 12/3.

Mrs. Nancy Basye, of Bourbon county. Died at the residence of her daughter, Nov. 20, 1845, aged 80 years. She had been a resident of Bourbon county more than 50 years. OR 12/3.

John Holton, constable of Bracken county. Killed at Brooksville, Monday Nov. 30, 1845, by James Hamilton. OR 12/3.

Nathaniel P. Long, of Lexington. Died Dec. 7, 1845. OR 12/13.

Major William S. Dallam, of Lexington; a native of Maryland, but resident of Lexington for nearly 40 years. Died Wednesday Dec. 10, 1845, aged 73 years. OR 12/13.

1845-46

Jesse Lamme, of Fayette county. Died Friday Dec. 12, 1845, aged 73 years. OR 12/17.

Miss Jane McKinney, of Versailles. Died Dec. 12, 1845. OR 12/20.

Mrs. Hannah McKinney, relict of Capt. John McKinney, of Versailles. Died Dec. 16, 1845, aged 85 years. She came to Kentucky before Lexington was laid out as a town. OR 12/20.

Mrs. Sarah Ward, of Lexington, consort of the late Rev. John Ward, and daughter of the late Thomas Clifton, of Philadelphia. She had been a resident of Lexington for 30 years. Died Wednesday Dec. 10, 1845, aged 63 years. OR 12/20.

Mark Peterson, of South Carolina, a member of the Medical Class. Died Thursday Dec. 18, 1845, aged 23 years. (Presume this to mean . . . of Transylvania University.) OR 12/20.

Mrs. Frances R. Smith, consort of Thomas P. Smith, of Paris. Died Wednesday Dec. 17, 1845. OR 12/24.

James Little, of Charleston, South Carolina. Died in Lexington, Kentucky, December 26, 1845. OR 12/27.

Miss Lavina B. Flournoy, daughter of Major T. B. Flournoy. Died at the Woodford county residence of her grandfather, E. M. Blackburn, Dec. 25, 1845. OR 1/3/1846.

Mary Ann, daughter of Daniel Allen, of Havilandsville, Ky. Died Dec. 30, 1845. OR 1/7/1846.

Augustus W. Hughes, only son of Jacob Hughes, of Fayette county. Died Dec. 12, 1845, aged about 27 years. OR 1/7/1846.

Miss Susan G. McKinney, of Versailles. Died Thursday Jan. 8, 1846. OR 1/10.

Lewis Reese, infant son of Dr. H. B. Bascom. Died Monday Jan. 5, 1846, aged 7 weeks. OR 1/10.

Amanda, wife of Capt. Joseph Hearne, of near Leesburg. Died Jan. 8, 1846. OR 1/14.

Samuel Bullock, infant son of Rev. J. G. and S. B. Simrall, of Fayette county. Died Jan. 8, 1846, aged 6 months. OR 1/14.

Miss Eliza, daughter of Mr. L. Chamberlin, of Verona, New York. Died at Lexington, Ky., at the residence of Hugh B. Payne, Thursday, Jan. 16, 1846. OR 1/17.

John G. Campbell, formerly of Lexington. Died in Shelbyville, Jan. 6, 1846. OR 1/24.

Mrs. Mary Ann Wallace, consort of John H. Wallace, of Frankfort, and daughter of William Hickey, of Fayette county. Died Jan. 15, 1846. OR 1/24.

Lucien Wingate, of New Orleans, son of H. Wingate, of Frankfort, Ky. Died at the former place Jan. 3, 1846, aged 26 years. He was buried at Frankfort. OR 1/24.

Mrs. Frances Kidd, widow of the late Edward Kidd. Died Jan. 14, 1846, aged 65 years. OR 1/24.

Henry M. Horine, a native of Jessamine county for several years a resident of Lexington. Died Saturday Jan. 10, 1846, aged 24 years. Buried in Jessamine county Sunday Jan. 11, 1846. OR 1/24.

Mrs. Elizabeth, consort of George H. Ketchum, and only surviving daughter of the late George T. Cotton. Died at the residence, near Versailles, of her mother at 30 minutes past 12 o'clock, Jan. 15, 1846. OR 1/24.

LeGrand, only child of Richard Higgins, of Lexington. Died Jan. 27, 1846, aged about 2 years. OR 1/28.

Mary, infant daughter of John and Josephine Lutz, of Fayette county. Died Jan. 25, 1846. OR 1/28.

Rev. William Hickman, of Franklin county. Died Dec. 24, 1845, aged 78 years. OR 1/28.

Dr. Willis Webb. Died in New Orleans. Buried at Georgetown, Ky. See notice in OR 1/31.

James Logan, of Shelby county. Died Monday Jan. 19, 1846, at an advanced age. OR 1/31.

Thomas H. Kane, son of Thomas Kane, of Louisville. Killed in a duel, at New Orleans, fought with a Mr. Hyman, an Englishman. Died Jan 21, 1846. Buried at Louisville, Ky., OR 2/4.

F. B. Geohegan, M. D., of Trimble county, Ky. A graduate of Transylvania University; married in Trimble county. Died in Lexington, Jan. 28, 1846. OR 2/7.

Mrs. Catherine L. White, consort of Col. William F. White, of Montgomery county, Ky. Died in the vicinity of Nashville, Tenn., Jan. 26, 1846, leaving her husband and four small children. OR 2/7.

Euclid L. Johnson, a native of Kentucky. Died near Little Rock, Ark., Jan. 13, 1846, aged 40 years. OR 2/7.

Mrs. Mary G. Pope, consort of William F. Pope, and daughter of the late Major Nicholas Peay. Died near Little Rock, Ark., Jan. 9, 1846, aged 25 years. OR 2/7.

Nathaniel Guthrie, of Fayette county. *A soldier in the Revolution.* Died Jan. 14, 1846, aged 83 years. OR 2/11.

Conrad Cornelison, of Clarke county. *A soldier in the Revolution.* Died Jan. 26, 1846, aged 84 years. OR 2/11.

Mrs. Lucy P. Todd, only surviving sister of Mrs. Madison. She married George S. Washington, nephew and one of the heirs of Gen. George Washington; she married, second time, Hon. Thomas Todd, of Kentucky, whom she survived for many years. She died Friday Jan. 30, 1846, at Megeville, Virginia, seat of her son, William Temple Washington. OR 2/11.

Samuel W. Chamberlain, member of the Law Department at Transylvania University. He was a native of Verona, N. Y. He died in Lexington, Ky., Feb. 9, 1846. OR 2/14.

Mrs. Martha L., consort of R. W. Downing, of Lexington. Died Feb. 6, 1846, aged 26 years. OR 2/14.

Col. John C. Rogers, a son of the late Jeremiah Rogers, and a native of Fayette county. Died in Fayetteville, Tenn., Jan. 31, 1846, aged 29 years. OR 2/14.

Ferdinand Frediricic, of Crab Orchard, Ky. Died Sunday Feb. 1, 1846. OR 2/14.

Mrs. Elizabeth Springle, of Lexington. Died Monday Feb. 9, 1846, at a very advanced age. OR 2/18.

James O'Mara, of Lexington, a native of Ireland. Died Friday, Feb. 13, 1846. OR 2/18.

Rev. Hardy M. Cryer, of Sumner county, Tenn. Died Feb. 7, 1846. OR 2/18.

Milton Mills, Representative from Wayne county to the Kentucky State Legislature. Died in Frankfort, Feb. 20, 1846, aged 36 years. OR 2/25.

Mrs. Catherine Jane Ellis, consort of H. C. Ellis, and daughter of Evans Price, of Fayette county. Died Monday Feb. 23, 1846. OR 2/25.

Mrs. Sarah Taylor, relict of George Taylor, of Clarke county, and daughter of Jacob and Phebe Fishback. Died Wednesday Feb. 11, 1846, aged 59 years. OR 2/25.

Mrs. Frances M. Taylor, of Clarke county. Died Wednesday Feb. 18, 1846, aged 36 years. OR 2/25.

Capt. Samuel Fitch, of Lexington. Died Thursday Feb. 26, 1846, aged 54 years. OR 2/28.

William Isles, of Bath county. Drowned near Licking, in February, 1846. OR 3/4.

Capt. Chauncey B. Shepard, of Lewis county. Died Feb. 25, 1846, aged about 55 years. OR 3/4.

Captain James Ward, of Mason county. A pioneer of that county. Died at his residence near Washington, Ky., in February, 1846. OR 3/4.

Mrs. Elizabeth Jacob. Died near Columbia, Mo., Feb. 21, 1846, aged 94 years. OR 3/11.

Henry Vawters, an old citizen of Franklin county. Died Saturday, March 7, 1846. Coroner's verdict: suicide by hanging. OR 3/14.

Edward Davis, of Christian county. Killed in May, 1845, by Alonzo Pennington. See story in OR 3/14.

John Ellis, of Glasgow, Ky. Died Mar. 10, 1846, aged about 25 years. OR 3/18.

Mrs. Anna Mary Boyer, of Lexington, Died Mar. 6, 1846, aged 78 years. OR 3/18.

Mrs. Ann Grace, daughter of Capt. Andrew Harper. Died in March, 1846, in St. Louis. OR 3/21.

Catherine, daughter of Dr. Samuel B. Richardson, formerly of Lexington. Died in Louisville, Sunday Mar. 15, 1846. OR 3/21.

Mrs. Helen D. Peck, consort of Dr. Peck. Died near Vicksburg, Tenn., Mar. 5, 1846. OR 3/25.

Miss Ann Jouett, daughter of the late Matthew Jouett. Died at the Lexington residence of her mother, Saturday Mar. 21, 1846. OR 4/25.

Michael Salter, of Garrard county. *A soldier of the Revolution.* Died in Lancaster, Mar 8, 1846, aged 92 years. OR 3/28.

Archibald P. Williams, of Rapides Parrish, and a native of Kentucky. Died Mar. 22, 1846, at an advanced age. OR 4/1.

Mrs. Martha Tutt, consort of James N. Tutt, of Winchester. Died in Lexington, at the residence of Samuel Long, Thursday Apr. 2, 1846. OR 4/4.

Miss Eliza, daughter of Charles B. Lewis, of Scott county. Died March 25, 1846, age 18 years. OR 4/4.

Gen. W. Lee D. Ewing, Auditor of Public Accounts of Illinois. Died at Springfield, Mar. 25, 1846, age 52 years. OR 4/18.

Elmira, infant daughter of Charles Coolidge, of Lexington. Died Monday Apr. 6, 1846. OR 4/8.

Mrs. Julia Ann Hughes, consort of Thomas Hughes, of Fayette county. Died Mar. 18, 1846, aged 36 years. OR 4/8.

Reason H. Dorsey, of Fayette county. Died Mar. 31, 1846, aged 71 years. OR 4/8.

Joseph Allen, of Scott county. Died Mar. 29, 1846, aged about 50 years. OR 4/18.

Beverly Murphy, of Louisville. Suicided Apr. 10, 1846. OR 4/15.

Mrs. Elizabeth Kay, consort of Robert Kay, of Fayette county. Died Mar. 24, 1846, aged 63 years. See obituary in OR 4/15.

Rev. William R. Preston, of Clarke county. Died Apr. 9, 1846. OR 4/15.

Thomas Downton, formerly of Fayette county. Died at his residence in the vicinity of Danville, Apr. 8, 1846, aged 63 years. OR 4/15.

Wesley W. Keas, formerly of Clarke county, Ky. Died at his residence on Brown's Prairie, Ill., March 25, 1846. He was 57 years of age. OR 4/15.

Mrs. Jane S. Higgins, consort of Dr. W. M. Higgins, of Lafayette county, Mo. Died Mar. 27, 1846, aged 36 years. OR 4/15.

Mrs. Elizabeth Milton, consort of William E. Milton, of Lexinton. Died Tuesday Apr. 14, 1846, aged 34 years. Funeral from their residence on Main Street, Wednesday morning, April 15, 1846. OR 4/15.

Mrs. Nancy A. Kidd, of Lexington. Her funeral took place Wednesday morning April 15, 1846 from the residence of Samuel A. Kidd, the service by the Rev. Thomas P. Dudley. OR 4/15.

R. North Todd, formerly of Fayette county, Ky., and son of the late General Levi Todd. Died at his residence near Columbia, Mo., April 11, 1846. OR 4/22

John Hart, Sr., of Fayette county. Died Apr. 20, 1846, aged 74 years. OR 4/25.

Mrs. Mary H., wife of James S. Jacoby, of Maysville. Died Thursday Apr. 23, 1846, aged 29 years. OR 4/25.

John Trimble, late Clerk of the Carter Circuit Court. He died at Grayson, Carter county, April 16, 1846, aged 49 years. OR 4/29.

Alfred Z. Boyer, of Frankfort. Died there Thursday Apr. 30, 1846. Buried in Episcopal Burying Ground at Lexington. OR 5/2.

Francis W. Ellis, eldest son of Capt. Thomas O. and Mary L. W. Ellis, of Stamping Ground, Scott county, Ky. Died May 1, 1846, aged 18 years. OR 5/6.

Mrs. Nancy Pigg, consort of Lewis Pigg, of South Broadway, Lexington. Died Tuesday, May 5, 1846. OR 5/6.

Miss George Ann Montgomery, daughter of William Montgomery. Died at the Lexington residence of her brother-in-law, Dr. John B. Payne, Tuesday May 5, 1846. OR 5/6.

Mrs. Anne Hennen Jessup, wife of Gen. Thomas S. Jessup, of the United States Army, and daughter of the late Major William Croghan, of Kentucky. Died in Washington, D. C., Apr. 24, 1846. OR 5/6.

John Somerville, of Nashville. Died Apr. 26, 1846, aged 76 years. OR 5/6.

Catherine, daughter of William S. D. Megowan, formerly of Lexington. Died in Bowling Green, Apr. 24, 1846, aged 5 years and 10 months. OR 5/9.

Elijah W. Craig, Jr., late of Lexington, Ky. Died in New Orleans, Tuesday Apr. 28, 1846. Buried in Woodford county, Ky., in May. See obituary in OR 5/9.

Norman Tankersley, son of Fountain Tankersley, of Lexington. Drowned Saturday May 9, 1846. He was a student of the City School. OR 5/6.

F. D. Pettit, formerly of Frankfort, Ky. Died in Columbus, Iowa, in May, 1846. OR 5/16.

Mrs. Martha D. January, wife of Samuel F. January, of Cynthiana. Died May 9, 1846, aged 28 years. OR 5/20.

Mrs. Susan W., consort of Gen. Bushrod T. Boswell, of Leesburg, Harrison county, and daughter of George A. Smith, of Bourbon county. Died May 7, 1846, aged 28 years. OR 5/20

Peter Hull Keiser, son of Benjamin C. Keiser, of Lexington. Died Wednesday May 20, 1846, aged 10 years. OR 5/23.

Mrs. Catherine Emison, of Scott county. Died May 6, 1846, aged 44 years. OR 5/23.

Mr. W. S. Jones, of Bourbon county. Died May 15, 1846, aged 62 years. OR 5/23

Thomas Bryan, son of Enoch Bryan. Died Wednesday May 20, 1846, aged 23 years. He "had been married but nine months to an amiable lady of Fayette county." OR 5/27.

Mrs. Rebecca Davis, wife of Henry C. Davis. Died in New Orleans, May 11, 1846. Buried in the Episcopal Grave Yard at Lexington on May 22, 1846. OR 5/20.

Capt. John Whitehead, Sr., of Claysville, Harrison county, Ky. Died May 12, 1846, aged 81 years. OR 6/3.

David H. Weigart, of Lexington. Died Sunday May 31, 1846, while drilling as a volunteer in Capt. Beard's Company. He was an old man. OR 6/3.

Mrs. Ana Ellen Rust, of Lexington. Died Mar. 23, 1846. See obituary in OR 6/3.

Hon. John J. Marshall, of near Louisville. Died Wednesday June 3, 1846. See story in OR 6/6.

Martha Laura, youngest daughter of Dr. John T. Lewis, of Lexington. Died Thursday May 28, 1846, aged 6 years, 2 months and 11 days. OR 6/6.

Margaret Virginia, infant daughter of William B. and Catherine S. E. Emmal. Died Sunday June 7, 1846. OR 6/10.

Patterson Bain, of Lexington. Died Sunday June 7, 1846, aged 70 years. He was a native of Maryland; came to Lexington with his widowed mother when he was 12 years of age. See obituary for further details of his life. OR 6/10 and 6/13.

Joel Johnson, of Lexington. Died June 16, 1846. See his obituary in OR 6/17.

Mrs. Catherine E. Sheppard, consort of Dr. H. H. Sheppard, of Fayette county. Died Friday June 19, 1846. OR 6/20.

Bartlett Haggard, of Clarke county. *He was at the battle of Yorktown, and witnessed the surrender of Cornwallis,* being then a lad of 16 years. He died May 18, 1846, aged 82 years and three months. OR 6/20.

Thomas J. Warner, of Lexington. Died June 8, 1846, leaving a wife and 1 child. OR 6/24.

Mrs. Margaret Johnson, mother of Ex-Chief Justice Robertson, of Lexington. Died at the Frankfort residence of her son-in-law, Ex-Governor Robert P. Letcher, Saturday June 13, 1846. OR 6/17.

A. B. Richardson, son of Capt. Thomas Richardson, of Madison county., and one of the Company of Cavalry, from Madison county, commanded by Capt. Stone. Died in Louisville, Saturday June 20, 1846. OR 6/27.

Mary Rebecca, infant daughter of Charles Wheatly, of Lexington. Died Thursday July 2, 1846. OR 7/4.

Julia Craig, only child of J. W. and Laura H. Craig, of Louisville. Died Tuesday June 30, 1846, aged 7 years. OR 7/4.

Charles Clarendon, son of Dr. Henry J. Peck, of Lexington. Died July 10, 1846, aged 7 years. OR 7/5.

Mrs. Sarah Cooper, of Ray county, Mo., relict of Captain Joseph Cooper, of Scott county, Ky. Died at Lexington, Ky., residence of Mrs. Hansbro, July 9, 1846, aged 51 years. OR 7/18.

John Tillitte, of Clarke county. Died July 15, 1846, aged 86 years. OR 7/18.

Labon Smith, formerly of Snow Hill, Maryland. Died at the Lexington City Hospital and Work House on July 16, 1846, aged 82 years. *He was a soldier in the Revolution.* OR 7/18.

Jose Debare, commonly called Jesse Devary, of Clarke county. He was a native of Havana, and a Spanish soldier in New Orleans when Louisiana belonged to Spain. He died July, 1846, aged about 104 years. OR 7/18.

Col. Thomas A. Russell, of Fayette county. Died Monday evening July 20, 1846, see obituuary in OR 7/22.

Mrs. Arabella Kohlhass, wife of Theodore Kohlhass, and daughter of James W. Keith. Died in Winchester, Monday July 20, 1846, aged 26 years and 10 months. OR 7/29.

Mrs. Elizabeth W., consort of Francis J. Keen, of Arkansas. Died at Lexington, Ky., at the residence of Richard Higgins, Sunday Aug. 2, 1846. OR 8/5.

George Blackford, son of Judge Isaac Blackford, of Indiana. Died at Mrs. Layton's, in Lexington, Ky., Sunday August 2, 1846, aged 24 years. OR 8/5.

Nathan Crane, of Lexington. Died Aug. 3, 1846. OR 8/5.

Francis D. Bonfils, son of Dr. S. F. and Martha D. Bonfils, of St. Louis. Died in Lexington, Ky., Aug. 7, 1846, aged 21 months. OR 8/12.

John, infant son of Isaac Cook, of Lexington. Died Aug. 9, 1846. OR 8/12.

Mrs. Prudence Morton, wife of Henry C. Morton, of Louisville. Died at the Woodford county residence of her son, Dr. C. J. Blackburn, August 8, 1846. OR 8/15.

Miss Harriet Emeline Shy. Died at the Fayette county residence of her brother, Samuel Shy, Aug. 16, 1846, aged 20 years. OR 8/19.

Victor Carr, son of Dr. William Carr Lane, of St. Louis, Died at the Phoenix Hotel, Lexington, Aug. 18, 1846, aged 15 years. OR 8/19.

William Tandy Bush, 1st Sergeant of the Clarke (County) Company of Volunteers. He died at Labaco Bay, Texas, July 25, 1846, aged 22 years. He left his young wife and 2 small children. He was the son of Colonel P. Bush. OR 8/19.

Paul Allen Prewitt, son of Gen. W. C. Prewitt. Died Aug. 19, 1846, aged 18 years. OR 8/22.

Mrs. Mary A. Holley, widow of the Rev. Dr. Holley, late President of Transylvania University. Died August 2, 1846, aged 60 years. See long obituary in OR 8/22.

John Lyle, Sr., of Fayette county. Died Aug. 6, 1846, aged 79 years. He was a native of Virginia, and came to Kentucky about 50 years ago. He married a Miss Tompkins. OR 8/19 and 8/22. This Miss Tompkins was a sister of Judge Tompkins.

Martin D. H. Wickliffe, son of Nathaniel Wickliffe, of Bardstown. Died Aug. 16, 1846, aged 22 years. OR 8/29.

Daniel E. Jones, late Representative from Jefferson county. Died Aug. 24, 1846. OR 8/29.

Mrs. Martha C. Hart, consort of Thomas M. Hart, of Montgomery county, Ky. Died at the Fayette county residence of her father, Captain John Cavins, August 16, 1846, aged 32 years. OR 8/29.

Ellen Ross, daughter of John Estess, of Lexington. Died Tuesday Aug. 25, 1846, aged 2 years. OR 8/29.

Benjamin Smith, of Louisville. Died Sept. 4, 1846. OR 9/5.

Mary Ellen, infant daughter of George Stoll, of Lexinton. Died Sept. 3, 1846. OR 9/5.

George Gaines, formerly of Fayette county. Died in Scott county, Thursday Sept. 3, 1846. OR 9/5.

William B. Oldham, a native of Lexington, Ky. Died at the residence of his mother, in Palmyra, Mo., Aug. 26, 1846. OR 9/5.

Robert Tevis, of Shelby county. Died Aug. 25, 1846, aged 95 years. OR 9/5.

Dr. Alexander H. Innes, of Claysville, Harrison county. Died Sept. 7, 1846. See account in OR 9/12.

John Vanmeter, son of Abram Vanmeter, of Fayette county. Died Friday Sept. 4, 1846, aged 19 years. OR 9/9.

Mrs. S. C. Plunket, consort of W. F. Plunket, of Lexington. Died Saturday Sept. 4, 1846, aged 19 years. OR 9/9.

Mrs. Polly Coulter, consort of Joseph Coulter, of Scott county, and daughter of the late Thomas Barry, of Clarke county. Died Sept. 8, 1846, aged 61 years. OR 9/12.

Samuel Daniel Breck, son of the Hon. Daniel Breck, of Madison county, Ky. Died Aug. 24, 1846, aged about 21 years. He died at St. Joseph, Mo., having but a short time previous emigrated there from Kentucky. OR 9/16.

Joseph, second son of John S. and Mary C. Todhunter. Died Thursday September 17, 1846, age 1 year, 2 months, and 15 days. OR 9/23.

James E., eldest son of Gray Briggs, of near Benton, Miss. Died Sept. 1, 1846, aged 7 years. OR 9/23.

James Robertson, Register of the Land Office of Kentucky. Died in Frankfort Friday Sept. 18, 1846, aged 64 years. OR 9/26.

Nicholas Brindley, of Bourbon county. Died Sept. 17, 1846. OR 9/26.

Mrs. Ann, consort of John Vimont, of Millersburg. Died Sept. 23, 1846. OR 9/26.

Col. Cyrus Stark, a member of the Bar, and a native of Bourbon county, Ky. Died in Palmyra, Mo., Sept. 10, 1846. OR 9/26.

Martin Duralde, son of Martin Duralde, of New Orleans, and grandson of the Hon. Henry Clay. Died in Philadelphia, Sept. 17, 1846, aged 23 years. OR 9/30.

John Land, Sr., of Madison county. *A soldier in the Revolution.* Died Sept. 22, 1846, aged 93 years. OR 10/7.

Miss Ann Maria Bosworth, daughter of David H. Bosworth, of Fayette county. Died Friday Oct. 9, 1846. OR 10/14.

William Whestly, of Henderson county. Died Oct. 3, 1846. OR 10/14.

Capt. Newbold Crockett, of Fayette county. Died Oct. 16, 1846, at an advanced age. OR 10/17.

Mrs. Matilda C. Hanson, consort of Samuel Hanson, of Winchester. Died Oct. 9, 1846, aged 46 years. OR 10/17.

Hon. William L. Kelly. Died at Springfield, Ky., at the residence of his son, Charles Kelly, Sept. 22, 1846, aged 78 years. He was the Judge of the Springfield Judicial Court. OR 10/17.

Mrs. Ann M. Sudduth, consort of William L. Sudduth, of Bath county, and youngest daughter of George Howard, of Mount Sterling. Died at the latter place, Oct. 9, 1846, aged 26 years. See obituary in OR 10/21.

Dr. Charles C. Frazer, of Woodford county. Died Monday Oct. 19, 1846, at an advanced age. OR 10/21.

Lieut. T. J. Chambers, Leander Ford and J. S. Johnson, all of the Frankfort (Ky.) Volunteers. The first two died at Camargo, the last at Monterey. OR 10/24.

Fortunatus Cosby, Sr., of Louisville, former Judge of the Jefferson Circuit Court. Died Oct. 19, 1846, aged 81 years. OR 10/24.

Mrs. Ann Hutchinson, consort of James E. Hutchinson, of Fayette county. Died Oct. 20, 1846. OR 10/24.

Lieut. Col. Alexander K. McClung, of the Mississippi Volunteers. He was a native of Mason county, Ky. Killed during Mexican War in 1846. OR 10/28.

Samuel Scott, of Woodford county. Died Sunday Sept. 27, 1846. See obituary in OR 10/28.

Isaac Sprake, of Scott county. Died Monday Oct. 26, 1846. He was formerly a resident of Lexington. OR 10/28.

Mrs. Ann Hunter, consort of John J. Hunter, of Lexinton, and daughter of John R. Campbell, of Mt. Sterling. Died Oct. 23, 1846, aged 21 years. OR 10/28.

Mrs. Sarah McDowell, of Boyle county. She was the eldest daughter of the late Governor Shelby. Died Friday Oct. 16, 1846. OR 10/31.

Mrs. Eliza M. Chinn, consort of R. H. Chinn, of New Orleans, and formerly of Lexington, Ky. Died at Galveston, Texas, Oct. 3, 1846. OR 10/31.

William H. January, of Cincinnati. Died Wednesday Nov. 4, 1846, aged 29 years. OR 11/7.

Miss Sarah Elizabeth, daughter of John Applegate, of Georgetown. Died Oct. 28, 1846, aged 22 years. OR 11/7.

William Kemper, of Montgomery county. Died Oct. 30, 1846, aged 82 years. OR 11/7.

Nelson Thomasson, of Scott county. Died Oct. 17, 1846, at an advanced age. OR 11/14.

Samuel Benton, of San Augustine City, Texas. Died Sept. 29, 1846, aged about 60 years. He was the youngest and last brother of the Hon. Thomas H. Benton. OR 11/18.

Major Moses V. Grant, of Kentucky. Died at Port Lavacca, October 5, 1846. OR 11/21.

John Fisher, of Louisville. Died Nov. 17, 1846. OR 11/21.

Mrs. Louisa C. Lawson, consort of Prof. L. M. Lawson, of Lexington. Died Nov. 20, 1846, aged 34 years. OR 11/25.

John M. Huggins, son of Thomas Huggins, of Lexington. Died in Nicholasville, Sunday Nov. 22, 1846. OR 11/25.

Mrs. C. Harper, relict of Mr. Harper, of Lexington, former cashier of the U. S. Bank. Died Nov. 25, 1846, aged 66 years. OR 11/28.

Richard Vawter. Died Nov. 26, 1846, at an advanced age. OR 11/28.

Edwin E. Berry, of Fayette county. Died Sunday Nov. 22, 1846. OR 11/28.

Sabert Offutt, of Scott county. Died Nov. 18, 1846. OR 11/28.

Thomas Faulconer, of Fayette county. Died Sunday, Nov. 29, 1846, at an advanced age. OR 12/2.

Enoch Benton, of Montgomery county. A volunteer in the Mexican War. Died at Camargo, Mexico, Oct. 22, 1846, aged 18 years. OR 12/5.

Mrs. Elizabeth, consort of Mr. L. P. Young, of Lexington, and daughter of the late Benjamin Field. Died Dec 9, 1846. OR 12/16.

Mrs. S. Q. J. Warren, consort of Dr. T. B. Warren, and daughter of William Z. Thomson, of Fayette county. Died Dec. 16, 1846. OR 12/19.

Horace Coleman, of Fayette county. A native of Spottsylvania county, Va. Came to Kentucky when he was a youth. He died Friday, December 18, 1846, aged 56 years. OR 12/23.

OBITUARIES

The abbreviations used denote:
KG—(Lexington) *Kentucky Gazette*
OR—Lexington (Ky.) *Observer & Reporter*

1847

William J. Higgins, of Montgomery county, Ala., a student at Translyvania University. Died Thursday, Dec. 31, 1846. OR 1/2/1847.

Mrs. America Porter, consort of Thomas P. Porter. Died Dec. 26, 1846, aged 23 years. OR 1/9/1847.

Oliver Gaines, of Bourbon county. Died Jan. 1, 1847, aged 30 years. OR 1/9.

Charles H. Seales, died Dec. 31, 1846. OR 1/9/1847.

Mrs. Mary Theobald, wife of G. P. Theobald, of Lexington. Died Jan. 6, 1847, aged 53 years. OR 1/9.

Mrs. Sarah Rochester. Died at the Danville residence of her son, Charles H. Rochester, Jan. 2, 1847, at an advanced age. OR 1/13.

Mrs. Elizabeth Goode, of Lincoln county. Died Dec. 26, 1846, aged 102 years, 9 months and 14 days. OR 1/13.

Thomas Cook, of Fayette county. Died in Frankfort, Jan. 8, 1847, aged 53 years. OR 1/16.

John T. Campbell, of Lexington. Died Jan. 10, 1847. OR 1/16.

Hon. James Slaughter, of Nelson county. Died Dec. 25, 1846, aged 82 years. OR 1/16/1847.

William H. Suddith, a volunteer in Capt. Milam's Company. Died at the Barracks, in New Orleans, in December, 1846. OR 1/16/47.

William Newton, a volunteer in Capt. Milam's Company. Died at the Camp opposite Camargo, Dec. 4, 1846. OR 1/16/1847.

Capt. James Jones, of Scott county. *A soldier in the Revolution.* Died Jan. 1, 1847, aged about 88 years. OR 1/16.

Agnes Ophelia, daughter of Dr. J. W. Bradford, of Georgetown. Died Jan. 10, 1847. OR 1/16.

Alice, infant daughter of L. B. and Sarah Rhoton, of Danville. Died Jan. 9, 1847, aged 1 year 6 months and 2 days. OR 1/20.

Col. John Moseley, of Jessamine county. Died Jan. 9, 1847, aged 81 years and a few days. He was a native of Virginia, and emigrated to Kentucky in 1776. See long obituary in OR 1/27.

Mrs. Henry Gilbert. Died Thursday, Jan. 21, 1847, at an advanced age. OR 1/23.

Dr. William J. Chenault, a volunteer in Capt. Stone's Company from Madison county. Died Sept. 16, 1846. OR 1/23/1847.

McKenzie Coyle, a volunteer in Capt. Stone's Company from Madison county. Died at Camargo, Dec. 12, 1846. OR 1/23/1847.

James, infant son of Joseph and Panthea Scrugham. Died Friday, Jan. 22, 1847. OR 1/23.

Samuel Downing, of Fayette county. Died at the residence of his son, Richard Downing, Friday, Jan. 29, 1847, at an advanced age. OR 1/30.

Mrs. Maria A. Cotton, consort of George T. Cotton, of Woodford county, and a daughter of R. C. Jackson. Died Jan. 17, 1847. OR 1/30.

James William Oots, son of Sampson Oots, of Lexington. Died Jan. 23, 1847, aged 16 years. OR 1/30.

George W., infant son of George W. and Susan M. Tabor, of Scott county. Died Wednesday Jan. 27, 1847, aged 37 days. OR 1/30.

Richard H. Chinn, formerly of Lexington. Died Wednesday Jan. 13, 1847, in the Parrish of Tensas, La. His body, and that of his wife, whose death had taken place some time before, were brought to Kentucky for interment. OR 2/3/1847.

Mrs. Richard H. Chinn. See above.

Mrs. Mary B. Slaughter, wife of J. H. Slaughter, of Woodford county, and daughter of Mrs. Lucy Weisiger, of Frankfort. Died in Woodford county, Jan. 29, 1847. OR 2/3.

Mrs. Grundy, relict, of the late Hon. Felix Grundy, of Nashville, Tenn. Died Jan 27, 1847. OR 2/3.

Mrs. Anna Maria Wharton, wife of Dr. William A. Wharton, of Richmond, Madison Parrish, La., and daughter of J. B. Harbin, of Lexington, Ky. Died Jan. 7, 1847, aged 26 years. OR 2/3 and 2/6.

James M. Frily, a corporal in Capt. Clay's Company of Mexican War Volunteers. Died near Camp Camargo, Dec. 16, 1847. Story in OR 2/6/47.

Mary Tilford, daughter of Thomas H. Hunt. Died Thursday, Feb. 4, 1847, aged about 11 years. OR 2/6.

Joseph H. Clay, of Bourbon county. Died Jan. 25, 1847, aged 42 years. OR 2/6.

John Smith. Died at Fayette county residence of his son-in-law, Solomon Rice, Saturday, Feb. 6, 1847, aged 82 years. OR 2/13.

James McDaniel, of Lexington. Died Feb. 16, 1847, aged 27 years. OR 2/20.

Lucretia Boon, infant daughter of James McDaniel, of Lexington (see above). Died Tuesday Feb. 16, 1847, aged 4 months. OR 2/20.

James Fair, of Lexington, Ky., a native of Bedford county, Va. He was a soldier "in the late war with Great Britain and a spy attached to Gen. Anthony Wayne's army." He died Feb. 10, 1847, aged 80 years. OR 2/24.

Joseph C. Price, son of Major D. B. Price. Died at Nicholasville, Feb. 18, 1847. OR 2/24.

Mrs. Mary A. Duke, wife of Capt. N. W. Duke, of the United States Navy. Died at the Bruen House, in Lexington, Feb. 24, 1847. OR 2/27.

Foster Collins, of Bourbon county. Died Feb. 22, 1847, aged 70 years. OR 2/27.

William, infant son of Zachariah and Jemima Herndon, of Henry county. Died at the Lexington residence of Henry Foster, Feb. 26, 1847, aged 4 months and 2 days. OR 2/27.

Mrs. Theodosia Raney. Died at the residence of her son-in-law, D. L. Zimmerman, Feb. 15, 1847, aged 66 years. OR 2/27.

Mrs. Elizabeth Ann Hollis, consort of Berry Hollis, of Jessamine county. Died March 5, 1847, aged 24 years. OR 3/13.

Mrs. Sophia Busby, consort of John Busby, of Richmond. Died Friday March 5, 1847. OR 3/13.

Miss Mary Matilda Barkley, daughter of James Barkley, of Fleming county. Died in Jessamine county, Friday Mar. 1847, aged 17 years. OR 3/17.

William F. Brown, son of ex-Senator Brown of Fayette, Mo. Died in Lexington, Ky., Mar. 6, 1847. OR 3/17.

Dr. Richland Wantyn, of Louisville. Suicided Thursday Mar. 12, 1847. OR 3/17.

Roy Stuart, son of John G. Stuart, of Clarke county. Died Mar. 10, 1847, aged 21 years. OR 3/20.

Mrs. Patsey Porter, consort of Richard W. Porter, and daughter of Capt. John Smith, dec'd. Died Mar. 3, 1847, at the mouth of Raven Creek, in Harrison county. OR 3/20.

Capt. Michael Davidson, of Lincoln county. Died Mar. 9, 1847, aged 69 years. OR 3/20.

Octavius Goodloe, of Lexington. Died Monday Mar. 22, 1847. OR 3/24.

Mrs. Francis B. Miller, of Lexington. Died Monday Mar. 22, 1847. OR 3/24.

Mrs. Effie McArthur Allen, wife of Hon. William Allen, Senator from Ohio. Died in Washington City, March 13, 1847. OR 3/24.

Rev. Gilbert Kelly, of Covington. Died Saturday Mar. 6, 1847. See obituary in OR 3/24.

Joseph Downing, infant son of Lewis L. and Elizabeth L. Mason, of near Mt. Sterling. Died Mar. 17, 1847, aged about 4 months. OR 3/24.

Mrs. Mary Ann, consort of Dr. William B. Wood, of the Parish of Point Coupee, La. Died Mar. 5, 1847. OR 3/24.

Col. Josiah Davis, of Montgomery county. Died March 1, 1847, aged 50 years. OR 3/27.

Mrs. F. M. Chapman, wife of O. H. Chapman, of Lancaster, Ky. Died Mar. 1, 1847. OR 3/27.

Howell Anderson, infant son of John H. Hunter. Died Saturday Mar. 20, 1847, aged 7 months. OR 3/27.

Mrs. Rosamond Noble, wife of Thomas H. Noble, of Lexington. Died Monday Mar. 29, 1847. OR 3/31.

Florence, infant daughter of Dr. William A. Wharton, of Madison Parish, La. Died in Lexington, Ky., Mar. 27, 1847, aged 8 months. OR 4/3.

James S. Allan, eldest son of the Hon. Chilton Allan, of Winchester. Died Mar. 22, 1847, aged 33 years. Or 4/10.

John Boggs, of Madison county. A soldier in the Revolution. Died April 5, 1847, aged 89 years. OR 4/10.

Alfred Shelby infant son of William and Mary H. Voorheis, of Woodford county. Died Monday Apr. 5, 1847, aged 11 months. OR 4/10.

William R. McKee, Edward M. Vaughn, A. G. Morgan, and William W. Bayles. Died at the battle of Buena Vista, Feb. 23, 1847. See Resolutions of Davies and Nelson Lodge, No. 22 in OR 4/17.

Edmonia Ferguson, second daughter of L. C. and Martha Randall. Died Apr. 13, 1847, aged 6 years. OR 4/17.

Jesse Brown, long known as the proprietor of the Indian Queen Hotel, Washington City. Died Apr. 7, 1847. OR 4/17.

Mrs. Nancy, consort of John Gibson, of Fayette county. Died Apr. 13, 1847, aged 58 years. OR 4/17.

Joseph Carroll, of Jessamine county. Died Apr. 11, 1847, aged 71 years, 6 months and 9 days. OR 4/21.

Capt. John Price, of Clarke county. Died Apr. 2, 1847, aged 83 years. OR 4/21.

Dr. Edward B. Church, formerly of Lexington, Ky. Died at his residence, Greenville, Bachelor's Bend, Miss., in April, 1847. He left his widow and three children. OR 4/24.

Capt. William T. Willis and Harvey Trotter, of Jessamine county, Ky. Fell Feb. 22, 1847, at the battle of Buena Vista. OR 4/28.

Alice Elizabeth, daughter of H. B. and E. L. Ingles, of Fayette county. Died Sunday April 25, 1847. OR 4/28.

Joseph T. Thomasson, of Scott county. Died Apr. 10, 1847, aged 59 years. OR 4/28.

Mrs. Louisa Jane Russell, wife of Robert M. Russell, and daughter of James Watson, of Bourbon county. Died Apr. 22, 1847, aged 18 years. OR 4/27.

Richard Isaac, son of William G. Skillman. Died Tuesday, Apr. 27, 1847, aged 7 years, 6 months, and 13 days. OR 4/28.

Mrs. Clara H. Pike, of Boone county, Ky., widow of Gen. Zebulon M. Pike. Died Sunday Apr. 18, 1847, aged 65 years. OR 4/28.

Jacob Creath Karsner, son of Major J. Karsner, of Jessamine county. Died in Lexington Saturday Apr. 24, 1847. OR 4/28.

Elkanah K. Hendley, of Lexington. Died Monday April 26, 1847. He was a soldier in the Revolution. OR 4/28 and 5/1.

Major P. N. Barbour, of Franklin county. Died at Monterey during the Mexican War. Buried near Frankfort, Ky., Tuesday, May 11, 1847. OR 5/8.

Capt. William Gorham. Drowned just below Island 69. He was formerly a resident of Portland, Me. OR 5/8.

Mrs. Julia Humbert Droz. Died at the Lexington residence of Mrs. Mentelle, Thursday May 6, 1847, aged 84 years. OR 5/8.

John N. Cabell, formerly of Virginia. Died in Lexington, Ky., May 3, 1847, aged 42 years. OR 5/8.

Miss Mary Jane, daughter of Isaac Barkley. Died at the Jessamine county residence of her mother, Mrs. Jane Barkley, May 5, 1847, aged 12 years. OR 5/12.

Mrs. Elizabeth Allen, of Jessamine county. Died May 6, 1847, aged 70 years. OR 5/12.

Col. James W. Rice, of Bourbon county. Died May 11, 1847, aged 43 years. OR 5/15.

William H. Goddard, only son of Mrs. Judith Goddard, of Maysville. Died at Santa Fe, New Mexico, Feb. 25, 1847, aged 26 years. OR 5/15.

Loren Spencer, formerly of Lexington, Ky. Died at St. Louis, May 3, 1847. OR 5/15.

Capt. ——— Maxey, son of Gen. Rice Maxey, of Clinton county, Ky. Died May 6, 1847, in New Orleans. See story in OR 5/19.

Elisha Warfield Ford, son of Charles F. and Rebecca A. Ford. Died in Franklin county, Ky. May 18, 1847, aged 15 years. OR 5/22.

The following men, members of Capt. John S. Williams Company of Volunteers, from Clarke county, Ky., were killed during the Mexican War: Corporal William F. Elkin; Private William Durham, and Alfred H. Hatton. OR 5/19.

Capt. John W. Hickman, of Boyle county. Died Thursday May 20, 1847, aged 61 years. OR 5/22.

James W. Neale, of Madison county. A volunteer in the Mexican trouble. Died Thursday May 20, 1847, aged 25 years. See obituary in OR 5/26.

Mrs. Frances Jeretta, consort of Joel Hickman, and only daughter of Lieut. John Wilson, who fell at the Battle of Eutaw Springs, during the Revolution. She died in Clark county, May 22, 1847, aged 80 years. OR 5/26.

Mrs. Sally Carneal, wife of Thomas D. Carneal. Died in Cincinnati, Friday May 21, 1847. OR 5/26.

Mrs. Sarah Stanhope, wife of William Stanhope, and eldest daughter of Joseph Bowman, of Fayette county. She died Sunday May 23, 1847. OR 5/29.

Elisha Dickerson, of Winchester. Died May 23, 1847, aged 67 years. OR 5/29.

Mrs. Ann F., consort of Dr. F. W. Major. Died at the Bourbon county residence of her father, Thomas P. Smith, May 25, 1847, aged 24 years. OR 5/29.

William P., son of John A. and Catherine Willis, of Lexington. Died May 24, 1847, aged 5 years. OR 6/2.

Barak G. Thomas, formerly of Charleston, S. C. Died in Lexington, Ky., May 28, 1847. OR 6/2.

John Peck, a native of Boston, but a resident of Lexington, Ky., since 1820. Died in the latter place, Monday May 31, 1847. OR 6/2.

Rev. Jacob F. Price, Pastor of Pisgah Church—located between Lexington and Versailles. Died in a stage, near Brownsville, Pa., Thursday May 27, 1847. Buried at Pisgah. OR 6/9.

Mary Robertson, infant daughter of Dr. Samuel M. Letcher, of Lexington. Died Sunday June 6, 1847. OR 6/9.

Mrs. Mary Elizabeth Graves. Died at the Trimble county, Ky., residence of her father, Samuel Dunn, May 30, 1847, aged 27 years. OR 6/9.

Castleman, infant son of Henry and Ann Kyle, of Baltimore, Md. Died at the Castleman residence in Fayette county, home of David Castleman, June 8, 1847. OR 6/16.

Dr. William A. Gaines, of Williamstown, Ky. Died May 28, 1847, aged 35 years. OR 6/16.

Dillard W. Hazelrigg. Died at the Bourbon county residence of James Hutchcraft, May 11, 1847, aged 28 years. OR 6/19.

Mrs. Mary Noble, of Lexington. Died June 18, 1847, aged 55 years. OR 6/23.

Mrs. Helen B. Young, consort of Richard B. Young, Lexington. Died June 27, 1847. OR 6/30.

Lewis Barry. Died at the Clarke county residence of his son-in-law, Hugh McDonald, Saturday June 26, 1847, aged 74 years. OR 6/30.

Nathaniel Dunn, Sr., of Fayette County. Died at Keene, Ky., the residence of William Bronaugh, June 23, 1847, aged 79 years. OR 7/3.

Dr. James M. Shannon, of Lewis county, Mo. Died May 22, 1847, aged 28 years. OR 7/3.

James Alexander, son of John H. Shannon, of Marion county, Mo. Died June 15, 1847. OR 7/3.

Mrs. Martha Farrar, consort of Asa Farrar, formerly of Lexington. Died in Frankfort, June 23, 1847, aged 71 years. OR 7/3.

Susan, infant daughter of Thomas S. Logwood, of Lexington. Died Thursday July 1, 1847. OR 7/3.

Benjamin A. Webb. Died in Owingsville, June 21, 1847, aged 28 years. OR 7/3.

Richard B. Simpson, Jr., a volunteer from Madison county. Died in New Orleans, on his return from Mexico, in June, 1847. OR 7/3.

Sarah J. A. Warren, infant daughter of Dr. T. B. Warren, of Lexington. Died Saturday July 3, 1847. OR 7/7.

Mrs. Elizabeth Ennis, consort of Josiah Ennis, of Lexington. Died Tuesday July 6, 1847. OR 7/10.

Jacob Blain, of Lexington. Died in Cincinnati, July 6, 1847. OR 7/10.

Daniel B. Hume, of Scott county. Died July 4, 1847, aged 42 years. OR 7/10.

William B. Carroll, formerly of Scott county, but for several years a resident of Georgetown. Died Tuesday July 6, 1847. OR 7/10.

Mrs. Louisa Harrison Fishback, consort of George T. Fishback, of Clarke county. Died July 6, 1847, aged 32 years. OR 7/10.

Anna Tompkins, infant daughter of John T. and Jane P. Lyle. Died July 6, 1847, aged 6 months. OR 7/14.

Lt. Col. Henry Clay, Jr., son of Henry Clay, of Lexington. Killed Feb. 22, 1847, at the battle of Buena Vista. OR June and July, 1847.

Mrs. Jane Harrison, relict of Hezekiah Harrison. Died at the Fayette county residence of her son-in-law, Richard Martin, Friday July 16, 1847, aged 72 years. OR 7/24.

Mrs. Elizabeth Miller, consort of Dr. Alexander Miller, of Madison county. Died July 13, 1847, aged 56 years. OR 7/24.

Dr. John W. Bradford, of Georgetown. Died July 18, 1847. OR 7/24.

Hon. Thomas P. Wilson, of Shelbyville. Died July 19, 1847, aged 53 years. OR 7/24.

Mrs. Sophronia Wheatly, consort of G. W. Wheatly, of Harrodsburg. Died July 21, 1847. OR 7/24.

Ella Louise, infant daughter of Charles and Henrietta T. Marshall. Died Monday July 19, 1847, aged 8 months. OR 7/24.

Frederick Ambos, infant son of Jacob Blain, dec'd., of Lexington. Died Wednesday July 21, 1847. OR 7/24.

Mrs. Olive R. Soczenski. Died at the Lexington residence of Mr. F. A. West, Saturday July 17, 1847, aged 38 years. OR 7/24.

Isaac Reed, of Lexington. Died Monday July 26, 1847, at an advanced age. OR 7/28.

J. M. Leauwell, son of Lieut. Leauwell, and nephew of Ex-President Tyler. Died Sunday July 18, 1847, aged 2 years and 2 months. OR 7/28.

Elijah Spates, of Fayette county. Died Saturday July 25, 1847, aged 35 years. OR 7/28.

John Simpson Cooke, of Louisville. Died July 25, 1847, aged 19 years. OR 7/31.

John C. Owings, of Owingsville. Died July 26, 1847, aged 29 years. OR 8/7.

Charles Coolidge, of Lexington. Died Aug. 6, 1847. OR 8/7.

William Davis, son of William D. Skillman, formerly of Lexington, Ky. Died in St. Louis, Mo., Thursday July 29, 1847, aged 8 years. OR 8/7.

Miss Mary Ann Bell, recently of Lexington, Mo., and a daughter of the late James Bell, formerly of Fayette county, Ky. Died Aug. 3, 1847. OR 8/7.

Charles Robinson, of Fayette county. Died Aug. 9, 1847. OR 8/11.

Miss Amanda E. Smith, daughter of Joseph Smith, dec'd., of Fayette county. Died July 20, 1847, aged 21 years. OR 8/11.

John M. Gray, formerly of Genesis, N. Y. Died in Athens, Ky., in August, 1847, aged 27 years. OR 8/11.

Mrs. Elizabeth Taylor, wife of Robert S. Taylor, of Clarke county. Died Aug. 2, 1847. Or 8/11.

Mrs. Susan Todd Bartlett, consort of J. H. C. Bartlett, of Lexington. Died Aug. 11, 1847, aged 23 years. OR 8/14.

Richard Tankersley, infant son of Mr. J. H. C. Bartlett, of Lexington. See above. Died July 22, 1847, aged 2 months and 8 days. OR 8/14.

Mrs. Maria E., consort of Dr. Joseph S. Halsted, of Lexington, and daughter of the late Joshua Worley, of Fayette county. Died Thursday Aug. 12, 1847. OR 8/14.

Mrs. Malinda Athey, consort of Presley Athey, of Lexington. Died Saturday Aug. 14, 1847. OR 8/18.

Richard D., son of Capt. W. S. D. Megowan, of Bowling Green. Died Aug. 9, 1847, aged 11 months. OR 8/18.

Capt. William Scott, of Paris. A soldier "in the late war." Died Aug. 13, 1847, aged 74 years. OR 8/21.

Dr. J. D. Shannon, of St. Louis, Mo., late of Frankfort, Ky. Died in the former place, Aug. 14, 1847. OR 8/21.

Mrs. Mary Ann Elizabeth Wood, second daughter of Joseph and Ann Case, of Bourbon county. Died Aug. 23, 1847, aged 26 years. OR 8/25.

Richard P. Whitney, son of Dr. W. W. Whitney, of Lexington. Died Wednesday Aug. 25, 1847, aged 22 years. Long obituary and military career of in OR /28.

Mrs. Susan Clark, relict of James Clark, of Fayette county. Died Wednesday, Aug. 25, 1847, aged 81 years. OR 9/1.

John Dunn, of Slickaway, Fayette county. Drowned in the Kentucky river, Monday Aug. 30, 1847. OR 9/4.

John G. Martin, of Paris, Ky. Died Aug. 27, 1847, aged 31 years. OR 9/4.

Courtney R. Lewis, a native of Jessamine county. Died at LaFayette, La., Aug. 20, 1847, aged 48 years. OR 9/4.

Francis Moore, of Kentucky. Died in New Orleans, Aug. 23, 1847. OR 9/4.

Col. Michael Flynn, of Clarke county. Died Aug. 17, 1847, aged 66 years. OR 9/4.

Hon. George H. Proffit of Evansville, Ind., formerly U. S. Minister to Brazil. Died in Louisville, Ky., Sept. 7, 1847. OR 9/11.

Mrs. Maria Trimble, relict of the late John Trimble, and daughter of James McConnell, of Fayette county. Died in Lexington, Monday Sept. 13, 1847. OR 9/15.

Mrs. Harriet Matilda, consort of J. R. Wendover, of St. Louis. Died Sept. 5, 1847, aged 23 years. OR 9/15.

Mrs. Lucretia C. Carouthers, a native of Penn. She came to Kentucky in a company with Col. Robert Patterson. She settled in Fayette county, and was one of the first to reside in Lexington. She died Sept. 12, 1847, at the residence of Samuel Busby, in Mt. Sterling. She was 86 years of age. OR 9/18.

Capt. David Bruton, of Montgomery county. Died Sept. 4, 1847. OR 9/18.

Mrs. Sidney Anderson, wife of Col. Thomas Anderson, of Louisville, formerly of Lexington. Died Monday Sept. 13, 1847. OR 9/18.

The following died of yellow fever in New Orleans, in September, 1847:

John Postelwaite, son of Capt. Postelwaite, of Fayette county, Kentucky.

Capt. M. W. Hinkle, of Louisville.

Dr. B. H. Hall, of Louisville.

Mrs. D. Hall, of Kentucky.

Vincent R. Hagan, of Kentucky.

John Young, son of John C. Young, of Frankfort. Died on board a steamer at St. Joseph, Sunday Aug. 29, 1847. He was buried at Fulton, Callaway county, Mo. OR 9/22.

Elder William R. McChesney, of Lexington, Ky. Died Thursday Sept. 16, 1847, at Cincinnati. He was 30 years of age. OR 9/22.

Benjamin Franklin, infant son of Capt. Courtney Talbot, of Fayette county. Died Saturday Sept. 18, 1847. OR 9/22.

Mrs. Jane Lamme, relict of Jesse Lamme, of Fayette county. Died Monday Sept. 20, 1847. OR 9/22.

William Adams, of Lexington. Died Sept. 18, 1847. R 9/22.

Mrs. Elizabeth Donohue, consort of John J. Donohue, and daughter of Joseph Barker, of Fayette county. Died at her home near Kiddville, Clarke county, Sept. 13, 1847, aged 33 years. OR 9/25.

Mrs. Amelia G. Owsley, consort of Hon. B. Y. Owsley, and daughter of Governor Owsley. Died in Frankfort, Tuesday Sept. 21, 1847. OR 9/25.

Hugh Frazer, of Harrison county. Suicided Saturday Sept. 25, 1847. OR 9/29.

Capt. Joseph Kelly, of Winchester. Died Monday Sept. 27, 1847. OR 9/29.

William B. Price, of Lexington, Mo. He was one of the first settlers of Fayette county, Ky. Died Sept. 8, 1847, aged 84 years. OR 9/29.

Francis Rivers Richardson, eldest son of F. R. and Sarah Richardson, dec'd., late of Amite county, Miss. Died at Harrodsburg, Ky., Saturday, Sept. 4, 1847, aged 14 years. OR 9/29.

Rowland Powell, a soldier in the Mexican War. Died at the Paris, Ky., residence of his brother-in-law, Thornton Gorham, Saturday, Sept. 25, 1847. OR 10/2.

John V. Varnum, of Louisville. Died Oct. 3, 1847, aged 47 years. OR 10/6.

Elizabeth, daughter of Isaac Worthington, of Miss. Died in Louisville, Ky., Thursday, Sept. 30, 1847, aged 5 years and 6 months. OR 10/6.

Mrs. Priscilla A. Yantis, relict of Col. John Yantis. Died at Dover, Mo., at the residence of her son-in-law, Judge J. W. Hall, Sept. 1, 1847, aged about 66 years. OR 10/6.

James Royster, of Garrard county. Died Sept. 26, 1847, aged 49 years. OR 10/6.

Dr. J. A. Armstrong, son of Capt. Andrew H. Armstrong, of Fayette county. Died in Mt. Sterling, Monday, Sept. 27, 1847. OR 10/9.

Rodolphus Conover, son of James Conover, of Lexington, Ky. Died at Mobile, Ala., Sept. 17, 1847, aged 27 years. He was buried in Mobile. OR 10/9.

Nancy F., daughter of Capt. W. S. D. Megowan, of Bourbon county. Died Thursday, Oct. 7, 1847, aged about 3 years and 6 months. OR 10/13.

Catherine Jane, daughter of Robert B. Hamilton, of Lexington. Died Oct. 9, 1847, aged about 8 years. OR 10/16.

James Ellis. Died in October, 1847. See Resolutions of Keene Division, No. 78, Sons of Temperance in OR 9/20.

John R. Campbell, of Mt. Sterling. Died Oct. 7, 1847, at an advanced age. OR 10/20.

Mr. J. C. Robinson, principal teacher at the Academy at Sharpsburg, Ky. Killed by two students, Monday, Oct. 11, 1847. OR 10/23.

Micajah Smith, of Harrison county. Died Wednesday, Oct. 13, 1847, aged about 64 years. OR 10/23.

Mrs. Susanna Smith McDowell, widow of Ex-Governor McDowell, of near Lexington, Va. Died Oct. 13, 1847, aged 48 years. OR 10/27.

Hugh White, of Clay county. Died in October, 1847. OR 10/27.

Mrs. A. A. Hanson, of Louisville, formerly of Lexington. Died Monday, Oct. 25, 1847, aged 63 years. OR 10/30.

Josiah S. Jewell, of New Orleans. Died Oct. 16, 1847. OR 10/30.

Mrs. Elizabeth Warren, of Lexington. Murdered Sunday, Oct. 31, 1847. Story OR 11/3.

Lucy Elizabeth, daughter of Dr. George B. Harrison, of Athens, Ky. Died Wednesday, Oct. 26, 1847, aged 2 years and 5 months. OR 11/3.

Col. George W. Bradbury, of Cincinnati. Died Nov. 1, 1847, aged 32 years. OR 11/6.

George E. Blackburn, formerly of Woodford county, Ky. Died on the Mississippi river, in October, 1847. OR 11/6.

Sallie G., child of J. S. G. and Kate T. Burt, of Cincinnati. Died Oct. 29, 1847, aged 4 years, 8 months and 23 days. OR 11/6.

Henry D. Elbert, of Scott county. Died Oct. 30, 1847, aged 80 years. OR 11/6.

Joseph Craig, of Fayette county. Died Saturday, Nov. 6, 1847, at an advanced age. OR 11/10.

Mrs. ——— Vaughn, consort of Cornelius Vaughn, Sr., of Fayette county. Died Nov. 6, 1947. OR 11/10.

Lewis Castleman, of Washington county, Mo., formerly of Lexington, Ky. Died Oct. 21, 1847. OR 11/10.

James Vallandingham, Sr., of Fayette county. A native of Virginia. Removed to Kentucky in 1789. Died Tuesday, Nov. 9, 1847, aged 84 years. OR 11/17.

Mrs. Ethelinda W. Besore, consort of John Besore. Died Nov. 15, 1847, aged 29 years. OR 11/17.

John Nelson, son of G. D. and Letitia Hunt. Died Nov. 13, 1847, aged 15 months. OR 11/17.

Mrs. Elizabeth Berkley, consort of Burgess Berkley, of Fayette county. Died Nov. 22, 1847, aged 50 years. OR 11/24 and 11/27.

Mrs. Nancy Daviess, widow of Col. Joseph Hamilton Daviess, who fell at the battle of Tippecance in 1811. Died in Washington county, Ky., Oct. 22, 1847. OR 11/27.

Nathaniel W. Keith, son of J. W. Keith, of Winchester, Ky. A soldier in the Mexican War. Died July 6, 1847, from wounds received at the battle of Cerro Gordo in the Spring of 1847. He was 20 years of age. OR 12/1.

Robert Bridger, of Miss. A student at Transylvania Univ. Died Sunday, Nov. 28, 1847, in Lexington, Ky. OR 12/1.

Edward, youngest son of Joseph Cooper, of Lexington. Died December 6, 1847. OR 12/8.

Mrs. Ann Willing, consort of Philip Willing, of Lexington. Died Wednesday Dec. 8, 1847. OR 12/15.

Mrs. Nancy Young, of Mercer county. Died Dec. 6, 1847, aged 65 years. OR 12/15.

William B. Blackburn, Jr., of St. Louis. Died Thursday, Dec. 9, 1847. OR 12/15.

John Bridges, late of Lexington, Ky. Died at Hot Springs, Ark., Nov. 24, 1847. He left his wife and 2 small children. OR 12/18.

Mrs. Anne, wife of George Lockerbie, formerly of Lexington, Ky. Died in Indianapolis, Nov. 29, 1847, aged 79 years. OR 12/22.

Benjamin Scott, of Fayette county. Died Dec. 14, 1847, aged 48 years. OR 12/25.

Mrs. Caroline H. Preston, of Louisville. Died Dec. 19, 1847. OR 12/25.

Mrs. Matilda Maury, relict of Francis Fontaine Maury. Died at the residence of her son-in-law, Rev. Edward F. Berkley, Rector of Christ Church, Lexington, Saturday, Nov. 6, 1847. She was 56 years of age. OR 11/10 and 12/25.

Mrs. Ann T. Reynolds, wife of W. B. Reynolds, of Louisville. Died at the Lexington residence of her father, John W. Hunt, Tuesday, Dec. 28, 1847. OR 12/29.

Mrs. L. A. L. Cross, wife of Professor Cross, recently of New Orleans, but now of Transylvania University, Lexington, Ky. Died Dec. 25, 1847, in Lexington. OR 12/29.

1848

Mrs. Mary T. Chiles, relict of Col. C. G. Chiles, of Ind., and eldest daughter of R. E. Brooking, of Clarke county, Ky. Died Dec. 19, 1847, at the Carroll county residence of her brother-in-law, A. G. Craig. She was 42 years of age. OR 1/1/1848.

James Doneghy, of near Danville. Suicided Friday, Dec. 31, 1847. OR 1/5/1848.

John B. Coleman, Sr. Died at the Lexington residence of his son-in-law, Robert Frazer, Jr., Saturday, Jan. 1, 1848, at an advanced age. OR 1/5.

Dr. William A. Wharton, of Madison Parish, La. Died in Lexington, Ky., Jan. 1, 1848. OR 1/5.

Miss Rachel Houghton, of Fayette county. Died Dec. 28, 1847, aged 24 years. OR 1/5/1848.

Benjamin Howard Thomas, of Mt. Sterling. Died Dec. 26, 1847, aged 23 years. OR 1/12/1848.

William Z. Thomson, of Fayette county, Ky. Died on board the steamer Alexander Scott, coming from New Orleans, Jan. 2, 1848. OR 1/12.

Henry Timberlake, of Paris, Ky. Son of Richard and Mary Timberlake, and born in Hanover county, Va., Sept. 18, 1777. Moved with his parents to Kentucky in 1786, settling on Paddy's Run, now a part of Harrison then in Bourbon county. He later settled in Paris, where he lived till his death, Jan. 2, 1848. Obituary in OR 1/12.

Mrs. Ruth Ann Sayre, consort of B. B. Sayre, of Frankfort, and daughter of Dr. Samuel Theobald, formerly of Lexington. She died in Washington county, Miss., Dec. 24, 1847, aged 24 years. OR 1/15/1848.

Mrs. Jane Hodges, relict of Daniel Hodges, formerly of Fayette county. Died in Franklin county, Ky., Jan. 10, 1848, at an advanced age. OR 1/15.

Mrs. Sarah A. Graves, daughter of Thomas Gibbons, of Fayette county. Died in Austin county, Texas, Dec. 27, 1847. OR 1/22/1848.

Miss Elizabeth Stevenson, daughter of Cassandre Stevenson, of near Georgetown, Ky. Suicided Jan. 13, 1848. OR 1/26.

Mrs. Woody J. Hopkins, of Mt. Sterling, formerly of Lexington. Died Jan. 18, 1848, aged 37 years. OR 1/26.

Capt. Frank Chambers, commander of the Color Company in Col. McKee's regiment at the battle of Buena Vista. Died at Frankfort, Ky., Jan. 20, 1848, aged 25 years. OR 1/26.

Charles S. Morton, formerly of Fayette county. Died at Charleston, Ill., Jan. 13, 1848, aged about 60 years. OR 1/26.

Lucy Jane, daughter of Enoch Clark. Died Jan. 27, 1848, aged 8 years. OR 1/29.

Rev. A. W. Campbell, of Paducah. Died Jan. 9, 1848, aged 45 years. OR 1/29.

Mrs. Julia Ann, wife of Dr. A. H. Peck, and daughter of Preston Merrifield, of Winchester, Vermont. Died at Port Gibson, Miss., Jan 17, 1848, aged 31 years. OR 1/29.

Nathan J. Putnam, son of Joseph Putnam, late of Lexington, Ky. He started in 1846 with the emigrants under Col. Russell for California, but changed his route to Oregon. He died at Williamette, Oregon, May 30, 1847. OR 1/29/1848.

Mrs. Catherine Whitehead, consort of J. N. Whitehead, of Winchester, and eldest daughter of the late Peter Flanagan, of the same place. Died Jan. 25, 1848. OR 2/2.

Laura Francis, youngest daughter of R. H. Ridgely, of Lexington, Mo. Died in Nicholasville, Ky., Jan. 30, 1848. OR 2/2.

Zachariah Garnett, of Jessamine county. Died Jan. 27, 1848, aged 83 years. OR 2/5.

Nathaniel McCluer, of Woodford county. Died Jan. 29, 1848. OR 2/5.

Joseph Bruen, of Lexington, a native of New Jersey. He came to Lexington in 1813. Died Jan. 28, 1848, aged 53 years. OR 1/29 & 2/16.

Miss Pauline Hatchet Singleton, daughter of Mason and Nancy Singleton, of Keene, Jessamine county. Died in Georgetown, where she was attending school, Monday, Feb. 14, 1848, aged 15 years and 25 days. OR 2/23.

Mrs. Martha Ann Snead, relict of John S. Snead, and daughter of the late Capt. John Postlethwaite, of Lexington. Died in Louisville, Feb. 17, 1848. OR 2/23.

Miss Eliza M. Bradford, youngest daughter of Capt. Simon Bradford, of Tenn. Died at Poplar Hills, near Frankfort, Wednesday, Feb. 9, 1848, aged 15 years. OR 2/23.

Francis J. Keen. Died in Arkansas, Feb. 19, 1848. He was a native of Lexington, Ky. OR 2/23.

Richard W. Downing. Died at the Fayette county residence of his mother, Saturday, Feb. 19, 1848. OR 2/23.

James G. Hutchinson, of Lexington. Died Saturday, Feb. 19, 1848. OR 2/23.

Lewis Pigg, Sr., of Lexington. Died Feb. 20, 1848, at an advanced age. OR 2/23.

John Young, of Fayette county. Died Feb. 8, 1848, aged 38 years. OR 2/23.

Gen. Peter R. Jordan, of Mercer county. Died Feb. 10, 1848, aged "upwards of 70 years". OR 2/26.

Dr. William R. Jennings, of Woodford county. Died Jan. 29, 1848, aged about 48 years. OR 2/26.

Rev. Laban Jones, of Jefferson county. Died Feb. 26, 1848, at an advanced age. OR 3/1.

Mary McNair, daughter of J. W. Patterson, of Lexington. Died Sunday, Feb. 26, 1848. OR 3/1.

Laura V., daughter of Rev. Ryland T. Dillard, of Fayette county. Died Feb. 28, 1848, aged 21 years. OR 3/21.

Franklin Young, of Mercer county. Died Feb. 4, 1848, aged 42 years. He left his wife and 2 children. OR 3/14.

Guinilda Spencer, only daughter of John and Rebecca Kennard, of Lexington. Died Saturday, Mar. 4, 1848, aged 4 years. OR 3/8.

Francis J. Keen, born, reared and married in Lexington, Ky. Removed in 1833 to Desha county, Arkansas, where he died Feb. 9, 1848, aged 33 years. OR 3/8.

Sarah Wilson, infant daughter of J. W. Patterson, of Lexington. Died Saturday, Mar. 4, 1848. OR 3/8.

Thomas O. Anderson, son of Col. Thomas Anderson. Died at the Kentucky Military Institute, near Frankfort, Feb. 25, 1848, aged 21 years. OR 3/8.

James H. Dixon, son of the late Levi Dixon, of Jessamine county. Died Feb. 24, 1848, aged 18 years. OR 3/8.

Samuel Meredith, son of John McCauley. Died Feb. 23, 1848, aged 2 years and 3 months. OR 3/11.

Louis Richardson, son of the late Dr. W. H. Richardson, of Fayette county. Died at Richardson Bend, Tchula River, Holmes county, Miss., Feb. 22, 1848, aged 37 years. He was buried March 11, 1848, at the family burying ground at Caneland, Fayette county, Ky. OR 3/11.

Caleb T. Hall, eldest son of John G. Hall, of Lexington. Died Mar. 12, 1848, aged 15 years. OR 3/15.

Dr. William B. Whitaker, of Woodford county. Died Wednesday, Mar. 8, 1848, aged 44 years. OR 3/18.

Wilson Hunt, Sr. Died at the Jessamine county residence of Harrison Hunt, Mar. 12, 1848, aged 93 years. OR 3/18.

Mrs. Martha H. Cost, of Winchester, Ky. Died Feb. 21, 1848, aged 58 years. OR 3/18.

Theodore F., youngest son of George P. Richardson. Died Mar. 15, 1848, aged 3 years. OR 3/22.

Sallie, daughter of John F. Leavy, of Frankfort. Died March 20, 1848. OR 3/22.

Mrs. Elizabeth Garnett Buckner, consort of Benjamin H. Buckner, formerly of Winchester, Ky. Died in Jackson county, Mo., Mar. 6, 1848, aged 58 years. OR 3/22.

Clemency, daughter of John and Lucinda Crim, of Clarke county. Died in Winchester, Thursday, Mar. 16, 1848. OR 3/22.

Ophelia, daughter of D. C. Wickliffe. Died Mar. 18, 1848, aged 2 years and 6 months. OR 3/22.

Mrs. Catharine Bailey ,daughter of Mrs. Ann Allen, of Fayette county. Died at Athens, Sunday, Mar. 12, 1848, aged 21 years. She left her mother, a sister and 2 brothers. OR 3/22.

Mrs. Frances Duvall, consort of Capt. John R. Duvall, dec'd., of Clarke county. Died at the Henry county residence of her son-in-law, John Lackland, March 2, 1848, at an advanced age. OR 3/22.

Alexander McCown, Sr., formerly a citizen of Kentucky. Died in Nashville, Mar. 11, 1848, aged 60 years. OR 3/22.

Miss Mary T. B. Hunt, eldest daughter of the late Charlton Hunt. Died at the residence of her grandfather, Dr. E. Warfield, Thursday, Mar. 23, 1848, aged 18 years. OR 3/25.

Griffin T., infant son of Daniel McPayne, of Lexington. Died Mar. 22, 1848. OR 3/25.

Henry Sidener, of Fayette county. Suicided Saturday, Mar. 25, 1848, at the Stamping Ground. OR 4/1.

Martha Graddy, youngest daughter of Robert and Julia Ann Gardner, of Woodford county. Died in March, 1848, aged 4 years and 9 months. Also on Mar. 24, 1848, Margaret Crochet, daughter of the same, aged 12 years and 8 months. OR 4/1.

Charles H., son of the late Charles Coolidge, of Lexington. Died Mar. 31, 1848, aged 1 year and 11 months. OR 4/5.

Col. Jason Rogers, of Louisville. Died Monday, Apr. 3, 1848; see obituary for military record. OR 4/5.

Clifton Thomson, infant son of John and Mary Brennan, of Harrodsburg. Died Apr. 9, 1848, aged 10 months. OR 4/12.

James G. Hazelrigg, of Mt. Sterling. Died April 11, 1849, aged 47 years. OR 4/19.

Mrs. Mary B. Warfield, wife of Dr. Lloyd Warfield. Died Monday, Apr. 17, 1848, aged 46 years. Obituary. OR 4/22.

Miss Juliett May, eldest daughter of G. W. and Laura G. Sutton, of Lexington. Died Monday, Apr. 17, 1848, aged 16 years, and 1 month. OR 4/22.

Mrs. Emily Glass, wife of Robert Glass, of Shelby county. Died Apr. 16, 1848, leaving her husband and 5 children. OR 4/22.

Charles Porter, son of David E. Oak. Died in Philadelphia, April 11, 1848, aged 15 months. OR 4/22.

Archibald Brooks, of Richmond, Ky. Suicided Sunday, Apr. 23, 1848. OR 4/26.

Richard P., son of Samuel and Amanda P. Downing, of Fayette county. Died Mar. 29, 1848, aged 4 years and 6 months. OR 4/26.

Mrs. Lucinda Crim, wife of John Crim. Died at the Clarke county residence of Daniel Duvall, Apr. 6, 1848, aged about 40 years. OR 4/26.

Mrs. Sarah Quin, consort of Rev. B. F. Quin, and daughter of William French, of Franklin county. Died Apr. 29, 1848, in Scott county at the residence of her father-in-law. OR 5/6.

Mrs. Mary P. Weigart, a resident of Natchez since 1810. Died Friday, May 5, 1848, aged 61 years. She was the mother-in-law of Jacob Crizer. OR 6/14.

Mrs. Elizabeth White, of Fayette county, relict of Jeremiah White. Died May 5, 1848, aged 65 years. OR 5/10.

Mrs. Nancy Jane Cochran, consort of William Cochran, of Bourbon county. Died May 9, 1848, aged 24 years. OR 5-13.

Mrs. Emeline Bowmar, consort of Herman Bowmar, Jr., of Versailles, Ky. Died May 12, 1848, at 4 o'clock p. m., at the residence of her father, A. C. Tunis, in Cincinnati. She was 38 years of age. OR 5/24.

Dr. James B. Fleece, of Danville. Died May 13, 1848, in his 26th year. OR 5/24.

Mary Ann, daughter of the late Thomas E. Hickman, of Winchester. Died May 13, 1848, at the residence of James L. Hickman, in Lexington. OR 5/20.

Mrs. Elizabeth J. Moreland, consort of Elexander Moreland, of Lexington, and daughter of Walker Hawkins, of Fayette county. Died Saturday night May 13, 1848. OR 5/17.

James Harlow, of Lexington. Died May 15, 1848, aged 30 years. OR 6/17.

Mrs. Elizabeth B., wife of George B. Worthen, both of Little Rock, Ark., formerly of Cynthiana, Ky. Died May 16, 1848. OR 5/17.

Sister Ann Spalding, the Superioress of St. Catherine's Academy, in Lexington. Died Tuesday May 16, 1848. OR 5/17.

James M., infant son of Henry and Bettie Buford. Died at the residence of James K. Marshall, in Bourbon county, Monday May 22, 1848. OR 6/3.

Susan Eleanor, daughter of B. and Ann S. Stout. Died Tuesday May 23, 1848, aged 3 years, 1 month and 14 days. She is buried in the family burying ground in Woodford county. OR 5/24.

John Lafon, of Jessamine county. Died at his residence, Fountain Head, May 24, 1848, aged 48 years. OR 6/14.

Thomas Goddard, Sr., of Scott county. Died May 25, 1848, aged 78 years. OR 6/10.

Mrs. Rebecca McIlvaine, wife of John W. McIlvaine, of Woodford county, and daughter of Col. William and Ann Wright, of Bourbon county. Died in former place, May 25, 1848, aged 30 years. Obituary, OR 7/12.

Col. T. C. Vallandingham, of Scott county. Died May 31, 1848, aged 59 years. OR 6/10.

Dr. Wallace E. Embry, of Madison county. Died June 2, 1848, aged 28 years. OR 6/10.

Thomas Ellis, of Fayette county. Died June 6, 1848, aged 73 years. OR 6/14.

Susan F., daughter of Judge Kenaz Farrow, of Montgomery county. Died June 7, 1848, aged 16 years. OR 6/14.

Elizabeth M., daughter of Francis J. and Elizabeth W. Keen, dec'd. Died Thursday June 15, 1848, aged about 5 years, at the residence of her grandfather, A. Legrand, in Lexington. OR 6/17.

William Buford, Jr., of Woodford county. Died June 18, 1848, aged 28 years. OR 6/21.

John Christy, of Clarke county. Died Monday night, June 19, 1848, aged about 80 years. OR 6/21.

Mary Elizabeth, second daughter of Mason S. and Narcissa E. Barkley, of Jessamine county. Died June 22, 1848. OR 7/8.

James W. Stuart, of Clarke county. Died June 26, 1848. He was a volunteer under Capt. Williams, and was at the storming of Vera Cruz, and at the battle of Cerro Gordo. OR 7/1.

Mrs. Harriet H. Slaughter, of near Bardstown, wife of Phil. C. Slaughter. Died June 26, 1848, aged about 50 years. She was the daughter of the late Gen. Jacob Castleman, of Kentucky. OR 7/5.

Miss Eliza Belle Skiles, of Kimlock, near Bowling Green. Died Monday morning June 26, 1848. She was the eldest daughter of James R. Skiles. OR 7/5.

William, infant son of Warren and Mary Outten, of Lexington. Died June, 30, 1848, aged 17 months. OR 7/1.

Patrick C. Beard, son of M. Beard, of Fayette county. Died Saturday evening July 1, 1848, aged 19 years, 8 months and 8 days. OR 7/5.

J. S. Henderson, of Rockcastle county. Died Saturday July 2, 1848. He was a State Senator. OR 7/8.

Dillard, second son of James F. and Elizabeth M. Barkley, of Jessamine county. Died July 4, 1848. OR 7/8.

Major Ezra R. Price. Died July 7, 1848, at the Lexington residence of Col. C. J. Sanders. He was 32 years of age. Obituary with military record in OR 7/15.

Thomas Edward, infant son of Thomas Bryan, dec'd., and Sophia Bryan. Died Friday July 14, 1848, aged 23 months. OR 7/19.

Hugh Brent, of Paris. Died July 16, 1848, aged 76 years. He removed from Virginia to Kentucky in 1789, living all his life at Paris, in Bourbon county. OR 7/22.

Mrs. Jane Breckinridge, consort of R. H. Breckinridge, of Lexington. Died July 18, 1848. She left her husband and three children. OR 7/29.

Mrs. Mary Brown, wife of H. B. Brown, late editor of the *Cincinnati Chronicle*. Died in Lancaster, Ky., July 20, 1848. OR 8/16.

John A. Scott. Died at the Weisiger House, Frankfort, July 25, 1848, aged 30 years. Obituary and war record in OR 8/5.

Mrs. Nancy A. Duncan, wife of William R. Duncan, of Clarke county. Died July 30, 1848, aged 30 years. OR 8/16.

Mrs. Eliza Withers, wife of William A. Withers, of Cynthiana. Died at the Lincoln county residence of her father, in August, 1848, aged 42 years. OR 8/12.

Rev. Robert Punshon, of Cincinnati. Died Aug. 1, 1848, aged 72 years. OR 8/5.

Col. John Graves, of Fayette county. Died Aug. 5, 1848, aged 76 years. Obituary in OR 8/23.

James Breckenridge, infant son of Alexander and Elizabeth Burch, formerly of Lexington. Died at Henderson, Ky., Aug. 5, 1848. OR 8/19.

Martha Eliza Faulconer, of Athens, Ky. Died Aug. 5, 1848, aged 19 years. OR 8/16.

William, infant son of Dr. J. W. and Margaret W. Welden, of Lexington. Died Aug. 7, 1848, aged 11 months and 23 days. OR 8/16.

Neville Blakemore. Died at the Fayette county residence of his mother-in-law, Mrs. Craig, Aug. 14, 1848. OR 8/16.

Enoch C. Orear, of Boone county, Mo., formerly of Kentucky. Died Aug. 15, 1848, aged 59 years. OR 9/2.

Gen. James Shelby, of Fayette county, the eldest son of Governor Isaac Shelby. Died Tuesday night Aug. 15, 1848, aged about 65 years. OR 8/19.

Emeline Josephine, infant daughter of William L. Reed, of Lexington. Died Sunday night Aug. 20, 1848. OR 8/23.

Susan M., eldest daughter of John F. Cautrill, of Scott county. Died Aug. 22, 1848, aged 17 years. OR 9/2.

James D. Glass, attorney at law, son of David Glass, of Fayette county. Died at Madison, Ind., Aug. 24, 1848, aged 31 years. OR 9/13.

George W. Gordon, of Fayette county. Died Aug. 24, 1848. OR 8/26.

Judge Lafayette Saunders, of Clinton, La., a native of Tenn. Died at Red Sulphur Springs, Va., Aug. 25, 1848. OR 9/27.

Louisiana, daughter of Thomas B. Stevenson, of Cincinnati. Died at the Weisiger House, Frankfort, Ky., Aug. 26, 1848, aged 5 years and 5 months. OR 9/2.

Mrs. Felicity Giron, of Maysville. Died Saturday Aug. 26, 1848. She was the consort of M. Giron, formerly of Lexington. "At her request her remains were brought to Lexington, where she long resided, for interment." OR 8/30.

Capt. James Devers, of Lexington. Died Aug. 26, 1848, at an advanced age. OR 8/30.

Garland Christy, of Lexington. Died Aug. 26, 1848, aged about 45 years. He left his wife and several children. OR 8/30.

William H. Summers, of near midway. Died Aug. 30, 1848. OR 9/6.

George E. Gillespie, of near Midway. Died Aug. 31, 1848. OR 9/6.

Mrs. Martha Cravens, of Lexington. Died at the residence of her son, E. B. Cravens, Sept. 1, 1848, aged 70 years. OR 9/13.

Mrs. Penelope Eastin, consort of Thomas N. Eastin, of Henderson county. Died at the Elizabethtown, Ky., residence of her father, Hon. Judge Churchill, Sept. 4, 1848, aged 30 years. OR 9/9.

Major Joseph Mosby, of Fayette county. Died at the residence of his daughter, Sept. 8, 1848, in his 93rd year, OR 9/23.

Jamison Samuel, of Hannibal, Mo. Died Sept. 10, 1848. He was for many years a resident of Frankfort, Ky. OR 9/20.

Mrs. Hannah Hood, wife of Dr. Andrew Hood, of Winchester. Died Monday Sept. 11, 1848. OR 9/16.

Mrs. Susan B. Evans, consort of Dr. G. S. Evans. Died Sept. 13, 1848, aged 22 years. OR 9/23.

Hugh Goddard, father of the editor of the *Richmond Chronicle*. Died in Richmond, Ky., Sept. 13, 1848, aged 66 years. OR 9/20.

Mrs. Elizabeth Jane Foster, of Fayette county. Died Sept. 13, 1848. OR 9/16.

Mrs. Louisa Robbins, of Paris. Died Sept. 17, 1848. OR 9/23.

Col. William Buford, of Woodford county. Died September 18, 1848. OR 9/27.

Mrs. Margaret McClure, relict of Nathaniel McClure, of Scott county. Died Sept. 18, 1848. OR 9/23.

John Duncan, of Lexington. Died Sept. 23, 1848, in his 72nd year. He was formerly of Madison county. OR 9/30.

Mrs. Susan E. Allen, consort of Capt. John Allen, and daughter of Richard S. Owen. Died at the residence of her father, in Shelby county, Sept. 25, 1848, aged 25 years. OR 10/7.

Mrs. Eliza Ross, relict of George Ross, and daughter of the late Dr. Richard Pindell. Died at her residence in Lexington, Monday morning Sept. 25, 1848. OR 9/27.

Mrs. Frances A. Atchison, consort of Daniel D. Atchison, formerly of Lexington, Ky. Died at Galveston, Texas, Sept. 28, 1848. OR 10/18.

Hon. William J. Graves, of Louisville. Died Sept. 28, 1848, aged 44 years. OR 9/30.

Mrs. Sarah Jane Cochran, wife of John B. Cochran, and daughter of James Hamilton. Died in Lexington, Sept. 28, 1848. OR 9/30.

Mrs. Elizabeth W. Parks, consort of Samuel Parks. Died in Louisville, Sept. 29, 1848, aged 22 years. Samuel Parks was formerly of Lexington. OR 10/7.

Rev. A. Goodell, formerly of Frankfort, Ky. Died at Hamburg, Miss., Oct. 1, 1848. OR 10/25.

Henry Goodloe, of Boyle county. Died Oct. 1, 1848. OR 10/11.

Mrs. Clara Hawes, relict of Richard Hawes, Sr. Died at her residence in Daviess county, Oct. 12, 1848, at an advanced age. OR 10/25.

Mrs. Eleanor S. Rhines, wife of Lansing Rhines, formerly of Lexington. Died in Danville, Oct. 12, 1848. OR 10/18.

Mrs. Nancy Pilcher, relict of Lewis Pilcher, of Fayette county (?). Died Oct. 13, 1848. Funeral Oct. 14, from the home of her mother, Mrs. Shaw, on Hill street. OR 10/14.

Mrs. Catherine Young, wife of John Young, and youngest daughter of the late Robert McNitt. Died in Lexington, Saturday night Oct. 14, 1848, aged 28 years. OR 10/18.

Mrs. Ellen E., consort of John F. Payne, and daughter of John Downing, of Scott county. Died at the latter's residence, Oct. 16, 1848. OR 10/21.

Samuel Oots, a teacher in the City School. Died at the Lexington home of his father, Oct. 17, 1848, aged 21 years. OR 10/18.

Edmund D. Langan, of Lexington, late of Woodford county. Died Wednesday Oct. 18, 1848. OR 10/21.

Emma F., only daughter of William H. and Ann Rogers. Died in Lexington Thursday night Oct. 19, 1848, aged about 12 years. OR 10/21.

Capt. Andrew F. Caldwell, of Laurel county. Died Oct. 20, 1848, aged 41 years. OR 11/4.

Mrs. Peggy Arnold, of Fayette county. Died Oct. 26, 1848, aged 92 years, 4 months and 2 days. OR 11/8.

Matthew R. Stealey, of Lexington. Died Tuesday evening Oct. 24, 1848. Buried Oct. 27 in the Frankfort Cemetery beside his wife and three children. OR 10/28.

Henry Goodloe, of Spring Hill, his residence. Died Nov 5, 1848. Obituary in OR 11/8.

Eugene Henry, son of William H. Rogers. Died Nov. 5, 1848. OR 11/8.

John F. Smoot. Died at the Lexington residence of John Gordon, Sunday Nov. 5, 1848. OR 11/8.

Bettie, daughter of John B. Raine, of Paris. Died at Vicksburg, Miss., Nov. 6, 1848. OR 11/18.

Capt. David R. Gist, of Clarke county. Died Nov. 6, 1848. OR 11/8.

Mrs. Mary Whitney. Died at the Lexington residence of her son, Dr. W. W. Whitney, Tuesday night Nov. 7, 1848, at an advanced age. OR 11/11.

James W. Fenwick. Died at the Scott county residence of Mrs. Jenkins, Nov. 17, 1848, aged 49. OR 12/9.

Miss Emily V. Offutt, daughter of Henry C. Offutt, of Shelby county. Died Nov. 18, 1848, aged 16 years. OR 12/16.

Robert Hicks, farmer. Died Nov. 19, 1848, aged 62 years. OR 11/22.

Mary Smith, youngest child of Remus Payne. Died Nov. 23, 1848, aged 5 years, 2 months and 19 days. OR 12/23.

William M., son of William H. Rogers, of Lexington. Died Nov. 23, 1848, aged 5 years. OR 11/25.

Mrs. Sophia Weaver, consort of Francis Weaver, of Lexington. Died Monday Nov. 26, 1848. OR 12/9.

David Bell. Died at the Lexington residence of his son, Dr. David Bell, Wednesday Nov. 29, 1848, at an advanced age. OR 12/2.

John J. Shiddell, of Lexington. Died Nov. 30, 1848, at an advanced age. OR 12/2.

Isaac Shelby, only surviving son of the late Alfred Shelby, and of the present Mrs. Dr. R. J. Breckinridge. He died on board the steamer "Crescent City" on the Gulf of Mexico. He was twenty-one years of age. His body was returned home to Traveller's Rest, Lincoln county, home of his grandfather, Governor Isaac Shelby, and there buried Jan. 2, 1849. OR 1/10/1849 and Nat'l Intelligence 1/31/49.

Mrs. Elizabeth P. Banks, widow of the late Capt. Cuthbert Banks, of Mt. Sterling. Died Dec. 5, 1848, at the home of her daughter, Mrs. Durrett, in Mason county. She was 71 years of age. OR 12/20.

William R. Griffith, of near Owensboro, Daviess county. Died Thursday Dec. 7, 1848, aged 55 years. OR 12/23.

Mrs. Margaret, consort of Mathew Markland. Died at Paducah, Dec. 13, 1848, aged 55 years.

Catherine W., second daughter of Joseph George, of Lexington. Died Dec. 16, 1848. OR 12/20.

William Rochester Beatty, of Washington, Ky. Died Dec. 17, 1848. He was the eldest son of Hon. Adam Beatty. OR 1/2/23.

Mrs. Agnes Wiseman, consort of William Wiseman, of Lexington. Died Saturday Dec. 23, 1848. OR 12/27.

William Franklin, youngest son of Willis P. and Mary Elizabeth Duvall, of Fayette county. Died Dec. 24, 1848, aged 1 year, 1 month and 16 days. OR 12/27.

Miss Frances Mary Miller. Died at the Fayette county residence of her uncle, James Hurst, Dec. 25, 1848, aged 15 years. OR 12/30.

Theodore Thompson, youngest son of John Williams, of Woodford county. Died Dec. 27, 1848, aged 6 years. OR 12/30.

Mrs. Mary Elizabeth Duvall, consort of Willis P. Duvall, of Woodford county. Died at the residence of her father, John Williams, Dec. 27, 1848, aged 25 years. OR 12/30.

1849

Cornelius Sullivan. Died at the residence of S. P. Kenney, Dec. 29, 1848, aged 93 years. He was a Revolutionary soldier. OR 1/3/1849.

Mr. V. U. Brooking, of Scott county. Died Jan. 4, 1849. OR 1/20.

Henry Clay Stewart, a son of Joseph and Susan F. Putnam, formerly of Lexington, now of Shippingport, Henry county. Died Jan. 1849. OR 1/10.

William Duerson. Died at the residence of Enoch Clarke, in Lexington, Jan. 8, 1840, at an advanced age. OR 1/10.

Joseph L., son of Marcus Downing, of Fayette county. Died Jan. 8, 1849, aged 18 months. OR 1/17.

Dr. John Croghan, of Jefferson county. Died Jan. 11, 1849. OR 1/13.

Mrs. Bettie Turner, wife of William L. Turner, of Richmond, Ky., daughter of the late Robert Crittenden. Died Sunday Jan. 14, 1849. OR 1/17.

John Allen Sr., of Fayette county. Died Jan. 1849. OR 1/17.

Julia Ann Davis, daughter of A. T. and E. R. Skillman, of Lexington. Died January 15, 1849, aged 14 years and 2 months. OR 1/17.

Clifton R. Ferguson, of Fayette county. Died Jan. 16, 1849, aged 54 years. OR 1/20 and 1/24.

John Tom (Thomas), son of William D. Skillman, formerly of Lexington. Died in St. Louis, Jan. 16, 1849, aged 2 years. OR 1/27.

Mrs. Catharine Fisher, relict of John Fisher, formerly of Lexington. Died in Louisville, Jan. 17, 1849, aged 66 years. OR 1/20.

Mrs. Celeste F. Candy, wife of John Candy, formerly of Lexington, and daughter of Mrs. Jane B. Robert, of Lexington. Died at Shelbyville, Jan. 17, 1849, aged 34 years. OR 1/24.

Joel R. Lyle, father of the editor of the Observer and Reporter (1849). Died at his residence in Paris, Ky., Jan. 18, 1849, aged 74 years, 1 month. Obituary in OR 1/27.

Col. Isaac Miller, one of the oldest residents of Cynthiana. Died Jan. 19, 1849, in his 70th year. He was born in Virginia on Mar. 15, 1779, and came to Kentucky when 16 years of age. Obituary in OR 1/24 and 2/3.

David Duck, of Lexington. Died Jan. 19, 1849. He was buried Jan. 21, by the Sons of Temperance, of which society he was a member. OR 1/24.

Mrs. Cannon Wingate, of Woodford county. Died Jan. 20, 1849, aged about 46 years. OR 1/31.

George C. Timberlake, of Lexington. Died Jan. 23, 1849. OR 1/24.

Mrs. Judith Goddard, relict of Col. William Goddard, and the widely known proprietress of the Lee House, Maysville. Died in Maysville Jan. 23, 1849, aged nearly 70 years. OR 1/27.

Mrs. Margaret Rainey, wife of Rev. W. H. Rainey. Died near Havilandsville, Harrison county, Jan. 25, 1849. She left her husband and several children. OR 2/3.

John T. Graves, son of R. C. and Susan Graves, of Jessamine county. Died Jan. 25, 1849. OR 2/7.

Josiah Gayle, of Owen county. Died Wednesday Jan. 26, 1849. Obituary in OR 1/31.

Mrs. Sarah Howard Bledsoe. Died at 3 o'clock a. m., Jan. 31, 1849, aged about 65 years. She was the wife of the late Judge Jesse Bledsoe, and the mother of Mrs. H. I. Bodley. Burial Feb. 1, at Lexington. OR 2/3.

Mrs. Villa Owsley, of Winchester, relict of John Owsley. Died Feb. 1, 1849, in her 85th year. She was born in Loudon co., Va., and came to Kentucky with her husband in 1789. OR 2/7.

Mrs. Mary Salmon. Died at the Lexington residence of her son, P. E. Salmon, Saturday morning Feb. 4, 1849, aged about 74 years. She came from Virginia in 1842. OR 3/7.

Miss Eusebe N. Higbee, daughter of the late Peter Higbee, of Lexington. Died there, at the residence of her grandmother, Feb. 4, 1849. OR 2/7.

Gen. William Smith, of Rockcastle county. Died Feb. 15, 1849, aged 76 years. OR 2/24.

Nathaniel Shaw, of Lexington. Died Thursday morning Feb. 15, 1849. OR 2/17.

James P. Crim. Died Feb. 20, 1849. OR 2/28.

Abraham Irvine, Jr., of Boyle county. Died Feb. 22, 1849, in his 53 year. OR 3/10.

James Morton Elliott, infant son of James M. and Julia R. Elliott. Died Thursday Feb. 22, 1849, aged 12 months. OR 2/24.

John Wiley, formerly a member of Transylvania Lodge No. 43, I. O. O. F., Lexington, Ky. Died at Chargres, Feb. 25, 1849. OR 4/18.

Mrs. R. L. Shelby, wife of Richard Shelby, of Mo. Died at Richland, Fayette county, the residence of Isaac Shelby, on Tuesday night March 6, 1849. OR 3/10.

Sidney Evans, infant daughter of John and Mary G. Hall, of Shelby county. Died Mar. 6, 1849. OR 3/17.

Elizabeth W., daughter of Isaac W. and Susan B. Scott. Died Thursday Mar. 8, 1849, aged 2 years and 6 months. OR 3/10.

Miss Lavina Frances, daughter of Mr. N. Long, of Scott county. Died Mar. 10, 1849, aged 19 years. OR 3/24.

Mrs. Margaret Graves, of Fayette county, relict of Col. John Graves. Died Mar. 11, 1849, at an advanced age. OR 3/14.

A. F. Shepard, of the firm of Elley & Shepard, Lexington. Formerly of Georgetown. Died Mar. 11, 1849, and buried at latter place. OR 3/14.

Gen. Robert B. McAfee, of Mercer county. Died Monday Mar. 12, 1849; he was one of the first settlers of Kentucky and author of "A History of the Late War in Western Country." OR 3/17.

Mrs. Barbary G. Chinn, consort of Dr. J. G. Chinn, formerly of Lexington. Died at Lexington, Mo., March 14, 1849. OR 4/4.

Mary M., eldest daughter of J. R. Sloan, of Lexington. Died Mar. 15, 1849, aged 13 years. OR 3/17.

Lewis Dedman, of Fayette county. Died Dec. 29, 1841. OR 1/1/42.

Oliver Keen, of Fayette county. Died Dec. 29, 1841, at an advanced age. OR 1/1/1842.

Miss Sarah M., daughter of Isaac Sprakes, of Lexington. Died Dec. 29, 1841. This was the third child of this family to die within three months. OR 1/1/1842.

Mrs. Sarah Hutchison, wife of James S. Hutchison, formerly of Bourbon county, Ky. Died in Cooper county, Mo., near Palestine, Sept. 23, 1842. LI 10/14.

General Joseph Desha, Ex-Governor of Kentucky. Died at Georgetown, Wednesday morning Oct. 12, 1842. LI 10/14.

Richard J., son of Mr. W. F. Plunkett, of Lexington. Died Oct. 12, 1842. LI 10/14.

Joseph Walker, of Harrison county. Died June 20, 1843, aged about 80 years. Protestant & Herald 6/29.

Charles M. Randall, of New Orleans, a member of the Bar of that city. Died Mar. 19, 1849. He was a former resident of Lexington, Ky., where he was graduated from the Law School of Transylvania University. He married a daughter of Judge James E. Davis, of Lexington. OR 4/7.

Samuel M. Peers, son of the late Rev. Benjamin O. Peers, of Lexington. Died in Philadelphia Mar. 19, 1849. OR 3/31.

Mrs. Mildred Darnaby, consort of Capt. John H. Darnaby. Died Mar. 20, 1849, aged 36 years. OR 3/28.

J. Dean Swift, recently of Richmond, Ky. Died Mar. 21, 1849, aged about 45 years. OR 3/24.

Mrs. Mary Ann Smith, consort of E. Smith, Jr., of Lexington. Died Mar. 22, 1849. OR 3/24.

Mr. Arjalon Price, of Lexington. Died Mar. 23, 1849, aged about 65 years. OR 3/28.

James W. Grant, of Georgetown. Died Mar. 24, 1849, aged 57 years. OR 3/31.

Benjamin G. Halleck. Died at the Bourbon House, Paris, on Mar. 25, 1849. OR 3/31.

Richmond Curle Goddin. Died in Richmond, Ky., Mar. 28, 1849. OR 3/31.

Bernard Donohoo, of Lexington. Died at Chiles' Apr. 2, 1849, aged 66 years. He was a native of Ireland, but a resident of Lexington since 1829. OR 4/4.

David H. Hickman, youngest son of John L. Hickman, of Paris. Died Apr. 4, 1849. OR 4/7.

Capt. Daniel Gano, on officer in the American Revolution. Died at his residence in Scott county, Apr. 8, 1849, in his 91st year. He was of the Order of the Cincinnatus (and believed to be the last) having a diploma signed by George Washington. OR 4/21.

Capt. William Ward, son of Junius Ward, of Fayette county. Died Apr. 9, 1849. Buried Apr. 10, 1849, with military honors by the cadets of the M. W. Institute of which he was a member. OR 7/14.

Mrs. Lucinda Vanpelt, consort of Sanford B. Vanpelt, of Lexington. Died Apr. 11, 1849. OR 7/14.

F. S. Hastings, of Lexington. Died at the residence of his father-in-law, Thomas B. Megowan, Apr. 11, 1849, in his early manhood. OR 7/14.

Mrs. Ann Shreve, widow of Judge William Shreve, of Jessamine county. Died Friday Apr. 13, 1849, at the residence of her son-in-law, Lewis Y. Martin, in Fayette county. She was in her 74th year. OR 4/21.

Mrs. Mary L. Verbryke, wife of William A. Verbryke, formerly of Lexington, now of Columbia, Mo. Died Apr. 16, 1849. She was a daughter of Stephen Young, dec'd. OR 5/5.

David Philips McConathy, son of Herbert McConathy, of Lexington. Died Apr. 18, 1849. OR 4/41.

Mrs. Susan Mary Salmon, wife of P. E. Salmon, of Lexington, and daughter of William Shannon, of Woodford county. Died Apr. 19, 1849 aged 28 years. OR 4/21, 4/25.

Michael Yates, of Fayette county. Died Apr. 23, 1849, aged 78 years. OR 4/28.

Mrs. Elizabeth Nelson, relict of Capt. Thomas Nelson, of Lexington, Ky. Died in Cincinnati Apr. 25, 1849, aged 66 years. OR 5/2.

Mrs. Sarah Wadsworth, consort of A. A. Wadsworth, of Maysville. Died Apr. 27, 1849, aged 47 years. OR 5/5.

George Nicholas, infant son of George R. and Amanda G. Trotter, of Main Street, Lexington. Died Sunday Apr. 29, 1849, aged 18 months and 10 days. OR 5/2.

Mr. S. N. Bowman, merchant of Danville. Died Apr. 29, 1849. OR 3/5.

John M. Conn, of Bourbon county. Died Apr. 30, 1849, aged 81 years. OR 5/5.

Dr. A. T. Cone, formerly of Lee, Mass. Died at Georgetown, Ky., May 1, 1849. OR 5/5.

OBITUARIES

The abbreviations used denote:

KG—(Lexington) *Kentucky Gazette*
OR—Lexington (Ky.) *Observer & Reporter*

1849

James Houston, of Ruddell's Mill, Bourbon county. Died May 1, 1849, aged 46 years. OR 5/5.

James D. Breckinridge. Died in Louisville May 6, 1849. OR 5/9.

Mrs. Martha Wheeler, wife of Warren Wheeler, and daughter of Starkè Taylor. Died May 10, 1849, aged 25 years. OR 5/12.

Richard Deering Craig, son of Parker Craig. Died May 10, 1849, aged 6 years. OR 5/16.

Mrs. Harriett Eubank, of Simpsonville, Shelby county. Died May 11, 1849, aged 47 years. OR 5/19.

John L. Hickman, of Bourbon county. Died at the residence of his son-in-law, James K. Marshall, of near Paris, Saturday May 12, 1849, aged 72 years. OR 5/19.

Mrs. Ruth Warrick Flanagan, relict of Peter Flanagan, of Winchester. Died May 13, 1849, aged 63 years. OR 5/16.

John Milton Craig, formerly a citizen of Kentucky. Died in Monroe county, Mo., May 14, 1849. OR 6/2.

Christopher Tempy, of Lexington. Died May 16, 1849, aged 47 years. He was a volunteer in Capt. Beard's company. OR 5/19.

Mrs. Mary W. Randolph, daughter of the late Judge Byrd, of Ohio. Died at the Jessamine county, Ky., residence of T. Woodson, May 16, 1849. OR 6/6.

Mrs. Veneshe Wingate, one of the oldest residents of Lexington. Died May 17, 1849, aged about 72 years. OR 5/19.

Mrs. Margaret Desha, relict of Governor Desha. Died May 20, 1849, aged 76 years. OR 5/26.

Charles Lewis Coppage, infant son of Charles F. and Maria T. Coppage. Died May 22, 1849, aged 8 months. OR 6/23.

Llewellyn, son of Henry Bell. Died May 22, 1849, aged 4 years. OR 5/26.

John McCann, of Paris. Died May 27, 1849, aged 81 years. OR 6/2.

William A. Verbryke, printer, of Columbia, Mo. Died May 27, 1849. He was formerly of Lexington, Ky. OR 6/20.

Thomas J. Brown, of Nicholasville. Died May 27, 1849. OR 5/30.

Alonzo H. Weaver, of Lexington. Died May 28, 1849. OR 5/30.

Henry Rogers. Died May 27, 1849. He was one of Fayette county's oldest citizens. OR 6/2.

David T. Hickman, of Paris. Died May 30, 1849. OR 6/2.

Mrs. Eliza Johnson, consort of Richard M. Johnson, of Georgetown. Died May 30, 1849. OR 6/2.

Grosvener, infant son of J. S. and Laura G. Brannin. Died June 3, 1849, aged 10 months. OR 6/9.

Milton Burch, of Scott county. Died June 4, 1849. OR 6/9.

Mrs. Jane Wilson, consort of James Wilson, of Fayette county. Died June 5, 1849, aged 67 years. OR 6/9.

Mrs. Matilda, wife of William B. Huston, of Maysville. Died at the Louisville residence of her brother, T. S. Forman, on June 9, 1849. OR 6/13.

Mrs. Davidella Buckner, consort of Joseph Rogers, of Fayette county, and the eldest daughter of Jesse D. and Lucy A. Winn. Died June 10, 1849, aged 19 years and 6 months. She left an infant one month of age. OR 6/16.

James Mahoney, of Lexington. A native of Ireland. Died June 11, 1849. He was a soldier in the Mexican War. OR 6/13.

Thomas O'Haver, of Lexington. Died of cholera June 11, 1849. OR 6/13.

Charles Wordell, of Lexington. Died of cholera June 12, 1849. OR 6/13.

Cornelia Bauman, youngest daughter of C. and E. M. Fitnam. Died June 13, 1849, aged 2 years and 2 months. OR 6/16.

James C. Todd, of Fayette county. Died at the Fayette county home of James H. Allen, Friday June 15, 1849. OR 6/16.

William Dallam Peter, son of Prof. Robert Peter. Died June 16, 1849, aged 10 years and 10 months. OR 6/20.

Rev. R. R. Dillard, of Georgetown, Ky. He was junior editor of the *Western Baptist Review,* a graduate of Georgetown College, and recently married. Died June 17, 1849. OR 6/30.

Andrew J. White, of Lexington. Died of cholera June 17, 1849. OR 6/20.

Mrs. Loud, wife of Richard Loud. Died of cholera June 17, 1849. OR 6/20.

John Doyle. Died of cholera, at Cooke's Coffee House, Lexington, June 17, 1849. OR 6/20.

Mrs. Beach, wife of Samuel Beach, of Lexington. Died of cholera June 17, 1849. OR 6/20.

Robert Boyd, merchant-tailor, of Lexington. Died of cholera June 17, 1849. OR 6/20.

John Herndon, of Scott county. Died June 18, 1849. OR 6/23.

Arthur Barker, of Lexington. Died of cholera June 18, 1849. OR 6/20.

Edward March, son of James March, of Lexington. Died of cholera June 20, 1849, aged 10 or 11 years. OR 6/23.

Mrs. Margaret Ross, relict of Thomas Ross, of Lexington. Died of cholera June 20, 1849. OR 6/23.

Thomas Moxley, blacksmith. Died in Lexington, of cholera, June 20, 1849, aged 18 or 19 years. OR 6/23.

Fabuis Hull, of Lexington. Died June 1, 1849, aged 32 years. OR 6/30.

Miss Mary O. Wilgus, a young lady of Lexington. Died June 22, 1849. OR 6/23.

Joseph L. Hopper, of Lexington. Died of cholera June 22, 1849. OR 6/23.

George Brisby, son of David K. Brisby. Died of cholera June 23, 1849, aged 13 or 14 years. OR 6/27.

Miss Martha McDowell, daughter of Charles McDowell, dec'd., of Fayette county. Died at the residence of her grandfather, Samuel Redd, June 25, 1849. OR 6/27.

James Baird, of Lexington. He was an old laboring man, an Irishman. He died of cholera Tuesday June 6, 1849, aged about 60 years. OR 6/27.

Mrs. Polly Henry, an elderly woman living in the western suburbs of Lexington. Died of cholera June 27, 1849. OR 6/30.

Miss Mary Watson, of Lexington. Died of cholera at the residence of her uncle, William Pulum, on Broadway, June 28, 1849, aged 15 years. OR 6/30.

Elisha I. Winter, one of Lexington's oldest citizens. Died at the Phoenix Hotel June 29, 1849. OR 7/4.

Miss Martha O. T. Hambleton, daughter of Mrs. .... Hambleton, who lived at the corner of Market and Second streets, Lexington. Died of cholera Friday morning at 7 o'clock, June 29, 1849. OR 6/30.

Mrs. .... Berryman, wife of Samuel Berryman, of Jessamine county Died of cholera in July, 1849. KG 7/28.

The following residents of Paris, K., died of cholera during the month of July, 1849:

Mrs. Mary Pomeroy, wife of A. S. Pomeroy.

Mrs. Ross, wife of William R. Ross.

Emma, infant daughter of William M. Taylor.

Mrs. Caroline Amelia, wife of Robert S. Morrow. OR 7/21.

Mrs. Catharine Higgins, consort of Thomas Higgins, of Lexington. Died of cholera July 1, 1849. OR 7/4.

John M. Powling, of Maysville. Died of cholera July 1, 1849. OR 7/7.

Mrs. John Hunt, of Maysville. Died of cholera in week of July 1, 1849. OR 7/7.

Mrs. Harlow Yancy, wife of Harlow Yancy, of near Helena, Mason county. Died of cholera in week of July 1, 1849, leaving her husband and 3 children. OR 7/7.

William Stafford, of Lexington. Died of cholera July 2, 1849, aged 17 years. OR 7/4.

Virginia E. Warren, of Lexington. Died of cholera July 3, 1849, aged 4 years. OR 7/4.

Stephen Manship, of Lexington. Died of cholera July 3, 1849. OR 7/4.

Miss Catherine Jane Graves, of Lexington. Died of cholera July 3, 1849, aged 15 years. OR 7/4.

Mrs. Catharine Kizer, consort of Jacob Kizer. Died Aug. 14, 1823. OR 8/18.

William J. Dunlap, of Lexington. Died of cholera July 3, 1849. OR 7/4.

Capt. Samuel M. Wallace, of Woodford county. Died of cholera July 3, 1849. OR 7/7.

James M. Eastham, of Georgetown, recently of Lexington. Died July 4, 1849, aged 25 years. OR 7/14.

Burnett R. Perry, of Lexington. He lived on Main Street, nearly opposite the old Baptist burying ground. He died of cholera July 4, 1849. OR 7/7.

Mrs. Mary M. Burrows, relict of Nathan Burrows, of High street, Lexington. Died of cholera July 4, 1849. OR 7/7.

Mrs. Nancy Markey, of Short street, Lexington. Died of cholera July 4, 1849. OR 7/7.

John Shy, who lived on the Winchester pike, in Fayette county. He was a brother-in-law of Samuel Shy. Died of cholera July 4, 1849. OR 7/7.

Capt. Benjamin Berry, of Fayette county. Died July 5, 1849, aged 84 years. OR 7/14.

Mrs. Catharine Huggins, consort of Thomas Huggins, of Lexington. She died July 5, 1849. OR 7/4.

Osceola, son of Hugh Jeter, of Lexington. Died of cholera July 5, 1849. OR 7/7.

Mary Scott, wife of William Scott, of Lexington. They lived opposite the Rail Road Warehouse, on Water street. She died of cholera July 5, 1849. OR 7/7.

Peter Donovan, an Irishman. Died of cholera at the residence of his brother-in-law, Jeff. Merrill, July 5, 1849. OR 7/7.

Mrs. T. W. Cridland, of Mulberry street, Lexington. Died of cholera July 5, 1849. OR 7/7.

James G. McKinney, of Lexington. Died of cholera July 5, 1849. OR 7/7.

Lewellyn Norton, who was connected with the Drug store of his brother, George W. Norton. Died of cholera July 5, 1849. OR 7/7.

James McMurtry. Died of cholera in his room on Short street, near the Post Office, July 5, 1849. OR 7/7.

Miss Kitty Hickey, daughter of Willis Hickey, of Water street, Lexington. Died of cholera July 6, 1849. OR 7/7.

Mrs. J. M. Hunt, wife of John M. Hunt, of Fayette county. Died of cholera July 5, 1849. OR 7/7.

Dr. William W. Whitney, of Lexington. Died of cholera July 6, 1849. OR 7/7.

Professor E. S. Bonfils, of Lexington. Died July 6, 1849. OR 7/7.

Mrs. Galway. Died of cholera at the residence of her son-in-law, Charles Carter, on S. Mill Street, Lexington, July 6, 1849. OR 7/11.

Vachel Keene, of Scott county. Died July 7, 1849, aged 73 years. Obituary OR 7/14.

George B. Twyman, of S. Mill Street, Lexington. Died of cholera July 7, 1849. OR 7/11.

William George, Sr., of Fayette county. Died of cholera July 7, 1849. OR 7/11.

A. S. Jouett, second son of Mrs. Jouett, of Lexington. Died at Harrodsburg, July 7, 1849, of cholera. Obituary OR 7/11.

Richard Vaughn, of High Street, Lexington. Died July 7, 1849. OR 7/11.

Miss Catharine Kelly, of Lexington. Died of cholera July 7, 1849. OR 7/11.

Mrs. Frances Buford, of Lancaster, consort of Col. Thomas Buford. Died July 8, 1849, aged 70 years. OR 7/18.

Noah Hunt, who lived on the old Paris road, Fayette county. Died of cholera July 8, 1849. OR 7/11.

John George, of Lexington. Died of cholera July 8, 1849. OR 7/11.

John W. Curd, of the firm Bodley & Curd, Lexington. Died of cholera at the residence of his mother, Mrs. Eleanor Curd, corner of Second and Upper Streets, July 8, 1849. OR 7/11.

Mrs. Catharine Armstrong, wife of Joseph Armstrong, Water Street, Lexington. Died of cholera July 8, 1849. OR 7/11.

Phebe Anne Burbridge, youngest daughter of Thomas and Elizabeth Burbridge, of Clarke county. Died July 8, 1849, aged 20 years. OR 7/11.

Mrs. Grady. Died of cholera at the residence of her son-in-law, James Bruin, July 9, 1849. She was from Franklin county. OR 7/11.

Mrs. S. Rollins, of High street, Lexington. Died of cholera July 9, 1849. OR 7/11.

Robert Kinkaid, Jr., son of Robert Kinkaid, of Lexington. Died of cholera July 9, 1849. OR 7/11.

James Peel of Lexington. Died of cholera July 9, 1849. OR 7/11.

William Dowden. Died at the Lexington residence of his son-in-law, R. N. Sharp, July 9, 1849. OR 7/11.

William Jenkins, son of Lewis Jenkins, South Broadway, Lexington. Died of cholera July 9, 1849, aged 14 or 15 years. OR 7/11.

James Stone. Died at the Fayette county residence of his son-in-law, Jefferson Blair, July 9, 1849. He died of cholera. OR 7/11.

Mr. Eute Perkins, of Jessamine county, formerly of Fayette. Died July 11, 1849. OR 7/28.

Andrew L. Wallace, son of the late Capt. Samuel L. Wallace, of Lexington. Died in Scott county, of cholera, July 11, 1849. He was 21 years of age. OR 7/14.

Edwin Stephens, of S. Mill Street, Lexington. Died July 11, 1849. OR 7/11.

Miss Harris, daughter, and Mrs. Colbert, mother-in-law of E. W. Harris, of Lexington. Both died of cholera, within an hour of each, July 11, 1849. OR 7/11.

Dr. James Jones, of Mill Street, Lexington. Died of cholera July 11, 1849. OR 7/11.

Grandison Mesmer, of Lexington. Died July 11, 1849. OR 7/14.

Tarlton Weigart, of Lexington. Died of cholera July 11, 1849, aged 18 years. OR 7/14.

John W. Trumbull, of Main Street, Lexington. Died of cholera July 11, 1849. OR 7/11.

Martha Ann, daughter of Alexander Maydwell. Died July 11, 1849, aged 8 years. She died of cholera. OR 7/14.

Eli Vaughn, of Lexington. Died of cholera at the home of John O. Sprakes, on Main Street, Lexington, July 11, 1849. He was 79 years of age. OR 7/14.

Polly, daughter of George B. Twyman, dec'd, of Lexington. Died of cholera July 11, 1849. OR 7/14.

Col. William G. Carter, of Lexington. Died of cholera July 11, 1849. OR 7/14.

Mrs. Amelia Stanhope, relict of William Stanhope, Sr., of Fayette county. Died July 11, 1849. OR 7/21.

James Murphy, blacksmith. Died of cholera at the residence of his mother-in-law, Mrs. Tudor, July 12, 1849. OR 7/14.

Samuel R. Bullock, member of the Lexington Bar. Died of cholera at his residence five miles from Lexington on the Richmond Pike, July 12, 1849. OR 7/14.

Presley Burton. Died of cholera at the residence of his sister, Mrs. Mary H. Cooper, near Lexington, July 12, 1849, aged 73 years. OR 7/14.

Barton W. Moore, eldest son of C. C. and Mary Ann Moore, of Fayette county. Died July 13, 1849. OR 7/2.

Dr. Lemuel Sanders, Druggist. Died of cholera at the residence of his father-in-law, H. M. Winslow, of S. Hill Street, Friday July 13, 1849. OR 7/14.

Miss Ella Herrine. Died of cholera at the residence of her nephew, Daniel Towels, of S. Mill street, Lexington, Friday July 13, 1849. OR 7/14.

Mr. C. B. Gillespie, of Midway, Woodford county. Died of cholera July 14, 1849, aged 21 years. OR 7/21.

Mrs. Ann Rowan, widow of Hon. John Rowan. Died at the Cincinnati residence of her son-in-law, Dr. Buchanan, July 14, 1849, aged 78 years. OR 7/18.

William Trabue, of Fleming county. Died of cholera at John Holland's Tavern, on Main street, Lexington, July 14, 1849. OR 7/18.

Joseph H. Hervey, Sr., of Lexington. Died of cholera July 14, 1849. OR 7/18.

Mrs. Mary Ann Nichols, wife of John Nichols, of Lexington. Died of cholera July 14, 1849. OR 7/18.

Mrs. .... Twyman, relict of George Twyman, of S. Mill street, Lexington. Died of cholera July 14, 1849. OR 7/18.

Col. A. C. Respess, of Maysville. Died July 15, 1849. He was an early graduate of Transylvania University. OR 7/18.

Matthew Wood, of Lexington. Died July 15, 1849. OR 7/18.

Benjamin Clemens, of Lexington. Died of cholera July 15, 1849. OR 7/18.

Miss Cordelia Nichols, of Lexington. Died of cholera at the residence of her brother-in-law, E. W. Dowden, S. Broadway, July 15, 1849. She was 15 years of age. OR 7/18.

Eliza Jane, daughter of Col. Neal McCann. Died July 16, 1849, 12 years of age. OR 7/21.

Peter Gatewood, of Fayette county. Died July 16, 1849, at an advanced age. OR 7/18.

Robert S. Todd, of Frankln county. Died July 16, 1849. He was buried at Lexington. OR 7/18.

Mrs. .... Elliott, wife of Smith Elliott, S. Mill street, Lexington. Died of cholera July 16, 1849. OR 7/18.

Mrs. James Jones, of Athens. Died of cholera July 17, 1849. OR 7/18.

William B. Thomas, of Athens. Died of cholera July 17, 1849. OR 7/18.

John Christian, of Athens. Died July 18, 1849, at an advanced age. OR 7/25.

Mrs. Lucy A. Winn, of Fayette county. Died July 18, 1849, aged 41 years. OR 7/25.

Walter G. Mastin, a native of Cayuga county, N. Y. Died at Athens, Ky., July 18, 1849, aged 25 years. OR 7/21.

Joseph Biggs, Jr. Died at his father's residence in Lexington, July 18, 1849, aged 20 years. OR 7/21.

Joseph P. Nixon, of Lexington. Died of cholera July 18, 1849. OR 7/21.

Mrs. Melinda Winter, wife of George Winter, of Scott county, and daughter of the late Robert Cunningham, of Clarke county. Died July 19, 1849, aged 50 years. OR 8/15.

Smith Burton, a journeyman cabinet maker, of Lexington. Died July 19, 1849, of cholera. OR 7/21.

Mrs. Maria C. Hume, wife of M. D. Hume, of Clarke county, and sister of Mrs. Belinda Winter, above. Died Aug. 7, 1849, aged 40 years. OR 8/15.

William, a son of John Kennard, of Lexington. Died of cholera July 19, 1849, aged 5 years. OR 7/21.

Dr. D. B. Flournoy, of Versalles, Ky., late of Lexington, Mo. Died July 20, 1849, aged 26 years. OR 7/25.

Miss Margaret Rollins, of Lexington. Died at the home of Joseph Ficklin, July 20, 1849, of cholera. OR 7/21.

Mrs. Jane Tudor, of Lexington. Died of cholera July 20, 1849. OR 7/21.

Mrs. Francis Ann Allen, wife of Wright Allen, and daughter of Capt. William G. Skillman, of Fayette county. Died July 21, 1849, aged 17 years. OR 7/25.

Percey, infant son of Col. D. S. Goodloe, of Lexington. Died July 21, 1849, at the Madison county residence of J. Speed Smith. OR 7/28.

Mrs. Theresa J. Leeds, consort of J. C. Leeds, of Paris. Died July 21, 1849.

Mrs. .... Sheely, wife of David Sheely, of Lexington. She died of cholera July 21, 1849. OR 7/25.

Mrs. Malvina Jones, wife of William Jones and daughter of Dr. C. W. Cloud, all of Lexington. Died of cholera July 21, 1849. OR 7/25.

Mrs. Anna Blair, relict of William W. Blair, and daughter of Dr. Walter Warfield, dec'd., all of Lexington. Died of cholera at the home of Rev. N. H. Hall, on South Mulberry street, Sunday July 22, 1849. OR 7/25.

Mrs. .... Ford, of Lexington. Died at the Lexington residence of her daughter, Mrs. Weigart, July 22, 1849, of cholera. OR 7/25.

Miss Jane Robinson, of Lexington. Died of cholera July 22, 1849, aged about 16 years. OR 7/25.

Mrs. Rosanna Barnett, of Jessamine county, relict of Judge Barnett, of Madison county. Died July 22, 1849, aged 70 years. She died at the Jessamine county residence of her son-in-law, P. E. Todhunter. OR 7/25.

Charles Carter, of Lexington. Died of cholera July 22, 1849. OR 7/25.

Emma, daughter of William Beach, of Lexington. Died of cholera July 22, 1849. OR 7/25.

Hugh Carlan, an aged resident of Lexington. Died of cholera July 22, 1849. OR 7/25.

John Kennar, an Irishman. Died of cholera at Rhody Henry's, on Water street, Lexington, July 22, 1849. OR 7/25.

Mrs. .... Towles, wife of Jonathan Towles, of Lexington. Died of cholera July 22, 1849. OR 7/25.

Mrs. .... McCann, wife of Benjamin McCann, who lived 8 miles from Lexington on the Richmond pike. Died of cholera July 23, 1849. OR 7/25.

Roger D., son of Major George W. Williams, of Paris. Died July 23, 1849, aged 17 years. OR 7/28.

Mr. Kelly, janitor of the Medical Hall (Transylvania University?). Died of cholera July 24, 1849. OR 7/25.

Mrs. Caroline E., wife of John S. Stansbury, of Ravenwood, Va., and daughter of Rev. James K. Burch, formerly of Lexington. Died June 24, 1849, aged 24 years. OR 7/7.

Thomas A. Pendleton, of Clarke county. Died June 24, 1849, aged 24 years. OR 7/7.

Caleb Jones, son of William Jones, of Lexington. Died of cholera July 25, 1849, aged 10 or 11 years. OR 7/28.

William H. Rogers, coach-maker, of Lexington. Died of cholera July 28, 1849. OR 8/1.

Mrs. .... Weigart, relict of David Weigart, of Lexington. Died of cholera July 6, 1849. OR 7/28.

James Winn, journeyman tailor. Died at Lexington, of cholera, July 29, 1849. OR 8/8.

Mrs. Dorcas Patrick, wife of James Patrick, of Bethel, Fayette county. Died July 27, 1849, aged about 75 years. OR 8/11.

Mrs. Penn, mother of Shadrach Penn, of Louisville. Died in Scott county, July 27, 1849, aged 87 years. OR 8/11.

Mrs. Sarah Bardsley, of Maysville. Died of cholera July 27, 1849. OR 8/1.

Mrs. Elizabeth Catterlin, widow of Col. Jacob Catterlin, of Dayton, Ohio. Died in Jessamine county, Ky., July 27, 1849, at the residence of her brother-in-law, William Murrain. She was 65 years of age. OR 8/1.

Dr. Lotan G. Watson, late Professor of the Theory and Practice of Medicine at Transylvania University. Died at Hillsboro, N. C., June 27, 1849, aged 55 years. OR 7/18.

Samuel Berryman, who lived on the Fayette and Jessamine county line. Died of cholera July 28, 1849. OR 8/8.

George Ware, of near David's Fork Meeting House. Died of cholera July 28, 1849, aged 71 years. OR 8/.

Samuel J., son of Thornton M. Cox, of Lexington. Died of cholera July 28, 1849, aged about 10 months. OR 8/1.

Mrs. Elizabeth M. Fitnam, wife of Christopher Fitnam, of Lexington. Died of cholera July 28, 1849. OR 8/1.

Mrs. Ellenora Mixer, of Lexington. Died of cholera July 28, 1849. OR 8/1.

Ann Rebecca Ferguson, daughter of A. L. and Mary K. Ferguson, of Lexington. Died June 28, 1849, aged 14 years, 2 months and 21 days. OR 7/7.

William Lafoe, of Fayette county. Died of cholera July 27, 1849. OR 8/4.

Alfred Rose, blacksmith. Died of cholera at the Lexington residence of George W. Morgan, July 29, 1849. OR 8/1.

Alice, aged 4 years, and Jane, aged 11 years, daughters of Christopher Fitnam, of Lexington. Died of cholera July 29, 1849. OR 8/1.

William, son of William H. Newberry, of Lexington. Died of cholera July 29, 1849, aged 13 years. OR 8/1.

Nathaniel P. Barnard, a young printer in the *Observer and Reporter* office. Died of cholera July 29, 1849, aged about 18 years. OR 8/1.

Mrs. Emma Walker, wife of Calvin Walker, of Lexington. Died of cholera July 29, 1849. OR 8/1.

Mrs. Baxter, of Lexington. Died of cholera July 29, 1849. OR 8/1.

James Estill, of Fayette county, recently from Madison county. Died July 29, 1849. OR 8/1.

J. S. Dooley, of the firm Besore and Dooley, Lexington. Died of cholera July 30, 1849. OR 8/1.

Mrs. Rebecca Dooley, wife of J. S. Dooley, dec'd., of Lexington. See above. Died of cholera July 30, 1849. OR 8/1.

Amanda, daughter of William H. Newberry, of Lexington. Died of cholera July 30, 1849. OR 8/1.

Andrew, son of John Chisham, of Lexington. Died of cholera July 30, 1849, aged 10 years. OR 8/1.

Oscar, son of Christopher Fitnam. Died of cholera July 30, 1849, aged 7 years. OR 8/1.

The following residents of Paris, Ky., died of cholera on Monday July 30, 1849:

James Wood
................Watts, a blacksmith
John Thurston
Thomas Rue, a child of Mrs. Ryan
Mrs. Taylor
Mrs. Lovely
Mrs. Haley
Squire Robertson
Dr. John A. Ingels. OR 8/1.

Mrs. Maria Henrietta Hockaday, wife of Philip Hockaday, of St. Louis, and daughter of Samuel Hanson, of Clarke county, Ky. Died June 30, 1849, aged 39 years. OR 7/11.

John Mulligan, of Lexington. Died at the Lexington residence of his brother, Dennis Mulligan, July 31, 1849. He died of cholera. OR 8/1.

Sarah Frances Monks, daughter of Thomas Monks, of Lexington. Died of cholera July 31, 1849. OR 8/1.

Chipley March, son of James March, of Lexington. Died of cholera July 31, 1849. OR 8/1.

John McMains, of Fayette county. Died of cholera July 31, 1849. OR 8/1.

Thomas Lowman, tailor of Lexington. Died of cholera Aug. 1, 1849. OR 8/4.

Mrs. Catharine McFarland, wife of Charles McFarland, of Lexington. Died of cholera Aug. 1, 1849. OR 8/4.

Mrs. Martha Stoll. Died at the Lexington residence of her son-in-law, William Beard, Aug. 1, 1849. She died of cholera. OR 8/4.

Mrs. Susan Thompson, wife of James K. Thompson, of Fayette county. Died Aug. 2, 1849, of cholera. OR 8/4.

Miss Elizabeth Oots, daughter of Sampson Oots, of Lexington. Died of cholera Aug. 2, 1849. OR 8/4.

Mrs. Mary O'Mara, mother-in-law of Charles McFarland, of Lexington. Died of cholera Aug. 2, 1849. OR 8/4.

John Alphonzo Jones, of Lexington. Died of cholera Aug. 2, 1849. OR 8/4.

Mrs. O'Neale, sister of John McCracken, of Lexington. Died at her home on Second street Aug. 3, 1849. OR 8/4.

Robert, son of Thomas Lowman, dec'd., of Lexington. Died of cholera Aug. 3, 1849. OR 8/4.

Judge A. K. Woolley, who lived in Lexington "opposite the College lawn". Died of cholera Aug. 3, 1849. OR 8/4.

Mrs. Susannah Richardson, of Westbrook, Fayette county. Died of cholera Aug. 3, 1849. OR 8/8.

Mrs. Clark, wife of James Clark, of Fayette county. Died of cholera Aug. 3, 1849. OR 8/8.

Josephine Virden, of Lexington. Died of cholera Aug. 4, 1849, aged 13 years. OR 8/8.

Mrs. Ann E., consort of C. G. McHatton, and daughter of M. W. Williams, of Scott county. Died in Georgetown, Aug. 4, 1849, aged 27 years. OR 8/11.

John W. Gess, of Athens. Died of cholera Aug. 6, 1849. OR 8/8.

Mrs. Eliza Jane Pullum, consort of William Pullum. Died at the Lexington residence of her brother, Col. Neal McCann, Aug. 8, 1849, aged 37 years. OR 8/11.

John Curtis, son of Dr. J. C. Darby, of Lexington. Died Aug. 9, 1849, aged 3 years. OR 8/11.

Mrs. Ann Bell, consort of William E. Bell, and daughter of George W. Clark, of Fayette county. Died at the residence of her mother-in-law, Mrs. Huldah Bell, in Lexington, Aug. 9, 1849. OR 8/11.

Samuel Woolley, of Arkansas. Died at the Phoenix Hotel, Lexington, Aug. 9, 1849. He was buried at Lexington. OR 8/11.

John Harris, of Madison county. Died Aug. 14, 1849, aged 70 years. OR 8/25.

Mrs. Mary Wilson, consort of David Wilson, of Bath county, and daughter of Capt. Samuel Herndon, of Mt. Sterling. Died Aug. 14, 1849. She married David Wilson in 1846. OR 8/22.

Mrs. Sarah Miller, consort of Isaac R. Miller, of Lexington. Died Aug. 15, 1849. OR 8/18.

Miss Mary M. Moore, of Bourbon county. Died Aug. 16, 1849. OR 8/25.

John A. Williams, of Madison county. Died Aug. 17, 1849, aged 31 years. OR 8/25.

Mrs. Ann Woolley, wife of John Woolley, of Lexington. Died Aug. 17, 1849. OR 8/18.

Mrs. Ficklin, wife of Joseph Ficklin, of Lexington. She died of cholera Friday Aug. 17, 1849. OR 8/18.

Amos Robert, of Lexington. Died of cholera Aug. 17, 1849. OR 8/18.

George Gorham, of Fayette county. Died Aug. 18, 1849. OR 8/22.

M. Walker Climes, formerly of Harrodsburg. Died Aug. 18, 1849. OR 8/22.

Andrew McClure, of Jessamine county. Died Aug. 18, 1849, aged 59 years OR 8/22.

Mrs. Elenor Halfpenny, of Clarke county. Died Aug. 21, 1849, at an advanced age. She was "a relict of a faithful soldier of the Revolution." OR 8/29.

Nicholas D. White, of Madison county. Died Aug. 21, 1849. OR 8/25.

John W. Hunt, of Lexington. Died Aug. 21, 1849, aged 77 years. OR 8/22.

Lucy Anderson, stepdaughter of J. Cunningham, of Lexington. Died of cholera Aug. 22, 1849, aged 17 years. OR 8/25.

John F. Busby, of Richmond, Ky. Died Aug. 23, 1849, aged 44 years. OR 8/25.

Henry W. Hampton, of Lexington. Died at the residence of his mother-in-law, Mrs. Dishman, Aug. 23, 1849, aged about 35 years. OR 8/18.

Mrs. Sophia, consort of Elder John T. Johnson, of Georgetown. Died Aug. 23, 1849. OR 9/1.

Mrs. Adaline Crittenden, daughter of Thomas S. Theobald, and wife of Robert Crittenden, 3rd son of Governor Crittenden. She died at the Governor's Mansion Aug. 23, 1849, of flux. Her husband was at that time on a visit in Europe. OR 9/1.

Laura Cates, daughter of Owen G. Cates, of Frankfort. Died Aug. 23, 1849, aged 15 years. OR 9/1.

Mrs. Anna Foster, relict of John T. Foster, of Bourbon county. Died Aug. 26, 1849, aged 54 years. OR 9/5.

Mrs. Elizabeth Chinn, of Georgetown. Died Aug. 27, 1849, aged about 60 years. OR 9/1.

Major Green Kerley, of Richmond, Ky. Died of cholera Aug. 27, 1849. OR 9/1.

William Raney, teacher, of Mt. Sterling. Died of cholera Wednesday Aug. 29, 1849. This was the only case of cholera in Mt. Sterling during the 1849 epidemic. OR 9/1.

James Owsley, of Winchester. Died Aug. 29, 1849, aged about 40 years. OR 9/1.

Daniel Bradford, of Georgetown. Died Wednesday Aug. 29, 1849, aged about 60 years. OR 9/5.

Mrs. Laura Brannin, wife of John S. Brannin, of Carroll Parish, La. Died Aug. 31, 1849, at the residence of her father, E. W. Craig, of Fayette county, Ky. OR 9/1.

Duncan F. Robertson, of Danville. Died of cholera Aug. 31, 1849. OR 9/8.

Samuel Pike, Jr., of Fayette county. Died of cholera in August, 1849. OR 8/8.

The following residents of Paris, Ky., died of cholera in August, 1849:

Mrs. Hubbard Taylor
Samuel McIlroy
George Barker
William Finlay
Dr. Quisenberry. OR 8/4.

The following residents of Richmond, Ky., died of cholera in August, 1849:

Mrs. Thompson, wife of Lambert Thompson, late of Lexington.
Sarah Lewis, daughter of John Lewis, late of Lexington.
Miss Martha Stephens, niece of John Lewis.
John Lawrence,
Lucy Lawrence, daughter of John Lawrence, Sr. (Capt.)
Daniel Lawrence, son of Capt. John Lawrence, Sr.

Miss Sophronia Mitchell, of Frankfort. Drowned in Aug., 1849, aged 30 years. OR 8/29.

James S. Duncan, son of Major Jeremiah Duncan, of Bourbon county. Died of cholera in Aug., 1849, aged 27 years. OR 8/25.

Mrs. Susannah Turner, of Bourbon county. Died of cholera in Aug., 1849, aged 69 years. OR 8/25.

Miss Margaret Moxley, of Lexington. Died of cholera in Aug., 1849. OR 8/25.

Mrs. Susannah Weber, relict of George Adam Weber, of Jessamine county, and daughter of Rolfe Eldridge, Sr., of Buckingham county, Pa. Died Sept. 1, 1849. OR 10/3.

Mrs. Laura C., consort of Dr. John A. Lyle, of Bourbon county. Died Sept. 1, 1849. OR 9/5. She was a daughter of John Chambers, of Mason county.

Mary Chambers, daughter of John Chambers, of Mason county. She died Sept. 1, 1849, a few hours after the death of her sister, above. OR 9/5.

Major Samuel McCown, of Mercer county. Died of cholera Sept. 2, 1849, aged 72 years. OR 9/15.

Mesheck Williams, of Danville. Died of cholera Sept. 2, 1849. OR 9/8.

Mrs. Catharine Paul, wife of Hugh Paul, of Woodford county. Died Sept. 3, 1849, aged 46 years. OR 9/12.

Presley Athey, of Lexington. Died of cholera Sept. 3, 1849. OR 9/5.

Mrs. Brand, wife of George W. Brand, of Woodford county, and daughter of David Griffin, of Natchez. She was adopted in early age by David Vertner, of Lexington. She died of cholera Sept. 4, 1849. OR 9/8.

Mrs. Catharine Rigg, mother of Alexander M. Rigg, of Owen county, Ky. Died at Mount Verd, near Jackson, Miss., Sept. 5, 1849, aged 76 years. OR 10/13.

Thomas Kane, of Louisville, formerly a resident of Lexington. Died in former place Sept. 5, 1849. OR 9/12.

Mrs. Rhoda Barnett, of Lexington. Died of cholera Sept. 8, 1849. OR 9/12.

Samuel Patterson, of Smithland, Ky., formerly of Fayette county. Died Sept. 9, 1849. OR 9/22.

James Russell, of Franklin county. Died at the residence of Capt. John W. Russell, Sept. 9, 1849, at an advanced age. OR 9/22.

John Brand, of Lexington. Born in 1775, a native of Montrose. Went to Dundee, Scotland, about the year 1794; came to America in 1801 or 1802; settled in Lexington, Ky., where he entered into a business with John W. Hunt, a partnership which continued 50 years. He died Sunday Sept. 9, 1849, at the home of his son-in-law, Edward Macalester, in Lexington. He died of cholera, in the 74th year of his life. OR 9/19.

Elzy Harvey, of Lexington. Died Sept. 10, 1849. OR 9/12.

Mrs. Margaret Gordon, relict of George W. Gordon. Died of cholera Sept. 10, 1849, at the residence of her father-in-law, John Gordon, of Lexington. OR 9/12.

Mrs. Mary Ann, relict of Elzy Harney, dec'd. Died Sept. 13, 1849, aged 28 years. She died at the residence of Charles R. Thompson. OR 9/19.

Mrs. Nancy Ware, relict of George Ware, of Fayette county. Died Sept. 14, 1849, aged 59 years. OR 10/3.

Col. Alvan Stephens, of Cass county, Mo., a native of Lexington. Died Sept. 15, 1849. OR 10/6.

Julia Maria, infant daughter of Elzy and Mary Ann Harney, both dec'd. See above. Died Sept. 17, 1849, aged 8 months. OR 9/19.

Mrs. Agnes M. Lyle, widow of Joel R. Lyle. Died at the residence of her son, William C. Lyle, Sept. 19, 1849, aged 66 years and 8 months. She was a daughter of Matthew Kenney, Sr., of Fayette county, and was born in Augusta county, Va. In 1807 she was married and settled in Paris, where, in its vicinity she resided until her death. OR 9/19.

Mrs. Verga J. Swift, consort of William Swift, of Millersburg, formerly of Lexington, and daughter of Lewis Vimont. She died Sept. 19, 1849, of cholera. OR 9/26.

James Weathers, Sr., of Fayette county. Died Sept. 22, 1849, aged 74 years. OR 9/26.

Henry Clay Harlan, son of Hon. James Harlan, of Frankfort. Died Sept. 29, 1849, aged 20 years. OR 10/3.

Maria A. Messick, consort of John Messick, of Jessamine county, and youngest daughter of the late Capt. Samuel Fitch, of Lexington. Died Sept. 29, 1849. OR 10/3.

Joseph Lyon, of Lexington. Murdered in Sept., 1849. See OR 9/22.

Hon. Benjamin Johnson, a Judge of the Supreme Court of Arkansas. Died at the Lexington residence of his brother, Capt. Henry Johnson, Oct. 2, 1849. Buried at Little Rock, Ark. OR 10/3.

Capt. Thomas Helm, of Woodford county. Died Oct. 6, 1849, aged 81 years and 2 months. OR 10/31.

Conrad Harp of Fayette county. Died Oct. 7, 1849, aged 67 years. OR 10/13.

Edgar Allen Poe, poet. Died at Baltimore, Sunday Oct. 7, 1849. OR 10/13.

Mrs. Frances Grigsby, consort of Lewis Kemp Grigsby, of Clarke county, and daughter of the late Col. J. V. Bush. Died Oct. 8, 1849, aged 46 years. OR 10/13 and 10/16.

Charles G. Young, of Lexington. Died Oct. 9, 1849, aged 38 years. OR 10/13.

Mrs. Eleanora March, of Lexington. Died Oct. 11, 1849. OR 10/13.

Mrs. Catherine H. Apperson, consort of W. W. Apperson, of Owingsville. Died at Mt. Sterling Oct. 12, 1849, aged 21 years. OR 10/31.

Mrs. Verlinda Offutt, consort of Barruck Offutt, dec'd., of Scott county. Died Oct. 15, 1849. OR 10/24.

Henry W., infant son of H. W. Hampton, dec'd., of Lexington. Died at the Lexington residence of Mrs. Dishman Oct. 18, 1849. OR 10/20.

Jacob Vanmeter, of Clarke county. Died Oct. 19, 1849, aged 27 years. OR 10/24.

John Roche, Professor of Ancient Languages at Transylvania University. Died Oct. 23, 1849, aged 55 years. OR 10/24.

John Wright, of Bourbon county. Died Oct. 24, 1849, aged about 63 years. OR 10/27.

Mrs. Elizabeth N. Offutt, consort of Urius M. Offutt, of Scott county, and daughter of Stephen L. Garrard, of Bourbon county. Died Oct. 27, 1849. OR 11/3.

William Brand of Aberdeen, Scotland, brother of the late John Brand, of Lexington, Ky. Died Oct. 31, 1849, aged 85 years. OR 12/8.

Claiborne T. Brasfield, formerly of Clarke county. Died in Harrodsburg Nov. 2, 1849, aged about 50 years. OR 11/10.

Rebecca Dunlap, oldest citizen of Fayette county. Died at the Lexington residence of her son, John R. Dunlap, Nov. 7, 1849, aged 99 years. She was born in Augusta county, Va., July 23, 1751. Obituary OR 11/14.

Rev. Orlando W. Craig, of Estill county. Died Nov. 10, 1849, aged 32 years, 11 months and 2 days. OR 11/28.

Mrs. Fanny Hampton, consort of Lewis Hampton, and daughter of Dr. A. Hood, all of Winchester. Died Nov. 11, 1849. OR 11/14.

Dr. Augustus W. Mills, of Winchester. Died Nov. 13, 1849, aged 43 years. OR 11/14.

William Wilson, of Lexington. Died Nov. 13, 1849. OR 11/14.

Benijah Bosworth, of Fayette county. Died Nov. 16, 1849, aged about 90 years. OR 11/17.

Henry Franklin, of Fayette county. Died Nov. 18, 1849, at an advanced age. OR 11/21.

Mrs. Sally E., wife of M. L. Broadwell, of Cynthiana. Died Nov. 4, 1849, aged 20 years. OR 11/28.

Isaac Arnold, of Garrard county. Died Nov. 26, 1849, at an advanced age. OR 12/5.

Samuel Clay, Sr., of Bourbon county. Died Nov. 28, 1849. OR 12/8.

Mrs. Ann Cromwell, wife of Alvin Cromwell, of Frankfort, and daughter of Charles McLèar, dec'd., of Fayette county. Died Dec. 1, 1849. OR 12/8.

Mrs. Elizabeth Hay Brand, relict of John Brand, Dec'd., of Lexington. Died Dec. 5, 1849, aged 68 years. OR 12/8.

Mrs. Rhoda Anderson, formerly of Lexington; died at the Louisville residence of her son, Col. Thomas Anderson, Dec. 5, 1849, aged 75 years. OR 12/8.

David Tingle, of Lexington. Died Dec. 10, 1849, aged 57 years. OR 12/12.

Adeliza Keen, daughter of George F. Keen, of Fayette county. Died Dec. 14, 1849, aged 17 years. OR 12/19.

Harvey McGuire, of Louisville, formerly of Lexington. He died Dec. 20, 1849, aged 48 years. OR 12/26.

Lewis Vimont, of Millersburg. Died in December, 1849, at an advanced age. OR 12/22. He died Dec. 11. See OR 1/9/1850.

Walter J. Lacy, of Flemingsburg. Died Dec. 21, 1849. OR 1/2/50.

John Bean, of Clarke county. Died Dec. 25, 1849, aged about 85 years. OR 1/2/1850.

Amanda, wife of James Kirkpatrick, and daughter of John Cain, of Louisville. Died there Dec. 5, 1849. OR 1/2/1850.

Mrs. M. E. Harris, daughter of Col. Joseph Woolfolk, of Woodford county. Died at her husband's residence, in Nelson county, Va., Nov. 22, 1849, aged 27 years. OR 1/2/1850.

C. G. Mead, son-in-law of Col. Joseph Woolfolk, of Woodford county. Died in Yazoo county, Miss., Oct. 26, 1849, aged 31 years. OR 1/2/1850.

John L., infant son of William and Catharine Duke, of Bourbon county. Died Dec. 27, 1849. OR 1/9/1850.

Arther Reese, of Lexington. Died Dec. 29, 1849. OR 1/9/50.

Mrs. Nancy W. Shelby, wife of Evan Shelby, of Lincoln county. Died Dec. 30, 1849. OR 1/9/1850.

Adeline Keene, of Fayette county. Died Dec. 14, 1849, aged 17 years. OR 1/9/1850.

William Moore, of Fayette county. Died Dec. 1, 1849, aged 30 years. OR 1/19/1850.

Green Clay Rodes, son of Col. William Rodes, of Madison county. Died Jan. 1, 1850. OR 1/5.

Richard Brent, of Lexington. Died Jan. 2, 1850, aged 66 years. OR 1/5.

William, infant son of D. C. and Virginia W. Wickliffe. Died Jan. 6, 1850. OR 1/9.

James W. Gibson, son of James Gibson, of Fayette county. Died Jan. 5, 1850, aged 30 years. OR 1/9.

Francis Garner. Died at the Fayette county residence of Mrs. Margaret Downing Jan. 1, 1850, aged about 60 years. OR 1/12.

John Sheely, of Fayette county. Died Jan. 9, 1850. OR 1/12.

OBITUARIES

The abbreviations used denote:

KG—(Lexington) *Kentucky Gazette*
OR—Lexington (Ky.) *Observer & Reporter*

1850

Mrs. Robinson, wife of William Robinson, of Bowling Green. Drowned Jan. 9, 1850. She had been married but 6 months. Her maiden name was Whitesides. OR 1/19.

Elias Knight, of Christian county. Suicided Jan. 14, 1850. OR 1/19.

John Stone, of Fayette county. Died Wednesday, Jan. 16, 1850, aged 60 years. OR 1/19.

Mrs. Catherine McHatton, relict of Hon. Robert McHatton. Died at the Georgetown residence of her son, Jan. 9, 1850, aged about 60 years. OR 1/19.

Emily, infant daughter of Lucellus and Margaret L. Lawes, of Lexington. Died Jan. 17, 1850. OR 1/23.

John Thomas Goodwin, of Fayette county. Died Jan. 11, 1850, aged 29 years. OR 1/23.

Abram Irvine, Sr. Died at the Boyle county residence of his son, James H. Irvine, Jan. 16, 1850, aged 84 years. OR 1/23.

Mrs. Elizabeth R. Parker, of Lexington. Died Jan. 21, 1850. She was one of the oldest citizens of this city. OR 1/26.

Samuel F. Patterson, son of Col. James Patterson, dec'd., of Scott county. Died in Versailles Jan. 22, 1850. OR 1/26.

Mrs. Sarah H., consort of Parker Otwell, of Georgetown. Died Jan. 21, 1850. OR 1/26.

Mrs. Lucinda McKim, consort of William McKim, of Millersburg, and eldest daughter of Capt. John Cunningham, of Bourbon county. Died Jan. 13, 1850. OR 1/26.

Mrs. Martha Beard, relict of Col. Henry Beard. Died in Lexington Jan. 29, 1850, aged 66 years. OR 2/2.

William Price, son of Willis Price, of Fayette county. Died Jan. 13, 1850, aged 22 years. OR 2/2.

Mrs. Margaret Craig, consort of Charles F. Craig, and daughter of Willis and Margaret Price, of Fayette county. Died in Lexington Jan. 25, 1850, aged 36 years. OR 2/2.

Mrs. Elizabeth C. Offutt, wife of Alfred D. Offutt, of Scott county. Died Jan. 22, 1850, aged 43 years. OR 2/2.

Henry Washington, of Breckenridge county. Died Feb. 1, 1850, aged 57 years. OR 2/9.

Mary Churchill Payne, formerly of Lexington. Daughter of James B. Payne, dec'd., of Fayette county. Died at Elizabethtown, Ky., Feb. 1, 1850, aged 19 years. OR 2/9.

Mrs. Fanny C. Spears, wife of Noah Spears, Jr., and daughter of Elder John A. Gano, of Bourbon county. Died there Feb. 4, 1850, aged 18 years. OR 2/9.

Lucy Mildred, daughter of Mrs. Mildred J. Anderson, of Lexington. Died Feb. 5, 1850, aged 8 years. OR 2/9.

Wharton R. Moore, of Fulton, Mo. Died Jan. 18, 1850, aged 67 years. OR 2/9.

Boston, celebrated race horse. Died Tuesday, Jan. 29, 1850 at the farm of Edward M. Blackburn, in Woodford county. OR 2/9.

Mrs. Elizabeth Calmes, of Winchester. Died Dec. 31, 1849, aged about 64 years. OR 2/13/1850.

Mrs. Nancy Johnson, relict of Col. James Johnson. Died at the Great Crossing, Scott county, Feb. 11, 1850, aged 73 years. OR 2/16.

Rt. Rev. Benedict Joseph Flaget, first Roman Catholic Bishop of Louisville. Died there Feb. 11, 1850, aged 87 years. OR 2/16.

Lieut. Thomas T. Sloan, a native of Lexington, Ky. Died at Brooklyn, N. Y., Feb. 11, 1850. OR 2/13.

Mrs. Mary Elizabeth, consort of Edward W. Dowden, of Lexington. Died Feb. 18, 1850. OR 2/20.

Rev. John M. Barnes, pastor of the Christian Church at Hopkinsville. Died Feb. 17, 1850. OR 2/23.

George W. Weissinger, of Louisville. Died Feb. 25, 1850. OR 2/27.

Lieut. James Johnson Moore, son of Col. Thomas P. Moore. Died at Harrodsburg Feb. 17, 1850. He served in the Mexican War. OR 2/27.

W. M. Bostwick, son of W. G. Bostwick, of Frankfort. Died Feb. 19, 1850. OR 2/27.

Mrs. Margaret Vance, of Fayette county. Died Feb. 14, 1850, aged 73 years. OR 2/27.

Mary Burrowes, of Lexington. Funeral held (after being postponed "some time ago") Sunday, March 3, 1850. OR 3/2.

Hannah Maria, daughter of Henry T. Duncan. Died Feb. 27, 1850, aged 9 years. OR 3/2.

Mrs. Elizabeth Williams, wife of John Williams, of Woodford county. Died Feb. 27, 1850, aged 50 years and 10 days. OR 3/6.

Mrs. ——— Hall, wife of Rev. N. H. Hall, formerly of Fayette county. Died in St. Louis Feb. 26, 1850. OR 3/6

Alney McLean, for many years a Circuit Judge in Kentucky, and member of Congress. Died in California in February or March, 1850. OR 3/13.

Rev. Porter Clay, a Baptist minister, and brother of Hon. Henry Clay. He was formerly of Frankfort, Ky. Died near Camden, La., Feb. 17, 1850. Obituary in OR 3/13.

John W. Graves of Fayette county. Died Feb. 26, 1850. OR 3/13.

Mrs. Mary Ann Spiers. Died at the Lexington residence of Zephaniah Spiers, Mar. 7, 1850, aged 70 years. OR 3/13.

Col. Preston W. Farrar, of New Orleans, a native of Lexington, Ky. Died Mar. 7, 1850. He married a daughter of Governor Scott, of La. Obituary in OR 3/16 and 3/30.

Charles Carroll, infant son of T. C. and Charlotte Fry. Died Mar. 10, 1850, aged 5 months and 15 days. OR 3/16.

Mrs. Elizabeth Frost, relict of Caleb Frost, of Anne Arundel county, Maryland. Died at Lexington, Ky., at the residence of her son, John M. Frost, Mar. 15, 1850 aged 84 years. OR 3/20.

John Adam Link, son of William R. Link, of Lexington. Died Mar. 17, 1850, aged 6 years. OR 3/20.

John Milton Breckinridge, son of John C. and Mary C. Breckinridge. Died Mar. 18, 1850, aged 7 months and 11 days. OR 3/20.

Dr. J. C. Bybee, formerly of Harrodsburg, Ky. Died at San Francisco, Calif., Jan. 7, 1850. OR 3/20.

Joseph N. Bell, of Scott county. Died Mar. 14, 1850. OR 3/23.

Mrs. E. H. Price, relict of Dr. William H. Price, and daughter of the late Judge James Haggin. Died at her residence in Frankfort, Mar. 16, 1850, aged 45 years. OR 3/23.

M. B. Cochran, of Louisville. Suicided Mar. 20, 1850. OR 3/23.

Annie Bell, daughter of Derrick and Martha B. Warner. Died Mar. 23, 1850, aged about 6 years. OR 3/27.

William Dunlap, infant son of Benjamin F. and Rebecca A. Dunn, formerly of Lexington, then of Danville. Died Mar. 20, 1850. OR 3/27.

Mrs. Hester Ann Robertson, of Jessamine county. Died Mar. 14, 1850, aged 50 years. OR 3/27.

Mrs. Rosa H. Anderson, consort of Rev. William H. Anderson, of Lexington. Died at the Richmond, Ky., residence of her father, Curtis Field, Sr., Mar. 17, 1850. OR 3/27.

David E. Harrison, of Garrard county. Died Mar. 20, 1850, aged 28 years. OR 3/27.

Jesse Hill, of Garrard county. Killed by Dr. Hezekiah Evans, Mar. 25, 1850. OR 3/30.

Mrs. Eliza Breckinridge, relict of Preston Breckinridge, formerly of Georgetown. Died in Louisville Mar. 22, 1850. OR 3/30.

Mrs. Martha W. Smith, wife of James W. Smith, of Fayette county. Died Mar. 30, 1850. OR 4/3.

William Tebbs Reid, son of Hon. Walker Reid, of Mason county. Died Mar. 29, 1850, aged 31 years. OR 4/3.

Robert Morrison, son of Major John Morrison, one of the early settlers of Kentucky. His mother was the first woman to take shelter in the old fort or blockhouse in Lexington. Died Mar. 12, 1850, in Butler county, aged about 68 years. OR 4/3.

Col. Benjamin Taylor, formerly of Fayette county, later of Arkansas. Drowned Mar. 6, 1850. OR 4/6.

Mrs. Ellen Letcher, consort of Dr. J. P. Letcher, of Nicholasville. Died Mar. 28, 1850, aged 26 years. OR 4/6.

Mrs. Mary Gibney, consort of Alexander Gibney, of Lexington. Died Apr. 5, 1850. OR 4/10.

James A. Welch, of Jessamine county. Died Mar. 28, 1850, aged 29 years. OR 4/10.

Caroline F., daughter of Charles and Sarah J. Roy. Died in Georgetown in April, 1850, aged 12 years. OR 4/13.

Mary Eliza, eldest daughter of Hon. Humphrey Marshall. Died Apr. 6, 1850, at Poplar Hill Academy, near Frankfort. She was 14 years and 9 months of age. OR 4/13.

Dr. Samuel C. Trotter, of Millersburg, formerly of Lexington. Died Apr. 14, 1850. OR 4/17.

William H. Eubank, of Franklin county. Died Apr. 2, 1850. OR 4/17.

Hon. Thomas J. Campbell, of Tenn., Clerk of the House of Representatives. Died Apr. 13, 1850. OR 4/17.

John J. Thomas, late a State Senator from Campbell county. Died Apr. 9, 1850, aged 50 years. OR 4/20.

Mrs. Eliza P. Coons, consort of Rev. John F. Coons, and daughter of Patterson Bain, dec'd. Died Apr. 17, 1850, at the Lexington residence of her brother, George C. Bain. OR 4/20.

Mrs. Martha Hunter, wife of Thomas Hunter, of Miss., and daughter of William Dowden, dec'd. Died at the Lexington home of her brother-in-law, Elisha B. Cravens, Apr. 18, 1850. OR 4/20.

George C. Hutton, formerly of Lexington, Ky. Died while on a trip to California in the Spring, of 1850. OR 4/20.

Elizabeth Winters, infant daughter of William Beach, of Lexington. Died Apr. 21, 1850. OR 4/24.

Hon. John Norvell, late U. S. Senator from Michigan. He was born in Garrard county; fought in the War of 1812; married in Philadelphia; was editor of the *Kentucky Gazette;* died Apr. 24, 1850, aged 58 years. Obituary S 5/1 and 5/8.

Gen. John Thomson Mason, second son of Stevens Thomson Mason, of Loudon county, Va., and the grand nephew of George Mason, author of the Bill of Rights. He was formerly a resident of Lexington, Ky. He died at Galveston, Texas, Apr. 17, 1850, aged 65 years. S 5/8.

Mrs. Lydia Anne Innes, wife of John P. Innes, of Fayette county. Died May 7, 1850, aged 29 years. S 5/11.

Dr. Caleb W. Cloud, of Lexington. Died May 14, 1850, aged 69 years. S 5/15.

Joseph T., infant son of Sylvester and Mary E. Lanchart, of Danville. Died May 1, 1850, aged 2 years, 2 months and 10 days. S 5/15.

Mrs. Elizabeth Church, relict of Edward Church. Died in Louisville May 2, 1850, aged 63 years. She was a native of London, and a daughter of John Bentley. S 5/15.

Mr. Rody Henry, of Lexington, a native of the Parish of Kilcronahan, County of Derry, Ireland. Died May 5, 1850, aged 36 years, leaving wife and 4 children. S 5/15.

Martin Hoagland. Sr., of Lexington. Died May 15, 1850. S 5/22.

Hon. William Hendricks, of near Madison, Iowa. Died May 16, 1850. S 5/25.

William H. Cunningham, of Fayette county. Died May 30, 1850, from injuries received when his horse jumped over a precipice near Slickaway. S 6/1.

Miss Ellen Bradford, daughter of Daniel Bradford, of Lexington. Died May 30, 1850. S 6/1.

J. N. Crane, infant son of J. P. and M. C. Crane, of Fayette county. Died June 5, 1850, aged 14 days. S 6/8.

Willis Muir, of Fayette county. Died June 4, 1850. S 6/12.

Mrs. Caroline T. Peters, wife of Waller L. Peters. Died at the Woodford county residence of Louis Peters June 12, 1850, aged 26 years. S 6/29.

John Melcher, oldest printer in the United States. He was an apprentice to Daniel Fowle, who introduced the first printing press in New Hampshire in 1766. Died June 9, 1850, aged 90 years. S 7/3. He died at Portsmouth, N. H.

Elizabeth Mitchell, infant daughter of Alexander J., and Mary R. Mitchell, and granddaughter of Gen. Leslie Combs. Died at Estill Springs July 12, 1850, aged 16 months. S 7/17.

Col. Manlius V. Thompson, of Georgetown. Died July 22, 1850. S 7/24.

Shelton, son of John H. and Augusta Hunter, of Lexington. Died July 18, 1850, aged about 2 years. S 7/24.

Pierre, son of Charles and Nancy Wheatly, of Lexington. Died of cholera July 25, 1850. S 7/27.

Mrs. Martha Farrar, wife of John M. Farrar, of Fayette county. Died July 25, 1850. S 7/27.

Dr. John T. Shotwell, of Cincinnati. Born in Mason county; entered office of Dr. Daniel Drake in his youth; became Professor of Anatomy in the Ohio State Medical College. Died of cholera July 23, 1850, aged about 43 years. S 7/31.

Sarah Brown, of Frankfort. Died of cholera July 22, 1850. S 8/3.

William Parker Johnston, son of M. C. N. Johnston, of Frankfort. Died of cholera July 22, 1850. S 8/3.

Mrs. Minas Williams, of Frankfort. Died of cholera July 22, 1850. S 8/3.

Miss Susan Dryden, of Ohio. Died at Frankfort, Ky., of cholera, July 26, 1850. S 8/3.

Mrs. Mary Ellen Moffett, of Frankfort. Died of cholera July 28, 1850. S 8/3.

Charles Williams, son of Mr. A. W. Brown, of Frankfort. Died of cholera July 28, 1850. S 8/3.

Benjamin Johnson, son of William Waller, Jr. Died at the Lexington residence of William S. Waller, July 25, 1850, aged 3 years, 4 months and 18 days. S 8/3.

David Murray, of Lexington, a printer. Died Aug. 5, 1850. S 8/7.

Eleanor Green, daughter of F. and Mary B. Mitchell, of Louisville. Died Aug. 5, 1850, aged 16 months and 2 days. S 8/10.

Mrs. Jane Epperson, of Lexington. Died Aug. 9, 1850, aged 38 years. She left three children. S 8/17.

Mrs. Sarah Sanders, of Nicholasville. Died Aug. 13, 1850. She was a sister of Mrs. Jane Epperson, above. S 8/17.

Mrs. Phoebe Woolfolk, of near Georgetown. Born in Caroline county, Va., in June, 1780. Emigrated to Kentucky in 1794. Died Aug. 18, 1850, in her 71st year. S 8/24.

Col. M. Taul, of Mardisville, Ala., formerly of Winchester, Ky. Died May 27, 1850, aged 65 years. Obituary written by his daughter Louisiana Bradford Taul. S 8/24.

John H. Bosworth, formerly of Lexington, Ky. Died in Oregon City, May 28, 1850, aged 29 years, 7 months and 11 days. S 8/28.

Matthew J. Patterson, of Scott county. Died Aug. 23, 1850, aged 46 years and 6 months. He left his wife, mother (aged) and two children. S 8/28.

Robert Wickliffe, Jr., of Lexington. Died Aug. 29, 1850, at 8:30 p. m. He was the only surviving son of Robert Wickliffe, Sr. S 8/31.

Dr. J. H. A. Fehr, late of Lexington. Died of cholera in Louisville in Sept., 1850. S 9/7.

Mrs. Louisa Wickliffe, consort of Charles H. Wickliffe, of Lexington. Died Sept. 6, 1850. S 9/7.

Rosalie, daughter of Dr. A. Otto H. and Harriet E. Hardenstein, of Lexington. Died Sept. 1, 1850, aged 2 years and a month. S 9/7.

Mrs. Margaret Ann Elbert, wife of Theodore Elbert, of Fayette county. Died Sept. 3, 1850, aged 28 years. She left her husband and 3 little daughters. S 9/7.

Bishop H. B. Bascom. Died in Louisville Sept. 9, 1850. S 9/11.

Maria Louisa, infant daughter of J. A. and G. A. Hall, of Lexington. Died Sept. 19, 1850. S 9/21.

Leonidas Baker Photon, of Danville. Died Sept. 17, 1850, aged 27 years. S 9/21.

David McBlain, of Lexington, a native of Ayr, Scotland. Died Sept. 22, 1850, aged 37 years. He left his wife and three children. S 9/25.

Charles Daniel, formerly Postmaster at Mt. Sterling. Died at Sibley, Mo., Sept. 9, 1850. S 9/25.

Mrs. Ellen Fischer, of Lexigton. Died Sept. 27, 1850. S 9/28.

Bishop Henry B. Bascom, of Louisville. See above. Additional notices in S 10/5.

James Sinclair, youngest son of Peter and Susan Haring, of Lexington. Died Oct. 2, 1850, aged 1 year, 5 months and 11 days. S 10/5.

Edward Protzman, of Lexington, a native of Pennsylvania. A volunteer in the war with Mexico. Died .... S 10/16.

Mrs. Lucretia Hoagland, of Lexington. Died Oct. 30, 1850, aged 82 years. S 11/2.

Thomas Clements. Killed by his brother, Madison Clements, Nov. 6, 1850. S 11/9.

Mrs. Elizabeth L. Holland, wife of Dr. R. C. Holland, of Louisville, and daughter of Nelson and Sarah E. Turner. Died Oct. 12, 1850 aged 25 years. She left four children. S 11/9.

Col. Richard M. Johnson. Died in Frankfort, Nov. 19, 1850. S 11/20.

Mrs. Caroline P. Arnold, daughter of John Cavins, of Lexington. She died in Henry county, Nov. 3, 1850, aged 24 years. S 11/27.

Robert Spalding Wilson, of Lexington. Died Nov. 29, 1850. S 11/30.

William Jackson, of Lexington, formerly of Virginia. Died Nov. 23, 1850. S 11/30.

Sarah Catharine, infant daughter of N. D. and Pelina Moore, of Fayette county. Died Dec. 4, 1850. S 12/7.

Mrs. E. Geohegan, of Lexington. Died Dec. 5, 1850. S 12/11.

William C. Kidd, of Lexington. Died Dec. 5, 1850. S 12/11.

John Hodge Stockwell, of Flemingsburg. Died Nov. 28, 1850, aged 31 years. S 12/11.

Mrs. Sarah Parker, consort of John Parker, of Fayette county. Died Dec. 24, 1850, aged about 36 years. S 12/28.

John Gordon, Sr., of Lexington. Died Dec. 29, 1850, aged 74 years. He came from Philadelphia to Lexington in 1800. S 1/4/1851.

Mrs. Margaret H. McConnell, wife of George W. V. McConnell, of Versailles. Died Oct. 23, 1850. S 1/4/1851.

Mrs. Julia DeClifford Evans, consort of Dr. George W. Evans, of Lexington. Died Jan. 14, 1851. S 1/15.

Septimus Wardle, of Lexington. Died Jan. 16, 1851. S 1/22.

Miss Matilda R. Bradford, daughter of Daniel Bradford, of Lexington. Died Jan. 23, 1851. S 1/29.

Charles Robinson, infant son of David F. and Mary H. Hogan, of Lexington. Died in Louisville, Jan. 19, 1851, aged 18 months. S 1/29.

Harrison Daniel, of Jessamine county. Died Jan. 15, 1851, aged 54 years. S 1/29.

Alice Young, daughter of Mr. L. P. Young. Died Feb. 1, 1851, aged 2 years and 9 months. S 2/5.

John M. Hewett, of Lexington. Died Feb. 2, 1851, at an advanced age. S 2/5.

Mrs. Fannie S. Shelby, wife of Thomas H. Shelby, Jr., and daughter of Dr. John Todd, of Springfield, Ill. Died at latter place Feb. 4, 1851, leaving an infant son 9 days old. S 2/8.

John Thompson, of Lexington, a native of Virginia. Died Feb. 7, 1851, aged 37 years. He had lived in Lexington since 1836. S 2/12.

Major Richard Spurr, of Fayette county. Died Feb. 8, 1851, aged 42 years. S 2/15.

Henry Clay Spurr, son of Major Spurr (see above). Died Feb. 8, 1851, aged 5 years. S 2/15.

Mrs. Sarah S. Wheelock, of Lexington. Died Feb. 22, 1851. S 2/26.

John F. Todd. Died Feb. 26, 1851, at Frankfort. S 3/1.

Platt Wilson, youngest child of Dr. George W. Evans. Died in Maysville, March 1, 1851. S 3/5.

Mrs. Susan Ann Wood, consort of Benjamin C. Wood, of Lexington. Died Mar. 22, 1851. S 3/26.

Robert Landreth, late of Charleston, S. C., but now of Lexington, Ky., where he died Mar. 19, 1851, aged 51 years. He was buried here with Military honors. S 3/29.

William G. Skillman, of Fayette county. Died in Harrodsburg Mar. 31, 1851. S 4/2.

Aurelius Willis, son of John A. and Catharine Willis, of Lexington. Died Apr. 1, 1851, aged 7 years, 2 months and 15 days. S 4/5.

Mary Eliza, eldest daughter of James March, of Lexington. Died Apr. 14, 1851, aged 17 years. S 4/23 and 4/26.

James Madison Kidd, of Lexington. Died Apr. 23, 1851. S 4/26.

Thomas Collins, of Lexington. Died Apr. 28, 1851. S 4/30.

Mary Ford, of Georgetown. Died Apr. 25, 1851. She was unmarried. S 4/30.

Mrs. Margaret Kinkead, wife of John Kinkead, of Woodford county. Died at the Bourbon county residence of her son-in-law, William Talbott, Apr. 23, 1851. S 4/30.

Cornelius Burnett, editor of the Henderson (Ky.) *Democrat Banner.* Died in April or May, 1851. S 5/10.

James Irvinge, of Jessamine county. Born in Mecklenburg county, Va., in March, 1754. He was in General Arnold's expedition against Canada in Sept., 1775; under General Washington at the siege and capture of Yorktown; at the Battle of White Plains, Germantown, Brandywine, Trenton, Princeton, Monmouth, Long Island, Red Bank, etc. He served throughout the War of Independence and was discharged at Charles City Va. He died Jan 3, 1851, in his 97th year. S 5/14.

Mrs. Caroline Elizabeth, consort of William P. Wilson, of Franklin, Ind., and daughter of Mrs. Ann E. Landreth, of Lexington, Ky. She was a native of Charleston, S. C., and was married in Lexington "several years ago." Died near Martinsville, Ind., Apr. 28, 1851, aged 20 years. S 5/28.

William H. Carpenter, of Lexington. An orphan. Reared by his uncle, George W. Dunlap, of Louisville. He was a volunteer in the War with Mexico. He was killed Sunday, May 25, 1851, by Jacob Cassell. He was in his 23rd year. S 5/28 and 5/31.

James Erwin, of Lexington, Ky., and New Orleans. Died in former city June 1, 1851. S 6/7.

Robert Frazer, of Lexington, one of the city's oldest inhabitants. He was never married. Died June 1, 1851. S 6/7.

John Utley, of Lexington. Died June 16, 1851, aged 55 years. S 6/18.

Mary Reed. Died May 31, 1851: Anna Reed. Died June 3, 1851. These were infant twins of James A. and Julia Wendover. They died of cholera. S 6/18.

Miss Mary B., daughter of Lucinda Deane, of Lexington. Died June 14, 1851, aged 20 years. S 6/18.

James A. Wendover, of St. Louis, Mo., and for 15 years a merchant of that city. Died of cholera June 4, 1851, aged 40 years and 23 days. S 6/18 and 6/25. Note children and wife of above.

Stephen Breckinridge, eldest son of Leo Tarlton. Died of cholera June 7, 1851, at Ion Plantation, Madison Parish, La., residence of his father. He was 14 years of age. S 6/25.

Mrs. Sytha E. Shiddell, of Lexington. Died June 18, 1851, aged 29 years. S 6/25.

Benjamin F. Higgins, M. D., of Fayette county, Ky. Died at Bridgeport, South Yuba River, California, May 6, 1851, aged 24 years. S 7/2.

Thomas Jefferson, second son of Michael and Lucinda Goodnight, of Fayette county. Died June 21, 1851, aged 15 years, 2 months and 12 days. S 7/9.

William Beach, of Lexington. Died July 6, 1851, aged 40 years. He left his widow and one child. S 7/9.

Mary Anne Browning, daughter of Mrs. Mary Browning, of Lexington. Died July 11, 1851, aged 19 years. S 7/12.

St. Clair J. Buford, of Woodford county. Killed at Versailles during a fight with George W. Carter, former sheriff. Died July 18, 1851. Carter was held blameless. S 7/23.

Larkin Scott, son of L. C. Randall, of Lexington. Died July 19, 1851. S 7/23.

Eugene, son of A. J. and Annie D. Haile, of Lexington. Died of cholera July 18, 1851, aged 1 year and 4 months. S 7/23.

Clement Hearne. Died at the Fayette county residence of Capt. Joseph Hearne, July 7, 1851, aged 66 years. S 7/23.

Lewis W. Morgan, late of Lexington, Ky. Died at Memphis, Tenn., the home of his brother, John L. Morgan, July 3, 1851, aged 45 years. S 7/23.

George P. Richardson, of Lexington, Ky., a native of Virginia. Died July 16, 1851. S 7/23.

Samuel Long, of Lexington. Died July 18, 1851, aged 71 years. S 7/23.

Dr. John Pryor, of Bourbon county. Died in July, 1851, at an advanced age. S 7/23.

William F. Houghton, of Fayette county. Died July 15, 1851, aged 32 years. S 7/23.

Andrew Adams, of Lexington, a member of the Union Fire Company. Died July 27, 1851, aged 22 years. S 7/30.

Edward P. J. Ward, son of George and Josephine Ward, of Lexington. Died Aug. 4, 1851, aged about 15 months. S 8/6.

Sarah Jane, infant daughter of Charles and Nancy Reiley, of Lexington. Died Aug. 5, 1851, aged 13 months and 28 days. S 8/8.

Major Peter Gordon Voorhies, a soldier in the War of 1812. He was born in Trenton, N. J., and in 1790 emigrated to Frankfort, Ky., and in 1812 he emigrated to Red River, where he died in July or Aug., 1851, aged 79 years. S 8/8.

Mrs. Polly Hieatt, consort of Allen Hieatt, of Woodward county. Died Aug. 9, 1851. S 8/13.

Ann Susan Lowry, daughter of Mr. N. Lowry, of Jessamine county. Died Aug. 15, 1851, aged 5 years. S 8/16.

Mrs. Fanny Ware, widow of Charles Ware, of Woodford county. Died in August, 1851, aged 77 years. S 8/26.

Mrs. Susannah Shiddell, of Lexington. Died Sept. 2, 1851, aged 56 years. S 9/2.

Florence, infant daughter of George and Sarah Heidelberg. Died Aug. 25, 1851, aged 17 months and 23 days. S 9/2.

William Flanagan, of Winchester. Died Sept. 1, 1851. S 9/5.

Miss Laura Virginia Peck, daughter of Dr. Henry J. Peck, of La., late of Lexington, Ky. Died at Drennon Springs, Sept. 4, 1851. S 9/5.

Mrs. John J. Crittenden, wife of Hon. John J. Crittenden. Died Sept. 8, 1851. S 9/12.

Edwin Irvine, son of Edwin B. and Josephine M. Settle, of Scott county. Died Sept. 14, 1851, aged 3 years and 1 week. S 9/19.

Annie Ellis, second daughter of Leo and Augusta Tarlton. Died at Ion Plantation, Madison Parish, La., Aug. 11, 1851, aged 6 years, 4 months and 17 days. S 9/19.

Eliza Jeannett Lowry, daughter of Nathaniel and Harriet C. Lowry, of Jessamine county. Died Sept. 20, 1851, aged 12 months. S 9/23.

Mrs. Sarah G. Ellis, relict of Hezekiah Ellis, and daughter of Capt. Peter Hurst, of Versailles. Died at Elliston, July 24, 1851. S 9/23.

Mrs. Patsey Quisenbury, wife of J. H. Quisenbury, of Clarke county, and daughter of the late Moses Bennett. Died Aug. 24, 1851. S 9/23.

Sallie Eliza, eldest daughter of Charles Grundy, of Washington county, Ky. Died Sept. 17, 1851, aged 19 years. S 9/23.

John H. Wilson, of Fayette county. Died Sept. 7, 1851, aged 58 years. S 9/26.

Harry Bodley, son of James P. and Elizabeth Megowan, of Lexington. Died in Bourbon county Sept. 23, 1851, aged 8 years. S 9/26.

Bettie, infant daughter of Benjamin F. and Edna M. Bridges, of Boyle county. Died Oct. 2, 1852, aged 15 months. S 10/1.

Reuben Bryant, formerly of Jessamine county. Died in Lincoln county, Sept. 28, 1852. S 10/1.

John Glacken, son of Charles and Ann Glacken, of Lexington. Died Sept. 23, 1852, aged 4 years. S 10/1.

Col. Colby H. Taylor, of Colbyville, Clarke county. Died Sept. 10, 1852, aged 73 years. S 10/1.

Emily J. Virginia, daughter of I. P. and Virginia A. Fisher, of Danville. Died Sept. 28, 1852, aged 9 years. S 10/1.

James Edward, infant son of James M. Lawrence, of Lexington. Died Oct. 11, 1852. S 10/12.

Thomas Scrugham, son of Col. Joseph Scrugham, of Lexington, Ky. Died in St. Clair county, Ill., Sept. 11, 1852, aged 32 years. S 10/15.

Lewis Lanckhart. Died at the Lexington residence of his uncle, Francis Hostetter. Died Oct. 9, 1852, aged 23 years. S 10/22.

Alice, daughter of J. C. and Nancy Montague, of Fayette county. Died Sept. 30, 1852, aged 2 years, 5 months and 25 days. S 10/26.

Emma Hale, daughter of Dr. J. T. and M. J. Warren, of Lexington. Died Oct. 20, 1852, aged 19 months. S 10/26.

Mrs. Mary Jane Chambers, wife of John Chambers, of Shelby county, and daughter of Mr. B. B. Bryan, of Fayette county. Died Oct. 24, 1852, aged 24 years, 8 months and 8 days. S 10/29.

Capt. William Boggs, of Louisville. Died Nov. 1, 1852. S 11/2.

Mrs. Huldah C. Bell, of Lexington. Died Nov. 9, 1852. S 11/9.

Dr. Ridgely Greathouse, recently of Versailles, Ky. Died of cholera in Sacramento City, Calif., Sept. 16, 1852. S 11/9.

Henry Clay, of Lexington. Born Apr. 12, 1777. Died in Washington, D. C.,

June 29, 1852. Best short biography in *Dictionary of American Biography,* Vol. IV.

Col. R. A. Patterson, of Princeton, Ky. Died Nov. 2, 1852. S 11/12.

Mrs. Maron Ingles, consort of John Ingles, of Lexington. Died Nov. 6, 1852. S 11/12.

Miss Hannah Elizabeth Harris, daughter of J. Harris, of Lexington. Died Nov. 11, 1852. S 11/16.

William Short, of Lexington. Died Nov. 20, 1852. S 11/23.

Julia, daughter of David T. Adams, of Lexington. Died Nov. 22, 1852, aged 4 years. S 11/23.

Mrs. Rachel F. Davis, consort of Hiram Davis, of Lexington. Died Nov. 21, 1852. S 11/23.

Mary Downing Brand, daughter of the late John Brand, of Fayette county. Died at the residence of her brother-in-law, Richard Higgins, Jr., of near Helena, Ark., Nov. 15, 1852, aged 21 years. S 11/23.

Dr. Charles Grundy, of Washington county. Died Nov. 4, 1852, aged 23 years. S 11/26.

Prof. Thomas J. Matthews, one time (1824) Professor of Mathematics at Transylvania University. Died Nov. 10, 1852, while a member of the faculty of Miami University. S 12/3.

Joel' Johnson, son of Isaac and Julia J. Johnson, of West Feliciana. Died Nov. 13, 1852, aged 4 months and 15 days. S 12/3.

Ann Maria, daughter of William Weigart, of Lexington. Died Dec. 2, 1852. S 12/3.

Sarah B. Tracy, daughter of Obadiah and Patsey A. Tracy, of Clarke county. Died Dec. 3, 1852, aged 18 years. S 12/10.

Abner Yates, of Lexington. Died Dec. 14, 1852. S 12/17.

Rosalie Adela, daughter of William and Mary Mahon, of Lexington. Died Dec. 14, 1852, aged 2 years, 2 months and 14 days. S 12/17.

Mary Virginia, daughter of Capt. B. C. Blincoe, of Lexington. Died Dec. 12, 1852, aged 11 months. S 12/17.

Ezra Price, son of K. F. and Elizabeth Price, of Jessamine county. He was a great grandson of Major William Price, an old pioneer of Ky., and a soldier in the Revolution. His grandfather, James Price, was killed at the battle of the River Raisin. Ezra died Dec. 16, 1852, aged about 21 years. S 12/21.

Mrs. Elizabeth Cartwell Barkley, daughter of Dr. Robert Best, dec'd., formerly of Lexington, and wife of Crawford H. Barkley. Died in Clarke county, Dec. 24, 1852, aged 24 years. S 12/28.

Mrs. Sarah Ann, wife of Waller Holliday, of Clarke county. Died Dec. 18, 1852, aged 32 years. S 12/28.

Mrs. Catharine W. Welch, wife of Samuel R. Welch, of near Nicholasville. Died Dec. 19, 1852. S 12/31.

Charles B., eldest son of J. C. and Mary McDaniel, of Lexington. Died Jan. 1, 1853, aged 3 years and 10 months. S 1/4.

Joseph Warren Holmes. Died at the Lexington residence of Mr. M. Thwaites, Dec. 31, 1852. S 1/4/1853.

James Laffoon, a resident of Fayette county since about 1793. A soldier in the Revolution, in the Virginia line. Died Dec. 27, 1852, aged 90 years. S 1/7/1853.

Mrs. Donley, wife of Charles Donley, of Lexington. Died Jan. 11, 1853. S 1/11.

Nanny, daughter of Rankin and Nancy Roberts, of Jessamine county. Died Jan. 18, 1853, aged about 4 years. S 1/21.

Teresa L. Turpin, of Kentucky, only daughter of Capt. Edward A. Turpin. Died in Angostura, South America, Nov. 27, 1852, aged 18 years. S 1/21.

William Metcalfe, of Lexington. Died Jan. 22, 1853. S 1/25.

Evan Shelby, of Fayette county. Died Jan. 24, 1853. S 1/25.

Frances H. Rogers, born and reared in Fayette county. Died Jan. 21, 1853, aged 70 years. She was mother of a large family. S 1/25.

John Barkley, President of the Danville and Lexington R. R. Died Jan. 21, 1853. S 1/21.

Mrs. M. Bruen, relict of Joseph Bruen, of Lexington. Died Jan. 27, 1853. S 1/28.

William B., son of Rankin and Nancy Roberts, of Jessamine county. Died Jan. 26, 1853, aged 9 years. S 1/28.

Mary Hanna Garger, of Lexington. Died Jan. 29, 1853. S 2/1.

Thomas A., infant son of Lucellus Laws, of Lexington. Died Feb. 2, 1853. S 2/4.

Dr. Philip Trapnall, of near Harrodsburg. Died Jan. 31, 1853. S 2/8.

Sears C. Walker, astronomer and mathematician. Died at Cincinnati, home of his brother, Judge Walker, Jan. 30, 1853. S 2/11.

Mrs. Polly Smith, consort of William Smith, of Clintonville, Ky. Died Feb. 9, 1853. S 3/8.

William Hays, son of Robert and Mary Hays, of Fayette county. Died Mar. 5, 1853, aged 18 years. S 3/11.

John Herbert Cronan, son of Mrs. Mary Cronan, of Lexington. Died Mar. 5, 1853, aged 12 years. S 3/11.

Mrs. Mary Mason, of Lexington. Died Mar. 9, 1853, aged 50 years. She left an only daughter. S 3/18.

Charles T., son of Abraham S. and Sarah C. Drake, of Lexington. Died Feb. 22, 1853, aged 1 year, 11 months and 12 days. S 3/18.

Isaac Johnson, ex-Governor of La. Died at New Orleans Mar. 15, 1853. S 3/22.

Mrs. Sarah O'Neil, consort of John O'Neil, of Harrodsburg. Died Mar. 7, 1853, aged 27 years. S 3/22.

James H. Daviess, of Georgetown. Died Mar. 14, 1853. S 3/22.

Addison E. Daniel, only child of E. A. and Francis P. Daniel, of Bath county. Died Mar. 10, 1853, aged 1 year, 5 months and 10 days. S 3/22.

James McConnell, of Fayette county. Died Mar. 21, 1853, aged 75 years. An old soldier. S 3/22.

John Kincaid, of Lexington. Died in March, 1853. S 3/25.

Major William K. Wall, of Harrison county. Died in March, 1853. S 3/29.

Miss Virginia L. Deane, of Lexington. Died Mar. 25, 1853. S 3/29.

Thomas Hill. Died at the Lexington residence of Mr. M. Outten, Mar. 27, 1853, aged 92 years. He was a soldier in the Revolution, and a resident of Fayette county since 1813. S 3/29.

Mrs. Ellen C. Ellis, wife of William A. Ellis, of Louisville, and daughter of Beverly A. and Mary C. Hicks, of Fayette county. Died Mar. 25, 1853. S 4/1.

Gen. Thomas Marshall, of Lewis county, a Brigadier General in the Mexican War. Shot and killed by a tenant on his farm, Mar. 29, 1853. S 4/5.

Major John W. Overton, born in Fayette county, Ky., but lived most of his life in Tenn. Died at the residence of his brother, D. C. Overton, Mar. 25, 1853, aged 62 years. S 4/5.

Mrs. Nancy H. Zimmerman, consort of David L. Zimmerman, of Lexington. Died Apr. 21, 1853, aged 38 years, 5 months and 2 days. She left her husband and four children. S 4/22.

Mrs. Judeth, consort of Joshua Coons, of Fayette county. Died Apr. 13, 1853, aged 69 years, 4 months and 4 days. S 4/22.

Mrs. Ann Eliza Ellis, wife of Benjamin Ellis, of Frankfort. Died Apr. 27, 1853, aged 25 years. S 4/29.

Capt. Thomas J. Todd, of Frankfort. Died at the home of his brother-in-law, Col. A. G. Hodges, April, 1853, aged 36 years. S 4/29.

James B., son of James and Ann McMains, of Lexington. Died Apr. 28, 1853. S 4/29.

Joel W. Rice, a student at Transylvania University, and native of Satartia, Miss. Died in April, 1853, aged 24 years. S 4/29.

Mrs. Mary Ann Scott, consort of P. Scott, of Lexington. Died May 1, 1853. S 5/3.

James Wardlow, of Woodford county. Died May 2, 1853. S 5/3.

Mrs. Jane Grooms, of Lexington. Died May 6, 1853, aged 78 years. S 5/13.

Judge James Burnet, of Cincinnati. Died May 10, 1853, at an advanced age. He was a pioneer of Ohio. S 5/13.

Flete Howard, son of R. and O. Prewitt, of Nicholasville. Died May 8, 1853, aged 9 years, 7 months. S 5/17.

Mrs. Sarah E. Lyne, consort of Daniel Lyne, of Jessamine county. Died May 12, 1853, at Keene. S 5/24.

Jeremiah Gaugh, son of Capt. Michael Gaugh, of Lexington. Died May 24, 1853. S 5/27.

Joseph Alexander, a native of North Carolina; spent his boyhood at Walnut Hill, Fayette county, Ky., and settled later in Fleming county. Died May, 1853. S 5/27.

William M. O. Smith, a member of the Fayette Bar. He was a native of Lexington. His wife died in 1852. He left 2 children. He died in Harrison county, June 2, 1853. S 6/3.

John Baptist, youngest child of John G. Daly. Died June 10, 1853, aged 23 years. S 6/17.

Mrs. Eliza D. Overton, wife of D. C. Overton, whom she married May 9, 1836, in Louisa county, Va. She was a daughter of Capt. Frederick Harris and Catharine Smith, of above county and state. She died .... S 6/17.

Thomas H. Hunt, Jr., eldest son of Thomas H. and Mary Hunt, of Louisville. Died at the Lexington residence of his uncle, C. C. Morgan, June 15, 1853, aged 11 years. S 6/21.

Philemon, son of George L. and Amanda Vallandingham, of Georgetown. Died June 24, 1853, aged 2 years and 18 days. S 7/1.

John Kelly, of Union township, Muskingum county, Ohio. He was born in North Carolina in 1755. A Revolutionary soldier, under Washington and Wayne. He was one of the first explorers and surveyors of Kentucky. He was the father of 9 children, 8 of whom survived him. He died June 11, 1853, aged 98 years. S 7/1.

John Pope Bruce, only child of John P. Bruce, editor of the *Somerset Gazette*. Died June 30, 1853, aged 16 years and 3 months. S 7/12.

Mrs. Judith Herndon, relict of John Herndon. Emigrated from Spottsylvania county, Va., to Kentucky in December, 1810. Died at the residence of Joseph Biggs, July 18, 1853, aged 86 years. S 7/19.

Sarah A., daughter of J. B. and Sarah Morton, of Lexington. Died June 10, 1853, aged 3 months and 3 days. S 7/22.

Caroline, daughter of J. B. and Sarah Morton, of Lexington. See above. Died July 17, 1853, aged 1 year, 9 months, and was sister to above. S 7/22.

Col. Orlando F. Payne, late of Lexington. Died in Paducah, July 15, 1853. Buried in Lexington in Presbyterian cemetery. S 7/26.

Mrs. Jessie W., wife of Joseph C. Mathews, of North Middletown, Bourbon county, and daughter of David H. Bosworth, of Fayette county. Died July 31, 1853. S 8/12.

Mrs. Ellen Rathvon, consort of Jacob Rathvon, late of Lexington, Ky. Died in Lexington, Mo., Aug. 10, 1853. S 8/12 .

Ernest, son of Thomas and Isabel Bradley, of Lexington. Died Aug. 12, 1853, aged 21 months and 8 days. S 8/16.

Mrs. Polly Moore, relict of Capt. John W. Moore. Died at the family residence in Fayette county, July 23, 1853. S 8/19.

Horace Holley, only son of Rev. Horace Holley, late President of Transylvania University. Died at the plantation of widow J. B. Labranche & Sons, Parish of St. Charles, Aug. 6, 1853. He was 35 years of age. S 8/23.

Mrs. Margaret T. Davis, formerly of Lexington, Ky. Died of yellow fever in New Orleans, Aug. 15, 1853. S 8/26.

Susan R., consort of Bernard G. Caulfield, of Lexington. Died Aug. 28, 1853, aged 24 years. S 8/30.

John Breckinridge McHatton, infant son of James McHatton, of Lexington. Died Aug. 29, 1853. S 8/30.

Dr. William Cochran, of Louisville. Died at Biloxi, Miss., Aug. 20, 1853. S 9/9.

Mr. C. Roach, of the Frankfort *Yoeman*. Killed Aug. 28, 1853. S 8/30.

Waller Bullock, of Fayette county. Died Sept. 7, 1853, aged 79 years. S 9/13.

Col. Pleasant Bush, of Clarke county. Died Sept. 9, 1853. S 9/13.

Rev. William Gunn, of Lexington. He was a member of the Methodist Church and Presiding Elder of the Lexington District. Died Aug. 23, 1853, aged 57 years. S 9/13.

Hubbard M. Beaseman, youngest son of Col. John O. Beaseman, dec'd., of Harrison county. Died Sept. 5, 1853, aged 21 years. S 9/13.

Mrs. Sue Todd, wife of Capt. Thomas Todd, of Shelby county. Died Sept. 3, 1853, aged 24 years. S 9/16.

Major Bland Ballard, of Shelby county. A resident of Kentucky since 1779, and soldier in the Indian Wars. Died Sept. 5, 1853. S 9/23.

Dr. ...... Lucien, of Frankfort, Ky. Died of yellow fever in New Orleans, Sept. 14, 1853. S 9/23.

Charles Edwin Morehead, formerly of Bowling Green, Ky. Died of yellow fever in New Orleans, Aug 9, 1853;

Emma Augusta Morehead, sister of above. Died same place of yellow fever, Aug. 22, 1853;

Charles D. Morehead, father of Charles Edwin and Emma above. For many years he was Postmaster at Bowling Green, Ky. Died of yellow fever in New Orleans, Aug. 23, 1853;

Mrs. Eliza A. Morehead, wife of Charles D. Morehead, and mother of Charles Edwin and Emma, listed above. She died Aug. 24, 1853. S 9/23.

Joseph F. M. Lemon, of Scott county. Died Sept. 21, 1853, aged 25 years. S 9/23.

J. J. McCabe, of Keene, Jessamine county. Died Sept. 15, 1853, leaving wife and 1 child. S 9/23.

Col. Parker Dudley, a native of Fayette county, Ky. Died in Palmyra, Mo., Sept., 1853. He served in the battle of New Orleans and was Receiver of the U. S. Land Office at Palmyra. S 9/27.

Emily J. Virginia, daughter of I. P. and Virginia A. Fisher, of Danville. Died Sept. 14, 1853, aged 9 months. S 10/1.

Bettie, infant daughter of Benjamin F. and Edna M. Bridges, of Boyle county. Died Oct. 2, 1853, aged 15 months. S 10/1.

Reuben Bryant, of Lincoln county, formerly of Jessamine county. Died in former, Sept. 28, 1853. S 10/1.

John Glacken, son of Charles and Ann Glacken, of Lexington. Died Sept. 23, 1853, aged 4 years. S 10/1.

1853 AND MISCELLANEOUS

Col. Colby H. Taylor, of Colbyville, Clarke county. Died Sept. 10, 1853, aged 73 years. S 10/1.

Major Charles Eastin, first white male child born in Lexington, Ky. Died at the Residence of his son, Capt. J. M. Eastin, Saturday, Sept. 16, 1865, aged almost 90 years. He married in Shelbyville in 1803, and from there emigrated to Indiana, settling in Madison. Served in the wars of 1812 and 1814, and was in Gen. Harrison's campaign in the Northwest. He moved to Kentucky from Ind., in the spring of 1830, and settled in Fayette county about 8 miles from Lexington. He was entirely blind for 6 or 7 years preceding his death. He was survived by his wife and 5 of 13 children, 3 daughters and 2 sons. OR 9/27.

John Folton, of Hartford county. Died Jan 29, 1821. He had been married Jan 26, 1821. About 10 o'clock on the evening of his marriage he was suddenly taken ill and remained entirely void of speech until his death. From the "B D Adv." LPA 2/17.

Dr. James Priestly, of Nashville, Tenn., president of Cumberland College. Died Feb. 6, 1821. LPA 2/17.

Mrs. Bryan, consort of John Bryan, of Fayette county. Died July 24, 1821. LPA 8/8.

Jacob Fishback, of Clarke county. Died Sept. 17, 1821, aged 73 years. LPA 9/29.

Henry Baily, of Lexington. Died of burns received when the *General Robertson* exploded. Lived until May 3, 1821. He was 28 years of age. He died at Eddyville. LPA 5/23.

Col. Richardson Owen, of Tuskaloosa, Ala. Died July 24, 1821, aged 78 years. A soldier in the Revolution. LPA 8/29.

Joshua Norvell, American consul for St. Bartholomews. Died at Havana, Aug. 11, 1821, aged 31 years. LPA 9/15.

Robert Thomas, of Fairfax county, Va. Died July 2, 1821, aged 107 years. LPA 8/29.

John B. Stevens, his wife and son, of Madison county, Miss. Killed Jan. 13, 1821, by John B. Duncan. There were two daughters not slain. LPA 1/24.

Mrs. Rebecca Beach, consort of Joseph Beach, of Lexington. Died Jan. 17, 1821, aged 25 years. LPA 1/24.

Mrs. ——— Harp, relict of Boston Harp, of Fayette county. Died Jan. 6, 1821. LPA 1/17.

William P. Greenup, son of Col. Christopher Greenup, Governor of Kentucky. Died July 9, 1821. LPA 7/18.

Richard Chiles, of Chilesburg, Fayette county. He came to Kentucky from Spotsylvania county, Va., about 1813. He died Oct. 7, 1853, aged 68 years. S 10/7 and 10/11.

Thomas Browning, member of the Lyon Fire Company of Lexington. Died in October, 1853. S 10/17.

Dr. Samuel Jeffrey Mays, of Nicholasville. He fought in the war with Mexico, and was at the battle of Buena Vista. He acted as assistant surgeon of Col. Marshall's regiment of Cavalry. He died Aug. 1, 1853, aged 30 years, 10 months and 11 days. S 10/18.

Dr. W. C. Galt, of Louisville. Died in October, 1853, aged 77 years. S. 10/25.

John T. Bruce, of Lexington. Died Oct. 22, 1853. S 10/25.

Grandison Owens, of Lexington. Died Oct. 24, 1853. S 10/25.

Mrs. Elizabeth Randall, consort of Dr. O. M. Randall, of Hardinsville. Died Oct. 25, 1853, aged 39 years. S 11/4.

Robert Atkinson, Jr., eldest son of Dr. R. J. Atkinson, of Lexington. Died in Selma, Ala., Oct. 18, 1853, aged 24 years. S 11/11.

Edwin T. Eastham, of Lexington. Died Nov. 12, 1853, aged 25 years. S 11/15.

Mrs. Theodocia Netherland, of Nicholasville. She was born near Salisbury, Rowan county, N. C., Aug. 10, 1766. Her father, *Col. Bramlette was an officer in the North Carolina Militia during the War of Independence,* and the family residence on the banks of the Yadkin was burned by British troops. For full story of her father's military career see obituary. She died Oct. 20, 1853, aged 86 years. See S 11/15.

John Karsner, of Owen county. He was born in Lexington, Feb. 11, 1789. Died Oct. 29, 1853. S 11/18.

Mrs. Jane Sea. Died at the Keene, Ky., residence of her son., L. M. Sea, Nov. 21, 1853, aged 57 years. S 11/25.

Patrick Heffernan. Killed Nov. 28, 1853, on the Maysville road, just beyond Lexington, by Frank Burns. S 11/29.

Abner H. Owings, of Danville. Died Nov. 29, 1853, aged 31 years. S 12/6.

Miss Sarah H., youngest daughter of Shadrach and Susanna Staples. Died in Lexington, Dec. 1, 1853, aged 16 years. S 12/13.

James Biscoe, of Franklin county. He was born in Maryland; *served in the Revolutionary War, was at the siege of Yorktown and the surrender of Corn-*

wallis. He also served as boatswain under Commodore Taylor, grandfather of Col. Edmund H. Taylor, of Frankfort, Ky. Died December 11, 1853, aged 94 years. S 12/20.

Samuel G. Jackson, of Fayette county. Died in Dec., 1853, obituary in S 12/23.

Benjamin S. Handy, of Harrodsburg. Killed Dec. 19, 1853, by William Thornton. Both were students at Missouri University. S 12/30.

L. C. Cushing, a clerk at Mr. Dalinghaus's Confectionary, in Lexington. Killed Dec. 29, 1853, by William Weigart. S 12/30.

Dr. Samuel McClellan. Died at Philadelphia, Jan. 11, 1854, aged 54 years. S 1/13.

Mrs. Elizabeth Hawkins, of Lexington. Died Jan. 5, 1854, aged 70 years. S 1/20.

Mrs. Mary Hollankamp, consort of G. H. Hollankamp, of Lexington. Died Jan. 19, 1854. S 1/20.

Gideon P. Burton. Died at the Lexington residence of his mother, Jan. 16, 1854. S 1/20.

Mrs. Mary Ford Offutt, wife of Dr. Z. C. Offutt, of Washington county, Miss., and daughter of B. B. Ford of Georgetown, Ky. Died Jan. 14, 1854. S 2/7.

Mrs. Sarah Blackwell, wife of Gen. Armstead Blackwell. Died in Clarke county, Jan. 25, 1854, aged 24 years. S 2/7.

Lucinda M., infant daughter of James M. and Mary E. Atkins, of Lexington. Died Feb. 9, 1854, aged 14 months. S 2/10.

William Atchison, Sr. He was born near Carlyle, Pa., Feb. 2, 1780. He lived for many years in Kentucky (Fayette county), and recently moved to Mo. Died at the Clay county, Mo., residence of his son, Jan. 29, 1854. S 2/17.

Mrs. Elizabeth Motague, wife of Thomas Montague, of Fayette county. Died Mar. 3, 1854. S 3/3.

Mr. J. W. Brawner, of Williamsburg, Ky. Died in Lexington, Mar. 9, 1854. S 3/14.

Curd Shelton, youngest son of R. B. and Nannie E. Shelton. Died Mar. 11, 1854. S 3/14.

Elder Jacob Creath, Sr., of Jessamine county. Died in Lexington Mar. 13, 1854, at the residence of his grandaughter, Mrs. Wendover. S 3/14.

James T. Lytle, Senator from the counties of Gonzales, Victoria, Jackson and Calhoun (Texas?). Born in South Carolina, reared and educated in Kentucky, and resident of Texas since 1846. Died there Mar. 5, 1854. Buried there. S 3/17.

George Neal, of Jessamine county. Died Mar. 21, 1854, aged 62 years. S 3/24.

Thomas J. Rogers. Died Mar. 16, 1854, aged 53 years. S 3/24.

Robert N. Sharp, of Lexington. Died Mar. 28, 1854. S 3/31.

Miss E. Jane Ellis. Died at the Lexington residence of her brother, William H. Ellis, Mar. 29, 1854, aged 23 years. S 3/31.

Mrs. Mary Jane, wife of Hiram B. Searcy, of Lexington. Died Mar. 27, 1854, aged 25 years. She had been married but 18 months. S 3/31.

Miss Sarah Ann Cromwell, daughter of Oliver Cromwell. She died at the Fayette county residence of her uncle, James C. Montague, April 5, 1854, aged 17 years. S 4/7.

Mrs. Margaret J. Lackens, consort of John R. Lackens, of Lexington. Died Apr. 5, 1854. S 4/7.

Georgie, daughter of J. L. and Mary Atchison. Died at the Lexington residence of Mrs. O. F. Payne, Apr. 5, 1854, aged 4 months and 5 days. S 4/14.

Lucy Frazer, only child of Dr. William T. and T. V. Shortridge, of Lexington. Died Apr. 6, 1854, aged 3 years and 10 months. S 4/14.

Elsie A. Wilson, daughter of Willam and Nancy Wilson, of Lexington. Died Apr. 14, 1854, aged 15 years. S 4/18.

Mrs. Nancy Woodruff, of Lexington. Died Apr. 22, 1854, aged 63 years. S 4/25.

David H. Bosworth, Jr., of Lexington. Died Apr. 20, 1854, aged 19 years. S 4/25.

Col. Calvin C. Morgan, of Lexington. Died Apr. 30, 1854, aged 55 years. S 5/2.

Hon. Richard French, of Kenton county. Died M 1, 1854. S 5/9.

John O'Neil, of Lexington. Killed May 14, 1854, during a fight with Patrick Rattigan, also of Lexington. S 5/16.

Miss Sally Chevis. Died at the Lexington residence of her brother, David Chevis, May 6, 1854, aged 57 years. S 5/16.

Mary and Willie, children of William and Lucy Sullivan, at one time of Fayette county, Ky., then residents of Montgomery county, Tenn. They died May 15, 1854. S 5/26.

Emily, daughter of Dr. Robert P. and Sallie Ward Hunt, of New Orleans. Died May 20, 1854, aged 4 months and 23 days. S 5/30.

Edward Slevin, of Louisville. Died in January, 1854. S 6/13.

Randolph Ballinger. He had recently graduated from Bethany College, in Virginia, and the Law Department of Transylvania University, and had begun practice of law in Harrodsburg, Ky., where he died June 1, 1854, aged 23 years. S 6/9.

Mrs. Jane B. Robert, of Lexington. Died June 18, 1854, aged 63 years. S 6/20.

Col. John Speed Smith, of Madison county. He was born in Jessamine county, near the Kentucky river, July 1, 1792. His father died when he was quite young and he was reared by his uncle, John Speed, of Jefferson county. His mother married a few years after his father's death. He studied law but gave up his practice to march to General Harrison's army on the Wabash. He fought in the battle of Tippecanoc. Returning to Kentucky he again practiced law, in Richmond, where he was admitted to the bar in June, 1812. Again in 1813 he fought Britain, this time becoming a Brig. Major. He married July 1, 1815, Eliza L., eldest daughter of Gen. Green Clay. He was elected a member of the Kentucky Legislature in 1819, and in 1821 to Congress. He authored the inscription on the marble block contributed by Kentucky to the Washington Monument. He was Attorney for the United States, District of Ky., for several years. His last public post was that of Superintendent of Public Works of Kentucky. During President Adams' administration he was offered two diplomatic appointments but declined both. Col. Smith was a fraction under six feet in height, his complexion fair, his hair light, thin even to baldness. His eyes were dark and penetrating. He died June 6, 1854, in Madison county. He was 62 years of age. S 6/6. 6/13 and 6/20.

Henry Parker, infant son of Abigail and Denmark Forsyth. Died June 20, 1854, aged 16 days. S 6/23.

Victor Charles De St. Mars, of Lincoln county, Ky. Died in June, 1854, aged 59 years. He was a French exile, decorated of July, and member of the Society of Horticulture of France. He left one son. S 6/27.

Capt. Alexander Black, of Salem Township, Champaigne county, (Ohio?). He was a soldier in the Indian wars in Kentucky and Ohio. Fought in the engagement at Maumee Rapids, under General Wayne, Aug. 26, 1794. He died June 16, 1854, aged about 89 years. S 7/7.

Joel Britts and his wife; Caroline Britts and her son, Cyrus, aged 2 years; Joseph Britts, Edward Britts, David Smith and his wife; Harriet Lycan. They were killed in an explosion which wrecked a cave the party was exploring, near Mount Vernon, (Ind.?). S 7/11.

Dr. Glass, of Shelbyville. Died of cholera July 10, 1854. S 7/11.

James, infant son of Isaac N. and Sarah Shepherd, of Lexington. Died July 9, 1854. S 7/11.

Mrs. Nancy Crittenden, of Lexington. Died July 10, 1854, aged 58 years. S 7/11.

Laura, daughter of Charles and Nancy Wheatly, of Lexington. Died July 12, 1854, aged 10 months and 22 days. S 7/14.

George Davis, son of Hiram Davis, of Harrodsburg. Died July 19, 1854, aged 19 months. Hiram Davis was formerly of Lexington. S 7/21.

George Cadwallader, of Lexington. Died July 15, 1854. S 7/25.

W. T. Bryan, of Jessamine county. Died July 8, 1854, aged 67 years. He left his wife and six children. S 7/25.

The following residents of Mt. Sterling died of cholera during the July, 1854, siege:

Levi Butler

Dr. W. P. Watrous

Mrs. James Kennard
Miss Dickey
Mrs. Dr. Stockton's son
Judge Daniel (John)
William Kennard
Martin Cartmell
Charles Fizer
Thomas J. Hood and child.
Mrs. Summersall
Edward, son of George J. Stockton, aged 13 years. S 7/28.

Miss Mary Ann, second eldest daughter of Samuel and Jane Lee, of Covington. Died Aug. 1, 1854, aged 18 years. S 8/18.

William H. Weigert, of Lexington. Hanged Saturday July 12, 1854, for the murder of Luther C. Cushing. S 8/15.

Mrs. Nancy E. Swetnam, of Fayette county. Died Aug. 10, 1854, aged 25 years. S 8/15.

Hon. S. W. Downs, collector of the Port of New Orleans. Graduated from Transylvania University, Lexington, in 1828. Died at Crab Orchard Springs, Ky., Aug. 13, 1854. S 8/18.

Theodore J. Sayre, of New Orleans, and for many years a resident of Lexington, Ky. Died at the former place Aug. 7, 1854. S 8/22.

Capt. J. S. Van Pelt. Died in August, 1854. S 8/22.

Mrs. Sussanah Murphy, an aged resident of Lexington, Ky. Died near Indianapolis, Ind., Aug. 16, 1854. S 8/25.

The following residents of Louisville were killed at 12 o'clock Aug. 27, 1854, when a hurricane demolished the Third Presbyterian Church, Eleventh and Walnut streets, there:

Mrs. Vildabee and her three children
Mr. Taylor and child
Mr. Godfrey
Mrs. Salisbury, wife of the city pump maker
Miss Headley, aged about 11 years
John McGowan
Mr. Sweeney
Mrs. Martin, wife of John N. Martin
Mrs. Wicks, wife of Capt. William Wicks
A niece of Mrs. Martin
Mr. Barbour
Mr. McLelland
R. Davies
Mr. McBride and child. S 8/29.

Willis W., youngest son of Garland Webb, of Lexington. Died Aug. 28, 1854, aged 12 or 13 years. S 8/29.

James F. Megowan, son of David Megowan, of Lexington. Killed in Louisville Aug. 31, 1854. S 9/1.

Mrs. Isabella Jane Plunkett, wife of William F. Plunkett, of Lexington. Died Sept. 18, 1854, aged 33 years. She left her husband, four children, her mother and an only sister. S 9/22.

John Murphy, Sr., of Indianapolis, Ind., formerly of Lexington, Ky. Died Sept. 16, 1854. S 9/22.

Mrs. Willy Jane, wife of Joseph Evans, of Lexington. Died Sept. 25, 1854, aged 27 years. S 9/26.

James O. Frazer, of Fayette county. Murdered Sept. 30, 1854. S 10/3.

Hon. Presley Ewing, a member of Congress from the Logan District. Died of cholera, at Mammoth Cave, in September, 1854. He was a young man. S 10/3.

Elisha A. McCurdy, Land Register for Kentucky. Died in Frankfort, Sept. 29, 1854. S 10/3.

Mrs. Miriam B. Brooking, wife of Robert J. Brooking, of Clarke county, and daughter of Capt. Marquis Richardson, of Montgomery county. She was born and educated in Virginia, and in early life removed with her parents to Kentucky. She died Sept. 11, 1854, aged 57 years. S 10/3.

Rev. London Ferrill, colored pastor of the first Baptist Church for colored persons, in Lexington. He was born in Virginia, a slave. Removed to Kentucky about 1820. He died Oct. 12, 1854. S/13.

Rev. John L. Waller, D. D. Died Oct. 12, 1854. S 10/13.

Jesse Tingle, of Fayette county. Died Oct. 15, 1854, aged 55 years. S 10/17.

Jeptha Bowen, of Lexington. Died Oct. 18, 1854. S 10/20.

Hugh A. Garland, of St. Louis, Mo. Born in Nelson county, Va. Elected to Legislature of that State in 1833, and chosen clerk of the House of Representatives in Washington in 1833. He is best remembered as the author of John Randolph's Life, published in 1854. He died Oct. 15, 1854. S 10/27.

Mrs. Catharine Robinson, widow of Capt. Benjamin Robinson, of Spottsylvania county, Va. She reared thirteen children. She died Oct. 11, 1854, aged 90 years. S 10/31.

Mrs. Mary Fowler, relict of James Fowler, of Madison county. Died Oct. 29, 1854, aged 22 years. She left a daughter. S 10/31.

William Hunter, of Washington City. He was a native of New Jersey, but his youth was spent in England, after having been captured by a French man-of-war and carried with his parents into France. He was left an orphan at an early age, and was placed in the printing trade as an apprentice. In 1798 he returned to the United States and established a French and American newspaper in Philadelphia. In 1795 he removed to Washington, Pa., where he established the *Telegraph*. In 1797 he married Anne Morrison, of Bedford, Pa., who outlived him, and removed to Washington, Ky., where he established the *Mirror*. Removing to Frankfort, Ky., he published the *Palladium*, and for ten years was elected State Printer. Early in General Jackson's administration, Col. Hunter moved to Washington City, and in 1829 received an appointment in the Fourth Auditor's office, which position he held until his death. He died October 22, 1854, aged 87 years. S 11/3.

Frederick G. Gedge, of Covington. Killed accidently or committed suicide Nov. 8, 1854. Story S 11/10.

Caroline, only child of Mrs. Harriet Long. Died Nov. 8, 1854, aged about 17 years. S 11/10.

Hiram, son of Richard Loud, of Lexington. Died Nov. 11, 1854, aged 12 years and 6 months. S 11/14

Theodore Riley, of Jessamine county. Died Nov. 6, 1854. S 11/14.

Mrs. Lucy Brashear, of Madison county. She was born in Virginia in July, 1761. Was present at the siege of Boonesborough in 1776, and was the first woman married in Louisville. She died in November, 1854. S 11/21.

Mrs. Sally Browning. Died at the Fayette county residence of her daughter, Mrs. O'Bannon, Nov. 18, 1854, aged 74 years. S 11/21.

Maria A. Anderson, consort of Bradley W. Anderson, of Barbourville, Ky., and daughter of Jeremiah and Isabella Smith, of Laurel county, who emigrated to Kentucky in 1806. She was married to Mr. Anderson in 1846. She died Nov. 1, 1854. S 11/21.

Thomas Rose, of Woodford county. Died Nov. 15, 1854, aged about 45 years. He left his wife and eight children. S 11/28.

William McAfee. Died at Evan's House, Lexington, Nov. 30, 1854, aged about 50 years. S 12/1.

INDEX

-C-

-D-

-E-

-I-

-J-

-N-

-O-

-P-

-Q-

-R-

-U-

-V-

-W-

-X-Y-Z